DIVE-BOMBER AND GROUND-ATTACK UNITS

of the Luftwaffe 1933-1945

DIVE-BOMBER AND GROUND-ATTACK UNITS

of the Luftwaffe 1933-1945

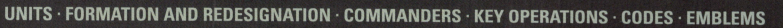

A REFERENCE SOURCE　　VOLUME 1

UNITS · FORMATION AND REDESIGNATION · COMMANDERS · KEY OPERATIONS · CODES · EMBLEMS

Henry L. de Zeng IV and Douglas G. Stankey

CLASSIC

An imprint of
Ian Allan Publishing

Henry L. de Zeng IV

Douglas G. Stankey

The Authors

Henry L. de Zeng IV has a BA in history, a BSBA in accounting and an MBA in business. He is a military veteran with a total of 11 years' active duty, and has worked as a corporate chief financial officer, a corporate vice president of mergers and acquisitions and lastly as an independent consultant.

Douglas G. Stankey holds a BSc in physics, a BEng in mechanical engineering and a PEng and had worked as an upper atmospheric weather observer in the arctic and more recently as an engineer for ABB-Daimler Benz and Bombardier.

Dive-Bomber and Ground-Attack Units
© 2009 Henry L. de Zeng IV and Douglas G. Stankey

ISBN (13) 978 1 903223 87 1

Produced by Chevron Publishing Limited
Project Editors: Chevron Publishing Limited
and J. Richard Smith
Cover and book design: Eddie J. Creek and Mark Nelson
Chevron Publishing would like to thank J. Richard Smith for his
assistance during the preparation of this work

Published by Ian Allan Publishing
Riverdene Business Park, Molesey Road,
Hersham, Surrey, KT12 4RG

North American trade distribution:
Specialty Press Publishers & Wholesalers Inc.
39966 Grand Avenue, North Branch, MN 55056, USA
Tel: 651 277 1400 Fax: 651 277 1203
Toll free telephone: 800 895 4585
www.specialtypress.com

With effect from 1st February 2010 distribution of all Ian
Allan Publishing Ltd titles in the United States of America
and Canada will be undertaken by BookMasters Distribution
Services Inc, 20 Amberwood
Parkway, Ashland, Ohio 44805.

Printed in England by Ian Allan Printing Ltd
Riverdene Business Park, Molesey Road,
Hersham, Surrey, KT12 4RG

Visit the Ian Allan Publishing website at:
www.ianallanpublishing.com

CLASSIC
An imprint of
Ian Allan Publishing

CONTENTS

Preface

This is the second installment in our multi-volume reference work on the flying units of the German Air Force during World War II. It covers the dive-bomber (*Sturzkampf-*) arm and the ground attack (*Schlacht*) arm of the *Luftwaffe,* which collectively was often referred to as the *Wehrmacht's* 'airborne artillery' because of their primary role in the direct support of the army in both attack and defence. In addition to operations on all fronts, the unit histories will take the researcher through the arm's transition from an emphasis on mostly dive-bombing with the slow and vulnerable Ju 87 *Stuka,* that usually required fighter escort to carry out its missions, to the fast, maneuverable and versatile ground attack versions of the Fw 190 single-engine fighter with the *Stuka* then being relegated to mainly the night harassment role.

While the reader should refer to our more detailed preface at the beginning of *Bomber Units of the Luftwaffe 1933-1945: A Reference Source,* Volume 1, where we describe what motivated us to focus on this subject more than 40 years ago, we would like to repeat a few words about our methodology. We have attempted to produce summarized or 'mini-histories' of the many Luftwaffe commands and units by taking the middle ground and making them intermediate in length and detail rather than acutely abbreviated or excessively long. This decision was largely dictated by the amount of primary material that survived the war and the practicalities of publishing. An estimated 97-98% of the *Luftwaffe's* records were either destroyed during Allied air attacks on the Berlin area, particularly the raid of 3 February 1945, or intentionally on *Reichsmarschall* Göring's orders during the first week of May 1945[1]. This has made the task of piecing together unit histories extremely difficult and forced us to rely on anecdotal and derivative sources more than we would have liked to. It should also be said that an understanding of the abbreviated histories require some general understanding of both the *Luftwaffe* and the course of the war on all fronts. It was not possible to more fully elaborate on the frequently shifting war situation on the various fronts due to space constraints.

We would also like to note a change in narrative style resulting from customer feedback and comment on the omission of a particular unit that was brought to our attention. In an effort to make the chronological narrative smoother and easier to read, we have moved the dates from the back to the front of the entries and inserted a colon to separate them from the text. At least one reviewer cited us for not including the *Luftwaffe's* Condor Legion which fought in Spain during the Spanish Civil War. In short, it was a provisional expeditionary ensemble rather than a regular *Luftwaffe* unit and therefore did not meet the criterion for inclusion in our books.

Finally, the alert reader will quickly become aware that Volume 1 does not contain all of the units while at the same time puzzle over the absence of appendices, bibliography and an index. These are all to be found in the second volume, which is planned for publication several months after the first volume.

We would like to extend our sincere appreciation and gratitude to a large number of institutions and individuals who assisted in the preparation of this work, the latter mainly by providing us with photocopies of documents, obscure articles, manuscripts, and other information from their files. The number of individuals who assisted us alone runs into the hundreds so it will not be possible to mention each and every one. But we thank those who are not named just as sincerely as we do those who are mentioned.

First, the archivists and staff of the U.S. National Archives in Washington, with a special mention to John Taylor, George Wagner, William G. Lewis, Amy Schmidt, Tim Mulligan and Harry Rilley, the Air Force Historical Research Agency at Maxwell AFB in Alabama, and at the *Bundesarchiv-Militärarchiv* in Freiburg-im-Breisgau all provided immense help in locating documents during more than 30 visits over a period of nearly 20 years. The inter-library loan staffs of the University of Central Florida, Seminole Community College and the Seminole County Public Library system deserve 'above and beyond the call of duty' awards for the more than one thousand inter-library loan requests they processed over the years in behalf of this research.

In England, Steve Coates, Martin Pegg, Nick Beale and Ian Jewison provided information and copies of numerous documents from the Public Record Office (now the British National Archives) in London, many of which were of vital importance to this work. In Germany, Georg Schlaug, Franz Selinger, Werner Horst, Christian Möller, Heinz Gülzow and Walter Waiss were most helpful with information for several types of units or specific units, particularly night attack, transport, weather and reconnaissance. Knut Maesel in Norway forwarded numerous packages full of copied documents and notes concerning *Luftwaffe* units that operated in that country and in Finland during the war. Jean-Louis Roba in Belgium likewise helped with document copies. In the United States, Dr. James H. Kitchens III, Russel J. Fahey, Barry Rosch and many others contributed significantly from their collections, while in Canada Dave Brown provided help of a technical nature.

Finally, our books would not be possible without the fine, professional talent contributed by the staff and associates of Chevron Published Ltd. in the United Kingdom. It has been often said that photographs and illustrations are what get a history book published, and that is certainly true in our case. Neither of the authors has ever collected photographs so we have had to rely on those selected from the extensive holdings of Eddie Creek. He not only selected the photos to be used to illustrate these volumes, but he also supervised the graphics and layout work, and even did some of it himself. Of equal significance is the work that went into writing the captions for each of the photos and the tedious job of proofreading the manuscript, not once but several times. This task fell to another long-time scholar of the *Luftwaffe* and well-known authority on German aircraft, 1933-45, J. Richard Smith. Without the knowledge and skilled assistance of Eddie and Richard, both authors of numerous works on the subject of the *Luftwaffe,* our books would have remained un-illustrated and possibly unpublished. For their superb efforts in particular, we are indeed most grateful.

Henry L. de Zeng IV
Douglas G. Stankey

---

[1]. The story of the destruction of the Luftwaffe's documents during the last few months of the war is fundamental for anyone interested in this subject and can be found in a short article (*The Fate of the Luftwaffe Archives at the End of WW II*) as this website: http://www.lwag.org/reference/fla001.pdf

Conventions used in this Book

Unit Titles:
The title is the unit name in the standard abbreviated form followed by the full unabbreviated form.

Units of Measure:
We have standardized on metric units of measure for weight and distance.

Layout of mini-histories:
A unit history is usually broken into a series of mini-histories for each of the major sub-units, each starting with its own title. Each mini-history consists of a series of 'paragraphs' which consist of distinct periods of operation. The first paragraph deals with the circumstances of formation: reason for creation, where, when, and from what contributions and initial subordinations. Each paragraph starts with a few words in bold face indicating the subject of the paragraph followed by a statement of the time period of operations in brackets. The final paragraph indicates the ultimate fate of the unit: dissolution, destruction, renaming. Each paragraph consists of a series of often terse phrases, each prefixed by a date of an activity or event followed by a period and a double space. This format is different from that used in our previous book, *Bomber Units of the Luftwaffe*, in response to comments from our readership and is intended to improve readability.

The paragraphs are followed by a statement of applicable unit identity codes only if they do not follow the 'orthodox' rules for unit codes or if they are notably obscure. These are followed by a summation of the known postal codes (FpNs).

Commanders are then listed in chronological order in the format:

Rank / First name/ Last name (awards listed) (start date – spot reference date – end date) fate details
For example:

Hptm. Friedrich-Karl *Freiherr* von Dalwigk zu Lichtenfels (RK) (14 May 1939 - 9 July 1940) KIA

Sources are listed last, firstly the unpublished sources, using standard abbreviations. The published sources are listed next using abbreviations for the books, which are keyed to the Bibliography at the end of the book. The sources listed contain information which might not be incorporated into the mini-histories but never-the-less were borne into consideration during the analysis.

Notations:
While we have made every effort to resolve the details stated in our mini-histories, it was unavoidable that some issues remain unsettled. In order to minimize 'myth-making' we have added notes to indicate the problems and the *pro and con* details. We leave it to others with more information to resolve them.

Abbreviations:
To the extent possible, we have used the abbreviations identical to that used by the *Luftwaffe* at the time concerned. Our guide has been the British Air Ministry A.I.12 document 'Manual of German Air Force Terminology'. However, where it has been deficient or ambiguous we have endeavored to follow a similar pattern of conventions. See our listing of abbreviations.

Place Names:
The names used are the correct English equivalents to those names used by the locals in the pre-war period. Every effort has been made to use the correct spellings, correct accents and avoid modern or Germanized names.

Ship Names:
Ship names are indicated in Italics and, where possible, are identified as to the type of vessel and nationality.

Dates:
To avoid confusion we are using a hybrid form, not quite European, 'day-month-year' but with the month spelled out. In the mini-histories, every action has an associated date. For commanders, the dates are the start and end dates of the individual's tenure as commander, and, if unknown, known dates while in command are stated , such as:

Lt. Hans Jurck (? – 22 June 1941 - ?)

Commanders:
Commanders names are stated as fully and correctly as known in the sequence/format:

(military rank, hereditary title, academic titles) (formal first name) (any nicknames in quotation marks) (any middle/second names or initials)(last name)

The name is followed by any military awards from any nation of DKS level or higher in ascending order. Awards had to have been those held at the time of completion of tenure as commander, the sole exception being posthumous awards. This may be followed by the reason for departure from the unit, if notable, e.g.: KIA, WIA, MIA, POW, illness, promoted, court-martialed, deserted.

In a number of cases, the appointments and assignments of commanders overlap, produce gaps, are inconsistent with previous listings or give rise to questions. We have tried to offer explanations in footnotes where possible, but not all of the inconsistencies can be explained with certainty. Many assignment orders were later amended by teletype message or telephone and no record of these exist today. To this is added the peculiar nature of *Luftwaffe* command assignments in that a first time commander was posted to the position on a provisional basis until he proved himself. Once that had occurred, sometimes many months later, his assignment was made permanent. Previously published listings often do not reflect this fact and that has led to confusion over appointment dates.

A comment should also be made concerning award dates. In the *Luftwaffe*, the individual would be recommended for an award and that recommendation would travel up the chain of command for endorsement and final approval, which was usually months – sometimes many months – after the initial recommendation. Meanwhile, the individual has transferred to another unit. So the date of the award does not necessarily correlate with his accomplishments while serving with his unit of assignment on that date. More often than not, the award is for accomplishments while serving in a previous unit.

Glossary:

Abt.	*Abteilung*	detachment, department or section
a.k.a.	—	also known as
a/c	—	aircraft
abkdrt	*abkommandierte*	temporarily assigned
AFB	—	Air Force Base
AFHRA	—	U.S. Air Force Historical Research Agency, Maxwell AFB, Montgomery, Alabama
Afp.	*Ausweichflugplatz*	Dispersal airfield (minor - no services)
AirMin	—	British Air Ministry
AMWIS	—	Air Ministry Weekly Intelligence Summary
A.O.K.	*Armeeoberkommando*	Army Supreme Command
Ausb.	*Ausbildung*	Training
BA-MA	*Bundesarchiv-Militärarchiv*	*Bundesarchiv-Militärarchiv* - Freiburg
(Bel)	*Beleuchter*	Illuminator
BKG	*Behelfskampfgeschwader*	Auxiliary bomber wing
BR	*Brillanten*	'Diamonds' – the highest level of Knight's Cross
BRT	*Bruttoregistertonnen*	Gross Registered Tonnage (GRT)
ca	circa	about, approximate
Ch.d.Stabes	*Chef des Stabes*	Chief of Staff
Dipl.Ing.	*Diplom Ingenieur*	Certified Engineer
DKG	*Deutsches Kreuz in Gold*	German Cross in Gold (a middle level award)
DKS	*Deutsches Kreuz in Silber*	German Cross in Silver (a middle level award)
DLH	Deutsche Lufthansa	German state airline
D.V.S.	Deutsche *Verkehrsfliegerschule*	German Civil Flight School
Eh.	*Einsatzhafen*	Operational Airfield (minor - limited services)
Ehrenpokal	*Ehrenpokal*	Honour Cup or Trophy
Eichenlaub	*Eichenlaub*	Oak Leaves to the *Ritterkreuz*
(Eis)	*Eisenbahn*	Railway or Railroad
E.K.	*Eisernes Kreuz*	Iron Cross
EL	*Eichenlaub*	Oak Leaves to the Ritterkreuz
Erg.	*Ergänzung*	Reserve training, replacement
Erg.KGr.	*Ergänzungs-Kampfgruppe*	Reserve training bomber group
(F)	*Fernaufklärungs*	Long-range reconnaissance
FAR	*Fliegerausbildungsregiment*	Basic training school for raw recruits in 1937-41
FBK	*Flugzeugbetriebskompanie*	Aircraft servicing company
FEA	*Fliegerersatzabteilung*	Basic training school for raw recruits in 1935-37
Ffp.	*Feldflugplatz*	Advanced Airfield (minor - limited services)
Fh.	*Flughafen*	Airport (major - full services)
Fh.(See)	*Flughafen (See)*	Seaplane Base (major - full services)
FHK	*Fliegerhorstkommandantur*	Airfield headquarters
FK	*Fernlenkkörper*	Remote control missile
Fl.Div.	*Fliegerdivision*	A tactical or regional command staff but smaller than a *Fliegerkorps*
Fl.Fü.	*Fliegerführer*	A tactical or regional command for a type of task
Fliegerkorps	*Fliegerkorps*	Air corps (having c 300 – 800 a/c)
Flh.	*Fliegerhorst*	Air Base (major - full services)
Fp.	*Flugplatz*	Airfield (major - full services)
FpN	*Feldpostnummer*	Military postal code
FTR	—	Failed to return
FuG	*Funkgerät*	Electronic or radio device
G	*Goldenen Eichenlaub*	Golden oak leaves, the unique special level of the Knight's Cross
GBM	—	Golden Bravery Medal
Gefechtsverband	*Gefechtsverband*	An ad hoc unit created from available units for a specific task for a limited time.
Gen.Major	*Generalmajor*	*Major* General
(H)	'Heer'	Refers to a reconnaissance unit established to directly support the Army (*Heer*)
Gruko	*Gruppenkommandeur*	Officially appointed commander of a *Gruppe*
HMS	—	His Majesty's Ship, ie: a Royal Navy ship.
Hptm.	*Hauptmann*	Captain
Ia op	—	operations officer in a headquarters staff
i.G.	*im Generalstab*	An officer appointed to the General Staff
(J)	*Jagd*	Fighter
J.Fl.Fü	*Jagdfliegerführer*	A fighter command staff controlling a certain region
Jabo	*Jagdbomber*	Fighter-bomber
JFS	*Jagdfliegerschule*	Fighter Pilot School

J.G.	*Jagdgeschwader*	Fighter wing with c 100-140 a/c
(K)	*Kampf*	Bomber unit
Kdo.	*Kommando*	A small special purpose unit; a detachment
K.G.	*Kampfgeschwader*	Bomber Wing
kg	*kilogram*	kilogramme
K.Gr.	*Kampfgruppe*	Bomber Group (c 30 a/c)
K.Gr.z.b.V.	*Kampfgruppe zur besondern Verwendung*	Bomber Group for special assignment
K.G.z.b.V.	*Kampfgeschwader zur besondern Verwendung*	Bomber Wing for special assignment
KIA	—	Killed in action
km	*kilometer*	kilometre
Koflug	*Kommando Flughafenbereich*	Airfield Regional Command
KSG.	*Kampfschulgeschwader*	Bomber School Wing
K.St.N.	*Kriegsstärke-Nachweisung*	Unit type establishment strength number
KTB.	*Kriegstagebuch*	War diary
Kü.Fl.Gr.	*Küstenfliegergruppe*	Naval air group or coastal air group
(l)	*'leichte'*	Light fighter (ie: single engined) unit
Lehrgang	—	course of instruction
Luftflotte	*Luftflotte*	An Air Fleet, with ca. 1,000+ a/c
L.G.	*Lehrgeschwader*	Experimental, developmental or instructional wing
LGr.	*Lehrgruppe*	Experimental, developmental, or instructional group
Lh.	*Leithorst*	Controlling Air Base (major - full services)
L.K.	*Luftkreis*	Air district
LKS	*Luftkriegsschule*	*Luftwaffe* Cadet College
LLG	*Luftlandgeschwader*	Air-Landing *Geschwader* or Wing
Lp.	*Landeplatz*	Landing Field (minor - no services)
LT	*Lufttorpedo*	Air-launched torpedo or aerial torpedo
Lt.	*Leutnant*	Second Lieutenant
Lw.Gr.Kdo.	*Luftwaffengruppenkommando*	An early period air district
Lw.Kdo.	*Luftwaffenkommando*	Similar to a *Luftflotte* but usually smaller
Major	*Major*	Major
mdWdGb	*mit der Wahrnehmung der Geschäfte beauftragt*	Detailed to deputize (for); temporary C.O.
mFb	*mit Führung beauftragen*	with command entrusted (a temporary command appointment usually becoming permanent after a period of probation)
MGFA	*Militärgeschliches Forschungsamt*	Military History Research or Studies Office of the BRD (Bundesrepublik Deutschland)
MIA	—	Missing in Action
Mq.	*Meldquadrat*	Map grid or square number
mWb	*mit Wahrung beauftragen*	with the management entrusted (an acting or provisional appointment)
n.l.t.	—	no later than
NARA	—	National Archives and Records Administration, Washington, DC
nicht wirksam	*nicht wirksam*	not effective – in case a documented change wasn't forthcoming after verbal instruction
N.J.G.	*Nachtjagdgeschwader*	Night Fighter Wing
N.K.V.D.	*Nadrodnyy Komissariat Venutrennikh Del*	People's Commissariat of Internal Affairs
N.S.D.A.P.	*Nationalsozialistische Deutsche Arbeiterpartei*	National-Socialist German Workers Party
NSGr.	*Nachtschlachtgruppe*	Night Attack Group
Ob.d.H.	*Oberbefehlshaber der Heer*	Army High Command
Ob.d.L.	*Oberbefehlshaber der Luftwaffe*	Air Force High Command
Ob.d.M.	*Oberbefehlshaber der Marine*	Navy High Command
Oberst	*Oberst*	Colonel
Oblt.	*Oberleutnant*	First lieutenant
Obstlt.	*Oberstleutnant*	Lieutenant Colonel
O.K.H.	*Oberkommando des Heer*	Army High Command (late period)
O.K.L.	*Oberkommando der Luftwaffe*	Air Force High Command (late period)
O.K.M.	*Oberkommando der Marine*	Navy High Command (late period)
ops	—	operations
PC	*Panzersprengbombe, cylindrisch*	Armour-piercing demolition bomb, cylindrical
Pl.Qu.	*Planquadrat*	Map grid square
PleM	*Pour le Mérite*	WWI high level award, the 'Blue Max'
POW	—	Prisoner of War
PRO	—	Public Records Office, London (now the National Archives)
(Pz)	*Panzer*	Refers to a tactical reconnaissance *Staffel* assigned to support a *Panzerdivision* (to 1942); later, refers to an anti-tank *Staffel*
Qu.	*Quartiermeister*	quartermaster
RAD	*Reichsarbeitsdienst*	Reich Labour Service
RAF	—	Royal Air Force
RDA	*Rangdienstalter*	seniority of rank

From Concept to Dive-Bombing and Ground-Attack

(Origins and Junkers Ju 87)

J. Richard Smith and Eddie J. Creek

WHEN the aeroplane was first pressed into service as a weapon during the First World War, there were conflicting views on how it could best be used. At first its role was purely that of aerial observation, extending the task already undertaken by the hot air balloon. As reconnaissance became more and more successful each side became aware that it would be a distinct advantage if these aircraft could be destroyed. Thus the fighter was born. By 1916 fighters were beginning to be used to strafe enemy trenches but these missions were haphazard and uncoordinated. Then, in 1917, the Germans began to use low-flying reconnaissance aircraft not only to collect information but also to attack targets of opportunity. Lighter, faster and more flexible CL-types, such as the Halberstadt CL.II, were issued to the newly formed *Schutzstaffeln* (or protection squadrons) in the second half of the year. Finally, in March 1918, the 38 *Schutzstaffeln* or Schusta were reorganised as *Schlachtstaffeln* (literally battle, or more accurately, ground attack, squadrons).

With the transfer of her forces from the eastern to the western front following the Russian revolution, Germany decided to launch a major attack on the Western Allies which it was hoped would lead to a successful conclusion to the war. Over 730 aircraft, one-third of total German aviation strength was concentrated to assist the offensive. When it began on 21 March 1918, a total of 27 *Schlachtstaffeln* were available. These became heavily engaged in supporting German forces on the ground by attacking enemy troops at very low altitudes in waves with both machine gun fire and hand grenades. In addition they also harassed enemy reinforcements for distances of up to 15 km behind the front line. The tactical efforts of the *Schlachtstaffeln* in their low level attacks were generally regarded as first-rate and sometimes of decisive value. The March 1918 offensive also saw the first anti-tank mission when a column of British tanks was halted by a *Jagdstaffel*.

Among the aircraft involved at this time were a handful of Junkers J.I sesquiplanes. This type can be considered the first aircraft in the world to be designed with the exclusive role of ground attack. It was of all-metal construction with 5 mm steel armour plates protecting the crew of two and the engine. It carried an armament of two forward-firing machine guns plus another flexible weapon in the rear cockpit. Nicknamed the 'furniture van', the J.I was a

difficult machine to shoot down, almost as fast as a fighter, and probably 15 years ahead of its time.

Following the German surrender in November 1918, the Treaty of Versailles placed severe restrictions on future aviation development. Nevertheless the success of previous ground-attack operations persuaded Germany to think how they could improve on the lessons learned. There was no doubt that the appearance of tanks on the battlefield had radically changed the face of warfare. Attack aircraft would now need heavy armament and cannon to pierce armour. But in the Twenties aircraft were not robust enough and lacked sufficient engine power to carry more than one 20 mm cannon or an adequate bomb load while still offering reasonable performance. Level bombing was not considered accurate enough to disable, let alone destroy, tiny and fast moving targets such as tanks. It would also be ineffective against supply targets behind enemy lines.

During the late 1920s several air forces began to think of delivering bombs in a steep dive which, it was realised, would be much more accurate than level bombing given the rudimentary bombsights then available. Probably the first such mission had been carried out by Second Lieutenant William Henry Brown of No.84 Squadron Royal Flying Corps flying an S.E.5a aircraft against German ammunition barges moored at Bernot. The success of this attack led the RAF to pursue similar experiments post war at the Royal Aircraft Establishment's Orfordness Armament Experimental Station, but peacetime constraints led to their abandonment.

The Junkers J.I (factory designation 'J 4') all-metal sesquiplane was extremely popular with its crews due to its immensely strong construction. Powered by a 200 hp Benz IV engine which gave it a maximum speed of 155 km/h (96 mph), the aircraft could carry a crew of two. Armament comprised two fixed forward-firing 7.9 mm Spandau machine guns with a single Parabellum gun of similar calibre in the rear cockpit.

German interest in the dive-bomber originated from a visit that Ernst Udet, Germany's second highest scoring fighter pilot of the First World War made during the summer of 1931. Udet, a superb aerobatic pilot, attracted the attention of the organisers of the American flying event, the National Air Races, centred in Cleveland, Ohio. During his visit to the city in September 1931, he was invited to fly the new Curtiss Helldiver then being evaluated by the U.S. Navy. Part of the performance of this stubby fighter-bomber biplane was a dummy high-speed diving 'attack' on the airfield to thrill the massed and enthusiastic American crowd.

The result was that Udet was so taken with the idea of dive-bombing that he asked Hermann Göring, a brother fighter pilot from the First World War, and soon to become commander of the new *Luftwaffe*, to provide the funds to buy two of the Curtiss F11C-2 Hawk II aircraft. Seeing his chance to get the charismatic Udet to join the Nazi Party, Göring immediately approved the purchase and on 19 October the two aircraft were mysteriously spirited through customs at Bremerhaven. In December 1933, they were transferred to the newly established *Erprobungsstelle* at Rechlin where they were extensively tested. One of the aircraft lost its tail while being demonstrated by Udet at Berlin-Tempelhof on 20 July 1934, but he managed to bale out. Despite this problem, the dive-bomber theory had been proved and the concept of the *Schlachtflugzeug* was abandoned for the moment at least.

After being flown by Ernst Udet at Cleveland in Ohio, two Curtiss F11C-2 Hawk IIs were bought by Germany and given the civil registrations D-IRIS and D-ISIS. After being tested at Rechlin, D-IRIS lost its tail while being flown by Udet at Berlin-Tempelhof in 1934. Four years later he gave a spectacular display with the remaining aircraft in front of Nazi Party officials at the Reichsparteitag gathering at Nuremberg.

In 1925 Germany established the army Weapons Bureau, a clandestine office designed to evaluate aircraft and keep a core of the disbanded German Military Aviation Industry in existence. Between 1927 and 1932 the Aviation Technical Group (WaPrw 8) under *Oberstleutnant* Hellmuth Felmy put forward, for the first time, a requirement for a *Sturzkampfflugzeug* or dive-bombing aircraft. Already the Heinkel company had produced such a machine, the He 50, to a specification originated by the Imperial Japanese Navy. Demonstrated at Rechlin in 1932, the second prototype, He 50aL, raised considerable interest among *Reichswehrministerium* (German Defence Ministry) officials who ordered three evaluation machines. They were powered by an uncowled Siemens 22B nine-cylinder radial engine rated at 600 hp for take-off. Though intended to be used as a single-seater in its dive-bombing role, provision was made to accommodate a rear gunner equipped with a single 7.9 mm MG 15 machine gun. A 500 kg bomb was to be carried in dive-bombing role, a 250 kg weapon to be delivered in level flight. The aircraft was also equipped with a fixed forward-firing 7.9 mm MG 17 machine gun.

Between 2 and 3 February 1935 two He 50s were tested at *Erprobungsstelle* (Experimental Station) Rechlin with various types of bomb racks. Immediately afterwards the Heinkels were transferred to Jüterbog were they carried out no less than 100 diving flights. In addition an experimental Junkers K 47 with bomb racks to carry two SC 50 bombs and fitted with a *Stuvi* sight, was held in reserve in case either aircraft went unserviceable. Following these trials two contracts were placed for a total of 60 He 50 As, deliveries to begin towards the end of 1933. Service trials were to show that the He 50 A was a great disappointment in both dive-bomber and ground-attack roles and it was quickly relegated to training

pending the availability of a new generation aircraft. It did, however, see a brief renaissance in 1943 when it was used by the *Nachtschlachtgruppen* on the Eastern Front.

The failure of the He 50 led the *Reichswehrministerium* to issue a new two-stage plan for a *Sturzkampfflugzeug* (*Stuka* or dive-bombing aircraft), the first phase being

The rather cumbersome Heinkel He 50 biplane dive-bomber was the first aircraft of its type to see service in the Luftwaffe. It was originally developed in answer to a Japanese specification, but later participated in dive-bombing trials at Rechlin and Warnemünde, dropping concrete bombs. Although a small number of He 50s saw service with the Luftwaffe, the machine was far from satisfactory.

Oberst Hellmuth Felmy

The Swedish-built Junkers K 47 light bomber can be said to be the forerunner of the Ju 87. Developed from the A 48 fighter, the aircraft had an aerodynamically pleasing airframe but was of rugged construction which enabled it to withstand the pull-out forces encountered when recovering from steep dives. The aircraft was powered by a 480 hp Bristol Jupiter radial engine which gave it a maximum speed of 270 km/h (168 mph). Primitive bombs were later fitted to the aircraft for diving trials which proved quite successful. A few of the type were delivered to the fledgling Luftwaffe and at least one was still flying in 1939.

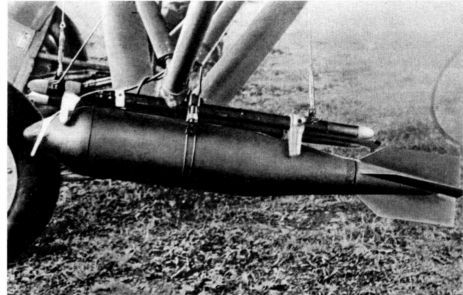

The Blohm und Voss competitor for the dive-bomber specification was the Ha 137. It had a similar cranked wing and spatted undercarriage to the Ju 87 but featured an open cockpit. The V1 and V2 were powered by BMW 132 radial engines, the V3 by a Rolls Royce Kestrel and the V4 (seen here) and the V5 by the Jumo 210 engine.

called *Sofort* or crash programme. Two manufacturers produced designs: Fieseler the Fi 98 and Henschel the Hs 123. Both were conventional biplanes, but the Henschel design was much cleaner, with no drag-producing wire bracing. First flown on 1 April 1935, the Hs 123 V1, although powered by the same 650 hp BMW 132 A-2 radial engine as the Fi 98, proved faster in climbing and level flight. Well before completion of the comparative tests, the choice was obvious. Three prototypes were built for official trials at Rechlin. During the course of the trials, two were lost when they broke up in mid-air, both pilots being killed. Subsequent investigation showed that the wing centre section had to be strengthened, these modifications being incorporated from the fourth prototype. This aircraft, the Hs 123 V4, was extensively tested at Rechlin and proved to be easy to pull out from dives at angles of over 80 degrees from any altitude. The type was ordered into production with the first version, the He 123 A-1, being delivered in the

summer of 1936. This version differed from the prototypes by its direct fuel-injection BMW 132 Dc engine rated at 880 hp for take-off. An improved version was also produced powered by a 960 hp BMW 132 K engine under the designation Hs 123 B-1.

The Henschel dive-bomber was seen as an interim type pending the development of a state of the art aircraft. A specification for this new *Stuka* was issued in September 1933 to Heinkel, Junkers, Arado and the Hamburger Flugzeugwerke (later Blohm und Voss). Because of their experience with the Junkers A 48 mentioned earlier and the fact that a mock-up of their new design had already been completed, Junkers were already odds-on favourites to win the order with their Ju 87. Two of the other entries for the competition, the Arado Ar 81 and the Blohm und Voss Ha 137, were quickly eliminated, but the Heinkel He 118 was also chosen for further development.

Arado's entry for the dive-bomber competition was the Ar 81. A sturdy biplane powered by a Jumo 210 engine, the aircraft was the least favoured of the four designs. Only three prototypes were completed, the V3, D-UDEX, seen here differing from the first two aircraft in having a single fin and rudder.

Ernst Udet seen here on his 40th birthday in April 1936. At this time he was Inspector of Fighters, eventually becoming Generalluftzeugmeister (chief of air armament). Even at this time he was taking drugs and drinking heavily, and his inability to fulfil the duties of his appointment led him to commit suicide on 17 November 1941. It was a sad end for a great fighter and aerobatic pilot.

A stiff competitor for the second dive-bomber specification was the He 118 which was powered by a DB 600 engine and had a retractable undercarriage. The type was finally abandoned after Udet crashed the V3 in June 1936. Although the crash was due to pilot error, it led to the abandonment of the Heinkel design.

Many historians have suggested that the more aerodynamically advanced He 118 with its retractable undercarriage should have been chosen in favour of the Ju 87. However, it should be stated that it only had a maximum dive angle of forty degrees and lacked the ruggedness of its Junkers competitor. In addition, and perhaps surprisingly, its maximum speed was almost

identical to the Ju 87. The final blow came to the He 118 programme on 27 June 1936 when Ernst Udet arrived at Rostock Marienehe to fly the aircraft for himself. Although briefed by Heinkel test pilot, Gerhard Nitschke, he failed to take in the instruction that the propeller should be set to coarse pitch before attempting a dive. Ignoring the caution, Udet climbed to about 4,000 m (13,000 ft) and then immediately put the aircraft into a steep dive. Completely forgetting Nitschke's caution, he failed to put the propeller into coarse pitch with the result that it 'ran away', shattering the reduction gear and severing the tail section. Udet baled out, but the accident sounded the death knell of the He 118.

Work on the Junkers design, the Ju 87, had begun as early as 1933 under the leadership of *Dipl.-Ing.* Hermann Pohlmann. The aircraft was to be fitted with a fixed, spatted undercarriage, projecting chin radiator, twin fins and rudders and cranked wings which enabled comparatively large weapon loads to be mounted below the fuselage. A radical feature of the design was the fitting of a dive brake under each wing. So confident were Junkers that they would win the RLM's endorsement, that they had begun to build three prototypes (the V1 to V3) during the summer of 1934. The first of these made its initial flight on 17 September 1935 with test pilot Willi Neuenhofen at the controls. However, early in its diving trials on 24 January 1936, it was destroyed in a crash after one of the vertical tail surfaces broke away during the pull-out. Test pilot Neuenhofen and his observer, Heinrich Kreft were killed.

Subsequent investigation of the crash led to a major redesign of the entire tail assembly, the twin fin configuration being replaced by a single fin and rudder on the second prototype. In addition the Ju 87 V2 was powered by a 610 hp Jumo 210 Aa inverted-Vee liquid-cooled engine in place of the 525 hp Rolls-Royce Kestrel which had been fitted to the V1. The new prototype made its first flight in March 1936 and was followed by the Ju 87 V3. This aircraft differed in that its Jumo engine was lowered to improve the pilot's forward view over the nose. It was also fitted with a larger rudder and a tailplane

with small endplate fins. The Ju 87 V4, completed in the late autumn of 1936, introduced more improvements including a further lowered engine, an even larger fin and rudder, revised landing gear spats, a modified rear canopy and full operational equipment.

The first pre-production Ju 87 A-0s came off the assembly line before the end of the year. They were powered by a 640 hp Jumo 210 Ca engine and equipped with one fixed and one flexible 7.9 mm machine gun. A normal bomb load of 250 kg could be carried, with this doubled under certain circumstances. Several other modifications designed to simplify mass-production were also incorporated. The first true production variant was the Ju 87 A-1 which was delivered by the Dessau factory from early 1937. By 1939 the Ju 87 A or *Anton* model had been replaced in *Luftwaffe* service by the Ju 87 B or *Berta*. Exchanging its Jumo 210 engine for the Jumo 211 with almost double the power, the B-series was faster and could carry a considerably heavier bomb load. It also introduced several aerodynamic refinements, perhaps the most notable of which was the wheel spats which were considerably reduced in size. Defensive armament was increased to three 7.9 mm machine guns. A further development, the Ju 87 R or *Richard* had increased range.

Meanwhile in October 1935, the *Luftwaffe's* first *Stukagruppe* to be formed, I./St.G.162 'Immelmann', was established at Schwerin. It was equipped initially with the unsatisfactory He 50 plus a few Ar 65s and He 51s. Even at this time there were doubts among several influential *Luftwaffe* officers about the *Sturzkampfbomber* concept. Some, like *Generalleutnant* Walther Wever, the Chief of Staff, *Major* Günter Schwartzkopff and *Hauptmann* Hans Jeschonnek, espoused the cause with enthusiasm, while

others, like *Oberstleutnant* Maximilian Ritter von Pohl, were at best lukewarm. One of the most prominent detractors of the Ju 87 programme was *Oberstleutnant* Wolfram von Richthofen at the RLM who, while not opposing dive-bombing as such, thought that the Junkers aircraft was far from the right vehicle to deliver it. Unsurprisingly there was no such opposition from Udet's Technical Office of course, and combat experience gained subsequently by the three *Stukas* (initially Ju 87 As and subsequently Ju 87 Bs) which participated in the Spanish Civil War only served to prove the success of the concept.

A wooden mock-up of the Ju 87 V1 photographed at Dessau during the autumn of 1934. The twin fins and rudders were a feature of this prototype but were found to be unsatisfactory.

The first prototype of the Ju 87, the V1, differed considerably from subsequent aircraft. It had double fins and rudders, was powered by a British Rolls-Royce Kestrel engine and had a much smaller radiator. Its first flight took place on 17 September 1935 with test pilot, Willi Neuenhofen, at the controls. There were already some doubts about the stability of the twin fins and this was confirmed when the prototype crashed on 24 January 1936, killing Neuenhofen and his observer, Heinrich Kreft.

Three Ju 87 Bs were delivered to 5.K/88 of the Legion Condor in Spain in time to see action in the Nationalist Catalonian offensive which took place between December 1938 and February 1939. They succeeded the three Ju 87 A-0s which had arrived in Spain during the previous year and proved equally successful. The machines managed to destroy the bridges at Meco and Fuentiduena de Tajo which were notoriously difficult targets to attack.

Richthofen, who was the last commander of the Condor Legion in Spain, was later credited by the British Air Ministry for much of the success of the aircraft in Spain: '*Richthofen had formed the far-sighted conception of creating a separate tactical air force for participation in land battles; it was to be an adjunct to, and not a substitute for a strategic air force. Not only did Richthofen encounter opposition to his wide plan, but it was only with the greatest difficulty that his ideas on army co-operation, which were to have such an extensive influence on air operations in the war of 1939, were accepted at all. Richthofen, like most of the stronger characters in the Luftwaffe, succeeded in carrying out his ideas without official sanction, and created ground-attack squadrons in the Luftwaffe. This far-seeing move was to prove Richthofen to be right; furthermore it was to pay handsome dividends in the victorious continental campaigns of 1940 and in the rapid German advance to the gates of Moscow in 1941.*'

Oberst Wolfram von Richthofen was not against dive-bombing as such, but considered that the Ju 87 was not the aircraft for the job. Between July 1939 and June 1942, he was to lead the VIII. Fliegerkorps which controlled most of the Luftwaffe's operational dive-bomber units.

Subsequent operations against Poland, France and the Low Countries were to prove equally successful but when the Ju 87 came up against effective fighter opposition as it did during the Battle of Britain, its inadequacies were highlighted. Several disastrous sorties over England resulted in huge losses with the result that the aircraft was temporarily withdrawn from operations. It was able to operate successfully in the campaigns in the Balkans and against the Soviet Union but as Russian fighter defences began to improve it again suffered badly.

The obsession in some parts of the *Luftwaffe* leadership with the dive-bomber meant that no *Schlacht* or ground-attack units were available until August 1938. In that month five such ad hoc units were formed as a temporary measure due to the Sudeten crisis. With the end of the problem all five units were disbanded in October 1938, but parts went towards establishing an experimental ground-attack unit, II.*(Schlacht)/Lehrgeschwader* 2, equipped with Hs 123 biplanes. Despite this the ground-attack arm remained woefully underdeveloped and neglected until the beginning of 1942.

Perhaps it would be useful here to remind ourselves of the often subtle differences between dive-bombing and ground attack. Dive-bombing was carried out from altitude with the aircraft launching its bombs in a steep dive. The resultant attacks were usually more accurate than level bombing given that the aiming devices

An Unteroffizier pilot kneels in front of an SC 250 bomb which is ready to be fitted under the fuselage of a Bf 109 F-4/B with a yellow-painted underside to the engine. The chalk inscription he has just written on the bomb reads 'The rest on the Kommandantur'. The unit could be the 10. Jabo Gruppe of either JG 2 or JG 26.

The Fw 189 V1 was rebuilt to compete with the Hs 129 for the heavily armed ground-support aircraft. This early adaptation, coded D-OPVN, first flew in the spring of 1939 and was powered by two Argus AS 410 engines, but its performance was disappointing.

available to the latter, particularly during the early part of the war, were unreliable. Objectives usually comprised ships of opposing navies, bridges, strong points and gun emplacements although troop concentrations were often targeted. Ground-attack sorties, on the other hand, were usually flown at low level against tanks, strong points, troops, and their supporting infrastructure.

From the beginning of 1942 the ground-attack arm was gradually expanded with the establishment of *Schlachtgeschwader* 1 and 2. Both were equipped with the Hs 123, bomb-carrying variants of the Bf 109 E fighter and the new Hs 129. Fortunately there were some in the *Reichsluftfahrtministerium* (RLM, or the Reich's Air Ministry) who realised the need for a specialised ground-attack and anti-tank aircraft. This resulted in a specification, issued in April 1937, for a small, twin-engine aircraft, armed with a combination of 20 mm cannon and heavy machine guns, which also had to be capable of delivering a bomb load. Two designs were produced to the specification, the modified Fw 189 V1b and the Hs 129. Both were heavily armoured to protect the pilot and were powered, initially, by two 465 hp Argus As 410 engines. Eventually the Hs 129 was preferred, and in its Gnome-Rhône 14 radial powered version, was to

This photograph clearly illustrates the crude and heavy construction of the armoured cockpit of the prototype Hs 129. The restricted pilot's visibility is further obscured by the gunsight, which is clearly evident.

This view of the Hs 129 V1 clearly shows the details of the Argus As 410 in-line engines fitted with two-bladed fixed pitch propellers. Note the slanted, pointed nose, the three-segment windscreen and short gun channels. The aircraft has also been fitted with two long, continuous bomb racks fitted under the front section of the fuselage.

The eventual winner of the RLM's Schlachtflugzeug tender, issued in April 1937, was the twin-engine Henschel Hs 129 which was the sole participant designed for the purpose of the ground-attack role. The Hs 129 V1, coded D-ONUD, W.Nr. 129 3001 is still in its factory finish and was later repainted in the green camouflage colours RLM 70/71 over RLM 65 light blue and re-coded TF+AM.

A factory-fresh example of an Hs 123. This design was used successfully in various roles throughout the war from training to Schlachtflieger and Nachtschlachtflieger operations. Note the striking factory-applied camouflage splinter pattern.

see limited service with the *Luftwaffe* especially in the anti-tank role.

In addition to the Hs 123, Bf 109 and Hs 129 mentioned previously, the ground-attack units began to make increasing use of bomb-carrying variants of Focke-Wulf's superb Fw 190 fighter. As the dive-bomber became more and more vulnerable to attack both by increasing numbers of enemy fighters and improved anti-aircraft defences, the *Stukagruppen* flew more and more specialised ground-attack sorties. New versions of the Ju 87 were produced including the Ju 87 D or *Dora* which was further aerodynamically refined and powered by a 1,400 hp Jumo 211 J engine. Several sub-variants were produced including the D-1 bomber, the D-3 ground-attack aircraft, the D-5 with extended outer wing panels and the D-7 fitted with flame-damping exhausts for use by the *Nachtschlachtgruppen*. The final version to see service was the Ju 87 G or *Gustav*. This was fitted with the devastating armament of two 37 mm cannon for use against tanks and other heavily armoured targets. Junkers also began work on the proposed Ju 87 F which, powered by a Jumo 213 F engine, was to have a retractable undercarriage and to carry even heavier loads. This was superseded by the Ju 187 project which was to have remotely-controlled defensive armament. A further development was the more aerodynamically refined Ju 287 'Super *Stuka*' which was fitted with a reversible fin and rudder to help improve the gunner's field of fire.

Already by the time of the Battle of Britain, the Junkers Ju 87 was showing signs of its limitations. A proposal for a faster, better armed and armoured replacement was put forward. The initial design work was drawn up around the basic latest configuration of the Ju 87 design. The new initial design was given the type number Ju 187. A wooden model of this proposal was built and tested in the wind tunnel at Braunschweig. A further design proposal was put forward under the designation Ju 287 as shown on the drawing. The new design had slatted dive brakes fitted near the trailing edge of the landing flaps and a retractable undercarriage which retracted rearwards and also rotated 90 degrees to lay flat

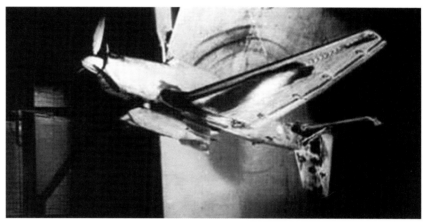

A wooden model of the Ju 187 shown suspended for tests in a wind tunnel.

under the wings. The aircraft was to be powered by a Jumo 213 A 12-cylinder liquid-cooled engine. As with the Ju 187 the new design also had the movable vertical tail fin and rudder, which could be moved 70 degrees downwards after take-off, thus clearing the field of fire for the rear gunner. Two men sat back-to-back in a pressurized cockpit with the defensive armament being located in a remote-controlled rear turret, consisting of one MK 151/20 20 mm cannon and one MG 131 13 mm machine gun. The proposed bomb load was one 500 kg (1,102 lbs) bomb under the fuselage. Although wind tunnel tests were carried out on a model of the Ju 287 and a full-size mock-up of the fuselage was built, the project was cancelled as the projected performance was not that much above the standard Ju 87 then in service.

By then, however, the *Stukageschwader* had been reorganized as *Schlachtgeschwader*. At the same time, October 1943, the two original Schl.Gs were also redesignated. The wheel had turned full circle.

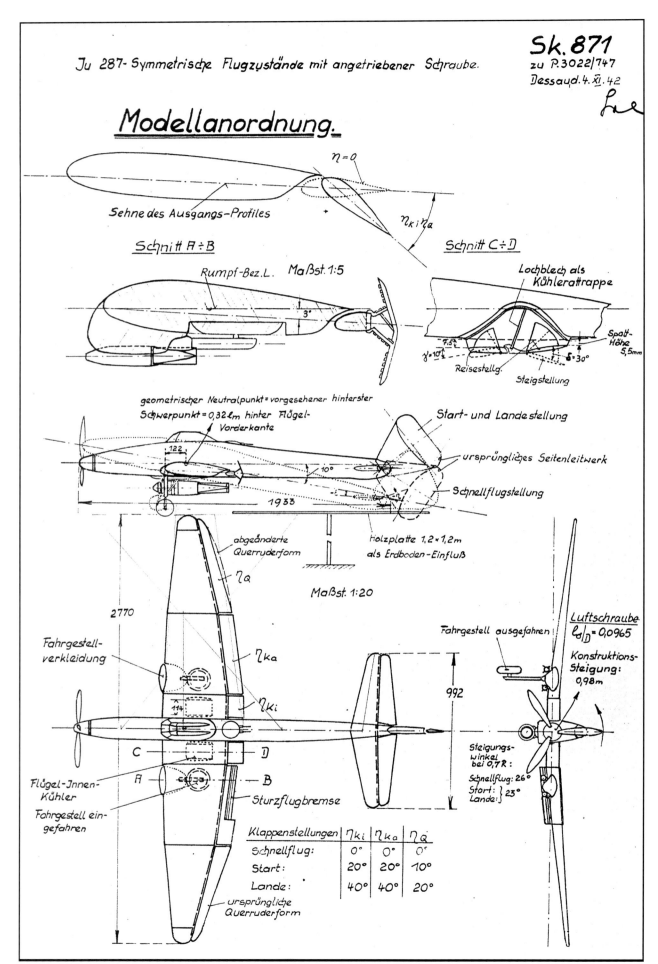

A drawing of the Ju 287 project dated 4 November 1942 clearly detailing the design proposal. The upward and downward rotation limitation of the tail fin and rudder assembly is clearly indicated. Also the subsequent timber mock-up (opposite page) shows that extensive time and effort were put into this design which eventually came to nothing.

ABOVE AND ABOVE RIGHT: Two photographs bearing Junkers company references, showing clearly the refined lines of the Ju 287 project.

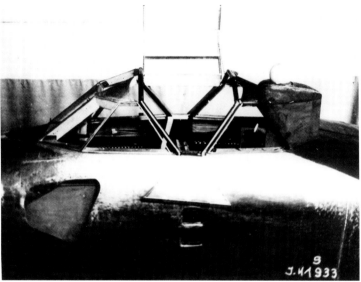

These four photographs of the full size timber mock-up of the Ju 287 fuselage show the detail of the canopy construction as well as the periscopic gunsight for aiming the remote gun turret situated on the upper fuselage behind the rear gunner's position. In the tail down position it would have given the rear gunner a much wider defensive firing radius.

The Role of Luftwaffe Dive-Bombers and Ground-Attack Units

By *Generalmajor* Hubertus Hitschhold

During September and October 1945, the Luftwaffe's former General der Schlachtflieger, Generalmajor Hubertus Hitschhold, wrote a survey of German dive-bomber and ground-attack units for British intelligence. The document forms an interesting personal adjunct to this book and the following is a slightly edited transcript of his report.

1. The Role of the Ground-attack Units in Action

First of all it should be emphasised that German ground-attack units possessed the ability to attack pinpoint targets. Special medium bomber units for the support of the army were lacking in the *Luftwaffe*, therefore twin-engined aircraft intended for strategic bombing were used for this purpose, although from the

beginning of 1943 most of these bomber units did engage in strategic bombing. Since that date, operations by medium bombers were almost completely lacking over German battle areas. Medium bombers were, however, able to combat area targets in support of the army. A ground force attack must consist of units which can combat area targets as well as forces which can bomb and shoot pinpoint targets. On the German side, the chief missions and targets of ground-attack units were:

A. For the support of the army

(1) Fighting – troops on the ground, troops in positions and troops on the march.

(2) Material – medium and heavy weapons, machine gun nests, anti-tank guns, artillery, rocket guns, anti-aircraft guns, tanks and tank columns.

(3) Transport – horse-drawn vehicles, locomotives, railways and shipping.

(4) Signals facilities – radio stations, telegraph/telecommunications (by attacks on entries and exits to villages), bridges, ferries, troops in villages, houses and troops in woods.

B. Coastal area – ships and vessels of all kinds, warships, landing places, etc

C. Air combat – destruction of enemy aircraft in the air and on the ground

Apart from its physical threat, the Ju 87 was fitted with a propeller-driven siren generator which had an often devastating effect on the morale of enemy troops. Known as 'the Trumpets of Jericho', this device was responsible for generating a piercing scream as the aircraft was put into a dive.

2. Types of Missions and Attacks

Daylight attacks

Ground-attack missions were usually carried out in *Gruppe, Staffel, Schwarm* or *Rotte* strength. Only in exceptional cases where large forces were massed did attacks in *Geschwader* strength take place. In the autumn of 1943 seven *Gruppen* had Fw 190s and the other 14 or 15 had Ju 87 *Stukas*. By the end of the war all but one of these Ju 87 *Stuka* units had been converted to the Fw 190. Radio control from the ground (*Egon* Procedure) was planned for the units but was not planned to be introduced until a time several months after the war actually ended. It was intended to use Egon procedure to lead the aircraft to the target in bad weather. After being led directly to the target only, they then conducted the attack after sighting the ground.

Ground-attack units released their bombs in a dive (80-60 degrees), a shallow glide (50-20 degrees) or at low level.

Armament of the Fw 190 ground-attack model was two 20 mm MG 151 cannon and two 13 mm MG 131 machine guns, one 500 kg bomb rack under the fuselage, and four 50 kg racks under the wings.

The choice of the mode of attack (dive, shallow dive, or low level) was dependent on the enemy's anti-aircraft and fighter defence, weather and the type of ammunition and bombs to be used. If the enemy anti-aircraft and fighter defences were disregarded, the most successful modes of attack were the shallow dive for dropping bombs and the low level attack for strafing. Very often it was the job of the ground-attack pilot to seek out the most important targets over the battlefield, and some of these targets were very well camouflaged. This forced him to fly at altitudes from which only a direct shallow dive or low level attack was possible. The shallow dive attack brought about the best possibility of hitting, and the type of bomb and fuse determined the dropping altitude. This was especially true with the type of

bomb container from which a great number of bombs were strewn and which required a certain dispersion to be effective. (For ground-attack aircraft like the Ju 87 and other aircraft with computing bomb sights, the dive attack is the most practical).

If anti-aircraft fire could be kept down or nullified, the ground attacks were flown as shallow dives or as low level attacks. It was often necessary to use part of the unit to suppress the anti-aircraft fire with suitable bomb load (containers with 1 kg anti-personnel bombs), in order that the greater part of the formation could carry out an effective attack with as little interference as possible from ground defences. If the suppression of anti-aircraft fire was not possible, dive attacks had to be flown. It repeatedly proved helpful to have friendly artillery keep down enemy anti-aircraft fire, when ground-attack units were attacking targets near the front line. If the anti-aircraft fire was too strong, a massed, closed-up dive attack had to be carried out in formation. In this manner the anti-aircraft gunners had only a short time to combat the attack and could not concentrate their fire on individual targets. Approach altitude and the beginning of the attack dive were, if possible, so arranged that they lay outside the effective range of the anti-aircraft fire.

Close-up of the slatted dive brake beneath the port wing of a Ju 87 D shown in the extended position. It was this feature that enabled the aircraft to make such steep dives.

Two photographs showing the cockpit interior of the Ju 87. (ABOVE) is the port side of the pilot's position; (RIGHT) is the radio operator's or 'back-seater's' equipment.

3. Escort for Ground-Attack Units

Besides anti-aircraft defence, fighter defence rendered difficult the conduct and effectiveness of ground-attack missions. It was proved on the Western Front and in Italy that ground-attack missions were impossible when the attacking side did not have air superiority, at least over the battle area during the time of the attack. Otherwise the losses of ground-attack aircraft were too high in relation to what was accomplished. The ground-attack pilot had to be able to carry out his attack without being threatened by enemy fighters. If fighter opposition was absent, the ground-attack unit could carry out its strikes in loose formation, but if fighter opposition was present, it had to keep tightly together over the battle area. On the Eastern Front it was usually sufficient if part of the ground-attack formation took over the fighter escort for the rest of the mission. It was even possible to use bomb-carrying Fw 190s as fighter escort. This was done in the following way. At the beginning of the attack, one part of the formation remained at altitude and furnished fighter cover. This part was then relieved by another part of the formation which had already dropped its bombs. The top cover then went down to conduct its own ground attacks. In case of contact with the enemy, bombs had to be jettisoned, with fuses armed if over enemy territory.

If the enemy had air superiority, fighter escort furnished by regular fighter units was advisable. Strong fighter opposition would force the ground-attack formation to make greatly concentrated mass attacks (usually with approach at great altitude for a dive attack, or on occasion a low level attack with the element of surprise). Effective strafing attacks could not then be flown, because the effectiveness of the ground-attack units was thus already cut in half. The most effective weapon of the ground-attack Fw 190 were its 20 mm MG 151 cannon and its 13 mm MG 131 heavy machine guns. Bombs were less effective.

It was the goal of every ground-attack mission to combat the enemy to the last round of ammunition, to destroy all recognizable targets on the ground, and then by a prolonged stay over the battlefield to render impossible every movement of the enemy. (This time gave the army the opportunity to attack, to redeploy or to retreat with little hindrance). The weather partly decided the type of mission to be flown by ground-attack units and also the size of the formation, i.e. the worse the weather, the smaller the formation. A minimum ceiling of 6,000 to 8,000 feet was required for dive-bombing. Shallow diving attacks could be flown with a ceiling of 1,500 feet and low level attacks at still lower altitude. Attacks under low ceilings usually resulted in higher losses because anti-aircraft fire cannot be adequately combated and because the ground-attack aircraft are too easily sighted by enemy aircraft.

Anti-Tank missions

It was necessary to use special anti-tank ground-attack units against modern tank formations. In cases of unforeseen tank breakthroughs, the army was often not in the position to throw in enough of its own tanks or anti-tank guns to stop the advance.

American troops inspect a captured Ju 87 G-2 (W.Nr. 494200) tank-buster at Pilsen in the summer of 1945. The two 37 mm cannon were hung beneath the wings on removable mountings. This aircraft has a yellow band painted around the nose, this marking being introduced on the Eastern Front in the autumn of 1944 to aid in distinguishing German aircraft from those flown by the Russians. Note also the flame dampers fitted to the engine exhaust for night operations.

In the spring and autumn in Russia, the ground was so muddy, and roads so bad, that the transfer of tanks for defence against the breakthrough of enemy tanks was so uncertain that the only possibility of combating them was to use these special anti-tank ground-attack units. It was apparent that ordinary ground-attack units were not able to destroy enough tanks with their guns, cannons and bombs, but the special anti-tank units with armour-piercing cannon and special anti-tank rockets were very successful. Anti-tank aircraft were the Hs 129 with the 30 mm MK 101 and later the 30 mm MK 103 cannon, the Ju 87 *Stuka* with two 37 mm cannon, and the standard Fw 190 ground-attack model with rocket racks attached to its bomb racks. These aircraft were successfully used against tanks which had broken through on the battlefield and back as far as the rear areas. Missions against tank assembly areas were a great mistake because they were always protected with numerous anti-aircraft guns and resulted in high losses with relatively little success. For attacks on tank assembly areas it was better to use a formation which carried a large number of containers of 4 kg hollow charge armour-piercing bombs. These could be dropped partly outside the range of effective anti-aircraft fire. Enemy tanks which had broken into friendly troop areas could only be safely combated by special anti-tank ground-attack units, without endangering friendly troops.

Troop columns which had broken through could be easily combated if the anti-tank units fought the tanks and the regular ground-attack units attacked the more thinly armoured vehicles which accompany the tanks. In good weather, tank breakthroughs were, however, protected by strong fighter cover. The destruction of this fighter cover was a pre-requisite for successful employment of anti-tank ground-attack units. If bad weather was used for tank breakthroughs the anti-tank units could fly anyway, since they usually flew in at low level.

After neutralizing enemy fighter cover, combating of anti-aircraft defences was another condition for the successful use of anti-tank aircraft. After a long series of successful missions against armour, the enemy began to provide the tanks with anti-aircraft protection. This was steadily increased and by the end of the war, every nation had some sort of anti-aircraft tank which could protect the other tanks. Thus it was decided to use anti-tank units in conjunction with regular ground-attack formations to suppress anti-aircraft fire. When the ceiling was so low that ground-attack units could not effectively act against anti-aircraft defences, the anti-tank units had to operate with the element of surprise. Then the attack was carried out in the shortest possible time before the anti-aircraft tanks, not usually ready for combat, could open fire. Experience and practice in immediate recognition of tanks enabled them to be shot up in the first attack. This brought about good success without significant losses. In the final year of the war, Russian tank troops had become used to anti-tank formations and they camouflaged their tanks as much as possible. At the approach of anti-tank units they immediately sought cover near houses, tree clumps, or hay stacks. Often the tanks could only be found from their tracks and the Russians usually erased these by dragging branches behind the tanks.

Anti-tank units fought in *Rotte, Schwarm* and, at most, in *Staffel* formation. If larger anti-tank units were

used simultaneously over the battlefield they often hindered and confused each other. The attacks with armour-piercing cannon were conducted like ordinary strafing missions. To ensure hits, the pilots had to approach as close as possible, with the German cannon then in use. The best range was 100 to 150 yards. The gunnery run had to be very even and calm, and the direction of approach was determined by the ground situation and with the 30 mm and 37 mm weapons aimed at the most vulnerable parts of the tanks.

Night attacks

The role of the night ground-attack units was to combat or harass the enemy on the front and in rear areas in the same manner as the day ground-attack units.

The idea arose from the use of the Russian harassing aircraft, the Polikarpov Po-2. At first the German *Störkampfstaffeln* (or

The main target for the Luftwaffe's anti-tank units on the Eastern Front was the Soviet T-34 as seen here. This superb vehicle is widely regarded as having been the world's best tank when the Soviet Union became involved in World War II, and although its armour and armament were surpassed by later tanks of the era, it has been often credited as the war's most effective, efficient and influential tank design. The T-34 was continuously refined during the war to enhance effectiveness and decrease costs, allowing steadily greater numbers to be delivered. In early 1944, the improved T-34-85 was introduced, with a more powerful 85 mm gun replacing the 76 mm weapon.

harassing squadrons as they were known), used normal training aircraft such as the Arado 66, Gotha 145, Heinkel 46 and the Bücker 181. At the end of 1943 German ground-attack units in Italy could not operate by day without difficulty and heavy losses because of great Allied air superiority. Therefore some Ju 87 *Stukas* were used experimentally against the Nettuno (Anzio) bridgehead by night. The employment proved successful. Consequently, in 1944, conversion of night ground-attack units to the Ju 87 and the Fw 190 began. These units were able, when used in sufficient numbers, to disturb the enemy continually in the night, to hinder materially night marches, to hold down artillery fire and to hinder attacks. In this way considerable relief was often given to German troops. The targets for night ground-attack missions had to be small area targets; the combating of individual targets as by day was only possible to a limited extent. Good targets proved to be firing artillery, lighted transport columns, defiles, bridges, villages and areas and geographic points of importance recognizable at night as troop concentration areas. Most successful of all were missions against light targets, such as roads and firing artillery. Unlit targets had to be illuminated with flares dropped from the air or through target markers either dropped or shot from the ground. The lavish use of 2 kg fragmentation bombs especially just after darkness was found to restrict the enemy's use of roads during the remainder of the night. An effective employment of forces was the rolling attack – a series of heavy blows one after another. Such rolling attacks continuing throughout the entire night on the Russian front greatly hindered enemy preparations for attacks on the following day. The usual tactics of *Nachtschlachtstaffeln* were dive and shallow dive attacks; horizontal attacks were conducted only rarely and at very low altitude, and where large area targets were involved.

Weather requirements for missions were a ceiling of 3,000 to 6,000 feet and a visibility of 4 to 5 kilometres. Moonlight made the mission easier because the targets were, of course, more visible. Regular anti-aircraft fire could be suppressed even at night by repeated bombing. Heavy anti-aircraft fire made the mission more difficult. Night fighter defence against night ground attacks was not present in the east, but was very effective in Italy. Radar control (Egon) proved good in Italy and in the

West and was a great help in combat. Close co-operation with the army in the battle area produced great results. This was not always achieved because the continual retreats of the army made the co-operation between it and the air force more and more difficult. It was proved, however, that night ground-attack units well led from the ground, partly equipped with antiquated aircraft, could achieve considerable results and effectively support the army.

The choice of suitable bombs

This was mainly the job of the unit itself, but the command organization had to keep control and sometimes interfere. This matter is touched on in the following paragraphs:

The Ju 87 D-7 was the first variant to exchange its two fixed 7.9 mm MG 17 machine guns in the wings for 20 mm MG 151/20 cannon. This variant, which was developed for use by the Nachtschlachtgruppen, also had large flame-damping tubes which led the exhaust back over the wings.

The Russians pioneered the idea of night ground attacks using the Polikarpov Po-2 during the winter of 1941-42. These ageing biplanes, nicknamed 'sewing machines' by German troops, proved extremely effective and resulted in the Luftwaffe creating its Störkampfstaffeln. This captured Po-2 is being examined by German troops.

(a) Against ground troops – Ground troops in open country and in positions which offered no cover against air attacks were effectively bombed with small fragmentation bombs of 1, 2, 4, and 10 kilograms, in large containers if possible. Less effective were the 50 and 70 kg fragmentation bombs, even with projecting fuses to make them explode above the ground. These latter bombs had to be used often because of the supplies on hand. Their insignificant effectiveness was continually confirmed, while the smaller bombs dropped in large containers had a bomb carpet effect coupled with considerable destructive power. Special belting of ammunition was not used. The belting usually was: two HE, HE incendiary and two armour-piercing incendiary or ordinary armour-piercing shells.

(b) Against heavy weapons – These targets were bombed to destroy the servicing personnel with the same bombs used as (a) above. If the guns were in the open, without cover (being transported or simply dispersed), then 50, 70, and 250 kg fragmentation bombs, all with projecting fuses, were suitable.

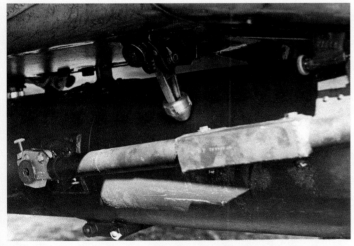

Close-up of a PC 500 armour-piercing bomb attached to a trapeze beneath a Ju 87 B. Contrary to myth, this device was not used to throw the bomb away from the propeller, but merely so that it was thrown free of the slipstream thus ensuring a clean and more accurate separation to the target. The most common bomb used by the Ju 87 was the general purpose SC 500 which had a diameter of 457 mm (18 inches), whereas the PC 500 had a diameter of 279 mm (11 inches) which meant that the trapeze beneath the fuselage was narrower and the bomb had to be carried off-set to the starboard side of the fuselage.

Strafing attacks were flown against the personnel and the lighter weapons, but they were useless against heavy equipment. On the other hand, Russian rocket batteries mounted on tracks were destroyed with the greatest effectiveness by strafing attacks. Armoured trains and railway guns were only successfully bombed with heavy bombs of 250 kg or more.

(c) Vehicles – Horse drawn and motor vehicles were bombed with 1 to 70 kg bombs. These were also used against lightly armoured vehicles. Tanks could be destroyed with 3, 3.7 and 7.5 cm cannon, with hollow charge shells or with 4 kg hollow charge bombs. Bombing with 50 to 500 kg bombs was not successful because the tanks presented too small a target. Destruction with such bombs was only accomplished if the bomb hit within 5 metres of the tank.

(d) Field fortifications – Field fortifications of all types could only be attacked with heavy bombs of 250 kg or more. Attacks on modern fortifications brought little success.

(e) Headquarters – Parts of towns and houses where headquarters or troops were quartered were attacked with bombs of 250 kg or larger. Wooden houses, especially with straw roofs, were best ignited with incendiary ammunition.

(f) Bridges – Bridge destruction was a difficult job and usually brought little success. Stone or concrete bridges were only damaged by direct hits with heavy bombs and then only temporarily. Complete collapsing of such a bridge was almost impossible.

Steel bridges were mostly invulnerable, because the blast effect usually dissipated through the steel work. Only in cases of some lucky hits was the destruction of such bridges possible.

Pontoon bridges were attacked with a mixture of 10 and 500 kg bombs. Even so, only temporary interruption of traffic was achieved. Repairs were especially easy for such bridges if continuous observation and bombing of the repair work was not possible.

In certain tactical situations, like pursuits, last escape routes out of surrounded areas, flank threats, and bringing up of reserves, bombing of bridges was of decisive importance and had to be carried out regardless of losses.

(g) Attacks on Airfields – These served as indirect support for the army. The main point of such attacks was the destruction of dispersed aircraft, which were bombed with small bombs of from 1 to 10 kg. Fixed installations were only attacked at the beginning of the war, because as a result of the ensuing dispersal such attacks were usually uneconomical.

(h) Railway bombing – This was an important target for ground-attack units, especially during the transportation of troops to and from the tactical area. Main points of attack were roads to and from these areas, and easily blocked sections like bridges and cuttings. Attacks on open stretches of road and on unoccupied stations brought no lasting effect. Most practical for this purpose were bombs of 250 kg or more. Trains in motion were wrecked with heavy bombs and troops streaming from them were strafed and bombed with small fragmentation bombs.

Special locomotive-busting missions were especially successful in areas where repair facilities were meagre. For the destruction of locomotives, hits with cannon of 30 mm calibre or greater or with rockets sufficed. Hits with smaller weapons or with fragmentation bombs only damaged the locomotives, but even this proved a great handicap in areas lacking repair facilities.

A 500 kg (1,100 lb) SC 500 (Sprengbombe Cylindrisch) – a thin-walled, high-explosive general-purpose bomb mounted beneath a Ju 87 B of St.G. 3. These weapons were usually painted buff or, occasionally, pale blue.

Two photographs of Ju 87s about to pull out of the dive just after releasing their bombs. In the photograph to left the aircraft has released its bombs in a steep dive with dive brakes extended, while to the right is an example of bombs being released during a shallow dive without the use of dive brakes.

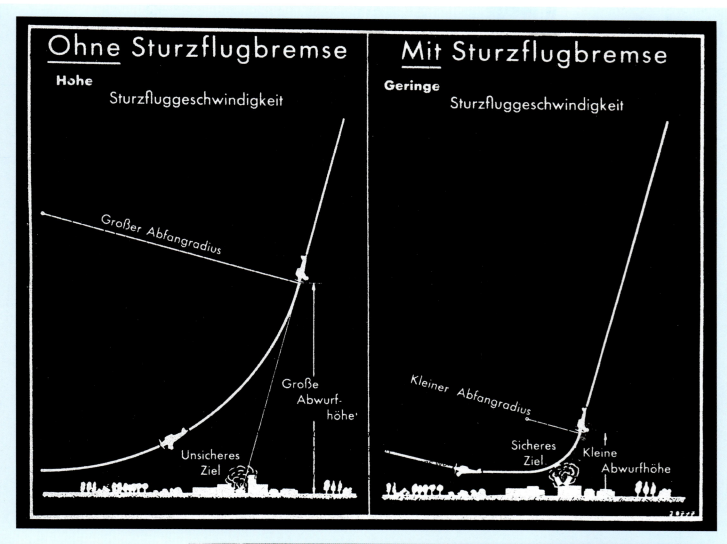

Ohne Sturzflugbremse

Hohe Sturzfluggeschwindigkeit

Großer Abfangradius

Große Abwurfhöhe

Unsicheres Ziel

Mit Sturzflugbremse

Geringe Sturzfluggeschwindigkeit

Kleiner Abfangradius

Sicheres Ziel

Kleine Abwurfhöhe

ABOVE: The principles of dive-bombing allowed an aircraft to place bombs accurately on relatively small or moving targets without the need for a sophisticated bomb sight. These illustrations, taken from a Ju 87 manual, show the comparison between attacking with and without dive brakes extended. In the drawing on the left, the aircraft's greater speed requires the pilot to pull out of his dive at a relatively high altitude, but with a loss in bombing accuracy. Conversely, the illustration on the right shows that by deploying dive brakes, the speed of the aircraft is reduced, allowing the machine to descend to a lower level before the pilot has to pull out of his dive. Although the pull-out radius is tighter, the aircraft has released its bomb very close to the target, hence the accuracy is improved.

RIGHT: Two photographs from a Ju 87 manual showing the dive brakes in the retracted and extended positions.

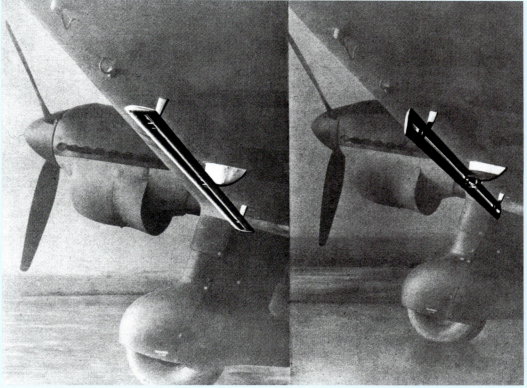

The Junkers Ju 87

The Ju 87 V3 – one of the prototypes leading to the 'A' series.

Dipl.-Ing. Ernst Zindel, seen here discussing a design issue with a colleague, was the Chief Designer at Junkers responsible for the Ju 87 'Stuka'. The name 'Stuka', an abbreviation of the German word 'Sturzkampfflugzeug' or dive-bomber aircraft, became synonymous with the Junkers aircraft, although it could be applied to any such type.

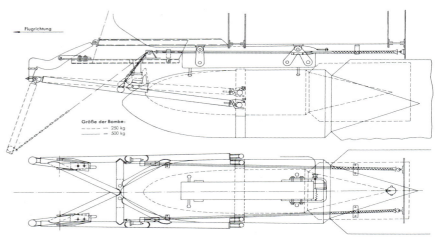

A handbook drawing showing the installation for carrying a 250 kg or 500 kg bomb.

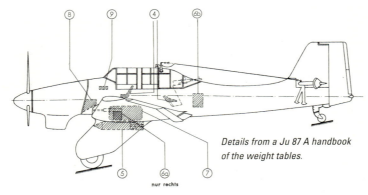

Details from a Ju 87 A handbook of the weight tables.

	Verwendungszweck		I	II
	Bombengröße	kg	250	500
1	Leergewicht	kg	2273 - 2290	2264 - 2281
2	Zusätzliche Ausrüstung	kg	247	164
3	Rüstgewicht	kg	2520 - 2537	2428 - 2445
4	Besatzung	kg	140 - 200	70 - 100
5	Bomben	kg	0 - 250	0 - 500
6	Munition a: starre Schußwaffe	kg	0 - 13	0 - 13
	b: bewegliche Schußwaffe	kg	0 - 20	
7	Kraftstoff γ = 0,76	kg	0 - 330	0 - 330
8	Schmierstoff γ = 0,92	kg	9 - 29	9 - 29
9	Leuchtpatronen	kg	0 - 1	0 - 1
10	Fluggewicht	kg	3365 - 3382	3401 - 3418

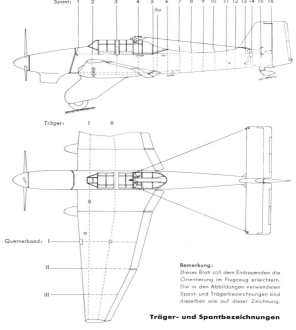

Wing main bearers and fuselage frames.

Ju 87 A

bomb release button

electrical switches for fuzing bomb

emergency bomb release lever

A view of the pilot's instrument panel also showing the control stick indicating the bomb release button at the top.

A detail photograph showing the location of the MG 17 machine gun and ammunition drum installation in the wing.

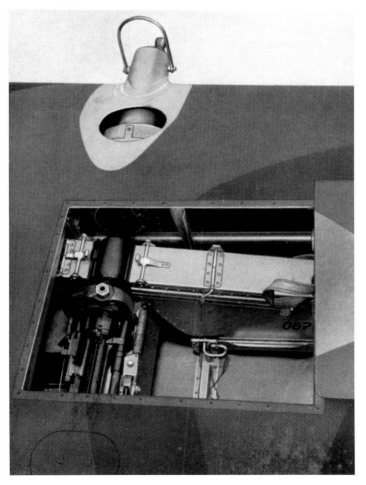

Close-up view of the swinging trapeze bomb carrier under the fuselage of a Ju 87 A in the closed position.

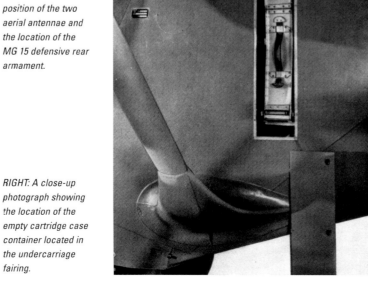

ABOVE: A detail photograph showing the location of the MG 17 machine gun and a view of the cockpit showing the position of the two aerial antennae and the location of the MG 15 defensive rear armament.

RIGHT: A close-up photograph showing the location of the empty cartridge case container located in the undercarriage fairing.

Ju 87 B

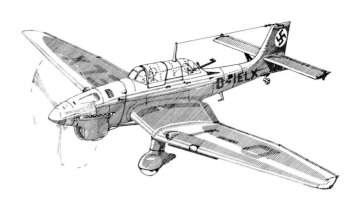

A drawing taken from an original Junkers/RLM handbook detailing the armament and weights for the Ju 87 B-1 and B-2.

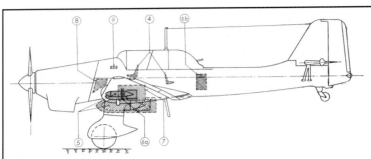

Dieser Ladeplan hat nur Gültigkeit für das seinem Verwendungszweck entsprechend vollständig ausgerüstete Flugzeug.

Die Besatzung besteht bis zu 500 kg Bombenlast aus 2 Mann.

Die Bombe hängt ungefähr im Schwerpunkt. Höchstzulässiges Fluggewicht 4300 kg.

Beanspruchungsgruppe: H 5.

Motor: Jumo 211 A.
Luftschraube: Ju HPC 3,4 m ∅.

				$4 \times 50 = 200$	1×250	$200 + 250 = 450$	1×500
	Bombenlast .... kg						
1	Leergewicht .... kg			2745	2745	2745	2745
2	Zusätzliche Ausrüstung .... kg			325	325	325	325
3	Rüstgewicht .... kg			3070	3070	3070	3070
4		Besatzung		140- 200	140- 200	140- 200	140- 200
5		Bomben		0- 200	0- 250	0- 450	0- 500
6	Munition	a: Starre Schußwaffe .		0- 26	0- 26	0- 26	0- 26
		b: Bewegl. Schußwaffe		0- 22	0- 22	0- 22	0- 22
7		Kraftstoff		5- 380	5- 380	5- 380	5- 380
8		Schmierstoff		9- 36	9- 36	9- 36	9- 36
9		Leuchtpatronen		0- 1	0- 1	0- 1	0- 1
10	Fluggewicht .... kg			3889-3935	3939-3985	4139-4185	4189-4235

Ladeplan Ju 87 B-1
(S 8700 - 5020 a)

Data tables taken from an original Junkers/RLM handbook detailing the armament and operational weights for the Ju 87 B-1 and B-2.

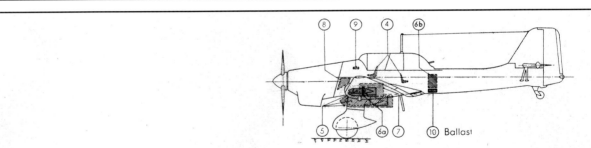

Motor: Jumo 211 D.
Luftschraube: VS 5 3,4 m ∅.
Gewichte in kg.

Dieser Ladeplan hat nur Gültigkeit für das, seinem Verwendungszweck entsprechend, vollständig ausgerüstete Flugzeug.

Die Besatzung ist stets 2 Mann.
Die Bombe hängt ungefähr im Schwerpunkt.
Landung mit 500 kg-Bombe vermeiden.
Notlandung mit 500 kg-Bombe verboten!

7. Ladeplan Ju 87 B-2
(S 8700 - 5033)

			Verwendungsgruppe: HK Beanspruchungsgruppe: 5 Höchstzul. Fluggewicht: 4400 kg		Schwerpunktslagen von Tm-Vorderkante für:	Leergewicht: 370 mm höchstzul. Vorlage: 550 mm höchstzul. Rücklage: 675 mm		
			Beladezustand und Bombengröße	I 1×500	II 1×250	III $1 \times 250 + 4 \times 50$	IV 4×50
1	Leergewicht		2800 ÷ 2880	2800 ÷ 2880	2800 ÷ 2880	2800 ÷ 2880	
2	Zusätzliche Ausrüstung		325	325	325	325	
3	Rüstgewicht		3125 ÷ 3205	3125 ÷ 3205	3125 ÷ 3205	3125 ÷ 3205	
4	Besatzung		160 ÷ 200	160 ÷ 200	160 ÷ 200	160 ÷ 200	
5	Bomben		0 ÷ 500	0 ÷ 250	0 ÷ 450	0 ÷ 200	
6	Munition:	a) Starre Schußwaffe	0 ÷ 26	0 ÷ 26	0 ÷ 26	0 ÷ 26	
		b) Bewegl. Schußwaffe	0 ÷ 22	0 ÷ 22	0 ÷ 22	0 ÷ 22	
7	Kraftstoff		5 ÷ 370	5 ÷ 370	5 ÷ 370	5 ÷ 370	
8	Schmierstoff		9 ÷ 43	9 ÷ 43	9 ÷ 43	9 ÷ 43	
9	Leuchtpatronen		0 ÷ 1	0 ÷ 1	0 ÷ 1	0 ÷ 1	
10	Ballast		20	20	20	20	
11	Fluggewicht voll		∼ 4400	∼ 4140	∼ 4340	∼ 4090	
12	Kraftstoff in Liter γ = 0,74		7 ÷ 500	7 ÷ 500	7 ÷ 500	7 ÷ 500	
13	Schmierstoff in Liter γ = 0,90		10 ÷ 47	10 ÷ 47	10 ÷ 47	10 ÷ 47	

electrical
connection
for Revi

switch and
test box

Revi C/12C
bomb sight

turning knob
for sighting
of Revi

gun firing
button for MG 17s
in safety position

steering column
type KG 12A

The instrument panel of the pilot's cockpit of the Ju 87 B-1 and B-2 showing the gun-firing position on the control column.

ABOVE and BELOW: A view of the rear cockpit showing the MG 17 defensive armament position.

The bomb release trapeze as fitted under the fuselage of a Ju 87 B shown in the down position.

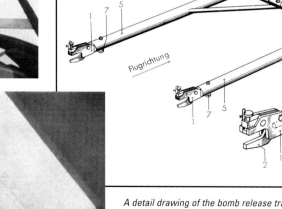

Flugrichtung

1 Gabelkopf
2 Klinke
3 Bolzen
4 Hülse
5 Traverse
6 Federbolzen
7 Rändelmutter
8 Traversen-Arme
9 Rastblech
10 Gummipuffer
11 Kugelköpfe
12 Seilhalterung

A detail drawing of the bomb release trapeze which also shows the possibility of width adjustment for carrying different size diameter bombs.

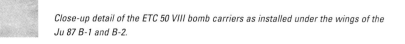

Close-up detail of the ETC 50 VIII bomb carriers as installed under the wings of the Ju 87 B-1 and B-2.

Ju 87 R

Handbook details of the weight tables for the Ju 87 R-2 Trop. and the R-4 Trop.

Ladeplan Ju 87 R-2 trop
S 8700—5061

Motor: Jumo 211 D
Luftschraube: VS 5 oder VS 11

Hierzu gehört Beladevorschrift S 8700—5062

Achtung! In der Bedienungsvorschrift-Fl festgelegte besondere Bedingungen für Überlastgewichte beachten.

Dieser Ladeplan hat nur Gültigkeit für das, seinem Verwendungszweck entsprechend, vollständig ausgerüstete Flugzeug (siehe Beladevorschrift).

Verwendungsgr.: **HK H H** Beanspruchungsgr.: **5 4 3** Höchstzl. Fluggew.: 4500 4850 5220 kg		Schwerpunktslagen hinter Tm-Vorderkante für	Leergewicht: **450 mm** höchstzulässige Vorlage: **550 mm** höchstzulässige Rücklage: **712 mm**	
		ohne abwerfbare Behälter		**mit** abwerfbaren Behältern	
Beladezustand		I	II	III	IV
		Gewichte in kg			
	Bombengröße	1 x 500	1 x 250	1 x 500	1 x 250
1	Leergewicht	2980÷3060	2980÷3060	2980÷3060	2980÷3060
2	Zusätzliche Ausrüstung normal	355	355	400	400
3	Zusätzliche Ausrüstung für Achse	120	120	120	120
4	Rüstgewicht	3455÷3535	3455÷3535	3500÷3580	3500÷3580
5	Besatzung	140÷200	140÷200	140÷200	140÷200
6	Bomben	0÷500	0÷250	0÷500	0÷250
7	Munition a: Starre Waffe	0÷26	0÷26	0÷26	0÷26
	b: Bewegliche Waffe	0÷22	0÷22	0÷22	0÷22
8	Kraftstoff a: Hauptbehälter	5÷370	5÷370	5÷370	5÷370
	b: Zusatzbehälter	—	—	0÷444	0÷444
9	Schmierstoff a: Hauptbehälter	9÷52	9÷52	9÷52	9÷52
	b: Zusatzbehälter	—	—	0÷23	0÷23
10	Leuchtpatronen	0÷1	0÷1	0÷1	0÷1
11	Fluggewicht voll	~4710	~4460	~5220	~4970
	Kraftstoff in Liter $\gamma = 0{,}74$	7÷500	7÷500	7÷1100	7÷1100
	Schmierstoff in Liter $\gamma = 0{,}90$	10÷57	10÷57	10÷82	10÷82

Die Besatzung ist stets 2 Mann. Die Bombe hängt ungefähr im Schwerpunkt.

Bei Landung brauchen **leere** Außenbehälter nicht abgeworfen werden.

Landung mit 500 kg Bombe möglichst vermeiden.

Zulässiges Höchstlandegewicht in Ausnahmefällen 5000 kg, das entspricht halb leergeflogenen Zusatzbehältern.

Vor Notlandung sind Bomben blind und Kraftstoffzusatzbehälter abzuwerfen.

Anlagen — Ju 87 R-2 trop, R-4 trop Tropenausrüstung — Flugbetrieb — II 03

Ladeplan Ju 87 R-4 trop
S 8700—5067

Motor: Jumo 211 H
Luftschraube: VS 11

Hierzu gehört Beladevorschrift S 8700—5068

Dieser Ladeplan hat nur Gültigkeit für das, seinem Verwendungszweck entsprechend, vollständig ausgerüstete Flugzeug (siehe Beladevorschrift).

Verwendungsgr.: **HK H H** Beanspruchungsgr.: **5 4 3** Höchstzl. Fluggew.: 4500 4850 5400 kg		Schwerpunktslagen hinter Tm-Vorderkante für	Leergewicht: **430 mm** höchstzulässige Vorlage: **550 mm** höchstzulässige Rücklage: **712 mm**			
		ohne abwerfbare Behälter			**mit** abwerfbaren Behältern		
Beladezustand		I	II	III	IV	V	VI
		Gewichte in kg					
	Bombengröße	1 x 500	1 x 250	—	1 x 500	1 x 250	—
1	Leergewicht	3155÷3255	3155÷3255	3155÷3255	3155÷3255	3155÷3255	3155÷3255
2	Zusätzliche Ausrüstung normal	355	355	355	400	400	400
3	Zusätzliche Ausrüstung für Achse	120	120	120	120	120	120
4	Rüstgewicht	3630÷3730	3630÷3730	3630÷3730	3675÷3775	3675÷3775	3675÷3775
5	Besatzung	140÷200	140÷200	140÷200	140÷200	140÷200	140÷200
6	Bomben	0÷500	0÷250	0	0÷500	0÷250	0
7	Munition a: Starre Waffe	0÷26	0÷26	0÷26	0÷26	0÷26	0÷26
	b: Bewegliche Waffe	0÷22	0÷22	0÷22	0÷22	0÷22	0÷22
8	Kraftstoff a: Hauptbehälter	5÷355	5÷355	5÷355	5÷355	5÷355	5÷355
	b: Zusatzbehälter	—	—	—	0÷444	0÷444	0÷395
9	Schmierstoff a: Hauptbehälter	9÷52	9÷52	9÷52	9÷52	0÷52	0÷52
	b: Zusatzbehälter	—	—	—	0÷23	0÷23	0÷23
10	Leuchtpatronen	0÷1	0÷1	0÷1	0÷1	0÷1	0÷1
11	Fluggewicht voll	~4890	~4640	~4390	~5400	~5150	~4850
	Kraftstoff in Liter $\gamma = 0{,}74$	7÷480	7÷480	7÷480	7÷1080	7÷1080	7÷1015
	Schmierstoff in Liter $\gamma = 0{,}90$	10÷57	10÷57	10÷57	10÷83	10÷83	10÷83

Die Besatzung ist stets 2 Mann. Die Bombe hängt ungefähr im Schwerpunkt.

Bei Landung brauchen **leere** Außenbehälter nicht abgeworfen werden.

Landung mit 500 kg Bombe möglichst vermeiden.

Zulässiges Höchstlandegewicht in Ausnahmefällen 5000 kg, das entspricht fast leergeflogenen Zusatzbehältern.

Vor Notlandung sind Bomben und Kraftstoffzusatzbehälter abzuwerfen.

II 04 — Flugbetrieb — Ju 87 R-2 trop, R-4 trop Tropenausrüstung

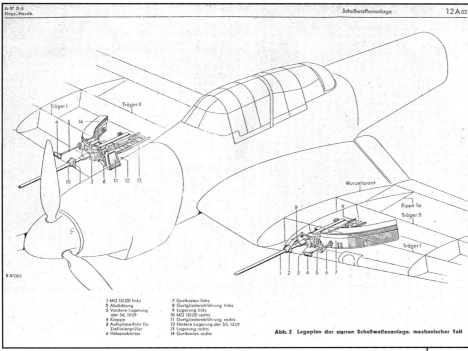

Handbook drawing of the wing armament of the MG 151/20 cannon.

View of the rear gunner and the rotating gun turret for the MG 81 Z machine guns.

Drawing showing the ammunition drums and empty cartridge container for the MG 81 Z machine guns.

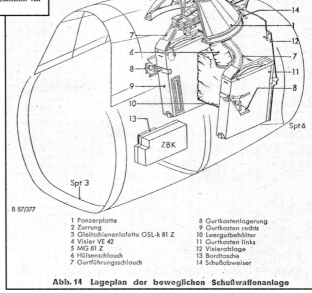

With the rear gunner's canopy slid over the rotating gun turret, an armourer is seen here cleaning the perspex.

The rear gunner loads the ammunition into the MG 81 Z machine guns with the canopy slid open over the rotating turret.

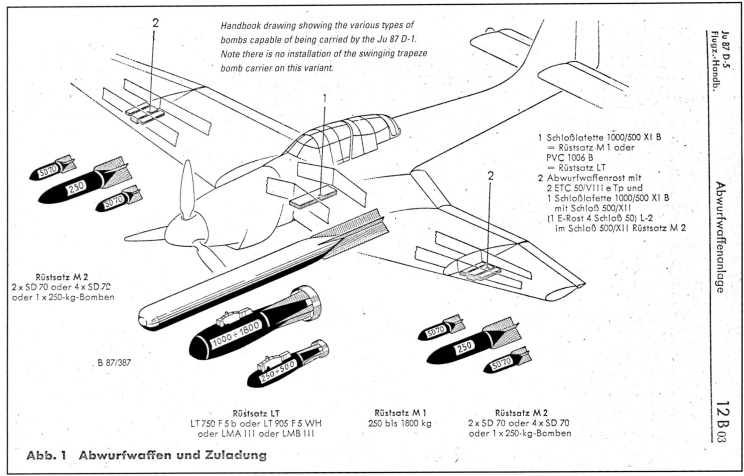

Handbook drawing showing the various types of bombs capable of being carried by the Ju 87 D-1. Note there is no installation of the swinging trapeze bomb carrier on this variant.

1 Schloßlafette 1000/500 XI B
= Rüstsatz M 1 oder
PVC 1006 B
= Rüstsatz LT
2 Abwurfwaffenrost mit
2 ETC 50/VIII e Tp und
1 Schloßlafette 1000/500 XI B
mit Schloß 500/XII
(1 E-Rost 4 Schloß 50) L-2
im Schloß 500/XII Rüstsatz M 2

SD 70
250
SD 70

Rüstsatz M 2
2 x SD 70 oder 4 x SD 70
oder 1 x 250-kg-Bomben

B 87/387

1000 ÷ 1800

250 ÷ 500

SD 70
250
SD 70

Rüstsatz LT
LT 750 F 5 b oder LT 905 F 5 WH
oder LMA III oder LMB III

Rüstsatz M 1
250 bis 1800 kg

Rüstsatz M 2
2 x SD 70 oder 4 x SD 70
oder 1 x 250-kg-Bomben

Abb. 1 Abwurfwaffen und Zuladung

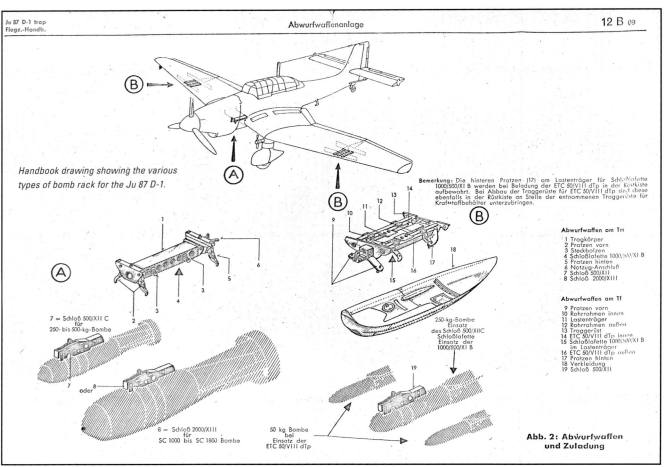

Handbook drawing showing the various types of bomb rack for the Ju 87 D-1.

Bemerkung: Die hinteren Pratzen (17) am Lastenträger für Schloßlafette 1000/500/XI B werden bei Beladung der ETC 50/VIII dTp in der Rüstkiste aufbewahrt. Bei Abbau der Traggerüste für ETC 50/VIII dTp sind diese ebenfalls in der Rüstkiste an Stelle der entnommenen Traggerüste für Kraftstoffbehälter unterzubringen.

Abwurfwaffen am Tm
1 Tragkörper
2 Pratzen vorn
3 Steckbolzen
4 Schloßlafette 1000/500/XI B
5 Pratzen hinten
6 Notzug-Anschluß
7 Schloß 500/XII
8 Schloß 2000/XIII

Abwurfwaffen am Tf
9 Pratzen vorn
10 Rohrrahmen innen
11 Lastenträger
12 Rohrrahmen außen
13 Traggerüst
14 ETC 50/VIII dTp innen
15 Schloßlafette 1000/500/XI B
   im Lastenträger
16 ETC 50/VIII dTp außen
17 Pratzen hinten
18 Verkleidung
19 Schloß 500/XII

7 = Schloß 500/XII C
für
250- bis 500-kg-Bombe

oder

8 = Schloß 2000/XIII
für
SC 1000 bis SC 1800 Bombe

50 kg Bombe
bei
Einsatz der
ETC 50/VIII dTp

250-kg-Bombe
Einsatz
des Schloß 500/XIIC
Schloßlafette
Einsatz der
1000/500/XI B

**Abb. 2: Abwurfwaffen
und Zuladung**

Ju 87 G

A mechanic makes some final adjustment to the engine of this Ju 87 G which is fitted with BK 3.7 tank-busting cannon under its wings.

Test-firing the 37 mm BK 3.7 cannon on a Ju 87 G.

A cloud of dust rises as two Ju 87 Ds of an unidentified unit take off from a Soviet airfield for another sortie. The aircraft in the foreground carries the Werknummer 110780 and the one behind carries bombs with the 'Stabo' device beneath its wings. This was a shaft extension from the nose that caused the bomb to detonate above ground to give better shrapnel distribution for use against ground troops.

The Henschel Hs 129

Hs 129 B

Dipl.-Ing. Friedrich Nicolaus, chief designer at Henschel and the creator of the Hs 129.

A photograph reproduced from a wartime German aircraft recognition manual showing an early Hs 129 B-0, coded KK+VP.

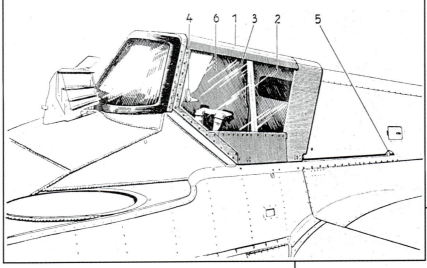

Details of the sliding canopy on the Hs 129 B-0.
1 – Dural metal frame to canopy
2 – Armour plated glass (Plexiglas) side panels
3 – Sliding panel
4 – Release catch for sliding panel
5 – Canopy runner and stop
6 – Detachable metal panel behind pilot

RLM Hs 129 B-0 Handbook drawing showing details of the nose armour and the Gnôme-Rhône 14M radial engines.
1 – Armour plated cockpit
2 – Panelling
3 – Fixed front windscreen
4 – Sliding hood
5 – Lower metal panelling
6 – Nose
7 – Additional lower panelling

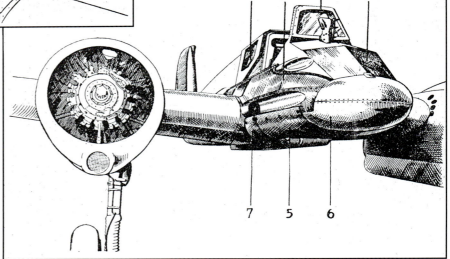

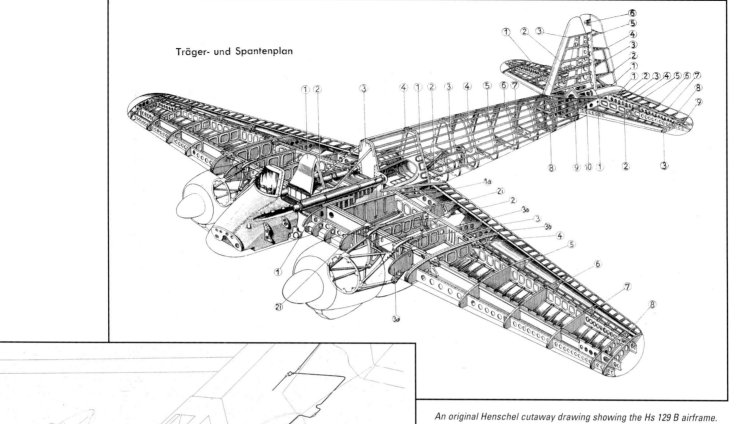

Träger- und Spantenplan

An original Henschel cutaway drawing showing the Hs 129 B airframe.

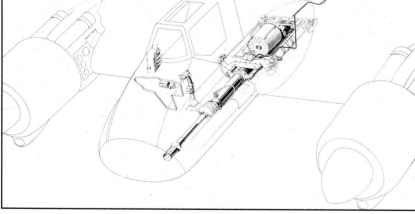

A handbook drawing detailing the installation of the 30 mm MK 101 cannon in the Hs 129 B.

This photograph shows one of the first Hs 129 B-1s fitted with the 30 mm MK 101 cannon. The gondola is shown in the down position so as to allow quick servicing of the main weapon. The drum containing armour-piercing shells has not yet been installed.

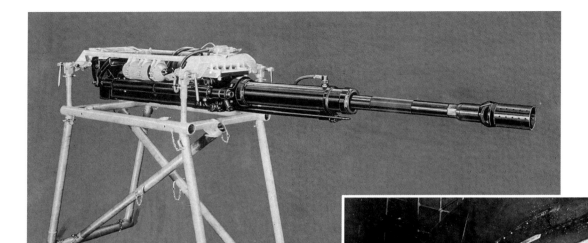

ABOVE: A 30 mm MK 101 cannon installed on a maintenance stand.

RIGHT: Close-up of the starboard side nose section of an Hs 129 showing the MK 101 cannon hanging in its maintenance position to allow access to the ammunition feed drum. Note the panelling covering the MG 151 has also been removed to allow complete access to the gun and its installation.

Close-up view of the MK 101 cannon as installed in an Hs 129 B-1.

An Hs 129 B-1 fitted with a MK 101 cannon is waved away by ground crew hoping for another successful mission.

LEFT AND ABOVE: Armourers work to reload the magazine of this Hs 129 B-2 with 30 mm armour-piercing shells for a MK 103 cannon. In order to gain easy access to the gun, the cover has been removed.

BELOW: Detail drawing showing the installation of the MK 103 cannon in an Hs 129 B-2.

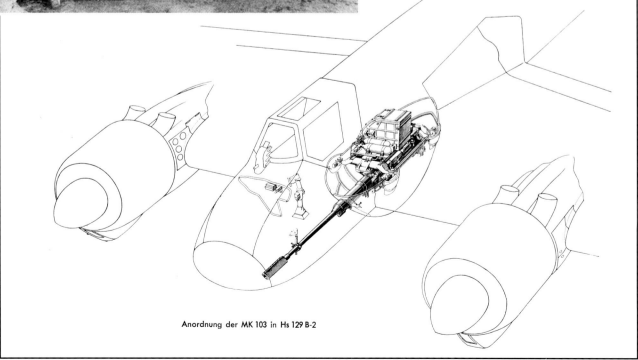

Anordnung der MK 103 in Hs 129 B-2

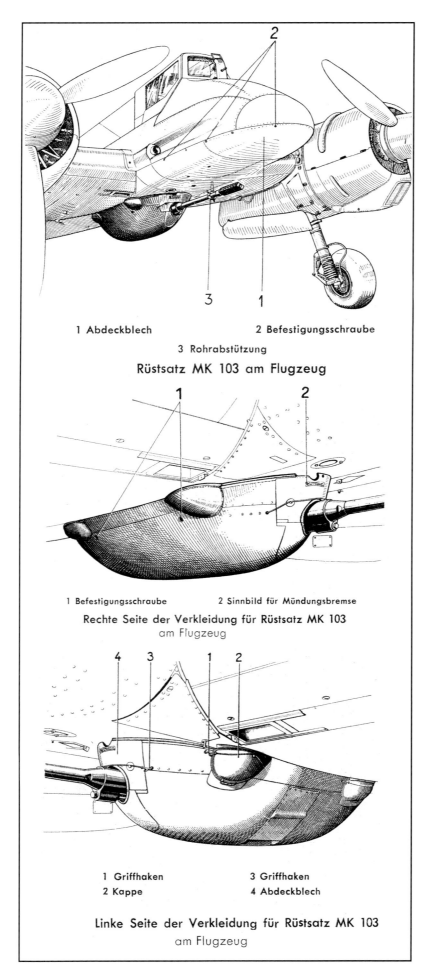

1 Abdeckblech   2 Befestigungsschraube

3 Rohrabstützung

Rüstsatz MK 103 am Flugzeug

1 Befestigungsschraube   2 Sinnbild für Mündungsbremse

Rechte Seite der Verkleidung für Rüstsatz MK 103
am Flugzeug

1 Griffhaken   3 Griffhaken
2 Kappe   4 Abdeckblech

Linke Seite der Verkleidung für Rüstsatz MK 103
am Flugzeug

An Oberfeldwebel closes the collars to secure the barrel of a MK 103 cannon beneath an Hs 129. The collar ensured that the barrel would not vibrate during flight and was also used to finely adjust the aim of the gun to harmonise with the gunsight.

LEFT AND BELOW: Handbook drawings showing various details of the MK 103 cannon installation in the Hs 129 B-2.

1 Hinteres Hebelrohr
Ein- bzw. Ausschwenken des Rüstsatzes MK 103

IV.(*Stuka*)/L.G.1

IV.(Stuka)/Lehrgeschwader 1

(Unit Code: L1+)

Formation and early history (November 1938 – August 1939) 1 April 1937: formed as IV.(St)/L.G. by the redesignation of I./St.G. 162 at Schwerin. 15 July 1937: moved to Barth. This redesignation made permanent the subordination of this *Gruppe* to *Stab*/L.G. which began as a temporary arrangement on 1 November 1936. 1937: became the unit responsible for working up the Ju 87 A and for developing tactics for its use. It had originally been equipped with a mixture of Hs 123 dive-bombers and He 70 as fast bombers. 20 September 1938: *Gruppe* had Ju 87 B at Barth. 1 November 1938: unit was renamed IV.(St)/L.G. 1 at Barth, as part of the general reorganization of the Lehr units. Also from about this time it was involved in conducting dive-bombing training, this continuing at Barth until mobilization on 25 August 1939.

Polish campaign (September 1939) 1 September 1939: had 3(3) Do 17 M and 39(37) Ju 87 B at Stolp-Reitz (104 km west of Danzig) under 1.Fl.Div.; hit Polish naval and harbour targets; struck targets at Dzialoszyn (near Lodz) in support of XI.*Armee*, then bombed troop concentrations south-east of Czestochowa. 2 September: struck naval base at Gdynia. 3 September: operations vic Warsaw. 6 September: relocated to Grieslienen. 11 September: transferred to Lyck. Between 6 and ?? September: attacked artillery positions and rail targets vic Warsaw. ?? September: relocated to Lyck/East Prussia. Second week of September?: struck rail targets vic Białystok. Third week in September: relocated to Radom

and flew last operations of campaign against Warsaw, Modlin and Novy-Dwór. 22 September: ordered under Lfl. 1. 24 September: subordinated to *Stab*/St.G. 77. 29 September: returned to Barth.

Standby and training in the West (October 1939 – April 1940) October, November: recovering at Barth. Late November or early December 1939: transferred from Barth to Dedelstorf under Lfl. 2. December 1939 - April 1940: regular training activities. End of April or beginning of May: deployed to Duisburg in the Ruhr for the forthcoming campaign in the West, although some sources maintain that the move to Duisburg took place in February 1940.

Attack on France and the Low Countries (May 1940 – June 1940) End of April or early May 1940: deployed to Duisburg. 10 May 1940: had 39 (37) Ju 87 B at Duisburg under VIII.Fl.Korps/Lfl. 2 via *Stab*/St.G. 77. *Gruppe* struck enemy defensive positions at Moerdijk/Holland and along the Albert Canal in support of paratroops and armour. 12 May: *Gruppe* remained subordinated to *Stab*/St.G. 77 after it was passed from Lfl. 2 to Lfl. 3. 13 May: struck targets vic Rotterdam while temporarily based at Neuenkampf. 15 May: attacked enemy armour and troop concentrations in the Nivelles–Villers-la-Ville area 28-30 km south of Brussels.

IV.(Stuka)/L.G. 1 pioneered the introduction of the Ju 87 into Luftwaffe service. This Ju 87 B, L1+JV of 11.(Stuka)/L.G. 1, W.Nr. 0236, suffered a flak hit during the campaign against Poland and was forced to land at Grieslinen in East Prussia. The anti-aircraft shell penetrated the starboard side of the fuselage, the resulting explosion blowing out the panelling on the port side.

For the attack on Poland, IV.(Stuka)/ L.G. 1 was based at Stolp-Reitz (104 km west of Danzig) and placed under the command of 1.Fliegerdivision. This photograph shows crews of two Ju 87 B-1s of the 10.Staffel relaxing prior to the invasion. L1+DU in the background still carries the early type fuselage Balkenkreuz with narrow white outlines and has the Hakenkreuz or swastika positioned across the fin and rudder.

16 May: *Gruppe* transferred from Kirchhellen to Aachen-Merzbrück - action vic Genappe. 17 May: dive-bombed enemy troops and columns withdrawing west vic Waals and Brussels. ca 17 May: moved to Neuenkampf and Bierset (west of Liège). 18 May: flew attacks on Belgian forts at Namur and Liège. 19 May: operating from Gymnich/south-west of Köln, attacked a British column along the road near Oudenaarde/north-west Belgium; at the end of the day, the *Gruppe* moved forward to a field strip at Hargimont/Belgium. 22 May: moved forward to Les Septanes, a field strip near Beaumont. 26 May: moved forward to Cambrai to better support the heavy fighting in north-eastern France. 27 May: attacked enemy troop movements and positions in the Mastaigne area and then around Seclin-Houplines. 25-31 May: attacked troop concentrations and shipping at Boulogne, Calais and Dunkirk. 2 June: flew two attacks on shipping off Dunkirk. 3 June: more attacks on shipping off Dunkirk. 4 June: transferred from Cambrai to Signy-le-Petit/35 km north-west of Charleville-Mézières. 4 June: transferred from Cambrai to Signy-le-Petit/35 km north-west of Charleville-Mézières. 5-18 June: flew operations in the Champagne region under VIII.Fl.Korps, supporting drive over the Somme, Seine and Loire Rivers. 8 June: operations in Soissons area. 9 June: moved to Barly/west of Arras. 10 June: hit the railway station at Dreux/72 km west of Paris. 14 June: transferred from Barly to Mannheim-Sandhofen to begin attacks on the Maginot Line forts in the Saarbrücken area. 21 June: at least 10.*Staffel* and possibly the entire *Gruppe* at Mannheim-Sandhofen to attack targets in Alsace – this was the *Gruppe's* last mission of the campaign. 22 June: the armistice ends the campaign this date. 22-ca 30 June: *Gruppe* at Mannheim-Sandhofen to recuperate. End of June or start of July 1940: *Gruppe* transferred from Mannheim-Sandhofen to Tramecourt (48 km south-east of Boulogne)/north-east France under II.Fl.Korps.

Air offensive against Britain (Battle of Britain) (July 1940 – December 1940) 11 July 1940: attacked convoy and Portland harbour. 14 July: attacked convoy off Dover, damaging coasters *Betswood* and *Bovey Tracey*. 25 July: attacked convoy CW 8 off Dover, shared in several sinkings. 25 July: transferred to Hesdin (Tramecourt)/33 km east of Merck-sur-Mer along the

Channel coast – attacked convoy CW 8 off Dover along with a/c from other units sank 5 ships and damaged 4 others – this was the *Gruppe's* first combat mission during the Battle of Britain. 29 July: raided Dover. 7? August: may have attacked a convoy. 11 August: action off Clacton. 12 August: attacked convoy in Thames Estuary. 13 August: had 36(28) Ju 87 B at Tramecourt under II.Fl.Korps/Lfl. 2. 13 August: attacked RAF Detling. 14 August: had action over Folkstone. 15 August: struck Hawkinge airfield. 18 August: after this, *Stuka* units generally withdrawn from the campaign. 29 August: struck at Dover harbour. 2 September: accident reported at Tramecourt. 3 September: transferred from Tramecourt (or nearby Hesdin) via Ghent to Amsterdam-Schiphol where the *Gruppe* spent the next two months providing dive-bombing training to new crews. 22 September: accident in Holland. 8 October: accident reported vic Paris. November 1940: reassigned from II.Fl.Korps to J.Fl.Fü 2. 8 November 1940: transferred from Schiphol back to Tramecourt. 8 November: attacked shipping in Thames Estuary. 14/15 November: at Tramecourt. 11 December: ordered transferred from Tramecourt to Kristiansand-Kjevik/southern Norway. Start of January 1941: move to Kristiansand begun.

Norway – anti-shipping operations; attack on the Soviet Union (January 1941 – January 1942) Early January 1941: upon arrival at Kristiansand-Kjevik, assigned to Fl.Fü. Nord for operations against maritime targets vic south-west Norway. 4 March: still at Kristiansand. Mid-March to end of April: 10.*Staffel* went to Banak, then Bardufoss and flew coastal patrols in area of Varanger Peninsula and North Cape. 16 April: Ju 87 R-2 accident noted. End of May or start of June: *Gruppe* left Kristiansand for Trondheim-Vaernes. 7 June: *Gruppe* joined 10.*Staffel* at Bardufoss. 21 June: moved from Bardufoss to Kirkenes with 33 Ju 87 Rs. 29 June: struck at airfields around Murmansk, then supported advance of XIX. *Gebirgs-Korps* (23-29 June); hit targets at Matunuovo. Summer 1941: the *Gruppe* operated in *Staffel- Schwarm-* and *Kette-*size units all along the front during the first hectic months of the advance. 30 June: action vic Litsa. 30 June: lost a Ju 87 R-2 after attacking Russian minelayers in Motovskiy Bay. 1 July: transferred from Kirkenes to Rovaniemi/Finland. 1-9 July: supported action vic Salla. 9? July: returned to Kirkenes. 10 July: action vic Kairala (110 km north-east Rovaniemi). 11 July: lost a Ju 87 R-1 and a Ju 87 B-1 during attacks on Russian minelayers, patrol craft and anti-submarine vessels in Litsa Bay. 12 July: action noted vic Alakurtti (207 km east of Rovaniemi). 14 July: Ju 87 R-2 shot down by a fighter over Kuotijärvi flew support operations for Finnish III Corps vic Kuotijärvi. 16 July: action vic Vuorijärvi. 18 July: action over Litsa Bay. 19-20 July: sunk destroyer *Stremitelny* and patrol boat *Shtil* near Murmansk. 21 July: saw combat near Ura-Guba/36 km north-north-west of Murmansk during an attack on a Russian airfield. 22 July: action over Motovskiy Bay. 30 July: lost Ju 87 B-1 (L1+EW) near Kirkenes during a carrier strike on Kirkenes and Petsamo airfields by 47 a/c from HMS *Victorious* and *Furious*. 1-7 August: supported Finnish III. Corps' drive on Kestenga (282 km east-south-east of Rovaniemi). 6 August: action vic Petsamo. 9 August: apparently attacked Varlamovo airfield during a maximum effort raid by *Luftflotte* 5 on enemy airfields around the city. 22 August: two *Staffeln* at Rovaniemi supported advance of XXXVI. *Korps* (August); attacked bridges at Kadda (not located; other sources give Kovda). 25 August: *Gruppenstab*, 10. and 11.*Staffeln* at Rovaniemi and 12.*Staffel* at Kirkenes. 28 August: attacked the Russian airfield at Alakurtti. 2 September: action vic Kestenga. 3 September: elements at Rovaniemi transferred to Kirkenes where they joined 12.*Staffel*. 9 September: action over Ura Bay vic Murmansk. 15 September: bombed ground targets along the front in the Litsa Bend area vic Murmansk. A few days later, a week of bad weather set in and air operations were curtailed. After end of September: operations reduced due to declining weather. By early October: based at Rovaniemi. 1-10 October: now operating mainly from Rovaniemi again, struck troop concentrations, supply columns, rail targets, etc. in area of Kandalaksha (200 km south of Murmansk). After 10 October: operations shifted to naval targets, such as naval base at Polyarnoya and port of Murmansk, where the *Gruppe* sunk a destroyer. 26 October: flew its last mission against targets on Rybachiy (Fischer) Peninsula, which was key to German operations in northern Finland. October-November: declining activity due to weather. 1 December: had two *Staffeln* at Rovaniemi and one *Staffel* at Kiestino (??). 16 December: switched to attacking Murmansk rail targets, using Alakurtti as a forward airfield (near end of year); attacked freight trains and troop barracks, vic Engozero on the Murmansk RR line 164 km south of Kandalaksha. 23 December: attacks on artillery positions east of Alakurtti. December 1941: operations came to a virtual halt as temperatures dropped as low as -50°C. January 1942: had 27 Ju 87 mainly at Rovaniemi. 27 January 1942: *Gruppe* was redesignated I./St.G. 5 at Rovaniemi. From 3 September 1940 to 27 January 1942, the *Gruppe* lost a total of 26 a/c, 21 men killed, 7 missing, 6 wounded and 3 captured.

Ergänzungsstaffel of IV.(St)/L.G. 1 (April 1940 – January 1942)

Information on this *Staffel* is extremely sparse but it was probably formed in 1940; however the first reference to it is dated on 15 April 1941 apparently at Kristiansand/Norway. In July 1941 it was temporarily transferred from Kristiansand to Kirkenes/northern Norway, in part to fly combat missions in the Murmansk region. 2 September 1941: it reported a combat loss of a Ju 87 R in the vicinity of Kestenga (282 km east-south-east of Rovaniemi). There are no further references until 27 January 1942 when it was redesignated 4.(Erg)/St.G. 5.

FpNs: IV.*Gruppenstab* (L 06687, 08798); 10. (L 16753); 11. (same as *Gruppenstab*); 12. (L 40409)

Codes: (L1+_E, U, V, W, F), where F applied to the Erg.St./IV.(St)/L.G. 1.

Kommandeur:

Obstlt. Hans-Hugo Witt (1 April 1937 - August? 1937)
Major Günter Schwartzkopff (1 November 1938 - 1 June? 1939)
Oberst Dr. Knause ? (? 1939 - ? 1939) – acting?
Hptm. Peter Kögl (1 June 1939? - 22 June 1940)
Hptm. Bernd von Brauchitsch (22 June 1940 - 31 July 1940?)
Hptm. Erwin Röder (1 August 1940 - 21 December 1940)
Hptm. Walter Klemme (21 December 1940 - 31 May 1941)
Hptm. Arnulf Blasig (RK) (1 July 1941 - 27 January 1942)

Sources for IV.(*Stuka*)/L.G. 1:

Unpublished and Archival:
BA-MA RL 2 III Meldungen über Flugzeugunfälle…..(Loss Reports – LRs);
NARA WashDC RG 242/T-971 roll 19, T-312 roll 1032/frame 460, T-312- roll 1052/frame 576;
PRO London AirMin AIR 40 intelligence documents based on radio intercepts and P/W interrogations;
PRO London ADM 223/OIC-SI Report 80.
PRO London AirMin signals intelligence documents AIR 40;

Knut Maesel collection via private correspondence.

Published:
[Anttonen – LiF] p. 15, 16, 62, 66-71;
[Balke – KG2V1] p. 393, 402, 409;
[Bateson – *Stuka*] p. 8, 9, 11, 23, 29, 30, 31, 35, 36;
[Bekker – LWD] p. 202, 215;
[Bergström – BCRS] p. 172, 177;
[Bingham – Blitz] p. 222-243;
[Brütting – SA] p. 158, 185, 189, 241, 264, 271;
[Dierich –VdL] p. 96, 202, 203, 204, 217, 223;
[Foreman – Forg] p. 56;
[Green –WotTR] p. 432, 434;
[Griehl – KFZ] p. 118;
[Hafsten – Flyalarm] p. 109, 110, 119;
[Held – SG] p. 16, 29, 31, 89;
[Kannapin – FPN] p. various;
[Mason – BovB] p. 550;
[Nauroth – StG2] p. 52;
[Obermaier – RK II] p. 84, 87, 96, 150, 165, 173, 174, 47;
[Plocher – Rus41] p. 193, 195, 196, 197;
[Plocher – Rus42] p. 27;
[Prien – JG77-1] p. 347;
[Ries – Lw] p. 111, 139, 170-173;
[Ries – PhotoCol] p. 203;
[Ries – PhotoRec] p. 170;
[Rohwer – Chron] p. 74;
[Shores – F] p. 19, 65;
[Smith – GA] p. 384, 385, 386;
[Smith – SAW] p. 19, 20, 37, 38, 40, 42, 43, 76, 77;
[Stipdonk – Schule] p. 218;
[Tessin – Form] p. 87, 225;
[Tessin – Tessin] p. 314, 325;
[Weal – *Stuka* 47-41] p. 34, 53-55, 77, 83;
[Zweng – Zweng] p. various;

[Archiv #9 – A-9] p. 26;
M.Holm website www.ww2.dk

IV.(Stuka)/L.G. 1 equipped with the Ju 87 R-2, was transferred to Kristiansand-Kjevik in January 1941 for operations against maritime targets off south-west Norway. This aircraft, L1+CV from the 11.Staffel, is pictured on a rough Norwegian airstrip.

Early in January 1941 IV.(Stuka)/L.G. 1 was transferred to Kristiansand-Kjevik in Norway. On 1 July it moved to Rovaniemi in Finland, often flying operations against Russian vessels in the Litsa Bay. Here two members of the ground crew relax on two 500 kg bombs. The Ju 87 R behind, L1+JV, belonged to the 11.Staffel. In the background can be seen Ju 52/3m and Fw 58 transports.

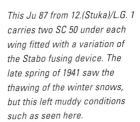

This Ju 87 from 12.(Stuka)/L.G. 1 carries two SC 50 under each wing fitted with a variation of the Stabo fusing device. The late spring of 1941 saw the thawing of the winter snows, but this left muddy conditions such as seen here.

This Ju 87 B, L1+GV of 11.(Stuka)/L.G. 1, overturned while attempting to make an emergency landing at Kemijärvi in Finland. Its crew was rescued by dint of levering the aircraft up and dragging them from their damaged cockpit. The aircraft was then put under guard before being recovered.

St.G. 1

Sturzkampfgeschwader 1

(Unit Code: A5+)

Stab/St.G. 1

Formation and Organization (November 1939 – April 1940) Formed 18 November 1939 at Jüterbog by renaming *Stab/Lehrgeschwader* 2. A *Stabsstaffel* was formed at the same time, probably by reorganizing and expanding the *Stabskette* of *Lehrgeschwader* 2 which had been equipped with Bf 109 fighters, and which immediately began converting to Ju 87 B and Do 17 M. A separate *Feldpostnummer* for the *Stabsstaffel* was not issued until the second half of 1941. Assigned to VIII.*Fliegerkorps* and transferred to Siegburg/23 km south-east of Köln in December.

Attack on France and the Low Countries (May 1940 – June 1940) 10 May: had 3 (3) Ju 87 B and 6 (5) Do 17 M at Siegburg, under II.*Fliegerkorps/Luftflotte* 3 and probably had II./St.G. 2 and I.(St)/Tr.G. 186 subordinated to it. Supported attacks on Belgian forts on the first day of the offensive, but specific activities of the *Stab* are unknown during the May-June period. 9 June: attacked Pont Ste-Maxence.

Air Offensive against England (Battle of Britain) (July 1940 – February 1941) July 1940: based at Angers/France under VIII.*Fliegerkorps*. 5 July: lost a Ju 87 B near Bapaume (45 km north-east of Amiens) due to engine failure. 20 July: Do 17 M crashed at Théville near Cherbourg, probably after being attacked by an RAF night fighter, 1 KIA and 2 WIA. 25 July: Do 17 M shot down by Spitfires at night to the south-west of London, 1 MIA and 1 WIA and captured. 13 August: had 3 (2) Ju 87 B and 2 (1) Do 17 M at Angers under VIII.*Fliegerkorps/Luftflotte* 3. 18 August: after heavy losses among the *Stuka* units, day combat operations over the Channel and southern England generally stopped. Beginning of September: transferred from Angers to St-Pol-Brias. 5 September: Ju 87 loss noted at St-Pol-Brias. 26 October: still based at St-Pol-Brias, but now under *Luftflotte* 2. Beginning of November: set up a forward command post at Ostend/Belgium for renewed attacks on shipping off Dover and over the Thames estuary. 29-30 November: Bf 110 shot down by fighters off Ramsgate/Kent during a reconnaissance flight. 22 February 1941: transferred from St-Pol-Brias to

Trapani in western Sicily and reassigned to X.*Fliegerkorps* for operations against Malta and the British Mediterranean Fleet.

Mediterranean, Greece and Crete (March 1941 – June 1941) March: while in Sicily, the *Stab* also used Comiso as a forward base. 12 May: transferred to Argos/Greece and reassigned to VIII.*Fliegerkorps* to support Operation *Merkur*, the invasion of Crete. 20 May: at Argos. June: relocated to north-east Poland.

Attack on the Soviet Union – Operations in Central Russia (June 1941 – December 1941) 22 June: had 3 (2) Ju 87 B and 6 (3) Bf 110 at Raczki (Radczki – 18 km south-east of Suwalki in north-east Poland) under VIII.*Fliegerkorps*. 24-30 June: *Stab* moved forward and briefly at Baranowicze/eastern Poland. 6 July: at Dokudovo (27 km east-north-east of Borisov). 15 July: now based at Orsha-South. 26 July: at Shatalovka, under *Nahkampfführer* 2/II.*Fliegerkorps*. 1 August: at Surazh/135 km west of Bryansk and with effect this date placed directly under *Luftflotte* 2. August - September: supported offensive operations near Roslavl, Rogachev, Gomel - Klintsy and in the Kiev pocket. 4 September: based at Seshchinskaya (40 km south-east of Roslavl). 30 September: reassigned back to *Nahkampfführer* 2/II.*Fliegerkorps*. October - November: supported the advance in Bryansk - Vyazma, Orel, Tula sectors, and towards Moscow. 27 October: *Stab* based at Yukhnov and still there at the beginning of December. December: transferred to Schwäbisch Hall in South Germany at the beginning of December to rest and refit.

Operations in North Russia (February 1942 – March 1943) 20 February: ordered from Schwäbisch Hall to Luga-Gostkino in north Russia for ops in the Leningrad area under I.*Fliegerkorps/Luftflotte* 1. 1 March: had 5 Bf 110 E-3 and 3 Ju 87 D-1 on hand. 7 May: Bf 110 D-3 accidently shot down by a German fighter near Vereskovo, *Oblt.* Hans Wolf + 1 WIA. June: transferred from Gostkino to Gorodets (23 km south of Luga). 3 June: Bf 110 D-3 accidently shot up by a German fighter near Volkhov. 30 August: base at Gorodets bombed and one Ju 87 destroyed. 20 September: reported 12 (5) Bf 110 and Ju 87 on strength at Gorodets.

Stab/St.G. 1 Emblem

*I./St.G. 1 Emblem
(First Formation)*

The crew chief looks on while ground staff from St.G. 1 push one of the unit's Ju 87 Bs into position. This aircraft, which was probably photographed during the Polish campaign in 1939, carries the code A5+AH with the individual letter 'A' in white. A narrow white band was also painted around the rear fuselage possibly indicating that this was the Staffelkapitän's machine.

27 September: Gorodets bombed again with slight damage to a Fi 156 liaison aircraft belonging to the *Stab*. 1 January 1943: reported 5 Bf 110 E, 3 Bf 110 D-3 and 3 Ju 87 D-1 on strength at Gorodets under 3.*Flieger-Div./Luftflotte* 1. 24-30 March: relocated from Gorodets to Bryansk in Central Russia for ops in the Kursk area under 1. Fl.Div./*Luftwaffen-Kdo. Ost*.

Operations in Central Russia (April 1943 – October 1943) 16 April: based at Bryansk. 29 April: transferred from Bryansk to Orel-North. 29 May: Bf 110 G-3 crashed at Orel-North due to pilot error, 3 injured. 12 June: Bf 110 G-3 shot down by AA fire over the Orel sector, 2 KIA and 1 MIA. 1 July: reported 2 Bf 110 E-3, 1 Bf 110 D-3, 4 Bf 110 G-3 and 3 Ju 87 D-3 on strength. 5 July: Orel-North – *Geschwader* commenced Operation *Zitadelle* this date, a massive German counter-offensive against the Kursk salient. 6 July: Bf 110 hit by ground fire in the vicinity of Samodurovka wounding *Hptm*. Werner Mikross. 16 July: Bf 110 G-2 shot down by a fighter over Optovo, 3 WIA. 23 July: *Stab* withdrew to Karachev/75 km west-north-west of Orel as Soviet forces closed on the city after the Germans lost the initiative at Kursk and the Russians began a powerful advance westward. 12 August: *Stab* now based at Krasnoye (45 km north-east of Orsha?) from where it directed attacks on Soviet forces advancing on Smolensk. September: at Mogilev/205 km east of Minsk. 18 September: Ju 87 D-5 crashed and burned east of Asinovo, *Hptm*. Paul Hoser + 1 MIA. Early October: still at Mogilev. 18 October: moved to Bobruisk about mid-October and redesignated *Stab*/S.G. 1 this date.

Codes: (A5+_A)

FpNs: *Geschwader*stab (L 19458); *Stabsstaffel* (L 42521)

Kommodore:
Oberst Eberhard Baier (18 November 1939 - June 1940)
Obstlt. Walter Hagen (22 June 1940 - 31 December 1942?)
    (Unknown) (January 1943 - March 1943)
Major Gustav Pressler (1 April 1943 - April 1943) – acting
Obstlt. Paul-Friedrich Darjes (May 1943 - 31 May 1943?) – acting
Oberst Clemens Graf von Schönborn-Wiesentheid (acting?) (June 1943 - 11 June 1943?)
Hptm. Siegfried Steinhoff (24 September 1943 - 18 October 1943) – acting

I./St.G. 1 (First Formation)

Formation and Training (May 1939 – August 1939) Formed 1 May 1939 at Insterburg/East Prussia by renaming I./St.G.160. Equipped with Junkers Ju 87 B dive-bombers.

Polish Campaign (September 1939) 1 September: at Insterburg and Elbing in East Prussia with 38 (38) Ju 87 Bs and 3 (2) Dornier Do 17 Ps as an independent *Gruppe* first under *Luftwaffenkommando Ostpreussen*, then under *Lw.-Lehrdivision* and later *Fliegerführer z.b.V.* Flew the first combat mission of World War II and suffered the first combat loss – 3 Ju 87s under Bruno Dilley were briefed to take out a twin railway bridge at Dirschau (Tczew) near Danzig, but unanticipated circumstance prevented total success. One Ju 87 B from 1.*Staffel* flew into the ground on the return flight killing the crew of two. The same day, struck radio stations at Babice and Lacy, near Warsaw. 2–27 September: attacked troop concentrations and positions, transport columns, airfields, radio stations and targets of opportunity in North Poland in support of advancing ground forces, moving forward behind the Army units to field airstrips and landing grounds at Grieslienen, Krasne, Brzezno, Gorowo and Oronsko/15 km south-west of Radom. 29 September: returned to Insterburg on conclusion of the campaign.

Ju 87 B-1s of I./St.G. 1 photographed at Insterburg in East Prussia around the time of the German invasion of Poland in September 1939. The aircraft nearest the camera, A5+BB, was possibly that of the Gruppen Kommandeur, Major Werner Rentsch, as it carries a distinguishing narrow white band behind the cockpit. At this time, many Ju 87s had their Hakenkreuz painted across both fin and rudder.

West – Phoney War and Standby (October 1939 – March 1940) October: relocated from Insterburg to Köln-Wahn in western Germany. October 1939 - March 1940: activities unknown but presumably involved in training as were most other units of the *Luftwaffe*. January 1940: moved to Koblenz-Karthause. March: transferred to Delmenhorst in North Germany where the *Gruppe* was outfitted with new Ju 87 R models equipped with jettisonable auxiliary fuel tanks for long-range anti-shipping missions, the first *Stuka* unit to receive these.

Occupation of Denmark and Norway (April 1940 – June 1940) 9 April: had 39 Ju 87 Rs at Kiel-Holtenau under X.*Fliegerkorps* – bombed artillery positions at Akershus and Fort Oskarsborg on Oslo Fjord, then attacked ships off Bergen, sinking a Norwegian destroyer. Towards the end of the day, the *Gruppe* relocated from Kiel-Holtenau, via Arhus/Denmark to Stavanger-Sola/Norway, with 1.*Staffel* detached at Oslo-Fornebu. 12 April: sent 7 a/c to bomb Trondheim-Vaernes airfield. 14 April: elements at Stavanger-Sola bombed by the RAF. 17 April: attacked cruiser *Suffolk*, hitting a turret. 19 April: 3 Ju 87 Rs dive-bombed British warships at Namsfjord without scoring any hits, but losing one *Stuka* to AA fire. 20 April: relocated from Stavanger to Oslo-Fornebu. 25 April: 1.*Staffel* lost 7 a/c in a series of raids on Trondheim-Vaernes by a/c from carriers *Ark Royal* and *Victorious*. 28 April: attacked shipping at Alesund and Andalsnes, sinking one small ship. 30 April: based at Trondheim-Vaernes under *Fliegerführer Drontheim*, sank 3 ships in Namsfjord. 1 May: flew an unsuccessful attack on the carrier *Ark Royal* off the coast north of Trondheim, one *Stuka* being shot down by fighters. 3 May: sank two destroyers, one French (*Bison*) and one British (*Afridi*), and damaged 3 other ships during convoy attacks off the Norwegian coast. 10 May: reported 39 (27) Ju 87 Rs at Trondheim-Vaernes under *Fliegerführer*

Drontheim. 22 May: raided Bodo harbour, sinking trawler *Ingrid*, and possibly freighter *Skerstad* at Rognan. 24 May: sank armed Norwegian trawler at Bodo. 27 May: bombed radio station at Bodo, destroying numerous houses. 28 May: flew first attack on Narvik, followed by heavier raids on 2 June which cost the *Gruppe* 3 Ju 87s, all downed by British fighters. 20 June: *Gruppe* left Norway for Évreux/France.

Air Offensive against England (Battle of Britain) (June 1940 – December 1940) ca 21 June: from Évreux, attacked fortified positions vic Cherbourg. Late June: transferred to Beauvais for rest and refitting. July: ordered to Angers at the end of July and commenced operations against Channel shipping and targets along the south coast of England using airfields around Caen for staging purposes. 8 August: attacked westbound convoy CW 9. 15 August: attacked Portland harbour and naval base without loss. 16 August: attacked Tangmere. 18 August: all *Stuka* units withdrawn from operations after this date. 25 September: Ju 87 R crashed on take-off from Angers airfield due to engine failure. September: ordered to move in whole or in part to St.Pol-Brias in north-eastern France around the end of September, but only a few combat missions were flown to the end of the year, mainly small-scale attacks on shipping along the Kentish coast and in the Thames Estuary. From November, elements of the *Gruppe* also operated from Bergen-op-Zoom in south-western Holland which afforded better positioning for operations along the south-eastern coast of England. 9 October: Ju 87 R-1 damaged landing at Évrecy/14 km south-west of Caen. October - December: flew a few attacks on coastal shipping. 30 October: Ju 87 R-1 collided with a Do 215 at Brest with moderate damage. November - December: with operations for the *Gruppe* in the West now concluded, the next two months were spent resting and

In March 1940 I./St.G. 1 at Kiel-Holtenau received its first Ju 87 Rs, having 39 of these longer range versions by the time it took part in the invasion of Norway on 9 April 1940. On this day the Gruppe bombed artillery positions at Akershus and Fort Oskarsborg on Oslo Fjord, then attacked ships off Bergen, sinking a Norwegian destroyer. The photograph shows an aircraft of the 2.Staffel.

Codes: (A5+_B, H, K, L)

FpNs: I. (L 30043, 37714)

Kommandeur:
Major Werner Rentsch (1 May 1939 - 18 October 1939)
Hptm. Paul-Werner Hozzel (1 June 1939 (or September 1939?) - 18 October 1939) – acting
Hptm. Paul-Werner Hozzel (18 October 1939 - 8 May 1940 - August 1941?)
Hptm. Helmut Sorge (DKG) (26 May 1941 - 13 January 1942 or 19 February 1942)
Hptm. Bruno Dilley (DKG) (December 1941 - December 1941) – acting?

I./St.G. 1 (Second Formation)

Formation (June 1943) Formed 17 June 1943 at Gorodets airfield/23 km south of Luga on the northern sector of the Eastern Front by renaming I./St.G. 5. Equipped with Junkers Ju 87 D dive-bombers.

Operations in North and Central Russia (June 1943 – July 1943) 18 June: 2 Ju 87 D-3s from 1. and 2.*Staffel* shot down by AA fire in the Mga area, *Oblt.* Hans Schrank + 1 MIA. 21 June: Ju 87 D-3 crewman WIA by AA fire over Alexandrovka in the Leningrad front area,

but the aircraft was not damaged. 22 June: Ju 87 D-3 damaged landing at Gorodets. 24 June: 2.*Staffel* Ju 87 D-3 crashed into the ground at Gorodets, 1 WIA. 28-29 June: departed Gorodets for Orel-West on the central sector of the front to support the massive German counter-offensive against the Kursk salient (Operation *Zitadelle*) that commenced on 5 July. In departing Gorodets, a DFS 230 glider belonging to the *Gruppe* crashed while being launched under tow from the airfield killing 2. 1 July: Orel-West – *Gruppe* reported 30 Ju 87 D-3 and 2 Ju 87 D-1 on strength. 7 July: 3.*Staffel* Ju 87 D-2 shot down by AA fire, *Staffelkapitän Hptm.* Kurt Pape + 1 KIA. 9 July: 2.*Staffel* Ju 87 D-3 shot down by AA fire over Nvosinovyy (Novosinnovyy?), 2 MIA. 10 July: 3.*Staffel* Ju 87 D-3 flipped on landing at Orel-Domnino airfield (Orel-West?) and totally destroyed. 11-12 July: 3 Ju 87 D-3s shot down by AA fire in the Bolkhov-Ulyanovo area to the north of Orel, 2 MIA. On 12 July 2.*Staffel* filed a claim for an La-5 fighter north-west of Bolkhov. 17 July: Ju 87 D-3 shot down by AA fire at Strelnikovo, *Hptm.* Friedrich Lorenz + 1 KIA. 22 July: 3.*Staffel* Ju 87 D-3 shot down by AA fire over the front, but the crew managed to bale out and evade capture. 23 July: withdrew to Karachev/75 km west-north-west of Orel as Soviet forces closed on the city after the Germans lost the initiative at Kursk and the Russians began a powerful advance westward. 29 July: 1.*Staffel* Ju 87 D-3 failed to return and believed shot down, 2 KIA.

West – Phoney War and Standby (October 1939 – March 1940) October: relocated from Insterburg to Köln-Wahn in western Germany. October 1939 - March 1940: activities unknown but presumably involved in training as were most other units of the *Luftwaffe*. January 1940: moved to Koblenz-Karthause. March: transferred to Delmenhorst in North Germany where the *Gruppe* was outfitted with new Ju 87 R models equipped with jettisonable auxiliary fuel tanks for long-range anti-shipping missions, the first *Stuka* unit to receive these.

Occupation of Denmark and Norway (April 1940 – June 1940) 9 April: had 39 Ju 87 Rs at Kiel-Holtenau under X.*Fliegerkorps* – bombed artillery positions at Akershus and Fort Oskarsborg on Oslo Fjord, then attacked ships off Bergen, sinking a Norwegian destroyer. Towards the end of the day, the *Gruppe* relocated from Kiel-Holtenau, via Arhus/Denmark to Stavanger-Sola/Norway, with 1.*Staffel* detached at Oslo-Fornebu. 12 April: sent 7 a/c to bomb Trondheim-Vaernes airfield. 14 April: elements at Stavanger-Sola bombed by the R.A.F. 17 April: attacked cruiser *Suffolk*, hitting a turret. 19 April: 3 Ju 87 Rs dive-bombed British warships at Namsfjord without scoring any hits, but losing one *Stuka* to AA fire. 20 April: relocated from Stavanger to Oslo-Fornebu. 25 April: 1.*Staffel* lost 7 a/c in a series of raids on Trondheim-Vaernes by a/c from carriers *Ark Royal* and *Victorious*. 28 April: attacked shipping at Alesund and Andalsnes, sinking one small ship. 30 April: based at Trondheim-Vaernes under *Fliegerführer Drontheim*, sank 3 ships in Namsfjord. 1 May: flew an unsuccessful attack on the carrier *Ark Royal* off the coast north of Trondheim, one *Stuka* being shot down by fighters. 3 May: sank two destroyers, one French (*Bison*) and one British (*Afridi*), and damaged 3 other ships during convoy attacks off the Norwegian coast. 10 May: reported 39 (27) Ju 87 Rs at Trondheim-Vaernes under *Fliegerführer Drontheim*. 22 May: raided Bodo harbour, sinking trawler *Ingrid*, and possibly freighter *Skerstad* at Rognan. 24 May: sank armed Norwegian trawler at Bodo. 27 May: bombed radio station at Bodo, destroying numerous houses. 28 May: flew first attack on Narvik, followed by heavier raids on 2 June which cost the *Gruppe* 3 Ju 87s, all downed by British fighters. 20 June: *Gruppe* left Norway for Évreux/France.

Air Offensive against England (Battle of Britain) (June 1940 – December 1940) ca 21 June: from Évreux, attacked fortified positions vic Cherbourg. Late June: transferred to Beauvais for rest and refitting. July: ordered to Angers at the end of July and commenced operations against Channel shipping and targets along the south coast of England using airfields around Caen for staging purposes. 8 August: attacked westbound convoy CW 9. 15 August: attacked Portland harbour and naval base without loss. 16 August: attacked Tangmere. 18 August: all *Stuka* units withdrawn from operations after this date. 25 September: Ju 87 R crashed on take-off from Angers airfield due to engine failure. September: ordered to move in whole or in part to St.Pol-Brias in north-eastern France around the end of September, but only a few combat missions were flown to the end of the year, mainly small-scale attacks on shipping along the Kentish coast and in the Thames Estuary. From November, elements of the *Gruppe* also operated from Bergen-op-Zoom in south-western Holland which afforded better positioning for operations along the south-eastern coast of England. 9 October: Ju 87 R-1 damaged landing at Évrecy/14 km south-west of Caen. October - December: flew a few attacks on coastal shipping. 30 October: Ju 87 R-1 collided with a Do 215 at Brest with moderate damage. November - December: with operations for the *Gruppe* in the West now concluded, the next two months were spent resting and

In March 1940 I./St.G. 1 at Kiel-Holtenau received its first Ju 87 Rs, having 39 of these longer range versions by the time it took part in the invasion of Norway on 9 April 1940. On this day the Gruppe bombed artillery positions at Akershus and Fort Oskarsborg on Oslo Fjord, then attacked ships off Bergen, sinking a Norwegian destroyer. The photograph shows an aircraft of the 2.Staffel.

refitting before being ordered to the Mediterranean. 26 December 40 - 10 January 1941: transferred to Trapani in western Sicily on or about this date with *Geschwaderstab/ St.G. 3* and *II./St.G. 2* and assigned to *X.Fliegerkorps* for operations against Malta and the British Mediterranean Fleet, especially the aircraft carrier *Illustrious* and shipping passing between Sicily and North Africa.

A cine camera was attached to the wheel spat of this Ju 87, replacing the wind-driven siren generator, so that propaganda film could be taken of a dive-bombing raid. The aircraft, which carries the emblem of I./St.G. 1, has its individual letter 'C' painted on the front of its spats to assist ground crews in marshalling their charges.

Central Mediterranean, Balkans and North Africa (January 1941 – June 1941) 10 January: attacked elements of the British Mediterranean Fleet between Sicily and Tunisia, scoring hits on the carrier *Illustrious* and the battleship *Warspite*; 2. and 3.*Staffel* each lost one Ju 87 on the mission. 11 January: helped sink cruiser *Southampton*. 15 January: Ju 87 R-2 damaged during RAF raid on Catania airfield/south-east Sicily. 18 January: attacked Luqa airfield on Malta losing a Ju 87 R to fighters. 19 January: dive-bombed the *Illustrious* in Grand Harbour/Malta losing 2 *Stukas* and one more damaged. 5/6 February: attacked HM Trawler *Tourmaline*. 5 February: made a tactical transfer from Trapani to Elmas/Sardinia to counter British naval 'Force H', which had sailed from Gibraltar and shelled Genoa harbour in north-west Italy on 9 February, but no contact was made

with the enemy surface force. 13 February: *Gruppe* elements transferred temporarily to Castel Benito/26 km south-south-west of Tripoli in Libya to begin supporting the planned offensive by the *Deutsches Afrikakorps* (DAK) and to attack British-held ports along the coast of Cyrenaica. 14 February: Ju 87 shot down over El Agheila by AA fire, 1 KIA. 18 February: attacked enemy positions near Marsa Brega with 12 Ju 87s of which 5 were claimed by RAF and Commonwealth fighters. 22 February: took part in an attack on the port of Benghazi during which the RN coastal monitor *Terror* was hit and damaged. 14 March: *Gruppe's* rear elements still at Trapani. 31 March: *Gen.Lt.* Rommel's DAK began his expected offensive aimed at driving the British out of Cyrenaica this date, sending his armour against the enemy in the Marada - Marsa el Brega area, but the *Gruppe* had returned to Trapani and did not participate. 1 April: transferred to Kraynitsi (Krainici)/42 km south-south-west of Sofia in Bulgaria on or about this date and attached to *Stab/St.G.2* (VIII.*Fliegerkorps*) for the Balkan campaign in Yugoslavia and Greece. On 5 April the *Gruppe* reported 24 Ju 87 Rs on strength at Kraynitsi. 7 April: reported first loss over the Balkans, losing a Ju 87 from 3.*Staffel* to ground fire near Veria in North Greece. 14 April: 2.*Staffel* Ju 87 shot down by a Greek PZL near Trikala in Central Greece. After returning to Kraynitsi following this mission, the *Gruppe* was ordered to return to Trapani. 25 April: all or elements now back at Castel Benito in Libya. 8 May: ordered to Elmas/Sardinia for action against the 'Tiger' convoy escorted by heavy British RN surface units in the western Mediterranean. Attacked the convoy this date with 28 *Stukas*, but no results were obtained. 12-13 May: transferred from Trapani to Argos/Greece for Operation *Merkur*, the airborne and air-landing assault on Crete. 19 May: 3.*Staffel*, preceding the rest of the *Gruppe* by nearly a month, returned to North Africa. 24 May: in the only apparent loss by the *Gruppe* during the Crete operation, which began on 20 May, a Ju 87 was forced to ditch off the north-west coast of Crete after receiving ground fire while supporting paratroops near Galatas at the western end of the island.

North Africa (June 1941 – January 1942) 1-15 June: departed Argos and returned to North Africa with station at Derna where I./St.G. 1 was assigned to support Rommel's *Afrikakorps* under *Fliegerführer Afrika*. 16 June: attacked targets in the Sollum, Bardia, Capuzzo area, with 2 *Stukas* claimed by Hurricanes, as British relief forces from Egypt attempted to advance towards surrounded Tobruk. 8 July: Ju 87 shot down by AA fire near Tobruk. 29 July: 4 Ju 87s claimed shot down by Curtiss Tomahawks in the Bardia area. 1 August: Ju 87 R/Trop bombed on ground at Malemes airfield on Crete. 2 August: dive-bombed a convoy off Sidi Barrani losing 2 Ju 87 R2/Trop to Hurricanes, both crews KIA. This was the last reported loss or accident for the *Gruppe* until 7 October, suggesting that it may have been on stand down to rest and refit with only a few operational sorties flown as needed. August: at Derna – continued supporting the siege of Tobruk. 7 October: Ju 87 R-4 crashed and burned near Tmimi airfield/Libya. 25/26 October: sank the Royal Navy's fast minelayer *Latona* (2,650 tons) off Bardia while she was transporting replacements and supplies to the Australian garrison surrounded at Tobruk in company with four other warships. 1 November: 5 Ju 87 R-2s moderately to

severely damaged during RAF raid on Derna. 20 November: 3 to 6 of the *Gruppe's Stukas* out of a formation of 12 claimed by RAF fighters when jumped in the Bir el Gobi area, but only one Ju 87 R-2/Trop was lost with 1 KIA and 1 MIA. 22 November: Ju 87 R-2/Trop shot up and crash-landed at Gambut airfield. 23 November: 2 Ju 87s claimed by Hurricanes in the Sidi Rezegh area. However, the *Gruppe* reported no losses that corroborate this claim. 4 December: 2 Ju 87 R-2s shot up by fighters at Bir bu Maades. 5 December: Ju 87 R-2/Trop force-landed near Gubi after being shot up. 10 December: Ju 87 shot down by naval AA fire while attacking a cruiser off Derna, *Oblt.* Heike Steinhagen + 1 MIA. 13 December: Ju 87 shot down by AA fire southeast of Gazala and crashed near Derna, 2 WIA. 18 December: *Hptm.* Gerhard Schmidt from the *Gruppe* KIA during Allied bombing of Benina airfield. December 1941 – 13 January 1942: variously identified as transferring from Derna to Arco Philanorum, Agedabia and El Agheila after British counter-attacks drove Rommel's forces out of Cyrenaica and back towards Tripoli on the Gulf of Sidra. 13 January 1942: renamed II./St.G. 3.

A British soldier examines an abandoned Ju 87 B-2 of the first 3./St.G. 1 in North Africa. The aircraft has sand yellow (RLM colour 79) upper surfaces with green (80) mottling and carries the code A5+HL, the indistinct individual letter 'H' painted in bright yellow.

I./St.G. 1 was transferred to Trapani in Sicily early in January 1941 and assigned to X.Fliegerkorps for operations against Malta and the British Mediterranean Fleet, in particular the aircraft carrier HMS Illustrious. On the 10th the Gruppe bombed the Illustrious and the battleship Warspite but lost two Ju 87s. Here, aircraft from the 1.Staffel fly over the North African coast, with A5+JH nearest the camera.

Three Ju 87 B long-range dive-bombers returning from a mission in the western desert. The aircraft nearest the camera, A5+FK of 2./St.G. 1, has its red individual identification letter 'F' painted above both wings outboard of the crosses. This letter was also repeated on both sides of the fuselage, in red thinly outlined in white.

Codes: (A5+_B, H, K, L)

FpNs: I. (L 30043, 37714)

Kommandeur:
Major Werner Rentsch (1 May 1939 - 18 October 1939)
Hptm. Paul-Werner Hozzel (1 June 1939 (or September 1939?) - 18 October 1939) – acting
Hptm. Paul-Werner Hozzel (18 October 1939 - 8 May 1940 - August 1941?)
Hptm. Helmut Sorge (DKG) (26 May 1941 - 13 January 1942 or 19 February 1942)
Hptm. Bruno Dilley (DKG) (December 1941 - December 1941) – acting?

I./St.G. 1 (Second Formation)

Formation (June 1943) Formed 17 June 1943 at Gorodets airfield/23 km south of Luga on the northern sector of the Eastern Front by renaming I./St.G. 5. Equipped with Junkers Ju 87 D dive-bombers.

Operations in North and Central Russia (June 1943 – July 1943) 18 June: 2 Ju 87 D-3s from 1. and 2.*Staffel* shot down by AA fire in the Mga area, *Oblt.* Hans Schrank + 1 MIA. 21 June: Ju 87 D-3 crewman WIA by AA fire over Alexandrovka in the Leningrad front area,

but the aircraft was not damaged. 22 June: Ju 87 D-3 damaged landing at Gorodets. 24 June: 2.*Staffel* Ju 87 D-3 crashed into the ground at Gorodets, 1 WIA. 28-29 June: departed Gorodets for Orel-West on the central sector of the front to support the massive German counter-offensive against the Kursk salient (Operation *Zitadelle*) that commenced on 5 July. In departing Gorodets, a DFS 230 glider belonging to the *Gruppe* crashed while being launched under tow from the airfield killing 2. 1 July: Orel-West – *Gruppe* reported 30 Ju 87 D-3 and 2 Ju 87 D-1 on strength. 7 July: 3.*Staffel* Ju 87 D-2 shot down by AA fire, *Staffelkapitän Hptm.* Kurt Pape + 1 KIA. 9 July: 2.*Staffel* Ju 87 D-3 shot down by AA fire over Nvosinovyy (Novosinnovyy?), 2 MIA. 10 July: 3.*Staffel* Ju 87 D-3 flipped on landing at Orel-Domnino airfield (Orel-West?) and totally destroyed. 11-12 July: 3 Ju 87 D-3s shot down by AA fire in the Bolkhov-Ulyanovo area to the north of Orel, 2 MIA. On 12 July 2.*Staffel* filed a claim for an La-5 fighter north-west of Bolkhov. 17 July: Ju 87 D-3 shot down by AA fire at Strelnikovo, *Hptm.* Friedrich Lorenz + 1 KIA. 22 July: 3.*Staffel* Ju 87 D-3 shot down by AA fire over the front, but the crew managed to bale out and evade capture. 23 July: withdrew to Karachev/75 km west-north-west of Orel as Soviet forces closed on the city after the Germans lost the initiative at Kursk and the Russians began a powerful advance westward. 29 July: 1.*Staffel* Ju 87 D-3 failed to return and believed shot down, 2 KIA.

Operations in Central Russia (August 1943 – October 1943) 3 August: still at Karachev – Ju 87 D-3 shot down by a fighter north of Krasnikovo, 1 KIA. 8 August: now operating from Bryansk – 2.*Staffel* Ju 87 D-3 shot down by AA fire south of Konevka. 12 August: 2.*Staffel* reported shooting down an La-5 near Gastilovo (not located). 13 August: 3.*Staffel* Ju 87 D-3 shot down by a fighter at Basavka, crew safe. 15 August: transferred north (possibly to Seshchinskaya or Smolensk-North) for operations around Smolensk in mid-August. 16 August: 2.*Staffel* Ju 87 D-3 shot down by a fighter at Subovka, 1 KIA. 18 August: 2.*Staffel* Ju 87 D-3 shot down by AA fire north-west of Prozt, 1 KIA. 21 August: 3.*Staffel* Ju 87 D-3 shot down by AA fire south of Pochinok, crew safe. 23 August: 1.*Staffel* Ju 87 D-3 crash-landed at Smolensk-North due to technical problems. 27 August: ordered back south on or about this date to cover withdrawal operations in the Glukhov-Konotop area. 28-30 August: 3 Ju 87 D-3/D-5s shot down by AA fire in the Glukhov area and 2 others destroyed in a mid-air collision, 6 KIA. 31 August – 3 September: 4 Ju 87 D-3s shot down and 2 more damaged by AA fire in the Glukhov-Konotop area, 4 KIA and 2 MIA. On 1 September, 2 Ju 87 D-3s were strafed on the ground at Borshchevo airstrip and damaged, one severely and the other slightly. The location of this airfield is unknown but presumably in the general Mogilev-Gomel area. 26 September: now at Bykhov airfield/42 km south of Mogilev. 6 October: ordered to move from Bykhov to Vitebsk. 15 October: transferred to Gorodok airfield/ 33 km north-north-west of Vitebsk on or about this date. 18 October: renamed I./S.G. 1 at Gorodok.

Codes: probably (L1+_B, H, K, L)

FpNs: I. (L 08798)

Kommandeur:
Hptm. Helmut Krebs (DKG) (17 June 1943 - 15 July 1943) – acting
Hptm. Horst Kaubisch (DKG, RK) (15 July 1943 - 18 October 1943)

Note: There is serious disagreement concerning who the *Kommandeure* of this *Gruppe* were with no two listings in accord with each other. Several creditable sources state that *Major* Kaubisch departed and the *Gruppe* was taken over at some point by a *Major* Martin Möbus (DKG, RK, EL), but this appears doubtful.

II./St.G. 1

Formation (July 1940) Formed 9 July 1940 at one of the several fieldstrips (St-Ingelvert?) around Marquise/12 km north-east of Boulogne in the Pas de Calais sector of north-eastern France by renaming III./St.G. 51. Equipped with Junkers Ju 87 B dive-bombers.

Air Offensive against England (Battle of Britain) (July 1940 – February 1941) 13 July: one *Staffel* from the *Gruppe*, escorted by Bf 109s from J.G. 51, attacked a convoy off Dover, but 2 of the *Stukas* were shot up by RAF Hurricanes and had to make forced landings on return to their base area. 20 July: flew a major yet relatively unsuccessful attack on convoy *Bosom* off Dover, sinking collier *Pulborough I* and destroyer *Brazen*, and damaging *Beagle* and one other ship. The convoy was well covered by Spitfires and Hurricanes and cost the *Gruppe* 2 Ju 87s with 4 more shot up and damaged. 25 July: attacked westbound convoy CW 8 sinking cement carrier *Summity* and collier *Henry Moon*. 29 July: flew a heavy

II./St.G. 1 Emblem

The II.Gruppe of St.G. 1 retained the emblem originally carried by III./St.G. 51. This comprised a red stylised eagle with a yellow comb and feet carrying green vine leaves. This Ju 87 B-2, which was operated by the former 7.Staffel, was coded 6G+DR, with the individual letter 'D' repeated on the outside of both wheel spats. The tip of the spinner was painted red followed by a narrow white band.

III./St.G. 1 Emblem

early morning raid on Dover harbour which caused little damage – 2 Ju 87s were shot down by Hurricanes. 13 August: *Gruppe* reported 38 (30) Ju 87 Bs on strength in Pas de Calais area under II.*Fliegerkorps/Luftflotte* 2. 13-14 August: aborted a strike on Rochester airfield in Kent when it could not be located and struck targets of opportunity instead; also sunk the Goodwin Sands lightship. 15 August: attacked Lympne and/or Hawkinge airfield. 18 August: all *Stuka* units withdrawn from daylight cross-Channel operations due to unacceptable losses. 26 October: at St.Pol-Brias/north-east France. 1 November: attacked shipping in the English Channel during mid-afternoon losing a 5.*Staffel* Ju 87 B; this was the first *Stuka* mission in close proximity to England since 18 August. November: all or elements moved to Ostend on the Belgian coast during November where the aircraft could more easily be brought to bear on small convoys and coastal shipping along the Kentish coast and in the Thames Estuary. 11/12 February: 5.*Staffel* Ju 87 B-2 shot down by naval AA fire while flying an experimental night dive-bombing raid on Chatham. 22 February: together with III./St.G. 1, transferred to Trapani/west Sicily for operations against Malta under X.*Fliegerkorps*; most missions were staged through Comiso at the other end of the island. The transfer was to replace I./St.G. 1 and II./St.G. 2 which had been ordered from Sicily to North Africa.

end of Crete. June: withdrew from the Mediterranean and Balkan theatres and rested and refitted for several weeks following the fall of Crete.

Attack on the Soviet Union – Operations in Central Russia (June 1941 – May 1942) 21 June: at (or near) Raczki (Radczki)/18 km south-east of Suwalki in north-east Poland for operations into Russia beginning the next day under VIII.*Fliegerkorps*; the *Gruppe* reported 39 (28) Ju 87s on strength. 24 June: lost 4 Ju 87s to Russian fighters while attacking targets in the Minsk area;

An Obergefreiter stares in surprise at the damage to the rear fuselage of this Ju 87 of 7./St.G. 1 as an Unteroffizier looks on. The aircraft carries the emblem first used by III./St.G. 51 and passed to II./St.G. 1 but on the cowling can be seen the legend 'Lee on Solent'. This probably refers to the attack on the Gosport area on 18 August 1940 when the Stuka units suffered severe losses to RAF fighters.

Central Mediterranean, North Africa and the Balkans (February 1941 – June 1941) 26 February: took part in a devastating raid on Luqa airfield/Malta that destroyed or damaged 17 to 19 British aircraft and most of the base hangars and workshops – 3 of *Gruppe's Stukas* failed to return. 11 April: 3 Ju 87s shot down by AA fire over Tobruk during an Axis drive across Cyrenaica. 29 April: 2 Ju 87 R-2/Trop crashed at Comiso airfield and moderately damaged. 9 May: attacked a relief convoy that had just arrived in Grand Harbour/Malta; the results of the attack were not determined. 11 May: one of the *Gruppe's Staffeln* was informally designated a '*NachtStaffel*' and comprised many of the night-qualified pilots from the night experiments that were conducted over England in February (see above). 12 May: transferred from Trapani and Comiso to Argos/Greece for Operation *Merkur*, the airborne and air-landing attack on Crete that commenced on 20 May. 24 May: lost 2 Ju 87s to non-hostile causes while supporting paratroops near Galatas at the western

During operations in the campaign against Greece and Yugoslavia several of St.G. 1's Ju 87s had animal badges painted on the noses. These photographs show three variants, a smiling hippopotamus, a rhinoceros and a lion, both of which were typical of this trend.

operated in the Bialystok-Minsk area to early July. 24 July: at Lepel-East/125 km south-west of Vitebsk – supported the advance on Smolensk to the end of July. 29 July: now at Surazh/135 km west of Bryansk. 8 August: 6.*Staffel* Ju 87 shot down by fighters in the vicinity of Velikiye Luki. 10 August: two of the *Gruppe's Staffeln* ordered to Bobruisk-South. 29 August: Ju 87 R-2 shot down by a fighter in the Toropets area, *Gruppen-kommandeur Hptm.* Keil KIA + 1 KIA. *Hptm.* Keil attempted a forced landing behind enemy lines but his Junkers flipped over killing both men. 31 August: *Gruppenstab* and elements at Seshchinskaya airfield/40 km south-east of Roslavl while other elements were at Novgorod Severski and later Konotop – flew attacks on enemy movements around Bryansk in front of XLVII.*Panzerkorps*; remained there to at least 21 September. 22 September: detached elements at Novgorod Severski and Konotop ordered to rejoin the rest of the *Gruppe* and move to Seshchinskaya to rest and refit for 3 days. 2 October: Ju 87 R-2 damaged taxiing at Seshchinskaya airfield. Operation *Taifun*, the drive to encircle and take Moscow, commenced this date along the front from Rzhev south to Bryansk and Orel. The *Gruppe* was assigned to support the advance on Rzhev towards Kalinin and on to the outskirts of the Soviet capital. 9 November: 1 Ju 87 destroyed and 2 badly damaged during a low-level Russian air attack on Yukhnov-North field airstrip east of Smolensk. 2 December: 2 Ju 87 R-4s shot down over the front area while attacking tanks near Naro-Fominsk to the north-west of Moscow, both crews MIA. Subsequent investigation stated that the two machines had actually collided during an evasive manoeuvre to avoid enemy fighters. Among the dead crew was *Hptm.* Joachim Rieger, *Staka* of 5.*Staffel*. December: while the operating component at Seshchinskaya, under *Nahkampfführer* 2/VIII.*Fliegerkorps*, supported the heavy defensive fighting west of Moscow, the rest of the *Gruppe*, mainly in the form of 6.*Staffel*, transferred to Schwäbisch Hall/Germany to rest and refit until mid-February; on return, the entire *Gruppe* moved to Dugino/65 km south of Rzhev. 30 December: elements resting and refitting at Schwäbisch Hall with Ju 87 D-1s; plans called for the entire *Gruppe* to begin moving around this date to Sicily for assignment to II.*Fliegerkorps*. These plans were subsequently cancelled as the defensive situation west of Moscow worsened. 15 February: 5.*Staffel* Ju 87 shot up and force-landed near Dugino between Rzhev and Vyazma. 1 March: *Gruppe* reported 42 Ju 87s on strength. 8 March: 2 Ju 87 B-1s shot down by AA fire near Kavkas, both crews MIA. 13 May: *Gruppe* ordered to operate from Rzhev during Operation *Nordpol*, an attempt to destroy the Russian 29th and 39th Armies in the Toropets-Nelidovo-Belyy area in the German A.O.K. 9 sector of the front. 17 May: ordered to transfer to Konstantinovka in the Donets Basin in South Russia as part of the planning for the German summer offensive towards Stalingrad and into North Caucasia. 19 May: Ju 87 D-1 damaged landing at Orsha. 21 May: Ju 87 R-4 shot down over Bolkhov to the north of Orel, *Gruppenkommandeur*

Hptm. Anton Keil poses in front of his Ju 87 B. He was born on 21 October 1910 in Plattling and joined the army in 1931. After transferring to the Luftwaffe in 1934, he became Staffelkapitän in III./St.G. 162 three years later. He led a Staffel of III./St.G. 51 during the Polish campaign and on 1 July 1940 became Kommandeur of II./St.G. 1. On 29 August 1941, during an attack on a railway station 1.5 km east of Skalowa, his aircraft was hit by ground fire. He attempted to make a forced-landing behind enemy lines but his Ju 87 flipped over and killed both him and his radio operator, Feldwebel Wilhelm Knof. On reaching the crash site, Soviet troops dragged Knof's body from the cockpit and stole all his possessions. Unable to reach Keil, they set fire to the Ju 87 with him still inside.

Hptm. von Malapert-Neufville KIA. Same date, the *Gruppe* began transferring to Kharkov-Rogan and then several weeks later to Volchansk airfield/62 km north-east of Kharkov to support the first phase of the summer offensive: the advance to the Don south of Voronezh. It seems clear from the record, however, that this move was either postponed for 3 weeks or at least one or two *Staffeln* remained behind for 3 weeks. 31 May: a Ju 87 B-1 bombed on the ground at Krasilina, a rarely used landing ground in the Rzhev-Dugino-Vyazma area.

South Russia – Operations in the Stalingrad Area (May 1942 – April 1943) 16 June: Ju 87 D-3 bombed on the ground at Kharkov and severely damaged. 17 June: flew an attack on partisans who had ambushed a train south-west of Shukovka in the Pz.A.O.K. 2 area. 27 June: still at Volchansk. 22 July: transferred to Tatsinskaya-South, this becoming one of the 5 or 6 principal *Luftwaffe* airfields on the western approaches to Stalingrad. 4 August: Ju 87 B-1 hit by ground fire and blew up near Rzhev, 1 KIA. August: supported the advance on Stalingrad, operating from Gorlovka, Lakedemonovka, Tatsinskaya and Oblivskaya (there 31 August) until September, then moved forward to Karpovka-West, just 40 km to the west of Stalingrad, from where the city and targets along the Volga were pounded over the next two months. 6-7 August: lost 3 and possibly 5 Ju 87s in action in the *Luftwaffenkommando Ost* sector in Central Russia this date but the location was not reported; at least 2 KIA (entry possibly wrong due to *Luftwaffe* reporting error). 26 August: shared in the destruction of 40 tanks during a breakthrough attempt by Soviet 63rd Army. 4 September: 4.*Staffel* Ju 87 B shot down by AA fire over Stalingrad, 2 MIA. 20 September: 4.*Staffel* Ju 87 R-2 shot up by AA fire over Kotluban in the Stalingrad area, 1 KIA.

25 September: Ju 87 R shot down by AA fire near Yërzovka, 25.5 km north of the centre of Stalingrad on the west bank of the Volga, 2 MIA. 5 October: Ju 87 R shot down near Volitsa near Stalingrad. 24-25 October: 2 Ju 87 Ds shot down by AA fire and fighters over Stalingrad, 2 KIA and 2 WIA. 5 November: Fi 156 liaison/spotter aircraft belonging to the *Gruppe* failed to return from a flight in the Stalingrad area, 3 MIA. 18 November: Bf 108 liaison/communications aircraft belonging to 5.*Staffel* crashed at Nikolayev airfield in south Ukraine and the pilot killed. This aircraft and pilot had probably been sent to the rear area for critically needed parts, this being a common practice for units at the front. November: as Soviet pincers closed on Stalingrad shortly after the Red Army began its powerful, surprise counter-offensive on 19 November, the *Gruppe's* aircraft and crews moved back to Oblivskaya and Morosovskaya, but most of the ground personnel from 4. and 6.*Staffel* were trapped in the Stalingrad pocket where many later perished in the fighting. 23 November: 4.*Staffel* Ju 87 shot down east of Morosovskaya, 1 KIA. December: handed over all remaining aircraft to St.G. 2 during the first part of December and transferred to Rostov to rest, refit and re-equip. 1 January 1943: *Gruppe* reported only a single Ju 87 R-1 on strength this date. 15-17 January: ground personnel casualties from the *Gruppe* listed at Rossosh, along the Don bend to the north-west of Stalingrad. 20-31 January: transferred from Rostov (or the Rostov area) to Nikolayev to re-equip with new aircraft. 20 February - 1 March: elements operated from Dnepropetrovsk-South under *Gefechtsverband Hozzel* in support of German counter-attacks against Soviet forces that had broken through the thinly-held front and were advancing towards the Dnepropetrovsk area; some of these missions were also flown from Poltava from around 27 February. 25-31 March: ordered to transfer to Bryansk on the central sector of the front to continue resting and refitting. 23 April: at Bryansk.

Central Russia – Counter-offensive at Kursk (April 1943 – October 1943) 29 April: transferred from Bryansk to Orel to begin pounding targets in the Kursk salient in preparation for the forthcoming German offensive there that began two months later. 10 May: Ju 87 D-3 shot down by a fighter over Shchigry/north-east of Kursk, 2 MIA; on the same date, another Ju 87 D-3 was shot down by a fighter east of Kursk, 2 MIA. In this engagement, *Oblt.* Franz (Heinz?) Roka and his gunner claimed a LaGG-3 fighter. 22 May: a very bad day (probably the *Gruppe's* worst in the war) – attacked Kursk marshalling yards with 36 Ju 87s, of which 8 Ju 87 D-3s were shot down by Russian fighters, 3 more shot up and severely damaged and 6 more lightly damaged with 1 KIA, 16 (8 crews) MIA and 2 WIA. 1 July: *Gruppe* reported 40 Ju 87 D-3 and 2 Ju 87 D-1 on strength. 5 July: 2 Ju 87 D-3s from 4. and 5.*Staffel* shot down over the Kursk salient during the opening day of Operation *Zitadelle*. 8 July: 6.*Staffel* claimed a LaGG-3 fighter over the front south-south-west of Orel. 19 July: Ju 87 D-3 rammed by enemy fighter and brought down at Stolbsheye, 2 KIA. 21-22 July: 2 Ju 87 Ds from 4.*Staffel* shot down by fighters over the Novaya Slobodka area, 3 KIA and 1 WIA. 22 July: elements (a *Staffel*?) of the *Gruppe* said to have been temporarily transferred to Krasnogvardeisk/44 km south-west of Leningrad on the

northern sector of the front to support defensive operations along the Volkhov River and then rejoined the *Gruppe* in Central Russia in early August. Although there was indeed a minor Russian offensive along the Volkhov than began on 22 July, the transfer of *Gruppe* elements to that area in the middle of Operation *Zitadelle* cannot be confirmed in the loss reports or other sources. 3 August: 3 Ju 87 Ds from 6.*Staffel* shot down by fighters in the Kromy-Shepelovo area, 3 KIA and 2 WIA. August: 12 experienced crews were sent to Baranowicze/east Poland to received night flying training and then rejoined the *Gruppe* at Orsha. 15 August: 5.*Staffel* Ju 87 D-3 shot down by AA fire at Pratnitskoye, 2 WIA. On the same date and possibly the same mission, 6.*Staffel* shot down an La-5 fighter a few kilometres south-west of Kharkov. 19 August: now operating against Soviet forces advancing along the front east and south-east of Smolensk, 5.*Staffel* Ju 87 D-5 blew up in the air north-west of Spas-Demensk, probably after a direct hit from an AA shell, 2 KIA. 22 August: 4.*Staffel* Ju 87 D-5 shot down by AA fire north of Ponitsovitse, 2 MIA. 28 August: 6.*Staffel* Ju 87 D-5 shot down by fighters over Moritsky, 2 KIA. 5 September: 4.*Staffel* Ju 87 D-5 shot down by AA fire east of Shatalovka/55 km south-east of Smolensk, 1 KIA. 14 September: 5 Ju 87 D-3/D-5s destroyed on the ground in Russian air raid on Shatalovka-East airfield, 7 more severely damaged and 7 more moderately damaged. These losses reduced the *Gruppe* to the strength of a single *Staffel*. 15 September: location after Shatalovka-East uncertain, but the shattered remnants of the *Gruppe* is believed to have withdrawn to Orsha where it had been maintaining a rear echelon. 18 September: 5.*Staffel* Ju 87 D-5 shot down by AA fire in the Kholm area north of Velikiye Luki. 22 September: 3 Ju 87 Ds shot down by fighters north-east of Kuchino/25 km south-south-east of Smolensk, 3 MIA and 1 WIA. 2 October: Ju 87 D-3 shot down by AA fire over the front line ca. 70 km east of Orsha, 2 KIA. 7 October: Ju 87 D-5 shot down by AA fire over Zushurokovo (not located and possibly misspelled), 1 MIA. 13 October: Ju 87 D-5 shot up by a fighter and force-landed south of P'yankovo/68 km north-north-west of Rzhev, *Gruppenkommandeur Major* Otto Ernst and *Oblt.* Erwin Möller both WIA. 18 October: renamed II./S.G. 1 at either Mogilev or Bobruisk, but probably the latter.

Codes: (6G+_D, R, S, T)

FpNs: II. (L 31790)

Kommandeur:
Hptm. Anton Keil (RK) (9 July 1940 – 29 August 1940 KIA)
Major Johann Zemsky (RK) (1 September 1941 – 28 August 1942 KIA)
Hptm. Robert-Georg Freiherr von Malapert-Neufville (DKG, RK) (13 January 1942 – 21 May 1942 KIA)
Major Otto Ernst (? – 1 October 1942 – 2 December 1942)
Hptm. Frank Neubert (DKG, RK) (9 December 1942 – August 1943)
Major Otto Ernst (DKG) (c 1 September 1943 – 13 October 1943 WIA) ★
Major Heinz Frank (DKG, RK, EL) (13 October 1943 – 18 October 1943) acting?
★ resumed command in late 1943 after recuperation.

ABOVE: III./St.G. 1 was formed from Trägersturzkampfgruppe I.(St)/Tr.G. 186 on 9 July 1940. The latter Gruppe had been formed to fly the specially modified Ju 87 C from the aircraft carrier Graf Zeppelin which had been launched in 1938. It was intended that the vessel should carry 10 Bf 109 Ts and 20 Ju 87 Cs, both variants having folding wings. Slow progress with the completion of the carrier led to the redesignation of Trägergeschwader 186 and the abandonment of both aircraft sub-types.

ABOVE: The Ju 87 Bs of III./St.G. 1 carried the code 'J9' originally adopted by I./Tr.G. 186. This aircraft had temporary white paint covering its dark green upper surface camouflage for operations during the early winter of 1941/42 in the Soviet Union and carried the letters 'LI' after the Balkenkreuz.

RIGHT: Two mechanics turn the starting handle of the Jumo 211 of this Ju 87 B of I./Tr.G. 186 prior to a sortie against Poland. This Gruppe was redesignated III./St.G. 1 in July 1940. The aircraft, which has had its spats removed to ease maintenance, carries the eagle and anchor emblem which was used by both units. The number '17' painted on the cowling and the band around the spinner were both in bright yellow.

BELOW: Prior to their operations in Poland, the Ju 87 Bs of 4./Tr.G. 186 carried large white identification numbers on both their engine cowlings and the outside of their wheel spats. These were probably adopted for easier identification in anticipation of operations from the aircraft carrier Graf Zeppelin. Starting from the front are numbers 18, 31, 14, 30 and 17.

Taken on 22 March 1939 these two photographs show work proceeding on the Graf Zeppelin at Kiel. The vessel had a displacement of about 33,500 metric tonnes (32,00 tons), was 262.5 m (861 ft 3 in) long with a beam 31.5 m (103 ft 4 in) and a draft of 7.6 m (22 ft 11 in). She was powered by geared turbines driving four screws which were to give her a maximum speed of 65 km/h (35 knots). A complement of 1,720 (including 306 flight personnel) was to be carried and armament comprised 16 x 15 cm (5.9 in) main guns and 12 x 10.5 mm (4.1 in) 22 x 37 mm guns and 28 x 20 mm anti-aircraft guns. The vessel was to carry 10 Messerschmitt Bf 109 T fighters, 20 Junkers Ju 87 C dive-bombers and 20 Fieseler Fi 167 torpedo bombers.

To much acclaim the aircraft carrier Graf Zeppelin is launched from the Deutsche Werft shipyard at Kiel on 18 December 1938. On the same day two Staffeln were formed to operate aircraft from the carrier as soon as she was commissioned. These were 4.(Stuka)/Trägergruppe 186 intended to be equipped with the Ju 87 C and 6.(Jagd)/Trägergruppe 186 which was to fly Bf 109 Ts.

ABOVE: At a conference with Hitler on 29 April 1940, Admiral Raeder proposed halting all work on the Graf Zeppelin because he thought that the carrier would be too late to see useful operations. Hitler agreed and, on 12 July 1940, the vessel was towed to Gotenhafen (now Gdynia) where she remained for about a year. Three days earlier, I./Tr.G. 186 with the Ju 87 was redesignated III./St.G. 1. This photograph, taken on 26 March 1940, shows the carrier still at Kiel.

Walter Hagen, (RK-EL)

ORN 16 March 1897 in Kiel, the son of a merchant, Hagen was a veteran of the First
World War, serving first in the *Kavallerie* then as a *Marineflieger*. On 1 September 1924 he
joined Junkers *Luftverkehr* as a civil pilot, transferring to *Severa* on 28 February 1926. He
became a *Flugkapitän* with the German airline industry and a test pilot for the test
establishments at Travemünde and Rechlin on 1 July 1928. He entered the *Luftwaffe* on 1
April 1935 with the rank of *Hptm.* (RDA 1 May 1935) and attended the *Infanterie Lehrgang*
in Königsbrück. On 1 June 1935 he transferred to *Erprobungsstelle* Travemünde and was
appointed flight operations director for the testing of aircraft there. He took up the important
post of *Referent für Flugsicherheit* (expert adviser for flying safety) with the RLM on 1 April
193 and became *Staka* of *Erprobungs-u.Lehrstaffel (See)* on 1 January 1938, being promoted to
Major a month later. On 15 November 1938 he was appointed *Staka* then *Kommandeur* of
4. *Trägersturzkampfstaffel* 186 (later I.(St.)/ *Trägergruppe* 186).

Hagen became *Kommodore* of St.G. 1 on 22 June 1940, being promoted to *Oberstleutnant*
on 1 July 1940. On 21 July 1940 he was awarded the *Ritterkreuz* (recommended while serving
as *Kommandeur* of I.(St.)/ *Trägergruppe* 186) and received the *Eichenlaub zum Ritterkreuz* (No. 77)
on 17 February 1942. Promoted to *Oberst* (see photograph) on 1 April, he was awarded the
Ehrenpokal on 10 August 1942. From 1 January 1943 he took up a number of staff positions
including provisional *Fliegerführer 1* (*Luftflotte 1*) and provisional *Fliegerführer 1* (Tunisia) 14 days
later. On 15 March 1943 he was appointed provisional *Fliegerführer 3* (Gabes) but was injured on 9 April 1943 in a Fi 156 crash in
Tunisia and sent to a hospital in Kiel.

After recovering, Hagen was appointed *Fliegerführer Albanien* in September 1943, a post which he held until 13 June 1944. On
30 April 1944 he was concurrently appointed *Fliegerführer Kroatien* and was promoted to *Generalmajor* on 1 July 1944. He became
Fliegerführer Nordbalkan on 29 August 1944 and was appointed commander of 17.*Fliegerdivision* on 1 February 1945. When the war
ended on 8 May 1945 he became an American POW, being released in 1947 to return to Kiel where he lived out the post-war years.
He died on 24 November 1963 in Kiel following a long illness.

III./St.G. 1

Formation (July 1940) Formed 9 July 1940 at Falaise
in Normandy by renaming *Trägersturzkampfgruppe*
I./Tr.G. 186. Equipped with Junkers Ju 87 B dive-
bombers.

**Air Offensive against England (Battle of Britain)
(July 1940 – February 1941)** 7 July: two days prior to
the redesignation, the *Gruppe* commenced operations
against British Channel convoys using Théville/12 km
east of Cherbourg for raid-staging, but no ships were
sighted. 25 July: in first major action over the Channel,
III./St.G. 1 attacked Portland harbour with 1 Ju 87 B
falling to a Spitfire and another shot up and damaged by
naval AA fire. 8 August: lost 2 Ju 87 Bs shot down by
Hurricanes off Swanage on the south coast of England
during a morning mission to seek out and attack
shipping. 13 August: now at Falaise (some sources say
Angers) with 38 (26) Ju 87 Bs under VIII.*Fliegerkorps/
Luftflotte* 3. 18 August: all *Stuka* units withdrawn from
daylight cross-Channel operations due to unacceptable
losses. 28 August: 2 Ju 87 B-1s destroyed in mid-air
collision off Deauville killing 3 – the aircraft had been
practice-bombing a target ship anchored off the town. 15
September: transferred to St.Pol-Brias but no missions
were flown until 29 October when a feint was made on
Folkestone for the purpose of drawing up RAF fighters
for *Luftwaffe* Bf 109s to ambush. November: flew several
successful attacks in mid-November with strong fighter
escort on shipping in the Thames Estuary. On
11 November the *Gruppe* damaged 3 merchantmen in the
estuary, but 2 Ju 87 Bs were shot down followed by the
loss of 2 more from 9.*Staffel* on 14 November during a
heavily escorted early afternoon attack on convoy *Booty*
off Dover by some 40 *Stukas* from St.G. 1. December:

now operating from Ostende (Oostende) on the Belgian
coast, flew occasional nuisance raids by single aircraft over
the Thames Estuary at night and during bad weather.
January 1941: continued low-scale evaluation and testing
of night dive-bombing techniques at both St.Pol-Brias

*A Luftwaffe mechanic fastens one of the oil filler access ports on the cowling of this Ju 87 of 5./St.G. 1.
The emblem of the unit, a brown Felix the Cat wielding Neville Chamberlain's famous umbrella, had
also been used by 8./St.G. 51. Felix the film cartoon cat (by Otto Messmer) had enjoyed enormous
international publicity from 1922 and several popular songs were written about him. During the Second
World War, his image was used as emblems by several Luftwaffe and United States squadrons.*

and Berck-sur-Mer/34 km south of Boulogne, with occasional night missions over south-eastern England. 5/6 February: Ju 87 B-1 shot down by a fighter while attempting to attack a trawler along the coast, and a Ju 87 R-2 crash-landed at St-Pol-Brias with slight damage due to icing. 13/14 February: 9.*Staffel* Ju 87 B-1 failed to return from night operations over the Thames Estuary.

Central Mediterranean, North Africa and the Balkans (February 1941 – June 1941)

13/14 February: 9./St.G. 1 flew missions over the Thames estuary. 19-23 February: transferred from St.Pol-Brias to Trapani/west Sicily for operations under X.*Fliegerkorps* against the British Mediterranean Fleet and convoys, the first mission being flown on 23 February against Malta followed by a heavy attack on Luqa airfield/Malta on 26 February. The transfer of II. and III./St.G. 1 to Sicily was made to replace I./St.G. 1 and II./St.G. 2 which had been ordered from Sicily to North Africa. 3-4 March: several crash-landings noted at both Trapani and Comiso, the latter airfield in eastern Sicily where the *Gruppe* staged its raids on Malta. 5 March: lost 2 Ju 87s during a raid on Malta. 22 March: attacked a Malta relief convoy (probably MW 6) and credited with hits on two ships. 23 March: attacked Valetta. 11 April: attacked airfield of Ta Venezia /Malta. 11 April: *Gruppenstab*, 7. and 8.*Staffel* transferred temporarily from Trapani to Derna/Libya to replace I./St.G. 1, which had been transferred to the Balkans, for operations under *Fliegerführer Afrika* against both land and maritime targets in support of the first major Axis drive across Cyrenaica. Meanwhile, 9.*Staffel*, which was equipped with the shorter range Ju 87 B model, flew day and night raids from Comiso on the harbour at La Valetta/Malta as well as other targets on the island. An Italian *Stuka* unit was attached to the *Gruppe* in North Africa to replace the absent 9.*Staffel*. 12 April: attacked ships in Tobruk harbour. 14 April: flew attacks on ships at Tobruk during the Axis offensive. 17 April: bombed the inner defences of Tobruk and later attacked a ship off the coast north-east of Sollum. 19 April: attacked Valetta harbour. 2 May: supported Italian troops during the advance on Tobruk. 4 May: attacked Valetta harbour. 8 May: departed Derna and returned to Trapani. 11 May: 9.*Staffel* ordered to standby for movement to the Italian mainland. 23 May: *Gruppe* transferred from Trapani to Argos/Greece to reinforce the air attacks on and around Crete, and then moved to Heraklion (Iraklion) in north-central Crete at the end of May. From Heraklion, attacked ships fleeing Crete for eastern Mediterranean ports, many of which were loaded with troops evacuated from the island. 3-4 June: transferred from Heraklion and Argos to Cottbus and Kitzingen in Germany for a brief rest, and then moved on 17 June to Dubowo-South (a.k.a. Raczki)/north-east Poland near Suwalki.

Attack on the Soviet Union – Operations in Central Russia (June 1941 – February 1942)

21 June: at Dubowo-South with 39 (24) Ju 87 Bs under VIII.*Fliegerkorps*/*Luftflotte* 2 for the attack into Russia that commenced on 22 June. 22 June: in the initial 10 days of the campaign, the *Gruppe* supported the advance towards Grodno, Bialystok and Minsk. 24 June: 9.*Staffel* Ju 87 R-2 shot down by fighters near Kasyn/ca. 25 km north-west of Minsk, 2 KIA; same date, *Gruppenkommandeur Hptm.* Helmut Mahlke was shot down over the city of Minsk and reported MIA but he

returned a day or so later. 27 June: 9.*Staffel* Ju 87 R-2 failed to return from an attack on Wolkowysk/Poland (100 km west of Baranowicze), 2 MIA. 28 June: moved forward from Dubowo-South to Baranowicze. 2 July: transferred from Baranowicze to Minsk; same date, 8.*Staffel* Ju 87 R-2 failed to return from an attack on troop concentrations 10 km east of Borisov, 2 KIA. 3 July: *Gruppenstab* Ju 87 R-2 failed to return from an attack on troop concentrations north-west of Beresino, 2 KIA. 5 July: advanced to Dokudovo/27 km east-north-east of Borisov. 7 July: attacked Mal Gorodino and troops near Gubailovichi east of Belavichi. 7 July: 9.*Staffel* Ju 87 R-2 shot down by ground fire near Malo Gorodino, 1 KIA, and another R-2 was shot down by ground fire near Gubailovichi (not located), 1 KIA and 1 WIA. 8 July: attacked tanks near Latigalskiye. 8 July: 2 Ju 87 R-2s, incl. one from the *Gruppenstab*, shot down by fighters while attacking tanks near Latigalskiye (not located), 1 KIA, 1 MIA and *Gruppenkommandeur Hptm.* Mahlke + 1 WIA. 17 July: transferred from Dokudovo to Orsha-South – from there supported the encirclement battle around Smolensk to the end of July. 17 July: attacked columns on road Krichev - Roslavl. 21 July: transferred to Shatalovka airfield 55 km south-east of Smolensk for operations under *Nahkampfführer* 2/II.*Fliegerkorps*. 21 July: attacked columns near Gusino. August: from Shatalovka, flew operations in the Roslavl-Gomel-Bryansk area. 1 August: attacked AA positions in the area of Voroshilovo. 2 August: 8.*Staffel* Ju 87 R-2 shot down near Moroshilovo, *Staffelkapitän Oblt.* Günter Skambracks MIA. 13 August: attacked aircraft on Shatalovka-East airfield. 9 September: attacked enemy positions at Konotop in support of *Panzergruppe* 2. 10 September: attacked rail line south of Romny. 17 September: attacked tanks north of Schatriza. 2 October: Operation *Taifun*, the drive to encircle and take Moscow, commenced this date along the front from Rzhev south to Bryansk and Orel. The *Gruppe* was assigned to support the advance on Orel and Tula while flying from Shatalovka, Orel and then Yukhnov. 7 October: 2 Ju 87s shot down near Dorogobuzh/north-east of Smolensk, both crews safe. 13 November: Ju 87 failed to return from an attack in the Serpukhov area 90 km south of Moscow, 2 MIA. 6 December: transferred from Yukhnov to Schweinfurt to rest and refit following two months of heavy action in support of the advance. On the day the *Gruppe* departed, the Russians opened their surprise counter-offensive along the Moscow front in sub-zero temperatures and quickly drove the exhausted, lightly clothed Germans back several hundred kilometres. January 1942: the Ju 87 B models were replaced with the new and greatly improved D model while at Schweinfurt, the *Gruppe* being just the second unit to receive them.

Operations in North Russia (February 1942 – June 1942)

13 February: ordered from Schweinfurt to Luga-Gostkino/135 km south-south-west of Leningrad on the northern sector of the Eastern Front. 13 February: attacked Krechno, south-west of Chudovo. 27 February: attacked AA positions near Glybochka. 28 February: unit's base at Gostkino hit by air attack. 1 March: *Gruppe* reported 33 Ju 87 D-1, 9 Ju 87 R-2 and 5 Ju 87 R-4 on strength. 15 March: moved from Gostkino to Gorodets/23 km south of Luga during the second half of March. 28 March: 8.*Staffel* Ju 87 D-1 shot down by AA fire near Soltsy, 2 KIA. 4 April: flew heavy attacks on the

Baltic Fleet at Leningrad and the naval base at Kronshtadt under I.*Fliegerkorps* as part of Operation *Eisstoss* – a major air operation to prevent the Fleet's deployment following the spring thaw. 13 April: 8.*Staffel* Ju 87 D-1 shot down by AA fire near Kholm, 2 MIA. 24 April: attacked Leningrad harbour. 29 April: 8.*Staffel* Ju 87 D-1 bombed on the ground during enemy air raid on Gorodets airfield and moderately damaged. 12 May: attacked armour near Lipowik. 22 May: attacked positions near Demyansk. 16 May: 8.*Staffel* Ju 87 D-1 shot down by AA fire near Malinovka, a suburb on the eastern outskirts of Leningrad, 2 MIA. 22 May: 8.*St.* and 9.*St.* each lost a Ju 87 D on operations, one of which fell to AA fire, 2 KIA and 2 WIA. 28 May: 8.*Staffel* Ju 87 D-1 shot up and force-landed near Schlüsselburg (Shlisselburg)/36 km east of Leningrad, 2 WIA. 29 May: 9.*Staffel* Ju 87 D shot down over Schlüsselburg during a raid on the Lake Ladoga port of Kobona by the entire *Gruppe*. Concentrated attacks were made on this target on both 28 and 29 May in an attempt to destroy Soviet efforts to ship supplies to besieged Leningrad. June: III./St.G. 1 flew armed reconnaissance over the southern reaches of Lake Ladoga during the first week of June, but only succeeded in sinking a few barges. The rest of the month was spent countering renewed Soviet attempts to break out of the Lyuban Pocket on the Volkhov front, and on 28 June the pocket was finally annihilated by the Germans and the Russian 2nd Shock Army destroyed. The *Luftwaffe* played a major role in this victory, including III./St.G. 1.

Crisis at Orel on the Central Sector (July 1942)
5-7 July: a week after the opening of the initial phase of the German summer offensive (Operation *Blau*) on the central sector of the front from east of Kursk towards Voronezh, Soviet West Front attacked 2.*Panzerarmee* in the sector north and north-west of Orel with 10th, 16th and 61st Armies. Elements of the *Gruppe*, possibly just 9.*Staffel* initially, were hurriedly dispatched to Orel on the central sector of the front on or about 6 July to support ground defensive operations aimed at blocking a Soviet West Front armour penetration in a weak sector of Pz. A.O.K. 2's line. The designation of the elements sent to Orel remain unclear, but they may have evolved into a provisional (ad hoc) unit identified in official documents as *Sturzkampfstaffel* Falke after its *Staffelkapitän*, Oblt. Günter Falke, which may be one and the same as either 8. or 9./St.G. 1. 7 July: the Orel element flew 29 Ju 87 sorties against tank concentrations in the vicinity of Kotovichi/138 km north-west of Orel claiming 7 tanks and 6 trucks destroyed. 8 July: flew 83 Ju 87 sorties in the same sector north-west of Orel claiming 20 tanks and 14 trucks destroyed, and 15 tanks damaged. 9 July: sent 52 *Stuka* sorties north-west of Orel hitting tank concentrations and claiming 4 destroyed and 6 damaged. 10 July: attacked positions around Slobodka/north-west of Orel in 44 *Stuka* sorties claiming 3 tanks destroyed, 7 damaged and 1 munitions dump detonated. 11 July: flew 33 *Stuka* sorties in the Gusevka area/north-west of Orel claiming 4 tanks destroyed and 5 more damaged. 12 July: return attacks at Kotovichi in 31 sorties, but only 2 tanks claimed and another 8 damaged. 13 July: dispatched 17 Ju 87 sorties in support of ground forces around Slobodka with 4 tanks reported destroyed or damaged; 2 Ju 87s had to force-land at Seshchinskaya airfield/40 km south-east of Roslavl with combat damage during the course of the day. By 12-13 July Soviet West Front halted its attack after

making little to no progress. 17 July: 2 Ju 87s belonging to the Orel contingent crash-landed at Smolensk.

Return to the Leningrad Front and Crisis at Rzhev (July 1942 – August 1942) 19 July: flew an attack near Staraya Russa. Same date, 2 Ju 87 Ds (main body) crashed at Tuleblya airfield/21 km south-south-west of Lake Ilmen after being badly shot up while avoiding enemy fire during an attack on tanks, 2 KIA, including *Hptm.* Hartmut Schairer, *Staka* 7.*Staffel*. 30 July: 8.*Staffel* Ju 87 D-1 slightly damaged taking off from Gorodets airfield. 30 July: Soviet West Front opened an offensive in the Rzhev area with five armies against German 9.*Armee* and 3.*Panzerarmee* which succeeded in driving the enemy back 40 km south-east of Rzhev and retaking the town of Zubtsov. Smaller gains were also made east of Vyazma. 5 August: elements (probably the Orel element) moved to Vyazma-Gradina/150 km east-north-east of Smolensk. 11 August: Pz. A.O.K. 2 and 4.*Armee* launched a counter-offensive (Operation *Wirbelwind*) towards Sukhinichi and Mosalsk in the Russian salient north-west of Orel. The *Gruppe* supported the attack from Orel. 13 August: Ju 87 D-3 crash-landed at Orel, crew WIA. 14 August: attacked positions 2 km north-east of Pochinok. 23 August: Ju 87

D-1 crashed at Orel due to pilot error, 2 KIA. 24 August: *Wirbelwind* failed to make any significant progress due to unexpected resistance, strong enemy positions and thick minefields which prevented the movement of armour. 26 August: with the situation along the central sector now under control, the Orel contingent of the *Gruppe* returned to Gorodets in North Russia.

Continuing Operations in North Russia (September 1942 – December 1942) 30 August: Ju 87 D-1 rammed by a He 111 at Gorodets and damaged beyond repair. Most operations to the end of the year were attacks on Russian artillery positions, bunkers and defensive works along the perimeter ringing Leningrad to the south. 10 September: operating from Lisino airstrip near Krasnogvardeisk, Ju 87 D-3 shot up by AA fire and crashed at Tortolovo (not located but probably a suburb of Leningrad), 2 KIA. 21 September: Ju 87 D-1 accidentally shot down by German artillery fire over Tortolovo, 2 KIA. 29 September: 2 Ju 87 D-1s from 7.*Staffel* bombed on the ground at Krasnogvardeisk airfield, one destroyed and the other severely damaged. 26 October: Ju 87 D-1 believed shot down by German artillery fire near Strelitsy/54 km south of Lake Ilmen (or around

III./St.G. 1 was still flying Ju 87 B and Rs as late as the summer of 1942. This aircraft carries the unit badge (originally adopted by Trägersturzkampf-gruppe I./Tr.G. 186) but its unit code, A5, seems to have replaced 'J9'. The code is also painted in small characters but individual aircraft identification seems to have been achieved by the application of large red numbers outlined in white.

Leningrad?), *Hptm.* Heinz Fischer + 1 KIA. 30 October: Ju 87 D-3 force-landed and burned out near Mga/45 km south-east of Leningrad after catching fire, 2 WIA. 7 November: Ju 87 D-1 crashed taking off from Krasnogvardeisk, 1 WIA. 30 November: Ju 87 failed to return from ops east of Korovye Selo/30 km north of Ostrov, 1 KIA; same date, a D-3 was shot down by AA fire at Poreyeva (not located) with 1 WIA. 4 December: Ju 87 D-3 shot down south of Strelitsy, probably by AA fire, 2 MIA. 10 December: attacked artillery positions 25 km east of Schlisselburg. 15 December: while the ground echelon remained at Gorodets, most of the aircraft and crews transferred to Idritsa on the central sector of the front to counter Soviet attacks aimed at Velikiye Luki.

Central Russia – Operations in the Velikiye Luki and Orel Area (January 1943 – February 1943)
30 December: attacked an armoured train east of Velikiye Luki. 30 December: 2 Ju 87 D-1s from 9.*Staffel* shot down west of Velikiye Luki, 2 KIA and 1 WIA. 1 January: *Gruppe* reported 18 Ju 87 D-1s and 13 Ju 87 D-3s on strength. 3 January: 8.*Staffel* Ju 87 D-1 rammed by a landing DFS 230 glider at Idritsa airfield/100 km west of Velikiye Luki. 11 January: Ju 87 D-3 shot up by AA fire in vicinity of Velikiye Luki and heavily damaged. January: aircraft, crews and a few key servicing personnel

III./St.G. 1 began to exchange its Ju 87 Rs for Ju 87 Ds at Schweinfurt during January 1943. On 13 February it was ordered to Luga-Gostkino, some 135 km south-south-west of Leningrad on the northern sector of the Eastern Front. These photographs show the unit's aircraft operating during the winter snows, one of them carrying the code J9+CK of the 8.Staffel.

transferred to Orel at the end of January; the *Gruppe's* main ground component followed from Gorodets several weeks later and arrived at Orel on 17 March. 31 January: force-landed Ju 87 D-1 destroyed by own troops west of Ostriki/121 km south-south-east of Orel to prevent capture. 1 February: flew 48 Ju 87 sorties against enemy columns east of Orel claiming 70 vehicles and 6 companies of infantry destroyed. 2 February: attacked enemy positions near Aleksandrovka south-east of Livny. 2 February: 33 Ju 87 sorties – struck enemy positions and columns east of Orel claiming 65 vehicles and 4 companies of infantry destroyed; a Ju 87 D-1 was shot down by ground fire at Peresukha/72 km north-north-east of Kursk, 2 KIA. 3 February: 53 Ju 87 sorties – hit enemy columns, tanks and vehicle concentrations claiming 11 tanks, 80 vehicles and 2 companies of infantry knocked out of action. 4 February: 49 Ju 87 sorties – attacked enemy columns east of Orel claiming 2 tanks, 23 vehicles and 3 companies of infantry; 1 *Stuka* was shot down by ground fire and several ground personnel from 7.*Staffel* were injured in an accident at Orel when a Ju 87 they were working on was rammed by a He 111 and severely damaged. 5 February: 40 Ju 87 sorties – smashed enemy columns east of Orel claiming 1 tank, 10-15 vehicles and 6 companies of infantry. 7 February: flew 9 Ju 87 sorties against enemy columns with no results reported. 9 February: 44 Ju 87 sorties – pounded enemy columns and occupied villages east of Orel claiming 10-15 houses and 6 companies of infantry destroyed. 11 February: 72 Ju 87 sorties – destroyed many motor vehicles and houses in occupied villages east of Orel. 12 February: 14 Ju 87 sorties – struck enemy columns and occupied villages east of Orel with good results. 20 February: 18 Ju 87 sorties – ordered to attack enemy tanks but forced to turn back due to low clouds and danger of icing. 21-23 February: 107 Ju 87 sorties on 21-22 February – hit tanks, troops and vehicle concentrations around Krasnyy and Polyani claiming 6 tanks, 60-65 vehicles and 300 infantry; 5 Ju 87 D-1s and D-3s shot down by fighters and AA fire in these operations east of Orel, 2 MIA and 2 WIA. 23 February: attacked troop concentrations in the vicinity of Katovichi.

Helmut Mahlke (i.G.). (RK, DKG)

MAHLKE was born 27 August 1913 in Berlin-Lankwitz, beginning pre-military flight training with the D.V.S. on 1 April 1932. On 29 August 1932 he entered service with the *Kriegsmarine* (German navy), beginning pilot training at the *Deutsche Verkehrs-Fliegerschule* (German Civil Aviation Flight School) at Warnemünde. Between 1932 and 1935 he served with the navy, attaining the rank of *Fähnrich zur See* (Ensign). He transferred from the navy to the *Luftwaffe* on 1 May 1935 and was ordered to Warnemünde for *Beobachter* (observer/navigator) training. He was promoted to *Lt.* on 1 October 1935 and assigned as a pilot training specialist (*Referent*) in *Stab/Kdo.d.Schulen (See)* at Warnemünde on 10 March. On 1 October 1936 he became a specialist and lead instructor with *Fliegerschule See* at Bug auf Rügen and *Fliegerschule See* at Parow. He was appointed specialist in *Stab/Kdo.d.Fliegerschulen* and *Flieger-Ers.Abt.* VI on 1 March 1937 and promoted to *Oberleutnant* a month later. On 1 March 1938 he was transferred to *Bordfliegerstaffel* 1./196 (based at Wilhelmshaven aboard the heavy cruiser/pocket battleship *Admiral Scheer*) as an observer/navigator. He departed for Spain on 29 June 1938 on the *Scheer* which gave support to Franco's Nationalists during the Civil War.

Mahlke returned to Germany on 1 September 1939 and was appointed *Staka* of 2./*Träger-Gr.* 186. He was promoted to *Hauptmann* on 1 April 1940 and awarded the E.K. II 15 days later and the E.K. I on 20 June 1940. On 9 July 1940 he became *Kommandeur* of III./St.G. 1, taking part in early operations during the Battle of Britain. He was hospitalized on 18 September but after recovery, again led III./St.G. 1 in operations against Malta and shipping in the Mediterranean. Following the invasion of the Soviet Union, Mahlke was shot down and wounded on 24 June 1941 over the city of Minsk and reported missing, but he returned to his unit a day or so later. He was shot down for a third time in Russia on 8 July 1941 and was taken to a forward surgical station in Borisov with bullet wounds in the left shoulder and second degree burns on both hands. On 16 July 1941 he was awarded the *Ritterkreuz* (recommended while serving as *Kommandeur* of III./St.G. 1). He transferred to the Ob.d.L./RLM officer reserve and was ordered to *Stab/XII.Fliegerkorps* for briefing on 4 December 1941 and 15 days later was appointed *Verbindungs-Offz.* (liaison officer) in *Stab/VIII.Fliegerkorps*. On 8 April 1942 he became Ia (operations officer) in *Stab/1.Fliegerdivision*, being promoted to *Major* on 1 June. At the end of the month he became Ia in *Stab/Luftwaffenkdo. Ost*. On 1 January 1943 he was transferred to the *Generalstab d.Lw.* This was purely on merit as he had not attended the *Luftkriegsakademie* as was usually the case. Appointed Ia/*Luftwaffenkdo. Ost* on 2 March 1943 and Ia op 1/1.*Fliegerdivision* on 5 April 1943. He became *Chef Führungsabteilung Gruppe* Ia/*Luftflotte* 6 on 6 May 1943, an appointment which he held until the end of the war. Mahlke was awarded the DKG on 31 March 1944 and promoted to *Oberstleutnant* (see photograph) on 1 May of the same year.

Mahlke was taken prisoner (probably by the Americans) on 8 May 1945 but was released on 9 September 1947. He joined the *Bundeswehr* on 16 November 1955 and, on 11 January 1963, was promoted to *Brigadegeneral*, heading the *Bundeswehr*'s naval aviation branch until the end of February 1966. He retired from the *Bundeswehr* on 30 September 1970 with the rank of *Gen.Lt.* and died on 26 December 1998 in Heikendorf near Kiel. Mahlke was credited with 150 combat sorties, received the *Verwundeten-Abzeichen in Silber* (wound badge in silver) and had been shot down three times behind Russian lines. He is also the author of *Stuka Angriff: Sturzflug* (Berlin: E.S. Mittler, 1993), ISBN 3-8132-0425-1.

Central Russia – Operations in the Orel and Kursk Area (March 1943 – August 1943): 6 March: 7.*Staffel* Ju 87 D-1 returned to Orel-West shot up by AA fire and severely damaged. 9 March: attacked tanks 5 km north of Zhizdra. 15 March: 9.*Staffel* Ju 87 D-3 shot down by a fighter south of Bulatovo, 2 MIA. 19 March: 3 Ju 87 D-1s and D-3s destroyed on the ground at Orel-West during enemy air attack, and 4 more damaged. 20 April: attacked AA positions near Gobachevka rail station. 20 April: Ju 87 D-3 shot down by AA fire north-east of Orel, 2 KIA. 28 April: 7.*Staffel* Ju 87 D-3 crashed taking off from Orel-East and reduced to salvage. 15 June: attacked armour assembly points near Tevemzy and Micheleikinski. 15 June: Ju 87 D-3 shot down by AA fire in the Orel sector, 2 KIA. 17 June: Ju 87 D-3 shot down by AA fire east of Orel, crew safe. 20 June: Ju 87 D-1 shot down by AA fire north of Bolkhov/53 km due north of Orel, 1 KIA. 21 June: struck artillery positions vic Chenyshino. 21 June: Ju 87 shot down by AA fire over Novosil'/65 km due east of Orel, 2 KIA. 1 July: *Gruppe* reported 31 Ju 87 D-3s and 11 Ju 87 D-1s on strength. 5 July: flew close air support for the massive German counter-offensive against the Kursk salient (Operation *Zitadelle*) which commenced this date, most of the *Gruppe's* crews flying 5 and 6 missions a day in the face of intense Soviet AA and ground fire and swarms of fighters. 5 July: attacked battery positions in small woods west of Malo Archangelsk (between Kursk and Orel), and attacked troop assembly areas vic Podolyan, just forward of the front line. During the first day's operations, 2 Ju 87 Ds from 7. and 9.*Staffel* were shot down by AA fire over the front area with 2 MIA and 2 WIA, and an 8.*Staffel* Ju 87 D-3 crashed at Orel-North with 1 KIA and 1 WIA. 11-12 July: 2 Ju 87 D-3s shot down by AA fire in vicinity of Pogorelovtsy/ 78 km due south of Orel, 2 MIA and 2 WIA. 13 July: attacked positions north of Setucha (vic Orel). 13 July: 7.*Staffel* Ju 87 D-3 shot down by AA fire, 2 KIA. 14 July: attacked armour advancing in area of Dudorovskiy - Dudorovo - Medyntsevo. 14 July: 2 Ju 87 D-3s shot down by fighters in the Dudorovka area/154 km north of Orel, 1 MIA and 2 WIA. 15 July: attacked Melechovo. 17 July: unit's bases at Konefka and Orel-East bombed. 19 July: attacked Vetrovo/15 km south-west of Bolkhov. 19 July: 2 Ju 87 Ds shot down in the Bolkhov area/53 km due north of Orel, 2 KIA and 1 WIA. 23 July: withdrew from Orel-East to Karachev/75 km west-north-west of Orel as Soviet forces closed on the city after the Germans lost the initiative at Kursk and the Russians began a powerful advance westward. 2-8 August: in desperate fighting to slow down the Russian westward advance, 5 Ju 87 Ds were shot down by fighters and AA fire in the Kolki-Kutafino area/50 km south-west of Orel and 3 others shot up and damaged, 4 KIA and 2 WIA; 2 August: attacked Vanovka, east of Larachev. Also, an 8.*Staffel* Ju 87 D-3 caught fire while fueling at Ivanovka fieldstrip (78 km S of Sumy?) on 4 August and burned out. 5 August: attacked Kutafino (50 km south-west of Orel). 8 August: attacked AA positions in the area of Studenka.

Central Russia – Operations in the Smolensk Area (August 1943 – September 1943) 12-15 August: moved from Karachev to Seshchinskaya/40 km south-east of Roslavl for operations against enemy forces advancing towards Smolensk from the east and south-east. 15 August: 2 Ju 87 D-3s shot down by AA fire at Otritsa/77 km north-north-east of Smolensk and Bolkotino, 2 KIA and 1 WIA. 19-20 August: 2 Ju 87 Ds shot down by AA fire around Sevsk/120 km south of Bryansk, 4 MIA. 20 August: attacked assembly areas in a forest south of Troyanovskiy south-east of Sevsk. 21 August: 7.*Staffel* Ju 87 D-1 damaged at Seshchinskaya due to technical problems. 28 August: 8.*Staffel* Ju 87 D-3 force-landed at Nikolskoye and then blown up by the crew to prevent capture by partisan bands. 28 August: 8.*Staffel* Ju 87 D-3 shot down by AA fire ca. 70 km south-east of Smolensk, 2 KIA. 1 September: 8.*Staffel* Ju 87 D-3 moderately damaged taking off from Seshchinskaya. 3 September: Ju 87 D-3 shot down by AA fire ca. 60 km south-east of Smolensk, 2 WIA. 12 September: Ju 87 D-3 shot down by AA fire north of Olsovyevka (not located), 2 WIA. 15 September: Ju 87 D-5 shot down by AA fire in the Tyshayevo-Dukhovshchina area/50 km north-north-east of Smolensk, 2 MIA, and another shot up and heavily damaged. 16 September: attacked about 40 tanks 10 km north of Dukhovshchina.

Operations in North Ukraine and Central Belorussia (September 1943 – October 1943) 16 September: from mid-September to 18 October, the *Gruppe* operated from Gomel and Bobruisk, largely in support of Pz. A.O.K. 4 operations in North Ukraine between Gomel and Kiev. 17 September: Ju 87 D-3 force-landed at the Unecha railway station/78 km north-east of Gomel due to engine failure; not being recoverable, the aircraft was made unserviceable and abandoned. 22 September: Ju 87 D-3 shot down by a fighter at Verbichi/81 km south of Gomel, crew safe. 26 September: Ju 87 D-3 exploded in mid-air over Aleksandrovka, 2 KIA. 9 October: 9.*Staffel* Ju 87 D-3 shot up by AA fire and crashed west of Kozlovo/62 km north of Vitebsk, 1 KIA and 1 WIA. 14 October: attacked factory north of Lenino, a tiny village 48 km east-south-east of Orsha. 14 October: 2 Ju 87 D-5s from 8.*Staffel* shot down by AA fire at Parfënovka/38 km east-south-east of Orsha and nearby Sysoyevo, 2 MIA. 18 October: renamed III./S.G. 1, probably at Bobruisk/138 km south-east of Minsk.

Codes: (J9+_B, H, K, L)

FpNs: III. *Stab* (L 33979); 7. (L 35315); 8. (L 35761); 9. (L 36646)

Kommandeur:
Hptm. Helmut Mahlke (RK) (9 July 1940 - 18 September 1941) – hospitalized.
Hptm./Major Peter Gassmann (DKG, RK) (19 September 1941 - 31 March 1943) – hospitalized from 4 December 1942 due to illness.
Oblt. Theodor Nordmann (DKG, RK) (ca. December 1942 - March 1943) – acting
Hptm. Friedrich Lang (DKG, RK) (1 April 1943 - 18 October 1943) – acting

The Geschwader code 'J9' was used successively by I.(St)/Trägergeschwader 186 from November 1938 until July 1940, by III./St.G. 1 until October 1943 and III./S.G. 1 probably until near its disbandment in May 1945. The Ju 87 B to the left, J9+AL, was piloted by Oblt. Karl-Hermann Lion.

IV.(Erg.)/St.G. 1

Formation and Organization (December 1940) Formed 8 December 1940 at Schaffen-Diest/53 km east-north-east of Brussels in Belgium (new) as *Ergänzungsstaffel/St.G. 1* to provide 6 to 8 weeks of operational formation and dive-bombing training to green crews fresh out of the schools that had been assigned to *Sturzkampfgeschwader* 1. The *Staffel* was also known informally as **10./St.G. 1**. During the second half of 1942 it was expanded to two *Staffeln* (1. and 2., or 10. and 11.?) and redesignated **IV.(Erg.)/St.G. 1** on 17 November 1942, but it continued to be referred to in the official records as **Erg.St./St.G. 1** which suggests that its existence as a *Gruppe* may have been short-lived or never fully brought into being.

West – Training in Belgium (December 1940 – January 1942) March - August 1941: routine Ju 87 B-1 training accidents and crashes at Schaffen-Diest, Coxyde airfield/23 km south-west of Ostende and various locations in north-east France and Belgium. September: the *Staffel* or elements of the *Staffel* based at Coxyde began limited combat operations against coastal shipping along the English coast, using powerful searchlights to illuminate the targets. There were no losses, although one Ju 87 R-2 did return to Coxyde shot up by AA fire on 30 September. 14 January 1942: transferred from Schaffen-Diest to Schweinfurt in Germany.

West – Continued Training in Germany (February 1942 – October 1942) 11-13 February: 10./St.G. 1 reported the loss of 2 Ju 87s on 11 and 13 February in combat operations around Malta. It is speculated that the *Staffel* either sent a detachment to Sicily around this time or some of its aircraft were taken away and reassigned to another unit there as replacements. II./St.G. 1 was supposed to be transferred to Sicily in January or early February but the orders were cancelled. Otherwise, routine Ju 87 B-1, D-1 R-1 training accidents at Schweinfurt and in the surrounding area through September. 6 October 1942: ordered to begin transferring to Nantes in western France.

West – Training in Western France (October 1942 – May 1943) 9 October: 5 DFS 230 gliders belonging to the *Staffel/Gruppe* damaged by a storm while parked at Fp.Schweinfurt. 17 October: 2 Ju 87 B-2s collided in mid-air over Nantes, 4 killed. November - December: routine training accidents and crashes. 1 January: *Gruppe* reported 25 Ju 87 B-1/B-2s, 10 Ju 87 D-1/D-3s and 7 Ju 87 R-1/R-2s on strength at Nantes. January - March 1943: routine training accidents and crashes. 1 April: *Gruppe* reported 32 Ju 87 B-1/B-2s, 13 Ju 87 D-1/D-3s and 7 Ju 87 R-1/R-2s on strength at Nantes. 17 May: renamed I./St.G. 151 at Nantes.

Codes: (A5+_U,V?)

FpNs: *Ergänzungsstaffel* (L 16602, 37989);
IV.(Erg.) (L 37989)

Armourers prepare to load the twelve 37 mm tungsten-cored explosive shells into the magazine of the starboard Flak 18 gun on this Ju 87 G-1. As can be seen, the shells were inserted into the guns in groupings of six. The first unit to fly the Ju 87 G operationally was the 1.Staffel/Versuchskommando für Panzerbekampfung (Experimental Anti-tank Detachment). This was successively redesignated Panzerjägerstaffel/St.G. 1 and finally 10.(Pz.)/S.G. 77.

Staffelkapitän/ Gruppenkommandeur:

Hptm. Lothar Schimitschek (22 December 1940 –
January 1942)

Hptm. Karl Schrepfer (DKG, RK) (May 1943 – 16 May
1943)

Pz.Jg.St./St.G. 1

Formation (June 1943) Formed 17 June 1943 at either Bryansk, Orel–North or Orsha on the central sector of the Eastern Front by renaming 1.*Staffel/ Versuchskommando für Panzerbekampfung* (Experimental Anti-tank Detachment). Equipped with Junkers Ju 87 G-1 dive-bombers outfitted with two wing-mounted 37 mm Flak 18 cannon as an anti-tank *Staffel*.

Operations in Central Russia (June 1943 – October 1943) 8 July: although little has come to light documenting the *Staffel's* day-to-day operations, it is thought to have been committed to the battle over the Kursk salient from Orel on this date. 12-13 July: the combined units under *Luftflotte* 6 claimed 67 or 68 enemy tanks destroyed in the Kursk salient on these two days and *Panzerjägerstaffel*/St.G. 1 is believed to have had a share of these. 14 July: Ju 87 shot down by AA fire east of Kolodyaztsy/64 km north-east of Bryansk, 1 KIA and 1 WIA. 29 August: Ju 87 G-1 shot up by AA fire and force-landed north-west of Esman, which is north-east of Konotop. The aircraft was destroyed in the crash. 18 October: renamed 10.(Pz.)/S.G. 77, possibly at Orsha.

FpN: (L 52762)

Staffelkapitän:
Unknown.

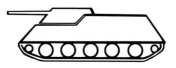

The *Panzer Jäger Staffel/St.G. 1* was formed on 17 June 1943 by renaming 1.*Staffel/Versuchskommando für Panzerbekampfung*. It was equipped with the Ju 87 G-1 which carried two 37 mm Flak 18 anti-tank cannon beneath the wings. The emblem of the *Staffel*, a white tank silhouette, was painted on both sides of the cowling. It probably flew its first operations during the battle over the Kursk salient in July 1943.

Pz.Jg.St./St.G. 1 Emblem

LS-Ausb.Kdo./St.G. 1

Formation and History (April 1943 – May 1943)
Formed 23 April 1943 at Wertheim as a training *Staffel* for glider towing (*Luftschlepp* - LS). Equipped with 2 Junkers Ju 87 dive-bombers and 21 DFS 230 gliders upon formation. Together with LS-Ausb.Abt./St.G. 77, renamed *LS-Ausbildungsstaffel für Stukaverbände* (Glider-Towing Training Squadron for Dive-Bomber Formations) on 22 May 1943 at Wertheim.

FpN: None known.

Kommandeur:
Unknown.

Sources for St.G. 1:

Unpublished and Archival:
BA-MA Freiburg: RL 2 III Gen.Qu.(6.Abt.) *Meldungen über Flugzeugunfälle und Verlust…* (LRs – Loss Reports).
BA-MA - *Flugzeug-Bereitstellungen* (Aircraft Availability Status Reports – FzB) in: Holm-op cit; all subsequent entries of this type are from this source.
BA-MA Freiburg: *Signatur* RL 20/274-77.
NARA WashDC: RG 242/T-311: H.Gr. Nord microfilms.
NARA WashDC: RG 242/T-312: roll 168/frame 941; roll 296/frame 937 (Lw.Kdo.Ost Ops Order Nr.66 for Operation *Nordpol*); roll 865/frames 380, 463, 525 and 930; roll 871/frame 230.
NARA WashDC: RG 242/T-313: roll 88/frame 045; roll 111/frame 249; roll 112/frames 167-538; roll 114/frame 895; roll 154/frames 511-12; roll 155/frames 057-939 scattered (2 February - 12 February); roll 156/frames 135-969 scattered (20 February - 22 February); roll 174/frame 830.
NARA WashDC: RG 242/T-321 roll 115/frame 001ff.
NARA WashDC: RG 242/T-971 roll 19.
Oberfeldkommandantur 672 daily report for 30 January 1942 provided by Jean-Louis Robas.
PRO London: ADM 223 Operational Intelligence Centre/Special Intelligence reports.
PRO London: AIR 40/file 1966, 1968, 1974, 1975, 1980, 1982, 1983, 1986, 1995, 1996.

Published:
[Aders – SG] p. 28, 33, 36, 39, 40, 43, 46, 47, 59, 60, 62, 67, 69, 100, 108;
[Balke – KG2V1] p. 404, 409, 410, 415, 418;
[Bateson – *Stuka!*] p. 8, 9, 13, 18, 19-21, 25, 29-31, 34-39, 42, 47, 52, 57, 59, 61, 63;
[Bekker – LWD] p. 11, 25, 167, 215, 223, 254, 284, 337, 434;
[Bergström – BC/RS-1] p. 120, 142, 246;
[Bergström – BC/RS-2] p. 196-190;
[Bergström – BC/RS-3] p. 99, 131-32;
[Brütting – BA] p. 118;
[Brütting – SA] p. 43, 142, 144, 149-151, 153-155, 181, 184, 185, 188, 189, 194, 195, 197, 198, 205, 206, 216, 217, 219, 224, 226-228, 234, 242, 243, 246, 253, 256, 264, 265, 268, 269, 271;
[Carlsen – CM2] p. 338-343;
[Dierich – VdL] p. 201, 202, 204-211, 215, 248, 270;
[Foreman – Forg] p. 13, 76, 90;
[Green – WotTR] p. 435-437, 440, 443;
[Griehl – KFZ] p. 119;
[Gundelach – Med] p. 99, 102, 109, 135, 140;
[Kannapin – FPN] p. various;
[Mahlke – Mahlke] p. 70-159, 177;
[Mason – BovB] p. 200, 552;
[Mehner – FT] p. 54;
[Nauroth – StG2] p. 208, 217;
[Obermaier – RK2] p. 48, 50, 56, 58, 60, 62, 64, 66, 78, 87, 98, 103, 108, 109, 118, 128, 137, 139-141, 145, 150, 152, 155, 174, 177, 180, 181, 185, 186, 198, 199, 205;
[Patzwall – LwR] p. various;
[Plocher – Rus41] p. 227;
[Plocher – Rus42] p. 144;
[Plocher – Rus43] p. 61, 76, 78;
[Ramsey – B-1] p. 146;
[Ramsey – B-2] p. 274, 305;
[Ries – Lw] p. 140;
[Ries – PhotoCol] p. 205-208, 216, 217;
[Ries – PhotoRec] p. 154, 158, 169;
[Rohwer – Chron] p. 92, 134;
[Scheibert – EP] p. various;
[Scherzer – DKG] p. 591-595;
[Shores – F] p. 16, 25, 99, 215, 236, 239, 241, 242, 244, 252, 274, 286, 296-298, 302-304, 315, 327, 332, 337, 339;
[Shores – FotD] p. 29, 30, 34, 45, 48-50, 64, 67, 77, 90, 207, 250;
[Shores – Malta-H] p. 105, 106, 109, 115, 119, 145, 155, 159, 162, 163, 171, 173, 183, 197, 200-202;
[Shores – Malta-S] p. 20, 79, 82;
[Shores – Yugo] p. 235, 244, 337, 359, 371, 398;
[Smith – GA] p. 383-386, 388, 389;
[Smith – SAW] p. 18, 19, 23, 31, 37, 39-41, 43, 44, 48, 72, 95;
[Smith – *Stuka*(1998)] p. 56-60;
[Smith – StG 77] p. 48, 67, 144;
[Tessin – Form] p. 223;
[Tessin – Tes] p. 328, 329;
[Weal – *Stuka* 37-41] p. 20, 83;
[Weal – Stu-Med] p. 57, 66?;
[Zweng – Zweng] p. 37, 38.

[Archiv #6 – A-6] p. 17;
[Archiv #8 – A-8] p. 12, 16;
[Archiv #9 – A-9] p. 28.

[Holm – Website www.ww2.dk]

St.G. 2 Emblem

St.G. 2 Immelmann

Sturzkampfgeschwader 2 'Immelmann'

(Unit Code: T6+)

The Geschwader Stab of St.G. 2 was formed at Köln-Ostheim by renaming Stab/St.G. 163 on 15 October 1939. The Stabsstaffel was equipped with one or two Dornier Do 17 Ps in addition to a small number of Ju 87s, these being used mainly for reconnaissance rather than bombing. The aircraft in the foreground was coded T6+FA.

Stab/St.G. 2

Formation, West – Phoney War, Training and Standby (May 1939 – May 1940)
Formed 15 October 1939 at Köln-Ostheim (new). The *Stabsstaffel* was equipped with Dornier Do 17 bombers and a small number of Junkers Ju 87 dive-bombers, these being used as much for reconnaissance and transport purposes as for combat. It remained at Köln-Ostheim for training until spring 1940.

Attack on France and the Low Countries (May 1940 – June 1940) 10 May: Köln-Ostheim under VIII.*Fliegerorps/Luftflotte* 2 with 3 (3) Ju 87 Bs and 6 (5) Do 17 Ms. At the start of the campaign, the *Geschwaderstab* had I./St.G. 76 attached to it, and after the first two days the *Stab* was reassigned from *Luftflotte* 2 to *Luftflotte* 3. A Ju 87 belonging to the *Geschwaderstab*

was shot down by a French Curtiss Hawk 75 at Bouillon/Belgium, 25 km east-north-east of Charleville-Mézières in north-eastern France during the second day of operations. On 25 and 26 May, aircraft from the *Stab* were taking part in operations over the Calais area and 1 Do 17 failed to return. As the offensive moved rapidly forward through Belgium and into France, the *Geschwaderstab* was located at Beaulieu/ 17 km north-west of Bastogne in South Belgium and then at Laon/north-east France. After the tail end of the campaign on 20 June, *Kommodore Major* Dinort was presented with the *Ritterkreuz* by Ernst Udet.

Air Offensive against England (Battle of Britain) (July 1940 – January 1941) July: the *Geschwaderstab* and *Stabsstaffel* moved to Saint-Malo in Brittany during July and were still there on 13 August with 4 (3) Ju 87 Bs and 5 (4) Do 17 Ms under VIII.*Fliegerkorps/Luftflotte* 3. 18 August: the *Stab*

controlled limited *Stuka* attacks on shipping, airfields and radar stations along the south coast of England during July and August until all *Stuka* units were withdrawn from cross-Channel daylight operations on this date due to high losses. From late August, the *Stab* supervised the *Geschwader's* training and replacement activities apart from occasional dusk raids on shipping. The *Stab* (and presumably the *Stabsstaffel*, too) was based at St-Malo until at least 5 January 1941; however it may have been briefly at Tramecourt near St-Pol in late October 1940, under Lfl 2. In December the *Geschwaderstab* and assigned units were placed on standby for possible use in Operation *Felix*, the planned invasion of Gibraltar that was subsequently cancelled for various reasons. Ordered to depart St-Malo in January for reassignment in the Balkans, with a one month delay en route at Kitzingen/S Germany for home leave and refit.

Balkan Campaign (February 1941 – May 1941)

10 February: transferred from Kitzingen to Otopeni 10 km/north of Bucharest in Romania and then on 6 March to Kraynitsi (Krainitsi)/42 km south-south-west of Sofia in Bulgaria for operations against Yugoslavia and Greece under VIII.*Fliegerkorps/Luftflotte* 4. For the start of the Balkans campaign on 6 April 1941, the *Stab* and *Stabsstaffel* moved forward to Belica-North (Belitsa) 85 km/south-south-east of Sofia on 27 March with 5 (4) Ju 87 Bs and 6 (6) Do 17 Ms. Subordinated for the operation were its own I. and III. *Gruppen*. On 11 April the *Stabsstaffel* lost a Do 17 M near Xanthe (Xanthi)/north-east Greece and on the 21st it lost another in the Larissa (Larisa) area. On 11 May the *Stab* was based at Corinth/south Greece, on the 17th it was probably at Molaoi, and on the 20th it was definitely at Molaoi. On 22 May aircraft from the *Stabsstaffel* hunted British ships north of Crete and on the 24th it lost a Do 17 M. Ordered from Molaoi to Cottbus in eastern Germany on 2 June to prepare for forthcoming operations against the USSR.

Attack on the Soviet Union – Central and North Russia. (June 1941 – June 1942)

22 June: *Stab* and *Stabsstaffel* now at Praschnitz (Przasnysz)/88 km north of Warsaw with 3 (3) Ju 87 Bs and 6 (4) Bf 110s under VIII.*Fliegerkorps/Luftflotte* 2. By 24 July, the *Stab* was at Lepel-East/125 km south-west of Vitebsk and 29 July at Surazh/40 km north-east of Vitebsk taking part in the capture of Smolensk. From 8 to 29 August it was based at Ryelbitsi, west of Lake Ilmen on the northern sector of the front, having moved north with the rest of VIII.*Fliegerkorps* for the advance towards Leningrad. In early September the *Stab* was reportedly at Tyrkovo/100 km south of Lake Ilmen, but in mid- and late September the *Stabsstaffel* was known to have been flying daily sorties against the Russian Baltic Fleet in the Gulf of Finland near Leningrad. At the end of September, *Stab*/St.G. 2 was ordered back to the central sector of the front to support Operation *Taifun*, the all-out drive on Moscow that commenced on 2 October, moving initially to Smolensk, and then around 8-10 October it moved forward to Kuleshevka/35 km north of Vyazma on the path of advance towards the Russian capital. In November, it moved ahead to Gorstkovo/80 km west of Moscow, and in mid-December it pulled back to Dugino/65 km south of Rzhev on 16 December following the powerful Russian counter-attack along the front west of Moscow. On 31 January 1942, a Bf 110 failed to return from operations in the Belyy area/96 km south-west of Rzhev. In February, the *Stab* left Dugino and moved 55 kilometres south to Vyazma where, on 1 March, it reported 9 Bf 110 Es and 1 Henschel Hs 126 on strength. On 6 March, one of its Bf 110 E-3s was destroyed during an enemy air attack on the airfield at Vyazma. It lost another Bf 110 E reported missing in the Staritsa area on 19 March and was still at Vyazma on 22 March. Sometime thereafter, probably in the first half of April after the desperate defensive fighting along the line west of Moscow had settled down, the *Stab* was transferred to Neukuhren in East Prussia, and then in May 1942 to Graz/Austria to rest and refit, remaining there until 22 June.

Stabskette St.G. 2 Emblem

The crews of St.G. 2 spent several periods at Graz in Austria for rest and refitting. This aerial photograph shows the practice dive-bombing area marked with the silhouettes of battleships which was used for dive-bombing training. Close study of the photograph plainly shows the bomb craters made during this training.

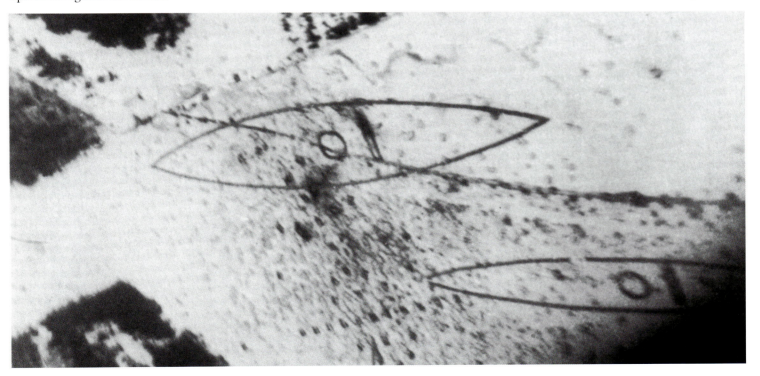

Dr.jur. Ernst Kupfer (RK-SW, DKG)

BORN on 2 July 1907 in Coburg/Oberfranken (Upper Franconia), Kupfer enrolled in law school at Heidelberg University between 1926 and 1928. Following this he entered service with the *Heer* (*Kavallerie*) and, on 1 December 1934, was promoted to *Oberleutnant*. In 1939 he transferred from the Army to the *Luftwaffe* with the rank of *Rittmeister* (equivalent to a *Hauptmann*) and began training at a reconnaissance flying school on 30 September 1939. In June 1940 he received further training at *Stukaschule* 2 (Dive-Bomber School 2) at Otrokowitz (Otrokovice)/Czechoslovakia.

After completing training he reported to the *Ergänzungs-Stukagruppe* at Lippstadt on 31 August 1940. He joined his first operational *Gruppe*, I./St.G. 2, as a pilot on 7 September 1940. On 1 October 1940 he was appointed *Staka* of 7./St.G. 2. On 22 May 1941 he was credited with a direct hit on the British cruiser *Gloucester* which sank off Crete with many of her crew of 693 officers and men. On 23-24 September 1941 he was credited with a direct hit on the Soviet battleship *Oktyabrskaya Revolutsiya*, which was caught in the area of the Leningrad Sea Canal. This caused heavy damage and put the ship out of action for some time. On 28 September he was severely wounded in a forced landing during operations in the Leningrad (St. Petersburg) area and was evacuated to Germany. After undergoing eight operations to repair numerous broken bones he underwent a period of extended convalescence.

On 23 November 1941, still as *Staka* of 7./St.G. 2, Kupfer was awarded the gold wound badge and the *Ritterkreuz* (Knight's Cross). He was promoted to *Major* on 1 January 1942 and appointed *Kommandeur* of II./St.G. 2 five days later. On 14 October 1942 he was awarded the *Ehrenpokal* (Honour Goblet for exceptional performance in air warfare) and next day the *Deutsche Kreuz in Gold* (German Cross in Gold). On 30 October 1942 he flew his 500th combat sortie and was awarded the *Eichenlaub zum Ritterkreuz* (Oak Leaves to the *Ritterkreuz*) (No. 173) on 8 January 1943. Appointed provisional *Kommodore* of St.G. 2 on 13 February 1943 and commander of *Stukaverband* Kupfer (a tactical formation) based at Kerch in Crimea in April for the Kursk offensive. Early in September 1943 (possibly the 11th) he was appointed *General der Schlachtflieger* (L.In.2/3)/RLM (General of the ground-attack branch in the Air Ministry in Berlin).

He was killed in the crash of an He 111 bomber/transport that went down in mountainous terrain 60 km north of Salonika/Greece during bad weather on 6 November 1943. He was returning to Berlin following an inspection trip to Greece where he had met, among others, *Major* Kurt Kuhlmey who was *Kommodore* of S.G. 3 at Argos airfield. Posthumously he was promoted to *Oberst* (RDA 1 November 1943) on 22 December 1943 and awarded the *Schwerter* (Swords to the *Ritterkreuz*) (No. 62) on 11 April 1944. At the time of his death, Kupfer had completed 636 combat sorties.

Ernst Kupfer steps down from the cockpit of his Ju 87 B of the Geschwader Stab of St.G. 2 which carries the unit's familiar emblem.

The Geschwader Stab of St.G. 2 was re-equipped with the Ju 87 D during early 1943. It is probable that this aircraft, T6+AA, was piloted by the Kommodore, Major Dr.jur. Ernst Kupfer. The badge of the Geschwader Stab, a black cross on a white shield edged in red, was painted just forward of the cockpit. After re-equipment, the Stab of the Immelmann Geschwader was ordered to Dnepropetrovsk-South to command ground-attack units brought in to stop Russian armoured spearheads moving rapidly towards the Dnieper River and the bridges at Dnepropetrovsk.

South Russia – Advance to Stalingrad (June 1942 – January 1943) 22 June: the *Stab* transferred from Graz to Akhtyrka (Achtirskaya)/115 km north-west of Kharkov on the southern sector of the Eastern Front for assignment to *Luftflotte* 4, and participated in attacks on Voronezh during the opening phase of the German summer offensive aimed at the Don River, Stalingrad and the oilfields of North Caucasia. On 20 July, it moved to Tatsinskaya along the advance west of Stalingrad, and on 29 July on to Oblivskaya along the Chir River 148 km west of the city where, on 20 September, it reported 10 (4) Ju 87s, Bf 110s and Fw 189s on strength. Transferred to Stalino-North at the end of September or beginning of October, and then on 13 October to Karpovka-West/40 km west of Stalingrad. The *Geschwaderstab* was based at Kalach/450 km south-east of Voronezh on 21 November 1942 when the airfield was overrun and it had to make a hasty retreat to Morosovskaya/202 km north-east of Rostov. At the end of December, the *Stab* pulled back to Makeyevka/12 km east of Stalino and then around 3 January 1943 it transferred to Nikolayev in the rear area of south-western Ukraine to rest and refit, remaining there for nearly two months.

Operations in Eastern Ukraine and Crimea (February 1943 – June 1943) On 22 February, the *Stab* was ordered to Dnepropetrovsk-South II to command ground-attack units brought in to stop Russian armour spearheads moving rapidly towards the Dnieper River and the bridges at Dnepropetrovsk. Moved forward to Poltava during the first week in March and then to Stalino. The last known aircraft reported lost by the *Stab* was a Ju 87 D-3 shot down by AA fire over the Izyum area to the south-east of Kharkov on 29 March. In April, it was based at Kerch IV in eastern Crimea for attacks on the Soviet landings at Novorossisk, and for support operations over the Kuban bridgehead. During 1 to 6 May 1943, the *Stab* was at Kharkov-North for operations under VIII.*Fliegerkorps* but from 9 May it was back at Kerch IV. In early June, the *Stabsstaffel* handed over all but 2 or 3 of its aircraft to other units in Russia and sent its 12 crews to II./LG 1 at Athens-Eleusis in Greece for retraining on Junkers Ju 88s and incorporation into the *Gruppe*. The *Geschwaderstab* reported 2 Ju 87 D-3s and 1 Ju 87 D-5 on strength on 1 July, and the next day received an official visit at Kerch from Albert Speer and Japanese General Otani.

Kursk and Retreat in Ukraine (July 1943 – October 1943) For the German offensive at Kursk (Operation *Zitadelle*) commencing 5 July, the *Stab* was initially based at Kharkov-East under VIII.*Fliegerkorps*/ *Luftflotte* 4, but due to Soviet counter-attacks during mid-July it was forced to move north to Orel and then to Karachev/75 km west-north-west of Orel from around 19 July. At about this time, the *Stab* was temporarily renamed *Stab/Gefechtsverband Kupfer* for tactical purposes and commanded the defensive operations of the ground-attack units in the area of Kursk and southward under *Luftflotte* 6. Ordered released by *Luftflotte* 6 on 25 August and transferred to Dimitrievka (Dmitriyevka)/84 km east of Dnepropetrovsk in South Russia for reassignment back to *Luftflotte* 4. The *Stab* took part in the defensive operations in eastern Ukraine as victorious Soviet forces drove the Germans back into Central Ukraine. In the latter part of September and during the first half of

The Geschwader Stab of St.G. 2 was equipped with one or two Bf 110s for reconnaissance and communications. This aircraft, T6+AA, possibly flown by the Kommodore, seems to have collided head-on with a Bf 109.

October, the *Stab* was located at Pervomaisk/90 km south-east of Uman and on 18 October 1943 it was renamed *Stab*/S.G. 2 Immelmann, probably at Pervomaisk.

FpNs: *Geschwaderstab* (L 21660, 38511); *Stabsstaffel* (L 00228)

Kommodore:
Oberst Oskar Dinort (16 October 1939 - 16 October 1941)
Major Paul-Werner Hozzel (RK) (16 October 1941 - 13 February 1943)
Major Dr.jur. Ernst Kupfer (DKG, RK, EL) (13 February 1943 - 10 September 1943)
Major Hans-Karl Stepp (DKG, RK) (20 September 1943 - 18 October 1943)

I./St.G. 2

Formation and Training (May 1939 – August 1939) Formed 1 May 1939 at Breslau in Silesia from the former I./St.G. 163 based at Cottbus. Equipped with Junkers Ju 87 B dive-bombers. It remained in training at Breslau until ordered to Welzow 25 km south-west of Cottbus on 19 August as part of the first phase of general mobilization for the anticipated attack on Poland.

Campaign in Poland (September 1939) 1 September: based at Nieder-Ellguth in Silesia, under 2.*Fliegerdivision*/*Luftflotte* 4 with 38 (37) Ju 87 B and 3 (3) Do 17 P bombers that were used mainly for reconnaissance and transport duties. On the first day of the Polish campaign, it struck the airfield at Krakow and possibly also that of Katowitz (Katowice) and Wadowice/38 km south-west of Krakow, then attacked cavalry near Wielun/111 km north of Katowice. Also on the first day, *Lt.* Frank Neubert of 1.*Staffel* is believed to have scored the first aerial victory of World War II when he and his rear-seat gunner, *Uffz.* Franz Klinger, attacked and shot down a Polish PZL P-11c around dawn while they were on a mission to dive-bomb the Polish airfield at Krakow. From 2 to 6 September, it repeatedly hit the railhead at Piotrkow which the Poles were using to offload troops and supplies for the front. In fact, the

Paul-Werner Hozzel (i.G.). (RK-EL)

HOZZEL was born 16 October 1910 in Hamburg, the son of a shipbroker. He joined the *Heer* (Army) in 1931 and was assigned to an artillery regiment. He was promoted to *Lt.* in 1934 and transferred to the *Luftwaffe* the next year. He became an *Oberleutnant* in 1936 and was appointed *Staka* in *Fliegergruppe* 20 (either 2. or 3.*Staffel*) on 1 September 1938. Promoted to *Hauptmann* in October 1938, he transferred to I./St.G. 160 at Insterburg on 1 November 1938. He was appointed provisional *Kdr.* of I./St.G. 1 on 1 June 1939 (or September 1939?), this position being made permanent on 18 October.

On 8 May 1940 Hozzel became the first *Stuka* pilot to be awarded the *Ritterkreuz* and is believed to have been promoted to *Major* at the same time. On 1 August 1941 he was appointed *Kommandeur* of *Stukaschule* 1 and *Kommodore* of St.G. 2 between 16 October 1941 and 13 February 1943. In May 1942 he also took command of the tactical *Gefechtsverband* (combat formation) Dugino. He transferred to the Ob.d.L. officer reserve and was ordered to *Luftflottenkommando* 4 for further assignment on 13 February 1943. He became *Kommandeur* of the tactical *Gefechtsverband* Hozzel at Dnepropetrovsk-South in the same month. On 13 March 1943 he was appointed *Kdt.* of *Flughafenbereich* Krim, Kuban *und* Schwarzes Meer (Airfield Regional Command Crimea, Taman Peninsula and Black Sea). He was awarded the *Eichenlaub zum Ritterkreuz* (No. 230) on 14 April 1943 and appointed acting *Kdt.* of *Koflug* 6/VI on 11 June 1943. Promoted to *Oberstleutnant* (see photograph) on 1 August 1943, he took part in general staff training between 1943 and 1944. He transferred to LKS Berlin-Gatow on 6 January 1944 and was appointed *Leiter der Führungsabteilung* (director of the headquarters command section) of *Luftflotte* 1 on 1 April 1944. He was recommended by *Luftflotte* 1 for promotion to *Oberst* on 22 November 1944 and was appointed acting Ch.d.*Stabes/Luftflottenkdo.* 1 on Christmas Day and *Chef d.Stabes* and Ia/*Luftwaffenkdo.* Kurland on 17 April 1945. On 8 May 1945 he was taken into Russian captivity and eventually confined in a camp in Sverdlovsk, not being released until 16 January 1956.

On his return to Germany, Hozzel joined the *Bundesluftwaffe* as an *Oberstleutnant*. He was appointed *Chef des Stabes der Offiziersschule der Luftwaffe* in Fassberg/Lüneburger Heide in 1956-57 and became a lecturer at the *Führungsakademie der Luftwaffe* in Bonn up to the summer of 1958, after which he was appointed *Chef des Stabes der Luftwaffendivision* at Münster/Westfalen. In early 1960 he was transferred to the *Generalstab* and promoted to *Oberst*. During the summer of 1967 he became *Chef des Stabes der Luftwaffengruppe Süd* in Karlsruhe and was promoted to *Brigadegeneral*. He was appointed *Chef des Stabes der Alliierten Streitkräfte Ostseezugang* in Karup/Dänemark (chief of staff of HQ Allied Forces Baltic Approaches in Karup/Denmark – HQ NATO BALTAP) on 1 October 1967. He finally retired on 30 September 1969 only to become an executive with the *Badischen Verwaltungs- und Wirtschaftsakademien* (Baden Academy for Administration and Economics) between 1971 and 1992. Hozzel died on 7 January 1997 in Karlsruhe.

Gruppe was credited with devastating a large force of Polish infantry that was detraining at Piotrkow on 2 September. Soon the unit was transferred to Czestochowa to support the Army's advance to Warsaw. On 17 September, I./St.G. 2 was involved in a large attack on Warsaw and also attacked the Polish Army HQ at Modlin. It also blasted retreating troops at rail yards at Radom, then supported Army attacks in the Kutno-Sochaczew area 50 to 100 km due west of Warsaw, around Modlin, the area west of Ilza, and south of Wierzbica.

Phoney War, Training and Standby in the West (October 1939 – April 1940) October: the campaign in Poland concluded towards the end of September and the *Gruppe* was transferred to Golzheim/28 km south-west of Köln under VIII.*Fliegerkorps* with orders to train and prepare for planned operations in the West. During the winter of 1939-1940 the *Gruppe* trained in the area of Hildesheim, specifically to knock out Belgian forts along the border between Liège and Maastricht. In January 1940, the *Gruppe* was possibly located at Marburg for a short time, probably in conjunction with training requirements or equipment modifications.

Attack on France and the Low Countries (May 1940 – June 1940) 10 May: at Golzheim (or Köln-Ostheim?) under VIII.*Fliegerkorps/Luftflotte* 2 (later *Luftflotte* 3) with 40 (33) Ju 87 Bs for operations in Belgium and France. On 10 May, attacked the Belgian fortress of Eben-Emael and nearby Belgian reserves. 11 May: attacked forts at Namur and Liège and supported

crossings over the Maas by 6.*Armee*, with heavy losses – 5 Ju 87 Bs were shot down by RAF Hurricanes over the Tirlemont area/42 km east-south-east of Brussels. 12 May: Ju 87 shot down by an RAF Hurricane at St-Trond/Belgium. 14-16 May: the *Gruppe* moved from Golzheim to Liège-Ans. A *Stuka* was lost to AA fire in the Liège area on 15 May and another there to the same cause on 16 May. 15 May: in action over Cortil-Noirmont, north-west of Gembloux. Moved forward to Guise/25 km east-north-east of Saint-Quentin in north-east France around 16-17 May. 25 May: moved north via Beaulieu and Cambrai and started attacks on the Dunkirk area, 2 Ju 87 Bs failing to return from operations this date. 25 May: attacked shipping off Calais. 26 May: attacked the docking areas of Calais losing one Ju 87 B. 29 May: attacked Dunkirk harbour at 0730 hours. Another *Stuka* was lost in the Calais-Dunkirk area on 29 May and operations against the British evacuation ended on 1 June. 2 June: attacked shipping east of Dunkirk. The *Gruppe* spent the next few days reorganizing. 5-7 June: supported the breakthrough of 9.*Armee* south of Laon. 8 June: began supporting the advance of 6. and 9.*Armee* over the Seine and the Marne, losing 3 Ju 87s on 8 June. 8 June: in action over Longpont along the north-east approaches to Paris. Over the following week, I./St.G. 2 supported battles near Peronne, Amiens, Roye, Chauny and Nogent. It also supported the Army's advances east of Paris over the Marne, Seine, Yonne and Loire. 12 June 1940: transferred to Laon-Couvron and retained there until early July. The campaign ended on 22 June with an armistice signed by Germany and France.

The pilot from 3./St.G. 2 looks on in some amusement as his ground crew are buffeted by dust kicked up by the propeller of his Ju 87 B. Two of the men hang on grimly to the handle which they have just turned to operate the inertial starting system. The aircraft carries SC 50 bombs beneath the wings but its wind-driven siren generators have been faired over.

3./St.G. 2 Emblem

Air Offensive against England (Battle of Britain) (July 1940 – January 1941)

2 July: at Laon-Couvron - began flying attacks on Channel shipping under VIII.*Fliegerkorps*, many or most of these missions being staged through forward airfields in the Pas de Calais area and elsewhere along the Channel coast of northern France. In late July or early August the *Gruppe* moved to Cherbourg and then a week or so later to St-Malo in Brittany. 5 August: Ju 87 B-2 damaged taking off from a forward field strip at Condé-sur-Ifs/22 km south-east of Caen. 8 August: attacked channel convoy CW 9 *Peewit* near the Isle of Wight, with unknown results, and suffered one aircraft damaged. 13 August: at St-Malo with 35 (29) Ju 87 Bs for attacks on Britain under VIII.*Fliegerkorps*. Same date, it was sent to hit Rochford airfield but the attack was aborted due to bad weather. 16 August: 5 Ju 87 B-2s shot down by Hurricanes during a raid on RAF Station Tangmere near Portsmouth plus 3 more shot up and damaged. 18 August: on this date a sister *Stuka Geschwader*, St.G. 77, lost so many aircraft to fighters

(a total of 22 destroyed or damaged) during an ill-fated raid on coastal airfields at Ford and Thorney Island and a radar station at Poling, that all *Stuka* units were pulled out of normal operations for the remainder of the campaign. It was the first decisive defeat for the German dive-bomber units which had generated great fear and respect for their prior successes. Following this debacle, the *Gruppe* and the rest of the *Stuka* formations stood down from the major cross-Channel activity and concentrated on training and occasional special missions, although small-scale dusk attacks on coastal shipping were carried out from October to the end of the year. September: the *Gruppe* was involved in the making of the Karl Ritter film *Stukas*, a big box-office hit of its day. December: I./St.G. 2 was tentatively assigned to Operation *Felix*, the invasion of Gibraltar, which was subsequently cancelled. 5-6 January 1941: transferred from St-Malo to Graz/Austria and then on to Otopeni/10 km north of Bucharest in Romania on 23 January for forthcoming operations in the Balkans under VIII.*Fliegerkorps*.

A group of interested spectators look on as British officials examine one of four Ju 87 Bs of 3./St.G. 2 which were shot down during an attack on Tangmere airfield on 16 August 1940. During this assault eight Ju 87s from I./St.G. 2 were destroyed or damaged, many of them shot down by Hurricanes of No.43 Squadron. III./St.G. 2 had little more luck, losing seven Ju 87s destroyed or damaged on the same day.

Balkan Campaign (February 1941 – May 1941)

27 January: after just 4 days at Otopeni, ordered to Kraynitsi (Krainitsi)/42 km south-south-west of Sofia in Bulgaria and then at the end of March (27th?) to Belica-North (Belitsa)/85 km south-south-east of Sofia. 5 April: at Belica-North with 30 Ju 87 B and 9 Ju 87 R. On 6 April, the opening day of the attack on Yugoslavia, the *Gruppe* attacked positions south-east of Petric and on the Metaxas Line. Early in the campaign it attacked Yugoslav airfields and may have taken part in the devastating air attack on Belgrade on 6 April. 9 April: attacked English troops at Arta in western Greece. Over the following days, I./St.G. 2 supported the ground advances on Skopje, Prilep, Veles and Salonika, struck Serbian positions where encountered, facilitated the breakthrough at Kastoria, the routing of the Greek Epirus Army, took part in the battles near Olympia, Larissa, Volos and Thermopylae, supported parachute drops into Corinthia, and the advance into Peloponesia. Along the way, the *Gruppe* used the airfields at Larissa (Larisa), Chalkis (Khalkis) and Corinth (Korinthos). 22 April: attacked British ships in the Gulf of Megara and by the end of the month it was based at Corinth and Molaoi preparing for operations on and around Crete. During the period 1 to 21 May the *Gruppe* flew concerted near-daily attacks on Allied ships in the waters around the island as part of the intense naval activity leading up to the great airborne and air-landing assault on Crete which commenced on 20 May. 22 May: operating from Molaoi and Argos, struck British ships off Maleme/Crete, sinking the destroyer *Greyhound*, the light cruiser *Gloucester* and contributed to the sinking of the light cruiser *Fiji*. 23 May: with a formation totalling 24 Ju 87s, sunk the destroyers *Kelly* and *Kashmir*. 30 May: operating from Rhodes, severely damaged the light cruiser *Orion* and the destroyer *Dido* 100 km south-east of Kasos Strait in the Dodecanese Islands off the Turkish coast, and helped sink the destroyer *Hereward*. By the end of the Crete operation, the *Gruppe* had claimed a total of 164,000 tons of shipping sunk. June: departed Rhodes for Cottbus in eastern Germany for a brief rest and refit, then moved to Praschnitz (Przasnysz)/88 km north of Warsaw.

Attack on the Soviet Union – Central and North Russia (June 1941 – September 1941)

22 June: at Praschnitz with 35 Ju 87 Bs under VIII.*Fliegerkorps*/*Luftflotte* 2 for the opening of the campaign into Russia. During the first three days, supported the breakthrough of 9.*Armee* and *Panzergruppe* 3 to the east and south-east of Suwalki in north-eastern Poland. 25 June: attacked a Russian tank concentration 80 km south of Grodno. Over the following days, flew support in the pocket battles of Grodno-Bialystok and around Minsk. Next, it supported the advance of *Panzergruppe* 3 on Vilnius (Wilna), Lepel and Vitebsk, and the bridgehead over the Dnieper. 28 June: attacked the supply point at Nowogrodek, between Grodno and Minsk, then moved forward to Sloboda/72 km south-west of Minsk and attacked the Vitebsk-Smolensk rail line on 11 July. 13 July: bombed the railhead at Yermachevo and the road from Polotsk to Nevel. 15 July: hit troop columns 2 km south-west of Mamonva and along the road 15 km from Velikiye Luki. 21 July: now at Lepel/125 km south-west of Vitebsk, supported the pocket battle of Smolensk, and hit a bridge over the Khmost' River, on the road between Minsk and Moscow. 22 July: bombed road and rail bridges near Ul'khovo/53 km north-east of Smolensk as well as other key targets in the area. 8 August: reassigned with the rest of VIII.*Fliegerkorps* to the northern sector of the Eastern Front to support the advance of 16.*Armee* over the Velikaya River between Idritsa and Pskov and towards Staraya Russa at the southern tip of Lake Ilmen, operating from Lepel, Yanovichi/33 km east-north-east of Vitebsk and probably several other airfields around Pskov and Dno to the west of Lake Ilmen including Ryelbitsi. Then it supported the advance along the Novgorod-Chudovo axis and in the direction of Lyuban on the approaches to Leningrad. 13 August: attacked retreating Soviet forces along the Volkhov River and knocked out a key bridge which disrupted the withdrawal. 27 August - 8 September: supported the advance by *Panzergruppe* Schmidt (XXVIII.*Armeekorps* and XXXIX.*Panzerkorps*) to Schlüsselburg at the mouth of the Neva River due east of Leningrad. On 29 August the *Gruppe* moved Tyrkovo/100 km south of Lake Ilmen to help deal with a strong Soviet counter-attack near Staraya Russa. At about this time, it aided *Panzergruppe* 4 in its advance towards Leningrad, rapidly changing bases from one hot spot to another. 9 September: attacked line-of-communication targets along the Moscow-Leningrad road and rail lines in the area about 40 km south of Leningrad. At about this time, it struck Soviet staging areas along the Lovat' River south of Lake Ilmen and around Lake Ladoga.

For operations in the Balkan theatre many Luftwaffe aircraft had yellow noses and rudders applied. The Ju 87 B of 2./St.G. 2 in the background carries the emblem of the Staffel, a white Scottish terrier on a black circle edged in red, painted forward of the cockpit. The wing of the aircraft nearest the camera has the individual letter 'J' painted outboard of the Balkenkreuz in black.

11 September: bombed troop positions south-east of Krasnogvardeisk near Leningrad. In mid September, I./St.G. 2 was based at Velizh/80 km north-east of Vitebsk, and attacked the rail line between Velikiye Luki and Rzhev. 19 September: now based at Lyuban on the Leningrad front from where it flew raids on Leningrad and the Red Banner Baltic Fleet in Kronstadt harbour, but lost several Ju 87s over the course of the day. On 23 September, Hans-Ulrich Rudel of I.*Gruppe* sank the battleship *Marat* with a single large bomb. 28 September: Ju 87 B-2 force-landed (location not reported), *Staffelkapitän Hptm. Dr.jur.* Ernst Kupfer + 1 WIA.

The Advance on Moscow (October 1941 – December 1941) 30 September: ordered back to the central sector of the front with other air units under VIII.*Fliegerkorps* to take part in Operation *Taifun*, the all-out drive on Moscow that commenced on 2 October. The transfer is believed to have been to Smolensk-North, although this cannot be confirmed. 2-9 October: struck positions, troop concentrations and other targets in the Vyazma pocket and then moved forward to Kuleshevka/35 km north of Vyazma on the path of advance towards the Russian capital. From there it supported the advance of *Panzergruppe* 3 and 9.*Armee* to Kalinin, and then became involved in the defensive battles in the same area. 7 October: 1.*Staffel* Ju 87 R-2 shot down by AA fire near Ivaniki, *Staffelführer Oblt.* Gerhard Weiss + 1 KIA. 17 October: operating from Dugino/65 km south of Rzhev – attacked targets in the Torzhok area/60 km north-west of Kalinin (Tver'). 21 October: ordered to Kalinin and over the next several days flew intense attacks on Soviet forces attempting to cut off and surround the 1.*Panzer-Div.* 27 October: from this date to December the *Gruppe's* airfield locations and dates are unclear due to the rapid advance towards Moscow immediately followed by a rapid retreat, but are believed to have included Gorstkovo/80 km west of Moscow, Staritsa/47 km north-east of Rzhev and then Kalinin-South until the first week of December. 26-28 November: supported the 2.Pz.Armee, and on 30 November supported *Panzergruppe* 4. 6 December: with the temperatures now dropping to -50 degrees Celsius (-58 Fahrenheit, so this must include a wind-chill factor) and with almost no serviceable aircraft remaining, the *Gruppe* was removed from operations and ordered to Stuttgart-Echterdingen in south-western Germany to rest, refit and re-equip.

Refit in Germany and return to North Russia (January 1942 – May 1942) December 1941 - January 1942: during the rest and refit period, the *Gruppe* re-equipped with Ju 87 D-1s and also made some contribution in personnel towards the creation of a new II./St.G. 2. 5 January: 4 Ju 87 D-1s destroyed in a training accident at Elbing airfield/55 km south-east of Danzig when they struck the ground during practice dive-bombing and low-level flying, 3 killed and 1 injured. 6 January: the operational part of the *Gruppe* moved from Neukuhren to Dno airfield, about halfway between Pskov and Lake Ilmen on the northern sector of the Eastern Front, for operations under *Luftflotte* 1. 17 January: shortly after arriving at Dno, began supporting the nearly 100,000 German troops cut off in the Demyansk pocket to the south of Lake Ilmen, then later helped stem an attack near Staraya Russa that began on 14 February. Both the Demyansk and Staraya Russa actions involved weeks

of heavy defensive and offensive fighting by 16.*Armee* and reinforcements brought in from elsewhere, including fleets of transport aircraft used to drop supplies to the surrounded ground forces. February: attacked tanks and road traffic between Staraya Russa and Bologoye, while helping to support the Demyansk pocket. 12 February: Ju 87 D-1 shot down by AA fire near Staraya Russa, 1 WIA and *Gruppenkommandeur Hptm.* Bruno Dilley initially MIA but later returned to German custody. 1 March: *Gruppe* reported 25 Ju 87 D-1s on strength. 13 March: 3.*Staffel* Ju 87 D-1 shot down near Lyubtsy, *Hptm.* Hans Breuer + 1 KIA. 17 March: *Staffelkapitän Oblt.* Friedrich Platzer was shot down near Devoyets. 7 April: 2.*Staffel* Ju 87 D-1 shot up by AA fire near Staraya Russa and heavily damaged. 24-27 April: took part in a series of relatively unsuccessful raids on the ships of the Red Banner Baltic Fleet in Leningrad harbour. The *Gruppe* sustained very few losses from January through April because its missions were usually escorted by Bf 109s from J.G. 54. May: ordered from Dno to Graz/Austria for rest and refit at the end of April or beginning of May. During the early summer while at Graz, the 1.*Staffel* was used to test the new Ju 87 G model.

Armourers prepare a Ju 87 B from 3./St.G. 2 for operations from a Russian airfield. The Staffel emblem is painted on both sides of the fuselage, just forward of the cockpit in black, white and red on a yellow shield, but the aircraft's individual letter 'H' was only applied to the front of the starboard wheel spat.

Typical detritus lies around this operational airfield comprising bombs, fuel drums, crates while two Ju 87 B 1s of 1./St.G. 2 stand ready for action. The aircraft carry the black Scottish Terrier emblem on a white circle which was adopted by the first Staffel of Geschwader Immelmann.

1./St.G. 2 Emblem

Central and South Russia – Advance to Stalingrad and Refit (June 1942 – January 1943) 20 June: ordered from Graz to the airfield at Akhtyrka (Akhtirskaya)/115 km north-west of Kharkov for operations under VIII.*Fliegerkorps*. From 22 June, the *Gruppe* supported attacks on Voronezh as part of the opening phase of the German summer offensive aimed at the Don River, Stalingrad and the oilfields of North Caucasia. 24 June: 3.*Staffel* Ju 87 D-3 damaged at Kiev - Post Volinski airfield and severely damaged due to technical problems; the aircraft was probably en route to Akhtyrka. 30 June: 2.*Staffel* Ju 87 D-3 failed to return from an attack in the vicinity of Chernovka (not located), 2 KIA. 9 July: the *Gruppe's* ground personnel lost 2 KIA and 5 WIA during Russian air attack on Rossosh airfield south-south-east of Voronezh. 20 July: moved forward to Tatsinskaya airfield along the path of advance west of Stalingrad. 4 August: Ju 87 D-1 shot down by ground fire (location not reported), 2 MIA. August: by mid-August the *Gruppe* was based at Oblivskaya, along the Chir River 148 km west of the city, and attacked dug-in tanks on north flank of Stalingrad. 7 September: 2.*Staffel* Ju 87 D-1 bombed on the ground at Oblivskaya during enemy air raid, 1 WIA. Around 7 September there is some creditable evidence in surviving documents that one or two *Staffeln* were either removed or ordered removed from the *Gruppe* and sent north to Krasnogvardeisk (Gatchina) to take part in Operation *Nordlicht*, Hitler's erstwhile plan to reduce the city of Leningrad to rubble. The plan was later abandoned after large numbers of

reinforcements had been shifted to the perimeter around the city, and the detachment from I./St.G. 2 is said to have rejoined the rest of the *Gruppe* at Karpovka-West around 1 November. 12 September: attacked targets in Stalingrad itself. 20 September: I./St.G. 2 reported 25 (16) Ju 87s on strength under *Luftflotte* 4. 23 September: 1.*Staffel* Ju 87 D returned to Oblivskaya shot up by AA fire and severely damaged. September: moved to Stalino in the Donets Basin of eastern Ukraine during the last week of September, probably to refit during a relative lull in the fighting, and then return to the front around Stalingrad on or about 13 October with station at Karpovka-West/40 km west of Stalingrad. 19 November: the Russians launched their powerful counter-offensive to the north and south of Stalingrad this date which very quickly succeeded in linking two armoured spearheads far to the west of the city, thereby cutting off and surrounding the entire German 6.*Armee* in the city and its suburbs. On the 21st the base at Karpovka-West was overrun by Russian tanks and troops. The *Gruppe's* ground personnel reverted to infantry and most became part of the forces trapped in the Stalingrad pocket. 26-27 November: the flying component of the unit reassembled at Morosovskaya/202 km north-east of Rostov and continued operations as best it could in extremely bad winter weather with fewer and fewer serviceable aircraft. 29 December: 2 Ju 87 D-3s from 2.*Staffel* hit by AA fire and collided over Donskoy, along the Don River west of Stalingrad. The crews baled out and were reported safe. December: moved to Makeyevka/12 km east of Stalino near the end of December and then around 3 January 1943 transferred to Nikolayev in the rear area of south-western Ukraine to rest and refit, remaining there for a month or so. 1 January: *Gruppe* reported 41 Ju 87 D-3 and 4 Ju 87 D-1 on strength. 3 January: 5 unserviceable Ju 87 Bs belonging to the *Gruppe* destroyed by German troops at Morosovskaya airfield/202 km north-east of Rostov to prevent them from falling into the hands of the enemy, this being done just hours before the airfield was evacuated by the last ground units defending it.

These two close-ups of the main bombing mechanism used by the Ju 87 show the arm which swung downwards prior to the bomb release. This enabled the weapon to clear the aircraft's slipstream during its steep dive. This machine carries the emblem of 3./St.G. 2, a black eagle atop an iron cross on a yellow shield inside a yellow circle which was the arms of the city of Breslau where the Staffel was formed.

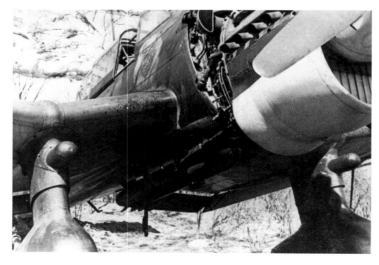

South Russia – Eastern Ukraine and Crimea (February 1943 – June 1943) 1–13 February: numerous ground personnel casualties reported at Voroshilovgrad, Rovenki and Gorlovka caused by enemy air attacks. All three of these locations were forward airfields just behind the front lines around 300 km west of Stalingrad. These men had been caught up in the desperate ground fighting and separated from the *Gruppe*. 15 February: the remnants of the *Gruppe* now at Samorsk/28 km north-west of Kerch in eastern Crimea under VIII.*Fliegerkorps*. 20–22 February: elements ordered to Dnepropetrovsk-South II as part of a contingent of ground-attack and other units brought in and assigned to *Gefechtsverband Hozzel* (*Geschwaderstab*/St.G. 2)/IV.*Fliegerkorps* to stop Russian armour spearheads moving rapidly towards the Dnieper River and the bridges at Dnepropetrovsk. 27 February: Ju 87 shot down by AA fire and another severely damaged during attack on the Russian Black Sea port of Novorossisk, 2 WIA. 1 March: operations in the Dnepropetrovsk area concluded and the *Gruppe* transferred to Stalino-North on or about this date. Its next operations were along the Mius front between Stalino and Taganrog, in the Donets Basin sector east of Stalino and in the area around Kharkov and Belgorod. During this period it was based for various periods at Stalino-North, Gorlovka and Kharkov-North. 6 March: 1.*Staffel* Ju 87 accident at Stalino-North and another on 14 March. 24 March: 3.*Staffel* Ju 87 accident reported at Kharkov-North and a 2.*Staffel* accident at the same location on 28 March. 1 April: 3.*Staffel* Ju 87 D-3 destroyed in a mid-air collision north-east of Rostov), *Staffelführer Hptm.* Kurt Hamann + 1 MIA. 16 April: transferred to Kerch IV airfield in eastern Crimea during the first half of April for operations over the Kuban (Taman Peninsula) with apparently some use made of the forward airfield at Anapa in North Caucasia, probably for staging purposes. On or soon after 16 April, the *Gruppe* hit targets in the area of Krymskaya. During this period, I./St.G. 2 was part of *Stukaverband Kupfer* under VIII.*Fliegerkorps*. 20–21 April: attacked enemy positions at Novorossisk on the Black Sea coast where Soviet naval infantry had staged a successful amphibious assault on 4 February and developed a significant bridgehead. 23 April: Ju 87 D-3 shot down by AA fire over Novorossisk, crew safe. 27 April: 2.*Staffel* Ju 87 D-3 shot down by AA fire over the Kuban area, 2 KIA. 1–6 May: based at Kharkov-North for missions east of Kharkov under VIII.*Fliegerkorps*. 13 May: moved to Kramatorskaya/ 82 km north of Stalino and then to Bagerovo back in eastern Crimea. 28–31 May: heavy action over the Kuban bridgehead with 1 Ju 87 D-3 shot down by AA fire and 3 more damaged. On 28 May *Oblt.* Egbert Jaekel claimed a Supermarine Spitfire a few kilometres north-west of Novorossisk. June: no information has come to light on the *Gruppe's* activities during June, but the absence of losses suggests it may have been on stand down in Crimea to rest and refit in preparation for the German Kursk offensive aimed at eliminating a huge salient driven into the front lines between Kharkov and Orel the previous February and March. 1 July: *Gruppe* reported 36 Ju 87 D-3 and 1 Ju 87 D-5 on strength. 2 July: still at Kerch.

South and Central Russia – Kursk Counter-offensive, Ukraine (July 1943 – October 1943) 4 July: departed Crimea and transferred to Kharkov-East for participation in Operation *Zitadelle* around Kursk.

Operations started on 5 July, supporting the advance in the area of Belgorod. However, as the Russians went over to the offensive, the *Gruppe* was forced to move to Karachev/75 km west-north-west of Orel and became part of *Gefechtsverband Kupfer* for defensive operations. 5 July: Ju 87 D-3 shot up by AA fire over the Kursk salient), *Oblt.* Franz Götzfried + 1 WIA. Same date, and possibly the same mission, *Oblt.* Egbert Jaekel from 2.*Staffel* claimed an La-5. 9–11 July: in 3 days of intense action over the Kursk salient, lost 1 Ju 87 D-3 to AA fire and 2 more damaged. On 9 July, *Hptm.* Alwin Boerst shot down an La-5 fighter ca. 65 km north-east of Belgorod. 12 July: transferred from Kharkov-East to Orel as the offensive faltered and the Germans were forced to switch to the defensive to try and stop the counter-attacking Red Army, particularly in the Orel-Bryansk sector. 17 July: Ju 87 D-3 shot down by a fighter east of Bol. Ochkasovo (Kursk salient), *Staffelkapitän Oblt.* Egbert Jackel + 1 KIA. 19 July: evacuated Orel and moved back to Karachev. 14 August: 1.*Staffel* Ju 87 D-3 returned to Poltava airfield shot up and heavily damaged by AA fire. 20 August: 3 Ju 87 D-3s from 2. and 3.*Staffel* shot down by fighters and AA fire in the Kalinovka area, 2 KIA and 2 MIA. 23 August: 2 Ju 87 D-3s from 3.*Staffel* shot down by AA fire along the Mius front south-east of Stalino, 4 KIA. 25 August: ordered to transfer to Dimitrievka (Dmitriyevka)/84 km east of Dnepropetrovsk. 29 August: 1.*Staffel* Ju 87 D-3 blown up by its own bomb detonation over Fedorovka (Roslavl-Gomel area), 2 KIA. 14 September: 1.*Staffel* Ju 87 D-3 shot down by a fighter over Nikolayevka, 1 WIA. 27 September: Ju 87 D-3 shot up by AA fire over the central Ukraine area south of Kiev), *Gruppenkommandeur Hptm.* Börst WIA. Same date, and possibly the same mission, 3.*Staffel* claimed a LaGG-3 fighter ca. 50 km north of Melitopol. October: transferred to Pervomaisk/90 km south-east of Uman in late September or early October. 10 October: 1.*Staffel* reported shooting down a LaGG-1 fighter. 18 October: renamed I./S.G. 2 *Immelmann*, probably at Pervomaisk. During 1943 the *Gruppe* used all or most of the following bases in approximate chronological order: Rostov, Gorlovka, Dnepropetrovsk, Stalino-North, Gorlovka (again), Kharkov-North, Kerch IV; Kharkov-North (again), Kramatorskaya, Kerch IV, Bagerovo, Kharkov-East, Orel, Karachev, Bryansk, Kharkov-South, Dimitrievka and Pervomaisk.

FpNs: I. (L 21650, 42675)

Kommandeur:

Major Oskar Dinort (1 May 1939 - 15 October 1939)

Hptm. Hubertus Hitschhold (RK) (16 October 1939 - 15 October 1941)

Major Bruno Dilley (DKG) (15 October 1941 - 3 January 1942)

Hptm. Dieter Pekrun (RK) (October 1941 - December 1941) – acting?

Hptm. Dieter Pekrun (RK) (ca. January 1942 - February 1942) – still acting?

Hptm. Otto Weiss (RE) (4 January 1942 - 22 October 1942) ?★

Hptm. Frank Neubert (DKG, RK) (September 1942 - ?) – acting

Hptm. Hans-Joachim Lehmann (RK) (? - 1 October 1942- ?) – acting

Major Siebelt Reents (23 October 1942 - January 1943)

*II./St.G. 2
(First Formation)*

Probably taken just after II./St.G. 2 had been formed from I./St.G. 162 on 1 May 1939, these two photographs show one of the unit's first Ju 87 B-1s. The aircraft nearest the camera carries the emblem of the Gruppe Stab, and the unit code T6+BC, the individual letter 'B' in green.

Hptm. Bruno Dilley (DKG, RK, EL) (8 January 1943 - 1 April 1943 - August 1943?)

Hptm. Wilhelm Hobein (April 1943 - 23 September 1943)

Hptm. Alwin Boerst (DKG, RK, EL) (24 September 1943 - 18 October 1943)

★ this is one of several aspects of Weiss's career which are uncertain.

II./St.G. 2 (First Formation)

Formation and Training (May 1939 – August 1939) Formed 1 May 1939 at Stolp-Reitz in Pomerania from the former I./St.G. 162 based at Jever: The four months prior to the outbreak of war were spent training and working up to peak operational efficiency. By late August, the *Gruppe* was still at Stolp-Reitz with 38 Ju 87 Bs.

Campaign in Poland, Training and Standby in the West (September 1939) 1 September: the *Gruppe* had 38 (36) Ju 87 Bs and 3 (3) Do 17 Ps based at Stolp-Reitz for the start of the Polish campaign and was subordinated directly under 1.*Fliegerdivision/Luftflotte* 1 in the northern sector and not through the *Stab* of St.G. 2. On the first day, the crews attacked various bridges, supply routes and positions, probably including naval and harbour targets in

the Bay of Danzig. 6 September: operated against the area near Rog-Wloclawek road about 125 km north of Warsaw and possibly against Kolo. On the 9th, it attacked infantry near Radom. Nothing is known of its remaining participation in the campaign, which concluded on 27-28 September with the end of the last organized resistance. Following operations in Poland, the *Gruppe* departed for the Köln area with orders to train and prepare for planned operations in the West.

Phoney War, Training and Standby in the West (October 1939 – April 1940) Reportedly based at Siegburg/23 km south-east of Köln, but this has not been confirmed. 15 March: in its first mention in the Loss Reports, a Ju 87 B-1 crash-landed at Göttingen airfield/207 km north-east of Siegburg, probably during a routine training accident. At the beginning of May 1940 the 5.*Staffel* was reportedly at Euskirchen-Odendorf airfield for a brief rest.

Attack on France and the Low Countries (May 1940 – June 1940) 10 May: at Siegburg with 38 (33) Ju 87 Bs for the *Blitzkrieg* into Belgium and France under *Stab*/St.G. 3, which in turn was subordinated to II.*Fliegerkorps/Luftflotte* 3, and initially charged with supporting the advance of 4.*Armee* through the Ardennes to the south of Liège towards the Meuse River at Dinant. On the first day, the *Gruppe* lost 1 Ju 87 B shot down by AA fire. 12 May: Ju 87 B shot down by a French fighter at Bouillon on the Belgian-French border 25 km east of Charleville-Mézières. 14 May: Ju 87 B failed to return from operations south of Sedan/18 km south-east of Charleville. 15 May: in heavy action near Roly, south of Philippeville. 15 May: Ju 87 B shot down by AA fire at Monthermé/13 km north of Charleville. 16 May: Ju 87 B failed to return from operations in the Cambrai area of north-east France. 19 May: Ju 87 B shot up by fighters over Maubeuge/52 km east of Cambrai. 20-24 May: transferred from Siegburg to Cambrai, although there may have been intermediate airfields in Belgium and France that were used, such as Guise/25 km east-north-east of St-Quentin in north-east France from 16-17 May. 25 May: attacked shipping off Calais. Same date, Ju 87 B failed to return from operations (location not reported). 29 May: Ju 87 B destroyed in a bomb explosion at Cambrai. 2 June: attacked shipping off Dunkirk. Same date, still flying missions in the Dunkirk area, the *Gruppe* took its heaviest losses of the campaign this date with 4 Ju 87 Rs shot down – one each at Fort Philippe, St-Quentin and near Dunkirk, and the fourth in a crash at Wertheim in Germany. 8 June: supported the advance of 5.*Panzer-Division* to Rouen losing a Ju 87 R-1 in that area. 8 June: in action east of Elbeuf. 18 June: in action in the vicinity of Nivillers, north of Beauvais. 22 June: campaign concluded with the signing of an armistice between Germany and France. In the last week of June the *Gruppe* was based at

A PK (the Propaganda Kompanie or military arm of Goebbels' Propaganda Ministry) photographer lies on the nose of this Ju 87 B-1 of 5./St.G. 2 probably some time in the winter of 1939/40. The aircraft, T6+HN, carries the emblem of the 5.Staffel, a furious comic penguin in black, white and grey, on its cowling. The nose of the spinner was painted red with a thin white band behind. The legend 'Frostschutz Glykol' (Glycol frost protection) was painted in red on the side of the radiator cowling.

5./St.G. 2 Emblem

Probably photographed at Quilly-le-Tesson during the invasion of France, these Ju 87 R-2s of 6./St.G. 2 have standard Luftwaffe camouflage of black green and dark green upper surfaces with pale blue beneath. The aircraft to the right, T6+AP, carries the Staffel's winged griffon badge.

6./St.G 2 Emblem

Lannion in Brittany under *Stab*/St.G. 3 (in turn under VIII.*Fliegerkorps*) and assigned to attack maritime targets.

Air Offensive against England (Battle of Britain) (July 1940 – January 1941) July: Lannion under VIII.*Fliegerkorps* – activity unknown, but probably resting and regrouping. 12 August: Ju 87 R force-landed at Lannion and severely damaged. 13 August: Lannion with 37 (31) Ju 87 R and 2 (2) Ju 87 B on strength. On this date it attempted to attack the radar station at Middle Wallop to the north of Southampton with a formation of 27 *Stukas* but was jumped by Spitfires before reaching the target and lost 6 Ju 87 Rs shot down; the rest of the formation turned back and returned to Lannion. 15 August: attacked RAF Station Hawkinge losing 4 Ju 87 Rs. The *Gruppe* flew no or very few operations after 16 August as they do not show up in the loss records nor otherwise mentioned. After the unacceptably high *Stuka* losses on 18 August (mainly from St.G. 77), all *Stuka* units were withdrawn from cross-Channel daylight operations in the West. 26 October: temporarily at Saint-Omer/north-east France recuperating, refitting and training; some of the personnel may have been sent back to the training schools in Germany as instructors. The respite was short-lived for by early December the *Gruppe* had been alerted for service in the Mediterranean. December: ordered transferred to Trapani in western Sicily for reassignment to X.*Fliegerkorps*, arriving there by 8 January 1941. Along with I./St.G. 1, the assigned mission was to carry out operations against Malta and the British Mediterranean Fleet, especially the aircraft carrier *Illustrious* and shipping passing between Sicily and North Africa.

Central Mediterranean (January 1941 – February 1941) January: while the *Gruppe* had been associated with *Stab*/St.G. 3 during 1940, the bond became stronger during its stay in the Mediterranean as it was to stay under *Stab*/St.G. 3 from then on. 10 January: attacked and hit the British carrier *Illustrious* and the battleship *Warspite* between Sicily and Tunisia, losing one Ju 87 R and another damaged. On 11 January it attacked ships near Malta, hitting the light cruiser *Gloucester* and sunk the light cruiser *Southampton*. 19 January: attacked Valetta harbour on Malta. 3 February: Ju 87 R-1 rammed by a taxiing Ju 52 at Trapani and demolished. 5 February: transferred from Trapani to Elmas/Sardinia to counter Royal Navy Force 'H', which shelled Genoa on the 9th, but no contact was made with the warships.

4./St.G. 2 Emblem

A Ju 87 B of II./St.G. 2 in flight over the North African sand dunes. At this time the newly-arrived Gruppe retained its black green and dark green upper surfaces, but this was obviously unsuitable for operations over the desert and was soon changed. This aircraft, which carries the palm tree emblem of the Afrika Korps, was probably T6+DM of the 4.Staffel.

North Africa (February 1941 – July 1941)

13 February: transferred to Castel Benito, near Tripoli in Libya, as a component of the German forces that began arriving at Tripoli on 12 February in accord with Hitler's decision of 20 January to establish a *Deutsches Afrika Korps* (Gen. Rommel) to assist Italian operations in North Africa. In the spring of 1941 the *Gruppe* supported the *Afrika Korps* in its offensive through Cyrenaica which commenced on 24 March at El Agheila and its successive bases following the advance were: Arco Philanorum (Marble Arch), El Agheila, Agedabia, Benghazi, Derna, and Martuba. Together with I./St.G. 1, the *Gruppe* also attacked British-held ports along the coast of Cyrenaica to interdict the enemy's flow of supplies. 19 February: Ju 87 shot down by a Hurricane while attacking targets in the Benghazi area in company with III./Z.G. 26. 22 February: took part in an attack on the port of Benghazi during which the RN coastal monitor *Terror* was hit and damaged. 31 March: *General* Rommel began his expected offensive aimed at driving the British out of Cyrenaica this date, sending his armour against the enemy in the Marada - Marsa el Brega area. 3 April: operated in the general area of Maraua – 3 to 6 Ju 87s shot down by Hurricanes while attacking forward troop positions east of Benghazi. 5 April: lost several aircraft in two separate engagements near Barce Pass/88 km north-east of Benghazi, including that of the *Staffelkapitän* of 4.*Staffel*; RAF and Australian Hurricane pilots filed claims for 14 of the *Gruppe's Stukas* during these mix-ups, but actual losses were considerably less. 14 April: attacked targets in and around Tobruk, with these continuing until at least 30 April when a Ju 87 was downed by AA fire over the town. 10 May: attacked British ships that had been shelling Benghazi. 12 May: hit targets in Tobruk harbour. 20 May: during the airborne and air-landing invasion of Crete this date (Operation *Merkur*), the *Gruppe* was temporarily based at Tmimi/Libya to attack ships in the Crete area. On 26 May, with 24 Ju 87s, it severely damaged the British carrier *Formidable* and damaged the destroyer *Nubian*. 3 June: lost 2 Ju 87 R-2s on the ground at Gambut/55 km south-east of Tobruk when the airstrip there was strafed by enemy planes. 17 June: ca. 3 Ju 87s claimed shot down by Hurricanes near Sidi Omar/112 km south-east of Tobruk on the Libyan-Egyptian border. 21 June: at Derna/Libya under *Fliegerführer Afrika*. Around this time while based at Derna, it flew support missions in the area of Tobruk-Bardia-Sollum. 15 July: jumped by fighters while flying along the coast between Tobruk and the Egyptian border and lost as many as 5 *Stukas*.

North Africa (July 1941 – January 1942)

July - October: a lull set in along the front after the severely mauled Allied forces pulled back into Egypt to re-form, replenish and reinforce in preparation for offensive operations that eventually began on 18 November (Operation *Crusader*). Not a single accident or loss was reported by the *Gruppe* between 15 July and 30 October, these being used, of course, to track the *Gruppe's* movements and activity. During August the *Gruppe* moved forward to Tmimi/62 km east of Derna and that much closer to Tobruk. 30 October: Ju 87 R-1 lost in the vicinity of Taladida to unknown cause,

1 KIA and 1 WIA. 15 November: *Oblt.* Hermann Kuchenbuch from the *Gruppe* reported WIA during Allied raid on Tmimi airfield. 19 November: II./St.G. 2 began supporting the retreat of the *Afrika Korps* from the Libyan-Egyptian border towards Tobruk. 20 November: Ju 87 R-2 shot up at Tmimi. The RAF claimed 18 *Stukas* were shot up on the ground during this raid but the *Gruppe* only reported this single Ju 87 as damaged. 22 November: lost 2 Ju 87 R-2/Trop south of Bir el Gobi and on 23 November 2 Ju 87 R-2/Trop were shot down by Hurricanes in the El Adem area and two others badly shot up while attacking Allied forces closing on Tobruk from the south-east during Operation *Crusader*. *Staffelkapitän Oblt.* Fritz Eyer and 2 crew members reported WIA. 30 November: flew attacks on the New Zealand Division around Sidi Rezegh/south-east of Tobruk. 4 December: *Gruppenkommandeur Hptm.* Leonhard Busselt and his radio operator/gunner both WIA when strafed by an enemy fighter near Bir el Gobi/south-east of Tobruk. No damage to the aircraft was reported. 7 December: had 15 aircraft intercepted by Hurricanes in the Bir el Gobi area to the west of El Adem, but its losses were limited to 2 Ju 87 R-2s. During December, the *Gruppe* withdrew along the Gulf of Sirte (Sidra) through the following bases: Gebel Akdar, Benghazi, Antelat, Agedabia (Ajdäbiyä)/150 km south of Benghazi, and En Nofilia (An Nawfalïyah)/125 km east-south-east of Sirte. 22 December: Allied fighters strafed Magrun (Al Magrün) airstrip/75 km south of Benghazi and claimed 5 Ju 87s; the *Gruppe* was getting ready to evacuate the strip at the time and move 53 kilometres farther south to Antelat (Antalät). These claims are not corroborated in the official loss reports. This was the last combat reference to the *Gruppe* in North Africa before being withdrawn to Italy to re-equip on Ju 87 D-1s. 2 January: an unserviceable Ju 87 R-2/Trop destroyed near Agedabia by its crew during the rapid westward retreat along the Gulf of Sirte. 13 January: renamed III./St.G. 3 at San Pancrazio in South Italy.

A pair of Ju 87 B-2s of 4./St.G. 2 swoop into the attack after spotting a convoy of enemy vehicles in the North African desert. II./St.G. 2 was the only component of the Geschwader to operate in this theatre. These aircraft, with T6+CM nearest the camera, had sand yellow (possibly RLM 79) stripes painted over their dark green upper surfaces.

21 March: 5.*Staffel* Ju 87 D-1 destroyed and 5 more D-1s damaged at Gostkino during enemy air attack on the airfield by Il-2s and LaGG-3s. 21-23 March: elements transferred from Neukuhren to Wels/Austria and then around 31 March ordered to Gostkino on the Leningrad front. 5 April: 5.*Staffel* Ju 87 D-1 shot down by AA fire while attacking targets around Chudovo on the Volkhov front south-east of Leningrad, 1 KIA and 1 WIA. 10 April: 6.*Staffel* Ju 87 D-1 failed to return from an attack in the vicinity of Makar'yevskaya around the Volkhov bridgehead on the Leningrad front, *Oblt.* Günther van der Bruck + 1 KIA. 17 April: 5.*Staffel* Ju 87 D-1 failed to return from operations over the Volkhov salient near Mostki/40 km north of Novgorod, 2 MIA. 24 April: 4.*Staffel* Ju 87 shot up by AA fire while bombing targets near Leningrad, 2 WIA. This was most likely during a series of raids on the ships of the Red Banner Baltic Fleet in Leningrad harbour from 24 to 27 April. May: ordered to Tulln/20 km north-west of Wien in Austria during the first half of May, except for one *Staffel* which remained on the Eastern Front. 14 May: Ju 87 D-1 crash-landed at Brieg airfield/42 km south-east of Breslau in Silesia. This is thought to have occurred during the *Gruppe's* movement from North Russia to Tulln.

This photograph shows the Ju 87 D-3 piloted by the Kommandeur of II./St.G. 2, Major Dr.jur. Ernst Kupfer, from a Russian base during the summer of 1942. The badge depicts 'Der Bamberger Reiter' (The horseman of Bamberg) painted in black and white on a red circle. Note the large white number '1' on the outside of the wheel spats and the white letter 'D' beneath the wing.

II./St.G. 2 Emblem modified for Kommandeur Ernst Kupfer.

South Russia – Advance to Stalingrad and Withdrawal (June 1942 – January 1943) June: transferred from Tulln/Austria to south Russia. 22 June: operating under *Luftflotte* 4, made attacks on Voronezh and towards Rostov. 28 June: based at Akhtyrka (Achtirskaya)/115 km north-west of Kharkov. 30 June: 6.*Staffel* Ju 87 D-1 shot down by AA fire near Bykovo/110 km west-south-west of Voronezh, crew safe. 1 July: 6.*Staffel* Ju 87 D-1 shot down by fighters near Bykovo, crew safe. 8 July: moved forward from Akhtyrka to Bykovo. 12 July: ground and air concentration shifted south and *Gruppe* now operating against targets around Millerovo to the west of Stalingrad; losses were few. 21 July: transferred to Tatsinskaya-West along the approaches to Stalingrad. 27 July: 6.*Staffel* Ju 87 D-1 shot down by AA fire near Beresov, *Staffelkapitän* Ernst Fick + 1 MIA, but both later regained German custody. 29-31 July: moved forward from Tatsinskaya to Oblivskaya/148 km west of Stalingrad. 5 August: 2 Ju 87 D-3s shot down by fighters, *Hptm.* Hans Gremm from 5.*Staffel* KIA. 6-7 August: attacked breakthrough attempts by strong enemy forces north-west of Kalach that were supported by tanks. 12 August: 2 Ju 87 D-3s bombed on the ground at Oblivskaya during Russian air attack. 26 August: shared in the destruction of 40 tanks out of 170 that led a strong Russian counter-attack just north of Stalingrad. 30-31 August: at the end of August the *Gruppe* was still based at Oblivskaya, and attacked tanks north of Stalingrad between the Don and Volga. 1 September: bombed vessels bringing up supplies and reinforcements along the Volga near Stalingrad. 4 September: attacked dug-in positions south of Stalingrad and during the month it generally supported troops south-west of the city. 13 September: 4.*Staffel* Ju 87 D landed at Tusov, a fieldstrip south-west of Kalach in the vicinity of Stalingrad, after being shot up by AA fire. 20 September: the *Gruppe* reported 25 (16)

Ju 87s on strength under *Luftflotte* 4. 21 September: 6.*Staffel* Ju 87 D landed at Gumrak airstrip on the outskirts of Stalingrad after being shot up by AA fire. 1 October: 5.*Staffel* Ju 87 D shot down over Stalingrad, 2 KIA. 10 October: 4.*Staffel* Ju 87 D shot up by AA fire, *Staffelkapitän Hptm.* Martin Möbus WIA. 13 October: transferred from Oblivskaya to Karpovka-West/40 km west of Stalingrad on or about this date. 27 October: 2 Ju 87 Ds from 4.*Staffel* destroyed in a mid-air collision over Stalingrad, 2 KIA. 29 October: 3 Ju 87 Ds from 5.*Staffel* failed to return from operations around Stalingrad and believed shot down, 3 KIA and 1 WIA. 10 November: 4.*Staffel* Ju 87 D crash-landed at Karpovka. 19 November: over a half-million Soviet troops under Marshal G. Zhukov, with powerful armoured forces and more than 1,000 combat aircraft, commenced Operation *Uranus* aimed at surrounding and cutting off the German front besieging Stalingrad. 22 November: 5.*Staffel* Ju 87 D failed to return from operations in the Stalingrad area, *Staffelkapitän Hptm.* Joachim Langbehn KIA. 25 November: elements of the *Gruppe* attacked target in Perelazovskiy/ca. 150 km north-west of Stalingrad. As a consequence of the chaotic retreats during the encirclement of Stalingrad, a part of the *Gruppe* (either 6.*Staffel* or a part of it) under *Oblt.* Heinz Jungclausen operated for a while in December from within the Stalingrad pocket itself. This so-called *Stuka Sonderstaffel* flew some 200 missions from within the pocket. December: the remainder of the *Gruppe* personnel were assembled at Morosovskaya in December and on 3 January 1943 they transferred to Tatsinskaya. 1 January: the *Gruppe's* aircraft status report for this date showed none on hand. 7 January: Tatsinskaya was overrun by Russian tanks and the *Gruppe* suffered heavy personnel losses. The crews from 4.*Staffel* were forced to blow up their sole remaining aircraft (probably unserviceable) to prevent it from being captured.

South Russia – Eastern Ukraine and North Caucasia (January 1943 – June 1943) 15 January: after pulling back and reassembling (at Makeyevka/12 km east of Stalino?), the *Gruppe* was ordered to Nikolayev/southwest Ukraine in mid-January to refit and re-equip with new aircraft and then nominally assigned to *Fliegerdivision Donez* from around this time until at least late February, when it began flying missions to stop the Russian advance towards Dnepropetrovsk. 19 January: Ju 87 D crashed at Vinnitsa/west Ukraine after running out of fuel, 1 injured. This is believed to have been a new aircraft being ferried to the *Gruppe* at Nikolayev. 20 February: at Nikolayev – ordered forward to Dnepropetrovsk-South II and became a component of *Gefechtsverband Hozzel* this date, which was charged with the command of ground-attack units brought in to stop Russian armour spearheads moving rapidly towards the Dnieper River

Late in December 1942, II./St.G. 2 was withdrawn from operations and transferred to Italy where it began to convert to the Ju 87 D-1. This photograph was probably taken just after re-equipment had been completed and shows the aircraft being escorted by five Regia Aeronautica Macchi C.200 fighters.

II./St.G. 2 Emblem

There were two second Gruppen formed within St.G. 2. Here, a large formation of Ju 87 B-1s from the first II./St.G. 2 sets out to attack Polish ground forces during the advance during September 1939. The aircraft nearest the camera carries the unit code T6+GN of the 5.Staffel, its red identification letter outlined in white.

and the bridges at Dnepropetrovsk. 1 March: now based at Stalino-North – flew missions from here, Gorlovka and/or Kharkov-North to support defences along the Mius River sector between Stalino and Taganrog, the Donets front, and in the vicinity of Kharkov and Belgorod. 2 March: 6.*Staffel* Ju 87 blown up by own bomb during a workshop test flight, 2 killed. 12 March: 2 Ju 87s failed to return from operations around Kharkov, 2 MIA and 2 WIA. 31 March: 6.*Staffel* Ju 87 D-3 crashed taking off from Proskurov airfield in western Ukraine, 2 killed. 1 April: 4.*Staffel* Ju 87 D-3 destroyed in a mid-air collision behind enemy lines over the Mius front between Taganrog and Rostov, 2 MIA. 2 April: 4.*Staffel* Ju 87 D-3 shot down by AA fire ca. 18 km south-east of Izyum where the Russians still held a salient developed the previous February, crew safe. 15 April: as part of *Stukaverband Kupfer*, II./St.G. 2 was involved in supporting the heavy defensive fighting in the Kuban bridgehead on the Taman Peninsula in North Caucasia. It was based at Kerch IV in eastern Crimea from around mid-April and to some extent at Anapa in North Caucasia proper, using this forward airfield mainly for staging purposes. 16 April: at Kerch IV – 5.*Staffel* Ju 87 D shot up over the Taman Peninsula), 1 WIA. 20-21 April: helped destroy the Russian amphibious landing at Novorossisk on the Black Sea coast. 1-10 May: temporarily back at Stalino during the first 10 days of May, but then returned to Kerch IV by 11 May. 14 May: at Kerch IV – 6.*Staffel* Ju 87 D-3 failed to return from operations in the Krymskaya area on the Taman Peninsula, 2 MIA. 23 May: 2 Ju 87 D-3s from 5.*Staffel* shot down by AA and ground fire over the Kuban bridgehead, 2 KIA. 28 May: 6.*Staffel* Ju 87 D-3 shot down by AA fire near Russkoye/11 km north-west of Krymskaya on the Taman Peninsula, 2 KIA. 3 June: 6.*Staffel* Ju 87 D-3 shot down by a fighter at Tambulovsky (not located, but probably Taman Peninsula), 2 MIA. 11 June: 6.*Staffel* Ju 87 D-3 shot down by AA fire over the Taman Peninsula, 2 KIA. 17 June: 4.*Staffel* Ju 87 D-3 shot down by AA fire over Krymskaya, 1 MIA. 27 June: 4.*Staffel* Ju 87 D-3 shot down by AA fire over the Taman Peninsula), crew safe. 1 July: *Gruppe* reported 28 Ju 87 D-3s, 6 Ju 87 D-1s and 2 Ju 87 D-5s on strength. 3-4 July: transferred from Kerch IV to Kharkov for the opening of the massive German offensive against the Kursk salient (Operation *Zitadelle*) that began on 5 July.

South Russia – Kursk Offensive and Withdrawal from Eastern Ukraine (July 1943 – March 1944)

5 July: 4.*Staffel* Ju 87 D-3 returned to Kharkov-North shot up by AA fire. 8 July: the *Gruppe* was in support of the offensive battles in the area of Yartsevo-Dukhovshchina. 13 July - 7 August: after the German assault failed and the Russians went over to the offensive, the *Gruppe* took part in the defensive battles in the area of Orel-Bryansk as part of *Gefechtsverband Kupfer*. 14 July: 5.*Staffel* Ju 87 D-3 blew up over the Kursk salient, *Staffelkapitän Oblt.* Günther Schmid + 1 KIA. 17 July: elements ordered south and temporarily operating from Kuteinikovo airfield/125 km north-west of Rostov – 3 Ju 87 D-3s shot down by AA fire over the Izyum area south-east of Kharkov and over the Muis defence line north-west of Rostov, 6 KIA. 18 July: 5.*Staffel* Ju 87 D-3 shot down by a fighter north-west of Rostov, 2 WIA. 23-27 July 1943: other elements evacuated Orel airfield and pulled back to Karachev. 6 August: 6.*Staffel* Ju 87 D-3 crash-landed at Kharkov-North. 20 August: 4.*Staffel* Ju 87 D-3 shot down by AA fire over the Donets area, crew safe. 2 September: a DFS 230 glider belonging to the *Gruppe* crashed at Poltava, 1 killed. September - October: participated in the defensive battles over the Nikopol bridgehead south-west of Zaporozhye, in the Kremenchug-Kirovograd area to the north-west of Dnepropetrovsk and over the Kherson bridgehead along the Dnieper Estuary where the river flows into the Black Sea. 7 September: 6 Ju 87 D-3/D-5s and 1 Fi 156 destroyed on the ground during Russian air attack on Krasnoarmeisk airstrip/48 km south of Simferopol in Crimea, 2 KIA and 2 WIA. 28 September: 5.*Staffel* Ju 87 D-5 shot down by a fighter over the Zaporozhye area, *Staffelkapitän Oblt.* Peter Keller + 1 KIA. 10-12 October: minor accidents reported at Bol. Kostromka airfield/42 km south-east of Krivoy Rog in central Ukraine. 18 October: following the mass reorganization of the ground-attack branch that was effective this date, II./St.G. 2 remained in existence in Ukraine under *Luftflotte* 4 without a change in its designation. Around the turn of the year, possibly in January 1944, 4.*Staffel* and 6.*Staffel* departed without aircraft for Neisse (Nysa)-Stephansdorf in Upper Silesia where they were renamed 10.(Pz)/S.G. 3 and 10.(Pz)/S.G. 77, respectively, on 7 March 1944. Shortly thereafter they were sent to Markersdorf in Austria to equip with Ju 87 Gs as anti-tank *Staffeln*. Meanwhile, the *Gruppenstab* and 5.*Staffel* were both disbanded effective 7 March. Regrettably, nothing seems to be known of the *Gruppe's* activity in Ukraine during November and December 1943.

FpNs: II. (L 43597)

Kommandeur:
Hptm. Dieter Pekrun (RK) (? – February 1942 – ?) ★
Major Dr.jur. Ernst Kupfer (DKG, RK) (6 January 1942 or 1 April 1942) ★
Hptm. Martin Möbus (DKG, RK) (13 February 1943 – 16 June 1943) – acting
Hptm. Hans-Joachim Lehmann (RK) (? May 1943 – ?) – intermittent acting
Major Hans-Karl Stepp (DKG, RK) (17 June 1943 – 9 September 1943)
Hptm. Dr.jur. Maximilian Otte (DKG, RK) (10 September 1943 – 18 October 1943)

The 'Horseman of Bamburg' emblem was carried by Ju 87s of II./St.G. 2 throughout its existence. The background of the emblem differed for the various sub-units, green for the Gruppe Stab, white for the 4.Staffel, red for the 5.Staffel and yellow for the 6.Staffel.

Hptm. Schütte (January 1942 -)

Hptm. Dieter Pekrun (February 1942 -)

Major Dr.jur. Ernst Kupfer (27 February 1942 - February 1943)

Hptm. Hans-Joachim Lehmann & *Major* Stepp (March 1943 - May 1943) – acting

★ **Note**: this seriously conflicts with the *StukaGeschwader 2 Immelmann* book by Nauroth, p. 363:

III./St.G. 2

Formation and Training (May 1939 – August 1939) Formed 1 May 1939 at Langensalza in Thuringia by renaming the former II./St.G. 163 based at the same location. The summer of 1939 was spent in training until around 26 August, when the order for general mobilization was issued, then deployed to Stolp-West (Slupsk) in Pomerania, near the Baltic coast and not far from Danzig and Annafeld (Annapole) near Schneidemühl (Pila) farther to the south.

Campaign in Poland (September 1939) 1 September: Stolp-West and Annafeld with 36 (34) Ju 87 Bs and 3 (3) Do 17 Ps under 1.*Fliegerdivision/Luftflotte* 1. On the first day of the Polish campaign, the *Gruppe* attacked various Polish naval targets and harbour installations such as at Gdingen (Gdynia)/20 km north of Danzig and probably key bridges, supply routes and troop positions in the same general area. During the early part of the campaign the *Gruppe* attacked coastal batteries by Gdingen and supported landings at Westerplatte. On 6 September it reportedly attacked targets at Kob (not located). 8 September: ordered to Vinné in eastern Slovakia and reassigned to *Luftflotte* 4 on the southern sector of the front in order to attack the Polish armies retreating towards Warsaw as well as railroads and troop concentrations in the area of Lvov. October: departed Vinné for Mannheim-East (a.k.a. Mannheim-Ostheim, Mannheim-Neuostheim, Mannheim-Stadt?) shortly after the conclusion of the campaign in Poland.

Phoney War, Training and Standby in the West (October 1939 – April 1940) November: transferred to Rotenburg near Bremen to defend against expected British naval attacks. Subsequently, the *Gruppe* moved to Ollesheim/24 km south-west of Köln and later to Hildesheim for specialized training over the winter on the technique of knocking out Belgian forts. March: now reportedly based at Düren. 25 March: reported a Ju 87 B force-landed near Nordhausen due to engine failure and badly smashed up.

Attack on France and the Low Countries (May 1940 – June 1940) 10 May: based at Nörvenich/26 km south-west of Köln under VIII.*Fliegerkorps/Luftflotte* 2 with 38 (27) Ju 87 Bs for operations into Belgium and France. Initially attacked Belgian forts, including Eben-Emael, just south of Maastricht, and supported the 6.*Armee* crossing over the Maas River. Subsequently involved in battles at Liège and Namur and supported crossings over the Oise River to the east of St-Quentin/north-east France. 10 May: attacked road traffic near Antwerpen. 11 May: attacked roads east of Tirlemont. 11 May: 4 Ju 87s shot down by Curtiss Hawk 75 fighters in the Bouillon area on the Belgian-French border/25 km east of Charleville-Mézières. 12 May: attacked armour near Gembloux at 0530 hours. 12 May: Ju 87 shot down by a RAF Hurricane over St-Trond/Belgium. 14 May: Ju 87 shot down by AA fire at Gembloux/16 km north-west of Namur and another was lost there the next day. 15 May: moved to Ochamps/St-Huberty, 32 km west-south-west of Bastogne in Belgium. 15 May: attacked armour near Gentinnes during the afternoon. 17-19 May: *Gruppe* credited with breaking up and destroying a major French tank attack under the command of Colonel Charles de Gaulle's 4th Armoured Division at Montcornet and the bridges at Serre in the St-Quentin area; most of the supporting French towed-artillery and motor transport was annihilated. 20-23 May: at Beaulieu between St-Quentin and Cambrai. 22 May: attacked British troops at Arras trying to break out of the encirclement that was being tightened around them by fast moving German armour spearheads; 1 Ju 87 B failed to return from operations. 22 May: hit targets south-east of Arques. 24 May: based at Guise, Laon and Cambrai to about 14 June. 25-26 May: attacked British evacuation shipping off Dunkirk and Calais, these missions continuing until 1 June. 26 May: in action near Estaires, west of Lille. 2-4 June: assigned to the breakthrough operation against French forces to the south following a few days of respite. 5 June: attacked troops near Morchain. 6 June: supported the attack of 6.*Armee* in the direction of Péronne, Amiens, Roye/42 km south-east of Amiens, and Chauny/26 km south of St-Quentin. 7 June: in action over Grécourt, 26 km south-west of St-Quentin. 8-18 June: supported the advance of 6.*Armee* and 9.*Armee* over the Marne and on towards the Seine. 8 June: flew an attack on enemy positions at Vierzy. On the 14th, the *Gruppe* moved to Chateau-Thierry/80 km east-north-east of Paris, then later to Auxerre/146 km south-east of Paris as the rapidly advancing Germans drove the defeated French Army to the south-west. Only 3 Ju 87s were reported lost during this 10-day period. 15 June: attacked targets between St-Sérotin and Voulx, north-west of Sens. 22 June: campaign concluded with the signing of an armistice between Germany and France. 30 June: transferred to St-Pierre-sur-Dives/south-east of Caen to rest and refit under VIII.*Fliegerkorps*.

Air Offensive against England (Battle of Britain) (July 1940 – January 1941) 4 July: the *Gruppe* began anti-shipping missions over the English Channel under VIII.*Fliegerkorps* and over the next month and a half was heavily involved in most of the convoy and related attacks in the Channel that constituted the preliminary phase of the Battle of Britain. 11 July: took part in an attack on Portland/south England and lost one Ju 87 B to a Hurricane over the harbour with the crew reported MIA. 8 August: attacked convoy CW 9 *Peewit* near the Isle of Wight at a cost of one aircraft shot up and damaged by fighters. 11 August: attacked Portland again along with ships in the vicinity without loss. 13 August: at St-Trond/Belgium with 31 Ju 87 Bs on strength – possibly assigned to the attack on Rochford airfield this date, but weather problems caused the mission to be aborted. 16 August: raided Tangmere airfield with 4 aircraft lost to fighters and AA fire and 3 damaged; later in the day attacked the radar station at Selsey Bill. After 16 August, the *Gruppe* was non-operational and reported no combat losses. Due to the high losses suffered by St.G. 77 on

18 August, all *Stuka* units were withdrawn from daylight combat in the Channel area. While the units remained in northern France and Belgium under VIII.*Fliegerkorps* as a threatening force in reserve and to standby for Operation *Seelöwe*, the invasion of England that was postponed and later abandoned, some of the crews were reassigned to the *Stuka* schools at Wertheim and Lippstadt as instructors. 25 August: Ju 87 B crashed taking off from a field airstrip at Ernes/25 km south-east of Caen due to engine failure while on a practice flight. September: together with I./St.G. 2, the *Gruppe* was involved in the making of the Karl Ritter movie *Stukas*, this consuming much of its activity during the month. November: with Operation *Seelöwe* now postponed indefinitely, the *Gruppe* was ordered to Kitzingen in Germany during the latter part of October or in November. 7 December: assigned for possible use in Operation *Felix*, the planned invasion of Gibraltar that was subsequently cancelled. 10 February: ordered from Kitzingen to Otopeni/10 km north of Bucharest in Romania for forthcoming operations under VIII.*Fliegerkorps*/*Luftflotte* 4.

Balkan Campaign (February 1941 – June 1941)

17 February: Ju 87 severely damaged in crash-landing at Balomir/Bulgaria. 6 March: moved to Kraynitsi (Krainitsi)/42 km south-south-west of Sofia in Bulgaria and then on 27 March to Belica-North (Belitsa)/85 km south-south-east of Sofia. 5 April: at Belica with 38 (35) Ju 87 Bs under VIII.*Fliegerkorps*. 6 April: commenced operations against Greece and Yugoslavia, attacking fortifications on the Metaxas line and airfields of the Royal Yugoslav Air Force. The *Gruppe* closely supported the advance of the Army through Skopje, Prilep, Veles, Salonika and against Serbian and Greek positions along the way; also aided in the breakthrough at Kastoria/north-west Greece, in defeating the Greek Epirius Army, and flew support missions for battles near Olympus, Larissa (Larisa), Volos and Thermopylae. The *Gruppe* then flew support for the airborne landings that seized the vital Corinth Canal on 26 April followed by the rapid advance into Peleponesia. During April and early May, III./St.G. 2 was based at Almyros, Mégara to the west of Athens and Argos/Peleponesia. 1-19 May: attacked ships in the Aegean and the area around Crete from bases at Larissa, then Mégara from 11 May. 20 May: now at Molaoi in southern Peleponesia and Scarpanto (Karpathos), an Aegean island halfway between Crete and Rhodes, the *Gruppe* struck targets on Crete in support of the airborne

9./St.G. 2 Emblem

All systems go as a crew from 9./St.G. 2 prepare for a sortie from a Bulgarian base during the invasion of Greece in April 1941. The Ju 87 has a yellow nose and the Staffel emblem, a black devil with a pitchfork on a yellow shield, painted on the nose.

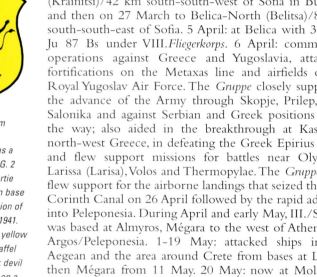

and air-landing operation on the island that began this date. 22 May: shared in the sinking of the British light cruiser *Fiji*. 26 May 1941: Scarpanto airfield was shelled with little effect by 2 British battleships and 2 cruisers. 29 May: took part in the sinking of the destroyer *Hereward*, the damaging of the destroyer *Decoy* and the damaging of the light cruiser *Ajax* in the waters off Crete. During operations off Crete, the *Gruppe* claimed 125,000 tons of shipping sunk and 20,000 tons damaged. 2 June: departed its bases in southern Greece and the Aegean and moved to Salonika/north-east Greece for two weeks to rest and refit, and then on 16 June transferred to Insterburg in East Prussia for operations in the East. Deployed forward to Praschnitz (Przasnysz)/88 km north of Warsaw a few days later.

Attack on the Soviet Union – Central and North Russia (June 1941 – September 1941) 21 June: Praschnitz with 39 (20) Ju 87 Rs for the advance into Russia that began in the pre-dawn hours the following day. For the start of the Russian campaign, the *Gruppe* supported the breakthrough of 9.*Armee* and *Panzergruppe* 3 east and south-east of Suwalki. 25 June: attacked a Russian tank concentration 80 km south of Grodno with little effect. Was subsequently involved in the pocket battles of Grodno-Bialystok and Minsk. July: supported the advance of *Panzergruppe* 3 through Lepel-Vitebsk to Smolensk, then supported Pz.Gr 2's bridgehead across the Dnieper. 20 July: at Lepel-East/north-north-east of Minsk. 22 July: hit enemy pontoon bridges over the Dnieper at Solov'yeva. 3 August: transferred with VIII.*Fliegerkorps* to *Luftflotte* 1 on the northern sector of the front to support the advance of the 16.*Armee* towards Lake Ilmen. During 8 to 29 August the *Gruppe* was based at Ryelbitsi, to the west of Lake Ilmen. From 7 to 23 August supported the advance south of Lake Ilmen and over the Lovat River. 23-26 August: supported the advance through Novgorod-Chudovo and towards Lyuban to the south-east of Leningrad. At about this time the *Gruppe* helped deal with a Soviet counter-attack near Staraya Russa. 27 August - 8 September: supported the advance of *Panzergruppe* Schmidt (XXVIII.*Armeekorps* and XXXIX.*Panzerkorps*) to Schlüsselburg (Shlisselburg) at the mouth of the Neva River due east of Leningrad. Moved to Tyrkovo to the south of Luga on 29 August. On 3 September attacked the Leningrad-Moscow rail line 17 km south-east of Slutsk. 9-28 September: supported attacks by *Panzergruppe* 4 on Leningrad and its line of communications. On 10 and 11 September the *Gruppe* attacked the fortifications in the Duderhof heights on the Leningrad perimeter to the south of Krasnoye Selo. 14 September: Ju 87 R-2 shot down by AA fire in the Mga area/south-east of Leningrad, 2 MIA. On the same date, *Hptm*. Steen knocked out a key railway bridge over the Volkhov River at Novogorod. 16 September: attacked Soviet warships off Leningrad that were shelling German troops and severely damaged the battleship *Marat* with a direct hit from a 500 kg bomb. 23 September: still at Tyrkovo – bombed ships in Kronstadt (Kronshtadt) harbour with one-ton PC 1000 bombs. The *Gruppenkommandeur*, *Hptm*. Steen, along with his gunner, was shot down in his Ju 87 R-2 while diving on the cruiser *Kirov* and killed in action on this mission. During the same or a similar mission a day or two later, the *Gruppe* was credited with heavily damaging the Russian battleship *October Revolution*, putting it out of action for a long time. 22 June - 30 September: III./St.G. 2

used the following airfields, in most cases only briefly, in the approximate order given: Raczki/13 km south-west of Suwalki in Poland, Lepel/125 km south-west of Vitebsk, Ulla/59 km west of Vitebsk, Surazh/40 km north-east of Vitebsk, Yanovichi/33 km east-north-east of Vitebsk, Dukhovshchina/51 km north-north-east of Smolensk, Ryelbitsy/50 km west-south-west of Lake Ilmen, and Tyrkovo/near Luga.

Central Russia – Advance on Moscow and the Aftermath (October 1941 – May 1942) 30 September: transferred on or about this date with VIII.*Fliegerkorps* to the central sector, probably moving to Smolensk initially, to support Operation *Taifun*, the all-out drive on Moscow that commenced on 2 October. 2-7 October: participated in the pocket battle of Vyazma, and then a few days later moved forward to Kuleshevka/35 km north of Vyazma on the path of advance towards the Russian capital. 8-14 October: supported the advance of *Panzergruppe* 3 and 9.*Armee* to Kalinin. 14-27 October: based at Kalinin-South and helped in repelling Soviet counter-attacks on the Kalinin front. 28 October – 5 December: supported the advance towards Moscow along the Klin-Dimitrov sector and in the vicinity of Tula. In early November the cold weather began to seriously interfere with operations. From 14 November to 15 December the *Gruppe* was based at Gorstkovo/80 km west of Moscow. 26-28 November: supported 2.*Panzerarmee*, and after the 30th it supported *Panzergruppe* 4. 5 December: due to the powerful Soviet counter-offensive that commenced this date along the entire front to the west of Moscow, the *Gruppe* was forced to pull back from Gorstovo to Dugino/65 km south of Rzhev on 16 December, losing 7 aircraft in the process. December: flew defensive operations east of the line Rzhev-Vyazma as part of *Gefechtsverband Dugino*, a provisional tactical formation that included elements of St.G. 2 and J.G. 51. During December and January 1942, II./L.G. 2 was attached to the *Gruppe* and between the two they were able to muster about 30 planes. 7 January: operating from Rzhev as well as Dugino. 16 January: attacked traffic between Suchevka and Rzhev. 18 January: Dugino airfield itself was under attack and the ground personnel were forced to revert to infantry. 21 January: Soviet 4th Shock Army took the German supply hub at Toropets and this began a period of intense fighting in the sector Toropets-Rzhev-Vyazma over the next 5 to 6 months in which III./St.G. 2 played a vital role until it departed the area in May. 22 January: 2 Ju 87 R-2s shot down in the Zhukovo area/ca. 55 km west of Rzhev, 4 MIA. 15 February: part of the *Gruppe* transferred from Dugino to Vyazma and remained there and at Dugino until April. 1 March: *Gruppe* reported 11 Ju 87 B-1s, 4 Ju 87 B-2s and 2 Ju 87 R-4s on strength. 6 March: 7.*Staffel* Ju 87 B-2 force-landed near Rzhev after being shot up and moderately damaged by a fighter during a mission against Soviet advances south-west of Kalinin towards Rzhev. 22 March: 2 Ju 87 B-1s from 9.*Staffel* collided over Murav'yevo/19 km east of Vyazma, both destroyed, 2 KIA and 2 WIA. 7 April: 2 Ju 87 B-1s from 7.*Staffel* failed to return from operations in the vicinity of Kruzinovo, 4 MIA. April: moved from Dugino and Vyazma to Smolensk and then to Vitebsk. After *Gefechtsverband Dugino* was dissolved at the start of May, III./St.G. 2 was ordered to Markersdorf near Wien in Austria for a month and half of rest and refit.

At the time of the invasion of the Soviet Union, III./St.G. 2 under Hptm. Gustav Pressler was based at Praschnitz and equipped with 39 Ju 87 Rs. This aircraft, T6+IR from the 7.Staffel, carried the Gruppe badge, a white cross of Lorraine above red mountains on a blue shield.

This superb close-up view of a Ju 87 B-1 of III./St.G. 2 was taken after the aircraft nosed over on rough ground at Prague-Ruzyne airfield in November 1941. The aircraft still carries the radio call sign NO+HP but with the addition of the letter 'A' just forward of the wing trailing edge and a variation of the emblem of the III.Gruppe. The bomb crutch aft of the radiator is plainly visible.

South Russia – Advance to Voronezh and the Don (June 1942 – August 1942) June: ordered to Akhtyrka (Achtirskaya)/115 km north-west of Kharkov on the south sector of the Eastern Front for assignment to VIII.*Fliegerkorps*/*Luftflotte* 4. 4 June: advance elements of the *Gruppe* began arriving at Kharkov-Rogan this date with the remainder of the aircraft and the ground element following along over the next several weeks. 28 June: now at Akhtyrka. June - July: participated in attacks from the Kursk area east towards Voronezh during the opening phase of the German summer offensive aimed at the Don River, Stalingrad and the oilfields of North Caucasia. 9 August: ordered to begin transferring to Vyazma, its former base on the central sector of the front. 11 August: operating from Bykovo/22 km north of Stary Oskol and from Voronezh-West.

III./St.G. 2 Emblem

Ju 87 D-3 from Erg.St./St.G. 2 with a DFS 230 glider in tow crashed at Melitopol airfield/110 km south of Zaporozhye in eastern Ukraine, 2 killed.

FpNs: *Ergänzungsstaffel/*St.G. 2 (L 44199, L 19339); IV.(Erg.)/St.G. 2 (L 19339)

Staffelkapitän/Kommandeur:
Oblt. Hans-Ulrich Rudel (DKG, RK) (March 1942 - October 1942)
Oblt./Hptm. Armin Thiede (DKG, RK) (February 1943 - 16 May 1943)

10.(Pz.)/St.G. 2

Formation (June 1943) Formed 17 June 1943 at Kharkov-East using elements of the former *2./Versuchskommando für Panzerbekämpfung* plus additional assets. Equipped with Junkers Ju 87 G-1 outfitted with two wing-mounted 37 mm Flak 18 cannon as an anti-tank *Staffel*.

Operations in Central and South Russia (June 1943 – October 1943) July: *Staffel* was involved in the German counter-offensive at Kursk (Operation *Zitadelle*) in July where it reportedly had considerable success against Soviet armour. It may have operated from Orel and Karachev with the rest of the *Geschwader* during the last 10 days of July. 4 August: Ju 87 G-1 returned to Kharkov-North shot up by AA fire and slightly damaged, 1 WIA. August - October: no information has been found concerning the *Staffel's* activities during this period. The absence of any entries in the Loss Reports raises many questions, since it is unlikely that it could have been in the thick of the heavy defensive fighting in eastern Ukraine with the rest of St.G. 2 and not had at least a few losses, crashes and accidents. 18 October: renamed 10.(Pz.)/S.G. 2, probably in Ukraine (Kirovograd? Bol. Kostromka?).

FpN: none found

Staffelkapitän:
Oblt. Helmut Schübel (? - 18 October 1943)

Sources for St.G. 2:

Unpublished and Archival:
BA-MA Freiburg: RL 2 III Gen.Qu.(6.Abt.) *Meldungen über Flugzeugunfälle und Verlust…* (LRs – Loss Reports).
BA-MA - *Flugzeug-Bereitstellungen* (Aircraft Availability Status Reports – FzB) in: Holm-op cit.
BA-MA Freiburg: *Signatur* RL 20/274-77.
NARA WashDC: RG 242/T-312: roll 205/frame 450; T-313: roll 258/frames 215 and 258.
PRO London: AIR 40/file 1968, 1978, 1982, 1983.

Published:
[Aders – SG] p. 28, 37, 59, 60, 63, 65, 99, 109, 111, 114, 115, 132, 150;
[Balke – KG 2V1] p. 393, 395, 402, 404, 410, 415, 418;
[Bateson – *Stuka!*] p. 8-13, 21-29, 31, 34, 35, 37-44, 47, 52, 54-56, 59, 61, 63, 64;
[Bekker – LWD] p. 18, 22, 24, 41, 127, 163, 164, 168, 180, 223, 228, 265, 278, 282, 284, 285, 323, 411, 421, 438;
[Bergström – BC/RS-1] p. 136, 185-189, 234;
[Bergström – BC/RS-2] p. 46, 64, 65, 92, 105;
[Bergström – BC/RS-3] p. 61, 131-132;
[Brütting – BA] p. 68, 118;
[Brütting – SA] p. 136, 149, 150, 152, 154, 155, 157-159, 171, 186-189, 191-193, 195, 196, 208, 210-213, 215, 217, 218, 222, 223, 231, 236, 241, 242, 247, 250, 252, 255, 256, 259, 266, 267;
[Carlsen – CM2] p. 338, 343;
[Dierich – KG51] p. 50, 51;
[Dierich – VdL] p. 211-218, 225, 226, 270;
[Griehl – KFZ] p. 119;
[Holm – Website www.ww2.dk];
[Just – Rudel] p. 76, 77, 85-88, 94, 95, 104, 107, 110, 114, 117, 118, 121, 122, 127, 133, 134, 136, 137, 139, 140, 142-146, 148-150, 158;
[Kannapin – FPN] various;
[Mason – BovB] p. various;
[Mehner – FT] p. 54;
[Nauroth – StG2] p. 48-50, 52-58, 65, 67, 70-72, 74-78, 80-82, 85, 89, 91, 93, 96, 104, 107, 108, 111, 112, 115-117, 119, 120, 127, 137-143, 145, 146, 148, 149, 152, 154, 163, 164, 167—178, 180-182, 186, 189, 191-193, 195, 196, 198, 205, 207, 208, 210, 214-218, 224, 226, 228, 231, 240-247, 261, 263, 265-269, 271, 273-275, 277, 358-359, 362-366;
[Obermaier – RK2] p. 44, 46, 48, 53, 55, 60, 62- 65, 67, 68, 72, 75, 76, 88, 92, 93, 95, 96, 98-101, 103, 104, 107, 108, 114, 120, 123, 126, 130, 132, 134, 137, 138, 142, 144, 147, 149, 150, 162, 164, 172, 176, 187, 189, 192, 196, 197, 202, 206, 210, 213, 216;
[Patzwall – LwR] p. various;
[Plocher – Rus42] p. 71, 280;
[Plocher – Rus43] p. 37, 76, 111;
[Prien – JG77] p. 609;
[Ramsey – B-1] p. various;
[Ramsey – B-2] p. various;
[Ries – Lw] p. 139;
[Ries – PhotoCol] p. 208-214;
[Ries – PhotoRec] p. 142, 169;
[Scheibert – EP] p. various;
[Scherzer – DKG] p. 598-611;
[Shores – F] p. 19, 81;
[Shores – FotD] p. 32, 33, 37, 45, 49, 66, 67, 71, 72, 74, 82, 91, 250;
[Shores – Malta-H] p. 106, 109, 115, 145, 205;
[Shores – Yugo] p. 240, 274, 337, 341, 352, 356, 358, 368, 378;
[Smith – GA] p. 183, 384, 385, 388-391;
[Smith – SAW] p. 19, 20, 30, 31, 37, 38, 41, 43, 54, 57-59, 61, 68, 76;
[Smith – *Stuka*(1998)] p. 58-62, 76, 92;
[Smith – StG 77] p. 49, 99;
[Tessin – Form] p. 223;
[Tessin – Tes] p. 306, 321;
[Weal – *Stuka* 37-41] p. various;
[Zweng – Zweng] p. 127-128.

[Archiv #8 – A-8] p. 13, 16;
[Archiv #9 – A-9] p. 28.

St.G. 3

Sturzkampfgeschwader 3

(Unit Code: S7+)

*Stab/*St.G. 3

Formation (May 1939) Formed with a *Stab* and *Stabsstaffel* at Dinard/France on 9 July 1940 by the redesignation of *Stab*/K.G. 28. It is possible that I./St.G. 3 was subordinated to it at the time of formation.

Air Offensive against England (Battle of Britain) (July 1940 - December 1940) 12 July: an He 111 H belonging to the *Stab* was shot up by Spitfires and force-landed near Cherbourg with heavy damage, 3 WIA. The aircraft is believed to have been flying reconnaissance over the Channel. 2 August: a Do 17 M from the *Stab* crashed at Dinant/Belgium due to engine failure, 3 KIA. 13 August: *Geschwaderstab* and *Stabsstaffel* now at Brétigny/28 km south of Paris under IV.*Fliegerkorps*/*Luftflotte* 3 for the opening of the main phase of the Battle of Britain. The *Stabsstaffel* reported 4 Dornier Do 17 Zs, 1 Do 17 M and 2 Heinkel He 111 Hs on strength. Most or all of these planes had originally belonged to the *Geschwaderstab* of KG 28. For a few weeks or months, the *Stabsstaffel* aircraft carried the code (2F+), which had been used by the *Stabsstaffel* aircraft of KG 28. 18 August: all *Stuka* units were withdrawn from cross-Channel daylight operations on this date due to heavy losses. Shortly after this date, the *Stab* and *Stabsstaffel* are believed to have returned to

Dinard. 4 October: Do 17 Z damaged landing at Dinard. 7 October: Do 17 Z-3 belly-landed at St Michel airstrip in Brittany. December: ordered from Dinard to Trapani/Sicily for assignment to X.*Fliegerkorps*, with the staff personnel and *Stabsstaffel* aircraft gradually arriving there between 2 and 9 January 1941. Subordinating I./St.G. 1 and II./St.G. 2, the assigned mission was to carry out operations against Malta and the British Mediterranean Fleet, especially the aircraft carrier *Illustrious* and shipping passing between Sicily and North Africa. En route, several weeks are said to have been spent at Echterdingen/13 km south of Stuttgart so holiday leave could be given to the officers and men.

Central Mediterranean and North Africa (January 1941 – March 1941) 28 February: just a few weeks after assembling on Sicily, the *Stab* together with its two assigned *Gruppen* transferred to Libya, possibly Bir Dufan/165 km south-east of Tripoli assigned to *Fliegerführer Afrika* for operations. This *Stuka* ground support element was a part of the German forces that began arriving at Tripoli on 12 February in accord with Hitler's decision of 20 January to establish a *Deutsches Afrika Korps* (Gen. Rommel) to assist Italian operations in North Africa. March: moved forward via Tamet and En Nofilia, both in the Sirte area. Late March: *Stab* ordered to Austria.

For a period of a few months the aircraft of the Stabsstaffel of St.G. 3 retained the code '2F' originally allocated to K.G. 28. This Bf 110 E-2, W.Nr. 4430, from the unit was found wrecked in North Africa. It has sand yellow (79) upper surfaces with sky blue (78) beneath and the individual letter 'G' was painted green.

After being assigned to Fliegerführer Afrika the Geschwader Stab of St.G. 3 was transferred to Libya in North Africa at the end of February 1941. In common with many other units based in Africa, the unit's aircraft had sand yellow camouflage sprayed in patches over their dark green upper surfaces. Initially, it is thought that this paint was borrowed from Germany's Italian allies, but shortly afterwards a dedicated RLM shade (colour 79) was developed.

Balkan Campaign (April 1941 – July 1941) 5 April: now at Graz-Thalerhof in Austria for assignment to *Luftflotte* 4 for the campaign in Yugoslavia and Greece. The *Stabsstaffel* reported 3 Ju 87 Bs on strength. April - May: advanced towards Athens via Larissa and Corinth, and by early May is said to have been at Argos to the south-west of Athens preparing for the airborne and air-landing assault on Crete that commenced on 20 May. 28 May: a *Stabsstaffel* Bf 110 crashed at Belgrade during a ferry flight. 22 June: several crashes by *Stabsstaffel* aircraft reported at Athens-Tatoi and Molaoi/150 km south-west of Athens. July: believed to have returned to North Africa between the end of July and the third week of August, probably to Derna/145 km north-west of Tobruk. On arrival, it took command of the two *Stukagruppen* in Libya, I./St.G. 1 and II./St.G. 2.

North African Campaign (August 1941 – November 1942) 13 August: Bf 110 E-2 belonging to the *Geschwaderstab* bombed on the ground at Heraklion (Iraklion) airfield on Crete and destroyed. 14 September:

Stab reported a Ju 87 lost at Gambut airstrip/52 km east-south-east of Tobruk. 9 October: Bf 110 E-2 crash-landed at Derna and moderately damaged. 14 November: Ju 87 R-4 bombed on the ground at Derna and destroyed. December: reportedly at Arco Philanorum (Marble Arch)/195 km south-south-west of Benghazi for a few weeks during December. January - February 1942: said to be at Agedabia/150 km south of Benghazi. 25 February: moved forward and now at Barce/90 km north-east of Benghazi. 1 March: *Geschwaderstab* reported 2 Ju 87 Rs and 1 He 111 H-5 on strength. 4 April: now at Berca/10 km south of Benghazi, but a week or two later moved back to Derna where it remained to 20 June. 21 June: transferred from Derna to El Adem/26 km south-south-west of Tobruk. July - September: *Geschwaderstab* advanced eastward into Egypt via the airfields at Fuka, Bir el Abd and Quasaba. 20 September: now at Haggag-Quasaba near the El Alamein line in Egypt. 12 November: *Geschwaderstab* withdrawn from North Africa to Crete to refit.

Central Mediterranean, Germany and Greece (December 1942 – October 1943) December: at Djedeida/24 km west-north-west of Tunis in Tunisia according to a single source, but this remains to be confirmed. The location of the *Geschwaderstab* is not mentioned in any of the surviving documentation for the period mid-November 1942 - mid-April 1943. It is possible that its personnel were used to staff the several *Fliegerführer* commands that were being set up in Tunisia towards the end of 1942. 1 January: *Stab* reported no aircraft on strength. March - April: supposedly at Ste-Marie du Zit/44 km south-south-east of Tunis, but corroboration is lacking. 16 April: now at Decimo (Decimomannu)/Sardinia. 27 April: transferred from Decimo to Herzogenaurach/Germany this date. 26 June: *Stab* began transferring from Herzogenaurach to Athens-Eleusis for reassignment to *Luftwaffenkommando Südost*. 1 July: *Stab* reported 2 Ju 87 D-3s on strength. 30 September: transferred from Eleusis to Argos/95 km south-west of Athens. 18 October: renamed *Geschwaderstab* and *Stabsstaffel/Schlachtgeschwader* 3.

This Ju 87 D-3, S7+AA, was flown by the Geschwader Kommodore of St.G. 3, Obstlt. Walter Sigel. It had black green (RLM 70) and dark green (71) upper surfaces overpainted with batches of sand yellow (RLM 79). The individual letter 'A' (positioned over the white rear fuselage band) and the tip of the spinner was painted blue. Sigel commanded the Geschwader between 1 March 1942 and 1 April 1943.

Codes: initially (2F+_A), later (S7+_A)

FpNs: *Geschwaderstab* (L 21402, 25927), *Stabsstaffel* (L 33847, 30137)

Kommodore:
Oberst Karl Angerstein (RkHS) (9 July 1940 – July 1940)
Obstlt. Hermann Edert (27 July 1940 – 7 February 1941)
Obstlt. Karl Christ (7 February 1941 – 1 March 1942)

Major Walter Enneccerus (RK) (1942) – occasionally acting
Obstlt. Walter Sigel (DKG, RK, EL) (1 March 1942 – 1 April 1943)
Major Kurt Kuhlmey (DKG, RK) (1 April 1943 – 18 October 1943)

Theodor Nordmann (RK-SW)

'Theo' Nordmann was born 18 December 1918 at Dorsten/Westphalia, the son of an attorney. He joined the *Luftwaffe* on 1 November 1937 and began basic and then flight training. On 1 December 1938 he was assigned to Aufkl.Gr. (H) 11 at Grossenhain and, on 1 February 1939, to the *Luftkriegsschule* at Berlin-Gatow. Promoted to *Leutnant* on 28 August 1939, he was sent to *Stukaschule* on the same day. On 31 March 1940 he was assigned to I.(*Stuka*)/*Trägergruppe* 186 which became III./St.G. 1 around 5 July. He received the E.K. I on 29 August 1940 following 66 combat missions and was appointed *Staka* of 8./St.G. 1.in October.

Around 11 April 1941, during a transfer flight from Sicily to North Africa, Nordmann's Ju 87 suffered engine failure and he was forced to ditch in the Mediterranean. He was rescued by an Italian seaplane after 28 days on a raft suffering badly from hypothermia. For this and nearly 200 combat missions *Leutnant* Nordmann was awarded the *Ritterkreuz* on 17 September 1941. He was then credited with the sinking of 5,000 tons of enemy shipping, damaging another 32,000 tons, destroying 21 tanks (19 of them Russian), 14 anti-aircraft batteries and placing direct hits on numerous harbour and airfield targets on Malta. Promoted to *Oberleutnant* (see photograph) on 1 October 1941, he completed his 600th combat sortie on 24 August 1942 as *Staka* of 8./St.G. 1. In September 1942 he was ordered to *Erprobungsstelle* Rechlin on temporary duty and on 20 October 1942 was awarded the DKG (recommended while serving with III./St.G. 1). He was appointed acting *Kommandeur* of III./St.G. 1 in December and awarded the *Eichenlaub zum Ritterkreuz* (No. 214) on 16 March 1943 and was promoted to *Hauptmann* on 1 April 1943, taking command of II./St.G. 3 on 14 August. With the reorganization of the ground-attack units on 18 October 1943, he became *Kommandeur* of II./S.G. 3 and was promoted to *Major* on 1 May 1944. On 14 September 1944 he claimed a lend-lease P-39 Airacobra in a dogfight over central Latvia and three days later was awarded the *Schwerter zum Ritterkreuz* (No. 98). He was ordered to *Stab/General der Schlachtflieger* in Berlin on 17 November 1944 but delayed his departure until his successor arrived and could be briefed and vetted as the new *Kommandeur* of II./S.G. 3. He was still waiting two months later!

Nordmann was killed on 19 January 1945 when his Fw 190 F-8 collided with that of his wingman during a mission near Insterburg/East Prussia in very bad weather. It is said that he inexplicably swerved sharply left into his wingman at an altitude of 300 metres (1,000 ft) and they both went down. One can speculate, but it is probable that he momentarily blacked out and lost control. Nordmann was credited with an amazing 1,191 combat missions over the course of the war and the destruction of at least 80 enemy tanks – amazing in that he flew into the maelstrom of fire 1,191 times and survived almost to the end. It was ironic that what finally brought him down was a freak flying accident in bad weather.

On 9 July 1940 I./St.G. 76 was disbanded at Barly near Arras and elements used to form both I./St.G. 3 and III./St.G. 77. The unit's code 'S1' passed to the former Gruppe which it retained until eventually replaced by 'S7'. This Ju 87 R-1 of 2./St.G. 3 has its red individual letter 'A' outlined in white and the familiar white rear fuselage band adopted by Luftwaffe aircraft operating in the Mediterranean area.

I./St.G. 3 Emblem

I./St.G. 3

Formation (July 1940) Formed on 9 July 1940 at Barly (17 km west-south-west of Arras in north-east France) with Ju 87 Bs using elements of I./St.G. 76.

Air Offensive against England (Battle of Britain) (July 1940 – January 1941) July - August: attacked convoys in the English Channel and targets along the south coast of England using Cherbourg-Théville and Picauville/33 km south-south-east of Cherbourg as forward staging fields. 8 August: from Théville, took part in a major attack on Convoy *Peewit* off the Isle of Wight which cost the British 4 ships sunk and 7 damaged, but

This Ju 87 D-3, S7+DL, has just landed after a mission. Note the I.Gruppe badge in front of the cockpit and the yellow painted nose and rudder, the distinctive marking of the Balkans Campaign.

the *Gruppe* lost 3 Ju 87 Bs to fighters plus 2 more shot up. 13 August: not listed in *Luftwaffe* order of battle for this date, so possibly on stand down or resting and refitting. 18 August: due to unexpected high losses (mostly by St.G. 77), all *Stuka* units were withdrawn from daylight cross-Channel operations. 19 October: Ju 87 B-1 slightly damaged in a taxiing accident at Barly airfield. 7 November: attacked shipping in the Thames Estuary, sinking one and damaging another – 1 Ju 87 was damaged. 8 November: flew a second raid on shipping in the same location, damaging several – 2 Ju 87 Bs were shot down. 7 December: temporarily assigned to VIII.*Fliegerkorps* for Operation *Felix*, the planned attack on Gibraltar through Spain that was aborted a short time later. December 1940 - January 1941: not mentioned in the surviving documents, but believed to have returned to Germany (Echterdingen near Stuttgart?) for rest, refit and the granting of home leave.

Balkan Campaign and Operations in the Eastern Mediterranean (February 1941 – November 1941) 17 February: Ju 87 crashed on take-off from Balomir airfield in Bulgaria, 2 KIA. 5 April: at Belica (Belitsa)/Bulgaria with 30 Ju 87 Bs and 9 Ju 87 Rs for the Balkan Campaign under VIII.*Fliegerkorps*. April - May: supported armoured and motorized spearheads advancing into Greece, moving forward via Sirbani (Sirbanovo)/Bulgaria, Larissa (Larisa), Corinth and then to Argos by around 10 May. 14 April: attacked British troops around Servia in north Greece, losing one *Stuka*, with another lost on 19 April while dive-bombing retreating

For operations in the Balkans, many of the Luftwaffe Ju 87s had the noses and rudders painted yellow. This aircraft, S1+NK of 2./St.G. 3, has armour plate fitted behind the pilot's seat and its drop tanks have short hollow tubes in their noses to assist in forcing air into the tanks to help improve the supply of fuel to the engine.

Two Ju 87 R-2s of 2./St.G. 3, S1+HK and S1+AK in flight, probably over the North African coast. This long-range version of the Junkers Stuka, which was designed mainly for anti-shipping combat, was widely used in this theatre of operations.

Probably photographed just after its arrival in the Mediterranean theatre, this Ju 87 B-2, S1+FH, carries a single SC 250 bomb under the fuselage and four SC 50 weapons beneath the wings. At this time, I./St.G. 3 retained its black-green (RLM colour 70) and dark green (71) upper surfaces with pale blue (65) beneath.

Walter Sigel (RK-EL, DKG)

BORN on 12 January 1906 in Ulm/Württemberg, Sigel entered military service in 1934 with *Infanterie-Rgt.* 10 in Dresden. He transferred from the *Heer* (Army) to the *Luftwaffe* in 1935 and was appointed *Staka* in I./St.G. 167 on 1 April 1937, now with the rank of *Hauptmann*. He became *Kommandeur* of I./St.G. 168 in 1938, remaining in command of this unit when it was redesignated I./St.G. 76 on 1 May 1939. On 15 August 1939, 13 of his *Stukas* and their 26 crew members were killed in a terrible accident at the Neuhammer training ground in Silesia due to ground fog. As *Gruppenkommandeur*, Sigel suffered the ignominy and burden of this event for the remainder of his career. Following the invasion of France and the Low Countries he was wounded on 14 May 1940 during operations over central Belgium. He was promoted to *Major* on 9 July 1940, and appointed *Kommodore* of I./St.G. 3. Awarded the *Ritterkreuz* on 21 July 1940 and became *Kommodore* of St.G. 3 on 1 March 1942. On 24 April 1942, as an *Oberstleutnant?*, he was awarded the DKG (recommended while *Kommodore* of I./St.G. 3), with the *Eichenlaub zum Ritterkreuz* (No. 116) following on 2 September 1942 (recommended while serving as *Kommodore* of St.G. 3 during the hard-fought campaign in North Africa).

On 1 April 1943 Sigel transferred to *Stab/General der Kampfflieger* (L.In.2), being promoted to *Oberst* (see photograph) on 1 December. On 6 February 1944 he became *Nahkampfführer Luftflotte* 2 and *Fliegerführer Norwegen* in April. He died on 8 May 1944 in a freak accident during an inspection flight from Trondheim-Vaernes to Hattfjelldal in Norway. The propeller of his Fi 156 F-1 (W5+BK, W.Nr. 1411) snagged a cable supporting camouflage netting near the battleship *Tirpitz,* causing the plane to stop and then fall tail-first onto a railway track at Faettenfjord.

I./St.G. 3 was formed on 9 July 1940 at Barly, some 17 km west-south-west of Arras in north-eastern France, from elements provided by I./St.G. 76. For some time it retained that unit's code 'S1'. These Ju 87 B-2s were photographed in Bulgaria just prior to the invasion of Greece in April 1941. The second aircraft in the line-up, S1+AB, was probably piloted by the then Gruppe Kommandeur, Major Walter Sigel. Sigel was promoted to Kommodore of St.G. 3 on 1 March 1942 and then served in various staff positions from April 1943. He was killed on 8 May 1944 in a freak accident in Norway.

enemy columns in the same area. Operations had reached the Athens area by 24 April. 20-31 May: took part in Operation *Merkur* (Mercury), the airborne and air-landing assault on Crete. 22 May: at Argos – 10 of the *Gruppe's* ground servicing personnel WIA when a 500 kg bomb exploded during the collision of two *Stukas* that were attempting to take off. 29 May: took part in attacks on Royal Navy forces evacuating personnel from Crete, losing a Ju 87 from 2.*Staffel*, which may have put a bomb into the forward gun positions of the cruiser *Dido* before

crashing into the sea. June: transferred to Maritza on Rhodes during the first half of June to attack Royal Navy surface units in the eastern Mediterranean as opportunities arose. 30 July: finding few targets, transferred from Maritza to Maleme on Crete. 13 September: 2 Ju 87 R-4/Trop from 2.*Staffel* damaged on the ground at Maleme during a raid on the airfield by RAF bombers. November: began transferring from Maleme to Derna in North Africa around mid-November.

North African Campaign – Retreat and Advance (November 1941 – May 1942) November 1941 - November 1942: supported Rommel's *Afrikakorps* during its advances and retreats across the deserts of Cyrenaica and western Egypt, taking part in the major actions at Bir Hacheim, Tobruk, El Alamein and El Ruweisat, with stations at Agedabia, Maraua and Tmimi. 25 November: Ju 87 shot down by AA fire near Tobruk. December: reportedly based at Arco Philanorum (Marble Arch)/195 km south-south-west of Benghazi during December. January 1942: moved forward and now at Agedabia/150 km south of Benghazi. 24 January: 2 Ju 87s shot down by fighters near Msus to the south-east of Benghazi – 1 KIA and 1 captured. However, the *Gruppe* reported it lost 3 Ju 87 R-2s in the Agedabia area to enemy fighters and AA fire this date with 4 crew members MIA. 28 January: Ju 87 claimed shot down by AA fire south of Magrun during operations in the Benghazi area. 1 February: 2 Ju 87s damaged while making crash-landings at Benina near Benghazi. February: moved forward to Martuba/23 km south-east of Derna and still there on 4 April. 12 February: 2 Ju 87 Rs shot down by Hurricanes south of Tobruk, 2 KIA and 2 MIA. 1 March 1942: *Gruppe* reported 23 Ju 87 R-2s and 12 Ju 87 R-4s on strength. 15 March: a Bf 108 belonging to the *Gruppenstab* was destroyed on the ground during an RAF raid on Martuba airfield. 20 March: entire *Gruppe* at Martuba. 27 March: attacked Tobruk with 15 Ju 87s, but jumped by P-40 Tomahawks, possibly losing one *Stuka* claimed shot down, *Hptm.* Naumann WIA. April: transferred to Derna around the end of March or beginning of April. 2 April: 12 Ju 87s from the *Gruppe* attacked a convoy near Tobruk, 2 of which were claimed by covering fighters, but the *Gruppe* only reported one loss, a Ju 87 R-4/Trop, crew

MIA. 11 April: 18 Ju 87s attacked motor transport columns in the Sidi Mansur area, losing 1 and 4 damaged to fighters. 25 April: 12 Ju 87s attacked shipping in Tobruk harbour. 7 May: 3.*Staffel* Ju 87 R-4 crashed at Derna, crew of 2 KIA. 20 May: moved forward again around this date, this time from Derna to Tmimi.

This Ju 87 B, S1+GK, was only slightly damaged after it nosed over on landing at a North African airfield during the summer of 1942. Most Luftwaffe aircraft operating in this theatre had white rear fuselage bands and white patches beneath the wing tips.

I./St.G. 3 began transferring from Maleme to Derna in North Africa around mid-November 1941. Shortly afterwards its Ju 87 B-2s were repainted with sand yellow (RLM colour 79) overall upper surfaces and sky blue (78) beneath. This aircraft also carries a white rear fuselage band, and white areas beneath the wing tips. The code, S1+HK was in black except for the individual letter 'H' which was red.

Annihilation (May 1942 – November 1942) 26 May: after six months of rapid retreat to El Agheila on the Gulf of Sirte (Sidra) that began with British Operation *Crusader* on 18 November 1941, and a rapid 12-day advance in late January to positions 50 km west of Tobruk, Rommel opened his third counter-offensive this date with the Suez Canal as his objective. 26 May: Ju 87 claimed shot down by AA fire during attacks on British positions around Gazala. 31 May: 3 Ju 87s claimed shot down by P-40 Kittyhawks along the front near Gazala. 3 June 1942: 4 Ju 87s claimed shot down – one over Gazala by AA fire and 3 near Bir Hacheim by P-40 Tomahawks. Relentless *Stuka* attacks on the Fort at Bir Hacheim, garrisoned by Free French forces, had begun several days before this and continued until the fort fell on 10 June. 4 June: 2 or 3 Ju 87s claimed shot down by fighters over Bir Hacheim; one of the casualties was *Gruppenkommandeur Hptm.* Heinrich Eppen, who was KIA. 20 June: 3 Ju 87 Rs shot down by AA fire during an attack on Tobruk and El Adem, 4 KIA and 2 MIA. July – August: advanced towards Egypt with bases at Fuka and Bir el Abd/72 km south-east of Fuka. 3 July: 3 Ju 87s shot down by Hurricanes between Fuka and El Alamein along the Egyptian coast. 15 July: Ju 87 shot down by AA fire near El Alamein. 12 August: temporarily transferred from Libya to Trapani/Sicily to take part in II.*Fliegerkorps* attacks on the *Pedestal* relief force and convoy moving across the Mediterranean from Gibraltar towards Malta. Scored hits on the aircraft carrier *Indomitable* on 12 August with two heavy bombs and three near misses, thereby forcing her out of action. Two Ju 87 Ds were shot down by carrier fighters during the attack. Further missions were flown on 13 and 14 August with hits on two more ships, including the cruiser *Dorset*, and another Ju 87 was shot down. Returned to North Africa during the second half of August and based at Quasaba/30 km south-east of Mersa Matruh. 6 September: Ju 87 D-3/Trop shot down by AA fire south of El Alamein, 2 MIA. 12 September: moved to Quasaba landing ground/30 km south-east of Mersa Matruh in north-west Egypt on or about this date. 31 October: Ju 87 shot down by AA fire over the El Alamein front area.

Crimea and North Caucasia (December 1942 – June 1943) 1 January: reported zero (0) aircraft on strength for this date, but during the course of the month received a full allowance of new Ju 87 D-3s. February: transferred at the beginning of February from Herzogenaurach to Bagerovo in eastern Crimea for operations over North Caucasia under VIII.*Fliegerkorps*. By 14 February, the *Gruppe* was fully in place at Bagerovo and ready to fly support missions for German forces that had retreated into the Taman Peninsula from deep in North Caucasia and set up defensive positions with their backs to the Kerch Strait. 11 February: casualties reported among the ground personnel during a Russian air raid on Bagerovo airfield. 24 February: more casualties among the ground personnel during another Russian air raid on Bagerovo. 24 March: 3.*Staffel* Ju 87 D-3 failed to return from operations, *Oblt.* Gerhard Kurz + 1 MIA. 25 March: 2 air crew personnel reported WIA by fire from a Russian fighter south-east of Gelendzhik on the coast just south of Novorossisk. 29 March: moved to Kerch IV airfield at the tip of eastern Crimea on or around this date. 1 April: 2.*Staffel* Ju 87 D-3 shot down by AA fire at Kurchevskaya, 1 KIA. 17 April: 2 Ju 87 D-3s shot down by AA fire over Novorossisk, both crews MIA. 29 April: Ju 87 D-3 shot down by a fighter over the Taman Peninsula to the east of Krymskaya, 2 MIA. 30 April: Ju 87 D-3 shot down by a fighter over the Krymskaya area, *Oblt.* Paul Krentz + 1 KIA. 13 May: 2.*Staffel* Ju 87 D-3 shot down by AA fire over Krymskaya, 2 MIA. 20 May: 3 Ju 87 D-3s destroyed and 2 more slightly to moderately damaged at Kerch IV

Commonwealth troops pose for a photograph on a wrecked Ju 87 D of 1./St.G. 3. The aircraft carries the badge originally used by I./St.G. 76, a white heraldic lion on a green shield positioned on a white circle. Several aircraft from the Gruppe were destroyed during operations in Tunisia early in 1943.

On 11 November 1942 I./St.G. 3 was virtually destroyed when 14 out of 15 Ju 87 Ds were shot down by SAAF Kittyhawks and USAAF P-40s while attempting to bomb British armour east of Tobruk. Following this debacle, the Gruppe returned to Germany for rest and re-equipment. This photograph of an Allied aircraft graveyard shows a Ju 87, S7+KL of the 3.Staffel, to the left.

During the second half of August 1942, I./St.G. 3 returned from Sicily to Quasaba in North Africa. However, in the next few months its losses began to mount and in December it was withdrawn to Herzogenaurach where it was completely re-equipped with brand new Ju 87 D-3s to replace those lost in North Africa. These included S7+AH shown here.

when a bomb accidentally exploded while being uploaded or downloaded on one of the aircraft – all 5 belonged to 3.*Staffel*. 2 June: Ju 87 D-3 shot down by AA fire over the Taman Peninsula, *Gruppenkommandeur Hptm.* Horst Schiller + 1 MIA. 11 June: transferred from Kerch via Bulgaria to Athens-Eleusis and reassigned to *Luftwaffenkommando Südost*. Moved to Athens-Kalamaki shortly after arriving.

Greece and the Eastern Aegean (June 1943 – October 1943) June: I./St.G. 3 was sent to Greece as part of large-scale reinforcements sent to the Balkans following the surrender of Axis forces in Tunisia on 10 May, and the rapid build-up of Allied invasion shipping in North African ports. Germany's Italian ally was also showing signs of instability and lack of resolve to continue the war, and Berlin did not want the ca. 660,000 Italian troops in the Balkans becoming a problem in the event of a surrender. The Balkans was not only a rich source of raw materials for the German war machine, but also their line of supply to the eastern Mediterranean and defensive rampart protecting south-eastern Europe. 27 June: Ju 87 D-3/Trop slightly damaged during Allied raid on Athens-Kalamaki. 1 July: reported 34 Ju 87 D-3/Trops on strength. July: moved from Kalamaki to Megara/35 km west of Athens at the beginning of July. July - August: exact nature of the *Gruppe's* activities during this period are not known with certainty but they did involve some support for anti-partisan operations underway in Greece at this time. Crashes were reported at Megara and at Kastelli/Crete during the summer, and on 22 August at Nis/Serbia. 16 September: Ju 87 D-3/Trop crashed west of Cephalonia Island off western Greece due to engine failure, crew rescued. The *Gruppe* was supporting German landings on the island and offensive operations to suppress the Italian division *Acqui*, which had refused to surrender with the rest of the Italian forces when Italy capitulated on 8 September. 17 September: Ju 87 D-4 force-landed on Cephalonia and caught fire, 2 WIA. 3 October: 2 Ju 87 D-4s shot down by AA fire and both crew members killed during operations to support German landings on Kos Is. in the eastern Aegean, which had been taken by the British following the capitulation of Italian forces on 8 September. Kos was successfully retaken by the Germans on 4 October, and this was followed by similar landing operations on nearby Samos. The *Gruppe* continued supporting the German offensive in the eastern Aegean until 18 October. 7 October: Ju 87 D-4 shot down into the sea south-east of Rhodes, probably by naval AA fire, 2 WIA. This plane all but certainly belonged to the formation of 18 *Stuka*s sent out by I. and II./St.G. 3 to attack a British task force between Rhodes and Karpathos in the Dodecanese which successfully damaged the cruiser *Penelope*. 9 October: Ju 87 D-4 shot down by AA fire east of Scarpanto (Karpathos), 2 MIA. 18 October: at Megara – renamed I./S.G. 3 this date.
Codes: initially (S1+_B, H, K, L) then (S7+_B, H, K, L)

FpNs: I. (L 07989, 33953)

Kommandeur:
Major Walter Sigel (RK) (9 July 1940 - 1 March 1942)
Hptm. Heinrich Eppen (RK) (1 March 1942 - 4 June 1942 KIA)
Hptm. Martin Mossdorf (DKG, RK) (5 June 1942 - 11 November 1942 POW)
Hptm. Horst Schiller (DKG) (1 December 1942 - 2 June 1943 MIA)
Hptm. Helmut Naumann (DKG, RK) (19 June 1943 - 18 October 1943)

II./St.G. 3

Formation (January 1942) Formed 13 January 1942 at either El Agheila or Agedabia along the Gulf of Sirte in Libya by renaming I./St.G. 1. Equipped with Junkers Ju 87 R *Stuka* dive-bombers.

North African Campaign (January 1942 – October 1942) 21 January - 4 February: supported the *Afrikakorps* (Rommel) rapid counter-offensive from El Agheila through Cyrenaica towards Gazala/50 km west of Tobruk. 14 February: Ju 87 shot down by ground fire over Gazala. 25 February: at Benghazi-Berca, but is believed to have moved forward to Martuba/23 km south-east of Derna a week or two later as the front stabilized around Ain el Gazala. 1 March: *Gruppe* reported 6 Ju 87 R-2s and 3 Ju 87 R-4s on strength. 7 April: moved to Bari/Italy to rest, refit and re-equip with Ju 87 D-1s. 24 May: transferred on or about this date from Bari to Derna/Libya to support the renewed offensive towards Tobruk by the *Afrikakorps* that commenced on 26 May. 29 May: 2 Ju 87 D-1s from 4.*Staffel* shot down by Kittyhawks over Gazala, 2 KIA and *Hptm.* Drescher + 1 MIA; Drescher later returned. June: moved forward to Tmimi in late May or early June. 1 June: Ju 87 D-3 shot down by AA fire over the front south-west of Tobruk, 1 KIA and 1 MIA. 4 June: Ju 87 shot down by AA fire over the fort at Bir Hacheim garrisoned by Free French forces which held out for two weeks under ceaseless *Stuka* and ground attack before capitulating on 10 June. 13 June: operating from Derna, attacked a British convoy en route from Alexandria to Malta and shared in the sinking of a Dutch merchantman, but lost two *Stuka*s to intense fire from the escort

II./St.G. 3 Emblem

destroyers. Among those lost was *Oblt*. Anton Ostler, *Staffelkapitän* of 6.*Staffel*. During a follow-up attack on 15 June with 35 Ju 87s, the *Gruppe* dive-bombed and sank the destroyer *Airdale*. 21 June: moved forward to El Adem/26 km south-south-west of Tobruk. 22 June: advanced to Fuka/72 km south-east of Mersa Matruh on the Egyptian coast, arriving by 1 July. 4 July: Ju 87 D-1 shot down by a fighter near El Alamein, 2 MIA. July – August: variously at Fuka, Bir el Abd and then moved to Quasaba. The lack of activity by the *Gruppe* during July and August suggests that it may have been standing down to rest and refit. 31 August: based at Quasaba/30 km south-east of Mersa Matruh – 2 Ju 87 Ds shot down by fighters and another by AA fire along the front at El Alamein, 4 MIA. 2 September: 3 Ju 87s believed shot down by Hurricanes out of 14 that attacked positions along the front west of El Alamein. 14 September: 2 Ju 87 Ds destroyed in a mid-air collision over Quasaba-North landing ground, 4 KIA. 29 October 1942: transferred from Quasaba to Trapani/Sicily and then on 7 November to Elmas/Sardinia to stand by for attacks on maritime targets in the western Mediterranean under X.*Fliegerkorps*.

A German propaganda photograph of the port of Tobruk under attack by Luftwaffe aircraft. St.G. 3 made regular attacks on the city in 1941 and 1942

Tunisian Campaign (November 1942 – December 1942) 9 November: transferred to Tunis-Aouina airfield in Tunisia with 24 Ju 87s to counter the Allied landings in Morocco and Algeria on the previous day (Operation *Torch*). On arrival, one Ju 87 D-3/Trop crash-landed and moderately damaged. 14 November: Ju 87/Trop shot down by a fighter to the west of Bône in eastern Algeria, *Staffelkapitän Oblt*. Hans Eichleiter + 1 MIA. 14 November: 2 Ju 87 D-3/Trop bombed on the ground at Tunis-Aouina and destroyed. 14 November: 2 Ju 87 D-3/Trop destroyed in a mid-air collision south of Mateur/Tunisia, both crews safe. 16 November: attacked Allied spearheads advancing near Tabarka to the west of Bône. 17 November: sent 15 Ju 87s to Bône for attacks on Allied shipping in the harbour. 20 November: transferred from Tunis-Aouina to Djedeida/24 km west-north-west of Tunis for operations under *Fliegerführer Tunis*. 22 November: 13 of its Ju 87s flew an afternoon raid on the rapidly developing RAF airfield complex at Souk el Arba claiming at least one aircraft destroyed on the ground. 24 November: struck Allied forces concentrating between Béja and Testour with 17 sorties. 25 November: advancing American tanks from the 1st Armoured Division overran Djedeida airfield and destroyed 4 of the *Gruppe's* Ju 87s and shot up or crushed 21 others, putting them out of action. The American tank crews claimed 30-36 aircraft in all. The *Gruppe* flew 48 sorties against the advance before the tanks reached the airfield. 26-30 November: still located at Djedeida, *Gruppe* stayed in combat, flying a few sorties a day with remaining a/c, and was soon brought back up to strength. 29 November: Ju 87 D-3/Trop badly shot up by AA fire and crashed on return to Djedeida, 2 KIA. 2 December: said to have moved to Protville/23 km north-north-west of Tunis and then to Bizerte a week or so later. Flew attacks on enemy vehicle concentrations in and around Tebourba. 2 December: Ju 87 D-3/Trop shot down by a fighter over Tebourba (Tabarqah) on the coast near the Tunisian-Algerian border, *Staffelkapitän Major* Hans Einwächter + 1 KIA. December: bombed Allied armour and infantry thrusts towards Tunis and supported German counter-attacks at Tebourba (1-10 December), in the Medjez el Bab area (10-12 December), Djebel el Ahmera (22-25 December). 14 December: now based at Bizerte. 22 December: escorted by Fw 190s from II./JG 2, hit enemy tanks and vehicles south of Medjez el Bab.

Tunisian Campaign (January 1943 – May 1943) 1 January: *Gruppe* reported 29 Ju 87 D-3s/Trop on strength. 1-2 January 1943: 2 Ju 87 D-3/Trop failed to return from operations during attacks on shipping in Bône harbour, 4 MIA. Together with aircraft from III./S.K.G. 10, the *Gruppe* shared in the sinking of 2 freighters and damage to the RN cruiser *Ajax* and 4 other ships during this raid. 3 January: Ju 87 D-3/Trop shot down by AA fire over Bône harbour, 2 MIA. 19 January: attacked British positions near El Aroussa/ca. 90 km south-west of Tunis. 20 January: Ju 87 D-3/Trop shot down by AA fire to the west of Pont du Fahs, 2 KIA. 1 February: ordered to transfer to Gabes in south-east Tunisia. 10 February: operating from a field strip near Zaghouan (Zaghwän/ca. 45 km south of Tunis near Ste-Marie du Zit) under *Fliegerkorps Tunis* – reported 29 (23) Ju 87 Ds on strength. 14-15 February: now operating under *Fliegerführer* 2 and only flying 9-12 sorties a day due to fuel shortages. The main action in Tunisia from 14-22 February was a powerful attack by 5.*Panzerarmee* from the Gafsa - Faid area that drove U.S. forces back 80 km through the Kasserine Pass towards Tebessa. 14 February: flew day-long attacks on Sidi bou Zid in support of German offensive operations in Central Tunisia that would culminate in the battle for the Kasserine Pass a week later. 15 February: struck elements of the U.S. 1st Armoured Division advancing towards Sidi bou Zid but without success. 26 February: began 4 days of intense operations in support of Operation *Ochsenkopf* (Ox Head), a 5.*Panzerarmee* offensive towards Béja in northern Tunisia. March: the British 8th Army began its attack on the Mareth Line in south Tunisia around the end of February, and most *Luftwaffe* ground support units were shifted there

Following the Allied offensive in November 1942, II./St.G. 3 was withdrawn to Elmas in Sardinia to stand by for attacks on maritime targets in the western Mediterranean. Several unserviceable aircraft had to be left behind such as this Ju 87 D-1/Trop of the 6.Staffel. Note the RAF Spitfire in the background of this photograph.

from northern Tunisia and remained there through March. 25 March: at Ste-Marie du Zit and still there on 11 April. 7 April: 3 Ju 87 D-3s shot down by fighters near Oued Zarga/ca. 65 km west of Tunis with 3 KIA and 2 MIA. These were part of a formation of 15 *Stukas* that had taken off to bomb Allied armour and artillery positions near Oued Zarga, but were jumped by fighters as they began their run on the target. 11 April: Ju 87 D-3 destroyed on the ground during Allied raid on Oudna. 11 April: Ju 87 D-3 shot down by AA fire 30 km south-west of Medjez el Bab, 1 KIA and 1 captured. The aircraft had been one of 12 *Stukas* from the *Gruppe* that had taken off from Ste-Marie du Zit and flown a dusk attack on enemy troop concentrations in the Medjez el Bab area, each with one 250 kg bomb and 4 x 50 kg bombs. 14 April: bombed Allied tanks, artillery and vehicles advancing along the roads in the Béja - Mateur - Oued Zarga area to the west

of Tunis. 19 April: a II.*Gruppe* Ju 87 D towing a transport glider reportedly shot down into the sea off Cap (Cape) Bon by a large formation of SAAF Kittyhawks; this is thought to have been the last *Stuka* lost by the *Gruppe* in combat during the campaign in Tunisia. 20 April: unable to continue operations due to prohibitive losses unless accompanied by large numbers of escort fighters, the *Gruppe* was ordered to fly its remaining 14 Ju 87s from Oudna/ca. 20 km south of Tunis to Reggio di Calabria in south Italy. 20 May: departed Italy and transferred to Herzogenaurach in Germany to rest, refit and completely re-equip.

Germany, Greece and the Eastern Aegean (June 1943 – October 1943) 31 May: Ju 87 D-3 crashed at Herzogenaurach due to pilot error. 1 June: ordered from Herzogenaurach to Argos/Greece and assigned to

As the Allies began their final advance on the North African front they collected together many wrecked Luftwaffe aircraft including these Ju 87s and Bf 109s at El Daba airfield in November 1942. The four Ju 87s in the foreground previously belonged to St.G. 3, the main Stuka unit to operate in this theatre. As can be seen, the original Geschwader code, 'A5', of the third aircraft in the line-up was painted out and replaced by the code of St.G. 3, 'S7'.

This wrecked Ju 87 D of 4./St.G. 3 was found in the western desert. The British applied RAF markings over the typical German sand yellow upper surfaces with dark green mottling. It still carries the unit code A5+HH originally used by 1./St.G. 1 from which it was formed.

Luftwaffenkdo. Südost to continue refitting with instructions prohibiting employment except in the event of an Allied landing in the Balkans. 16 June: 3 Ju 87 crashes near Argos and this date probably marks the arrival of the main body of the *Gruppe* from Herzogenaurach. 1 July: *Gruppe* reported 39 Ju 87 D-3s/Trop on strength. 1 July: Ju 87 D-3/Trop force-landed in a partisan infested area south-west of Larissa and blown up by its crew, 1 KIA. 9 September: Ju 87 D-3/Trop shot down by Italian naval AA fire west of Oxia/Greece, 1 WIA. September: took part in operations against the Italian garrison on Cephalonia off the west coast of Greece beginning in mid-September. The garrison, mainly the *Acqui* Division, had refused to surrender to the Germans following Italy's capitulation on 8 September and was viciously attacked by its former ally. 21 September: 2 Ju 87 D-3s destroyed during a dive on a target on Cephalonia when one of the bombs prematurely exploded, *Oblt.* Herbert Stry, *Staffelkapitän* of 6.*Staffel*, + 1 KIA. 26 September: operating from Agrinion airfield in south-west Greece. The *Gruppe* is believed to have moved here temporarily in mid-September since Agrinion was the German airfield closest to Cephalonia. 29 September: one pilot reported KIA during an Allied air attack on Argos-South. 3 October: commenced support for German operations aimed at recapturing Leros and other islands in the eastern Aegean off the Turkish coast that had been taken by the British on 14 September. 3 October: Ju 87 D-3/Trop downed by AA fire near Kos in the Dodecanese off south-west Turkey, crew rescued. 5 October: 2 Ju 87 D-3s blown up by explosives during a

night raid by Greek partisans on Argos airfield. 7 October: together with *Luftwaffe* bombers, 18 *Stukas* from I. and II./St.G. 3 attacked a British task force between Rhodes and Karpathos in the Dodecanese damaging the cruiser *Penelope*. 9 October: 7 Ju 87 D-3s shot down by U.S. P-38 Lightnings south-west of Rhodes plus another damaged, 3 KIA and *Hptm.* Peter von Heydebrand + 8 MIA. The *Gruppe* had attacked a Royal Navy task force spotted transiting the narrow passage between Rhodes and Karpathos, sinking the destroyer *Panther* and severely damaging the cruiser *Carlisle*. The USAAF P-38s had flown to the eastern Aegean from their base at Gambut in Libya. 13 October: Ju 87 D-3/Trop bombed on the ground at Maritza airfield on Rhodes and moderately damaged. 18 October: renamed II./S.G. 3.

Codes: initially (A5+_B, H, K, L), then (S7+_C, M, N, P)

FpN: II. (L 37714)

Kommandeur:
Hptm. Kurt Kuhlmey (DKG) (13 January 1942 – July 1942)
Hptm. Heinrich Heins (July 1942 – 1 April 1943)
Hptm. Hans Neumann (DKG) (1 April 1943 – 14 August 1943)
Hptm. Theodor Nordmann (DKG, RK, EL) (14 August 1943 – 18 October 1943) – acting?

III./St.G. 3

Formation (January 1942 – February 1942)
Formed at San Pancrazio/south Italy on 13 January 1942 by the renaming of II./St.G. 2 and equipped with the new and improved Ju 87 D. *Gruppe* spent the next two months rebuilding its strength.

Operations against Malta (March 1942 – May 1942)
1 March: *Gruppe* reported 29 Ju 87 D-1/Trop on strength. 22 March: rested and now back to full strength, transferred on or about this date from San Pancrazio on the Italian mainland to San Pietro/Sicily and commenced operations against Malta under II.*Fliegerkorps.* These raids were flown almost daily from 24 March, with frequently two or three missions of 15-30 *Stukas* each being mounted against the island on any given day. The targets were always the same: harbours and airfields. On 1 April, the *Gruppe* sank two submarines (*Pandora* and *P 36*) and a minesweeper/drifter and damaged 3 other vessels, and on 9 April claimed the destroyers *Lance* and *Gallant.* Two days later, on 11 April, its *Stukas* dive-bombed and severely damaged the destroyer *Kingston.* All of these ships were in port at the time. To the final raid on or about 13 May, III./St.G. 3 lost at least 17 planes, including 4 on 10 May, most of these falling to RAF fighters. 21-24 May: after being brought up to strength, transferred from San Pietro to Libya around this date with station probably at Derna/145 km north-west of Tobruk or one of its nearby auxiliary fields.

North African Campaign in Libya and Egypt (May 1942 – January 1943) 26 May: 2 Ju 87 D-1s shot down by AA fire during attacks on British positions around Gazala, 3 MIA and 1 WIA. Like the rest of the *Luftwaffe* in Cyrenaica (Libya), the *Gruppe* was assigned to support the renewed offensive towards Tobruk by the *Afrikakorps* (Rommel) that commenced this date. 14 June: one or possibly 2 *Stukas* shot down by P-40 Tomahawks while attacking motor transport columns between Tobruk and El Adem. 14 June: flew an attack on a British convoy off Tobruk, losing one *Stuka* without scoring any hits, but returned the next day and disabled the cruiser *Birmingham* without loss. 20 June: at Benghazi-Berca. Tobruk fell to Axis forces the next day and Rommel's rapid advance continued 500 km eastward until it halted at the end of June at a new Allied main line of resistance (MLR) running from El Daba - El Alamein south-west to the Qattara Depression. 22 June: advanced to Fuka/72 km south-east of Mersa Matruh on the Egyptian coast via

Tmimi, arriving around 1 July. 26 June: struck enemy positions at Mersa Matruh in western Egypt with some 20 *Stukas*, of which at least 6 were claimed by a large force of intercepting fighters. 8 July: Ju 87 shot down by P-40 Kittyhawks while taking off for a mission with others from Mumin Busaq airfield to the west of El Daba. 17 July: flew a strike on targets around El Alamein with around 30 planes, but the formation was largely broken up by intercepting Hurricanes. 31 July: operating from Shterasat (not located but believed to be an auxiliary airfield in the Fuka - Quasaba area). August: moved to Quasaba in mid-August and still there on 26 October. 29 August: Ju 87 D-1/Trop shot up by AA fire and crashed into the sea near El Daba on the Egyptian coast, crew rescued by the *Seenotdienst* (air-sea rescue service). 12 September: 25 Ju 87s flew a mission to El Alamein without loss, although several were claimed by defending Kittyhawks. 14 September: attacked British naval forces withdrawing after an aborted commando raid on Tobruk, scoring hits on the AA-cruiser *Coventry* and the destroyer *Zulu*, and sinking a motor torpedo boat. 1 October: at least 2 of 18 Ju 87s shot down by Kittyhawks over the El Alamein front. 23 October: superior Allied forces under General Montgomery began the El Alamein offensive which gradually drove the Axis out of Egypt and Libya. 26 October: 2 Ju 87s shot down by Hurricanes while returning from a mission, *Gruppenkommandeur Hptm.* Walter KIA when his parachute failed to open after baling out at low altitude. 31 October 1942: one or 2 Ju 87s shot down by fighters and 2 to 4 more through 3 November. 6 November: operating from Gambut/52 km east-south-east of Tobruk. Over the next 10 days the *Gruppe* reported a large number of combat losses and crashes as the *Luftwaffe* tried to pull back in the face of relentless RAF air superiority along the front. 12 November: transferred from Gambut to Arco Philanorum (Marble Arch)/195 km south-south-west of Benghazi. 24 November: now at Nofilia-North on the Gulf of Sirte along the route of retreat towards Tripoli. 15 December: a Ju 87 D-1 and a D-3 blown up by German troops at Nofilia-North to prevent capture by the enemy. 1 January 1943: *Gruppe* reported 12 Ju 87 D-1/Trop and 9 Ju 87 D-3/Trop on strength. 9 January: at Bir Dufan/165 km south-east of Tripoli operating under *Fliegerführer Afrika.* Over the next 10 days the *Gruppe* reported 2 Ju 87s lost in combat along with 4 crashes at Bir Dufan/165 km south-east of Tripoli. 17 January: moved from Bir Dufan to Mellaha (not located). 21-22 January: 3 Ju 87 Ds destroyed in combat in the Castel Benito area 26 km south-south-west of Tripoli. The *Gruppe* also blew up 2 Bf 109 E-1s, both of which were listed as belonging to it.

Luftwaffe colours 78 (himmelblau or sky blue), 79 (sand gelb or sand yellow) and 80 (olivgrün or olive green) were introduced around September 1941. This Ju 87 B of St.G. 3 has a typical example of a camouflage scheme adopted using these colours, 80 mottling over 79 upper surfaces with 78 beneath. A white rear fuselage band was applied to all Luftwaffe aircraft operating in the Mediterranean theatre.

This Ju 87 D-1/Trop of 8./St.G. 3 was shot down by an Allied fighter on 1 November 1942 over the North African desert. Both members of the crew, Uffz. Otto Eckhardt and Uffz. Herbert Wagner, were captured, wounded. Their aircraft, W.Nr. 2396, had a white rear fuselage band with the individual letter 'K' in yellow with the Staffel letter 'S' probably in the same colour.

British troops pose for the camera on this wrecked Ju 87 D of St.G. 3, the Geschwader having adopted the 'S7' code for all its aircraft by early 1943.

An Allied soldier stands in front of a wrecked Ju 87 D of 9./St.G. 3 with the remains of an Italian aircraft in the background. It appears that the swastika marking has been subjected to pot shots judging by the small holes in the fin. Between 11-16 April, III./St.G. 3 was forced to transfer from Oudna in Tunis to Alghero in Sardinia with 18 Ju 87s to rest and refit after losing many of its aircraft and crews during heavy fighting in Tunisia. The Gruppe was only able to stay in Sardinia for about two weeks until relentless Allied air attacks forced its return to Germany.

Campaign in Tunisia (January 1943 – April 1943)
24 January: now at Gabes-West/Tunisia supporting 5.*Panzerarmee* operations in central Tunisia. 1 February: 4 Ju 87 D-1s and D-3s shot down by fighters in the Sened-Fatnassa area in central Tunisia, 2 KIA and 5 WIA. 10 February: at Gabes-West with 19 (16) Ju 87 Ds on strength under *Fliegerkorps Tunis*. 14-22 February: supported Axis offensive operations from the Gafsa - Sidi bou Zid - Faid area which drove U.S. forces back 80 km through the Kasserine Pass towards Tebessa. 26 February: departed Gabes-West as British forces approached from the south and the airfield began coming under artillery fire, moving to Mezzouna-North in central Tunisia, about 80 km west of Sfax, where it remained for the next month. 4 March: *Major* Franz Albertshauser from the *Gruppe* WIA in a crash-landing by an unidentified aircraft south-east of Mezzouna-North. 6 March: Ju 87 D-3 forced down west of Medenine after being shot up by AA fire, *Staffelkapitän Hptm.* Fritz Eyer + 1 WIA. 21 March: 9.*Staffel* Ju 87 D-3/Trop shot up by a fighter and crashed at Mezzouna-North, 2 KIA. 25 March: transferred to El Djem in east-central Tunisia, but then moved to Oudna/ca. 20 km south of Tunis on 8 April. By now the front had been driven back into north-east Tunisia and *Gruppe* was mainly limited to missions flown by just 2 or 3 planes, since larger formations were easy prey for the overwhelming number of Allied fighters operating over Tunisia. These missions were flown primarily against U.S. and British tanks and motor transport columns pushing north towards Tunis. 11-16 April: transferred from Oudna to Alghero/Sardinia with 18 Ju 87s to rest and refit after losing many of its aircraft and crews during the heavy fighting in Tunisia, but relentless Allied air activity over Sardinia made a prolonged stay there impossible. 27-30 April: departed Sardinia for Herzogenaurach (or Echterdingen?) in Germany to rest and completely re-equip for employment in Russia.

Central and South Russia (June 1943 – October 1943) 5 June: transferred from Germany to Konotop in central Russia on or about this date and assigned to *Luftflotte* 6. June: Ju 87 D-3 crashed at Konotop but apparently no combat losses. July: moved forward from Konotop via Bryansk to Orel in late June or the beginning of July for the opening of the Kursk offensive (Operation *Zitadelle*) on 5 July. 1 July: *Gruppe* reported 36 Ju 87 D-3s/Trop and 3 Ju 87 D-1s/Trop on strength. 6 July: 7.*Staffel* Ju 87 D-3 shot down by AA fire at Gremyachevo, crew safe. 15 July: 7.*Staffel* Ju 87 D-3 shot down by AA fire at Zhizdra/60 km north-north-east of Bryansk, *Hptm.* Otto Patschkowski MIA plus 1 WIA. 16 July: operating from Orel – 7.*Staffel* Ju 87 D-3 shot down by a fighter over the Kursk salient, crew safe. 26 July: Ju 87 D-3 shot down by AA fire north-west of Kharkov, 1 KIA. 3 August: ordered from Ozerskaya/50 km north-east of Bryansk to Gavrishi/45 km west-north-west of Kharkov. 17 August: 9.*Staffel* Ju 87 D-3 force-landed west of Poltava due to technical problems. 30 August: 9.*Staffel* Ju 87 D-3 shot up and force-landed south of Yelnya (south-east of Smolensk). On the same date a Ju 87 D-3 from '10./St.G. 3' was reported as slightly damaged after being shot up by a fighter to the south of Yelnya. If this is not a clerical error, it suggests that the *Gruppe* may have been operating its own *Ergänzungsstaffel* in Russia, which carried the number 10. No corroborating mention of this so-called 10./St.G. 3 has

been found. 1 September: 7.*Staffel* Ju 87 D-3 shot down by fighters south-east of Kurnosovka/62 km north-east of Kursk, 2 MIA. 6 September: 8.*Staffel* Ju 87 D-3 crash-landed at Smolensk-North. 19 September: transferred to Novo Zybkov/72 km east of Gomel. 25-29 September: transferred to Bagerovo in eastern Crimea and reassigned to *Luftflotte* 4. 2 October: 9.*Staffel* Ju 87 D-5 shot down by AA fire over the Taman Peninsula, *Oblt.* Edmund Reichard + 1 KIA. 4 October: Ju 87 D-3 crash-landed at Zaporozhye airfield after being shot up by AA fire. As the Soviet summer offensive reached the Dnieper at the end of September, the *Gruppe* was assigned missions not only in the eastern Crimea - Black Sea area but also to the north in the Dnepropetrovsk - Zaporozhye area. 6 October: in four separate missions over the course of the day, attacked and sank the Soviet destroyers *Kharkov*, *Besposhchadny* and *Sposobny* in the Black Sea off Crimea. 12 October: 9.*Staffel* claimed an La-5 fighter near Tarsovka (not located). 15 October: 9.*Staffel* Ju 87 D-5 shot down by AA fire over the Dnepropetrovsk area, 1 WIA and 1 MIA. 18 October: renamed III./S.G. 3 at Bagerovo.

Codes: initially (T6+_C, M, N, P), then (S7+_D, R, S, T)

FpN: III. (L 07718)

Kommandeur:
Major Walter Enneccerus (RK) (13 January 1942 - 1 March 1942)
Hptm. Kurt Walter (1 March 1942 - 26 October 1942)
Hptm. Bernard Hamester (DKG, RK) (ca. 26 October 1942 - 17 June 1943) – acting ?
Hptm. Eberhard Jacob (DKG) (17 June 1943 - 18 October 1943)

IV.(Erg.)/St.G. 3

Formation and Organization (August 1941) Formed August 1941 at Würzburg as *Ergänzungs-staffel*/St.G. 3 by renaming 3./*Ergänzungs-Stukagruppe*. Equipped with Junkers Ju 87 *Stuka* dive- bombers. The *Staffel* provided 6 to 8 weeks of operational formation and dive-bombing training to green crews fresh out of the schools that had been assigned to *Sturzkampfgeschwader* 3. The *Staffel* was also known informally as 10./St.G. 3. During the second half of 1942 it was expanded to two *Staffeln* (10. and 11.) and redesignated IV.(Erg.)/St.G. 3 on or about 17 November 1942.

Training in Greece and Italy (October 1941 – January 1943) 15 October: at Würzburg with about 20 crews in training. 29-30 October: transferred from Würzburg to Salonika-Sedes in Greece. 2 December: Ju 87 R-1 crashed at Salonika-Sedes, 2 injured. 9-10 February 1942: transferred from Salonika-Sedes to Piacenza/north Italy with a brief stopover at Foggia in central Italy. 1 October: all or elements now at San Severo near Foggia. Trainees at this point were only with the *Staffel* for 6 weeks before being sent to one of the operational *Gruppen*. November - December: Ju 87 D-3 and Ju 87 B-1 training crashes recorded at San Severo. 1 January 1943: *Gruppe* reported 28 Ju 87 D/Rs and 1 Bf 109 E-4 on strength.

Training and Anti-Partisan Operations in Yugoslavia and Greece (January 1943 – May 1943)
15-20 January 1943: transferred from Piacenza to Zagreb/Croatia to provide *Stuka* support for Operation *Weiss*, a major anti-partisan offensive against Tito's communist bands in Croatia, Bosnia and Herzegovina. Over the course of *Weiss*, which ran from January into March, the *Gruppe* flew at least 106 combat missions. 12 February: Ju 87 R-4 burned out at Zagreb after the engine caught fire, 1 injured. 24 February: Ju 87 R-4 shot up by ground fire and crash- landed at Sarajevo. 2 March: *Gruppenstab* and one *Staffel* now at Athens-Kalamaki assigned to X.*Fliegerkorps* with a reinforced second *Staffel* at Zagreb. 23 March: 13 Ju 87s at Athens-Kalamaki and 21 at Zagreb. 1 April: *Gruppe* reported 2 Ju 87 R-1s, 10 R-2s, 4 R-4s, 4 D-1s, 8 D-3s, 4 Bf 109 E-7s and 1 Bf 109 E-4 on strength. 7 April: 9 of the Ju 87s at Zagreb transferred to Athens-Kalamaki and then on 11 April flew on to Alghero/Sardinia via Bari/Italy to help fill up III./St.G. 3. 6 May: *Gruppe* reported 19 (12) Ju 87s and 6 (3) Bf 109s at Athens-Kalamaki, and 9 (9) Ju 87s at Alghero/Sardinia. 17 May: renamed III./St.G. 151 at Zagreb.

Codes: initially (S7+_U), then (S7+_E?, U, V, W?)

FpNs: Erg.St. and IV.(Erg.) (L 40461, 31153)

Staffelkapitän/Kommandeur:
Hptm. Heinrich Heins (DKG) (1 February 1943 - April 1943) – acting
Oblt. Siegfried Göbel (DKG, RK) (April 1943 - 16 May 1943) – acting?

Sources for St.G. 3:

Unpublished and Archival:
AFHRA Maxwell AFB (Montgomery, AL) – Karlsruhe Collection;
AFHRA Maxwell/PRO London: CSDIC P/W interrogation AFHQ No. 13, 23 May 1943; No. 5, 12 May 1943.
AFHRA Maxwell/PRO London: P/W interrogation ADI(K) 320D/42.
BA-MA - *Flugzeug-Bereitstellungen* (Aircraft Availability Status Reports – FzB).
BA-MA Freiburg: RL 2 III Gen.Qu.(6.Abt.) *Meldungen über Flugzeugunfälle und Verlust…* (LRs – Loss Reports).
NARA WashDC: RG 242/T-311 *Heeresgruppe* E microfilms.
PRO London – AIR 40 AirMin /'Y' Sigint intelligence documents 40/1966, 1971, 1975, 1978, 1979, 1995, 1996.
PRO London: DEFE 3 ULTRA signals ML447, ML475, ML2779, ML5771, QT4934, QT6332, QT6786, QT6924, QT8644, VM859, VM1447, VM1878, VM2269, VM3049, VM3860, VM4173, VM4851, VM4900, VM5386, VM7337, VM7525, VM8771; VM8866, VM8947, VM9050, VM9100, VM9489, VM9837, VM9860, VM9933, plus others.

Published Sources:
[Arthy190] various;
[Aders – SG] p. 36, 59, 60, 66, 71, 73, 76;
[Balke – KG2V1] p. 408-415;
[Bateson – *Stuka*!] p. 30, 36, 39, 41, 48-51, 59;

[Bekker – LWD] p. 350, 355, 359, 360, 363-365;
[Brütting – SA] p. 143, 144, 171, 187, 191, 205, 220, 222 229, 230, 232, 247, 254, 267-269;
[Carlsen – CM2] p. 338-43;
[Dierich – VdL] p. 202, 219-221, 223-226, 270;
[Foreman – Forg] p. 14;
[Gundelach – Med] p. 55, 94, 463, 534;
[Kannapin – FpN] p. various;
[Held – Afrika] p. 71, 78, 137, 150, 155, 159, 174, 188, 205;
[Mason – BovB] p. 552;
[Mehner – FT] p. 54;
[Nauroth – StG2] p. 158, 244, 262;
[Obermaier – RK2] p. 42, 50, 57, 72, 83, 87, 91, 101, 102, 111, 120, 131, 145, 160, 161, 164, 179, 186, 201, 207;
[Patzwall – LwR] p. various;
[Plocher – Rus43] p. 37;
[Ramsay – B-2] p. various;
[Ries – PhotoCol] p. 169, 170;
[Rohwer/Hummelchen-Chronology: 186;
[Salmaggi – 2194] p. 318;
[Scheibert – EP] various;
[Scherzer – DKG] p. 611-614, etc.;
[Shores – Malta-H] p. 145;
[Shores – Malta-S] p. 146, 148, 151, 162, 165, 167, 168, 174, 178, 181, 214, 233, 238, 258, 266, 284, 349, 350, 357, 455, 489, 503;
[Shores – Yug] p. 180, 337;
[Shores – FOtD] p. 28, 52, 54, 67, 69, 90, 91, 93, 94, 98, 101, 102, 104, 113, 114, 116, 118-120, 131, 134, 143, 147, 148, 158, 167, 170, 173, 177, 178, 195, 200, 205, 207, 250;
[Shores – FOT] p. 10, 41, 55, 67, 70, 81, 82, 85, 122, 129, 131, 155, 159, 163, 164, 187, 205, 215, 228, 235, 237, 243, 257, 284, 298, 306, 327;
[Shores – MAW3] p. 108, 114, 115;
[Smith – GA] p. 384, 386, 388-390, 392;
[Smith – StG 77] p. 84;
[Smith – SAW] p. 41, 44, 81, 82, 84, 97-99;
[Tessin – Tes] p. 312, 352, 353;
[Tuider – LwOst] p. 118;
[Weal – Stu-Med] p. 57, 66-68, 83;
[Weal – *Stuka* 37-41] p. 67;
[Zweng – Zweng] p. 187, 188.

[Archiv – A-8] p. 13;
Jürgen Zapf letter in *Jet & Prop*, 3/1999: p.7.

[Holm – Website www.ww2.dk]

St.G. 5

Sturzkampfgeschwader 5

(Unit Codes: L1+ and J9+)

St.G. 5 consisted only of I. *Gruppe* and an *Ergänzungsstaffel*, with no evidence of any other components.

I./St.G. 5 (First Formation)

Formation (January 1942) Formed 27 January 1942 at Rovaniemi/north Finland and Kirkenes/north Norway by renaming IV.(*Stuka*)/*Lehrgeschwader* 1 with *Gruppenstab* and 1. – 3.*Staffel*. Equipped with Junkers Ju 87 R dive-bombers, the 'R' designating the long-range version.

Operations in Northern Norway and Finland (January 1942 – December 1942) February – August: at Rovaniemi and Kirkenes with smaller detachments up to *Staffel* strength at Alakurtti and Bodo in an average total inventory of 28 to 36 Ju 87 Rs. Supported ground operations along the front, and flew attacks on Soviet airfields and on the Murmansk railway line (mainly from Alakurtti) which connected the vital port of Murmansk with the Russian interior. Subordinated to *Fliegerführer Nord (Ost)/Luftflotte 5*. 24 March: Ju 87 R-4 failed to return from an attack on Murmansk, 2 MIA. This was one of two raids on the Murmansk port area by the *Gruppe* this date, and on one of them a direct hit was claimed on

I./St.G. 5 Emblem
First Formation

During December 1941 and January 1942 operations from northern Finland came to a virtual halt as temperatures dropped as low as -50°C. On 27 January IV.(Stuka)/ L.G. 1 was redesignated I./St.G. 5, the Gruppe remaining at Rovaniemi. Here one of the unit's Ju 87 Rs, still carrying the radio call sign, NC+WY, comes in to land.

a British merchant ship. 23 April: flew two raids on Murmansk port facilities and one of the city's airfields. 30 April: Ju 87 R-2 shot down by a fighter near Kestenga, crew safe. The *Gruppe* was supporting 6. *SS-Gebirgsdivision Nord* and the Finnish Div. *J* which were engaged in heavy defensive fighting during a powerful offensive in the Kestenga-Loukhi area by Soviet 14th Army which ran from 24 April to 23 May. 8 May: Ju 87 R-2 shot down by AA fire near Kiestinki, 2 MIA. 15 May: inflicted severe damaged on the Soviet submarine *Shch-403* and the U.S. freighter *Yaka* (6,187 tons) during a *Stuka* raid on the port of Murmansk. 17 May: attacked targets in the Kandalaksha area. 1-2 June: operating over Murmansk again, dive-bombed and sank the British freighter *Empire Starlight* (6850 tons) and damaged the Soviet submarine

Shch-404. During these two days of intense action over and around Murmansk, a Ju 87 R-4 was lost (probably to AA fire) on 1 June and 2 Ju 87 R-1s were shot down by fighters on 2 June. All 6 crew members listed as MIA, but one of the crew somehow found his way back to German lines. 14 June: 4.*Staffel* formed at Bodo by redesignating *Ergänzungsstaffel*/St.G. 5. 17 June: 2 Ju 87 Rs shot down by fighters over the front, 4 MIA. 24 June: sank the British minesweeper *Gossamer* in the Kola Inlet just north of Murmansk. 1 July: 3 Ju 87 Rs shot down by fighters and AA fire during raids around Murmansk, 4 MIA. 2 July: Ju 87 R-2 failed to return from a raid in the Murmansk area, 2 MIA. 7 July: Ju 87 R-4 shot down by a fighter in the Murmansk area during one of several raids this date on port facilities, shipyards and airfields, 2 MIA. 15 July:

LEFT AND OPPOSITE PAGE: These two colour photographs of Ju 87 Bs typify the often horrendous winter conditions in which I./St.G. 5 was called upon to operate during the Arctic winters. Not only did the crews have to battle with snow, ice and extreme temperatures, they often had only primitive equipment with which to service their aircraft. These two aircraft both have spectacularly coloured spinners.

From its formation in January 1942 until August of that year, I./St.G. 5 had an average total inventory of between 28 and 36 Ju 87 Rs. Most operations were flown in support of ground troops, in attacking Soviet airfields and against the Murmansk railway line (mainly from Alakurtti) which connected that vital port with the Russian interior. This aircraft still carries the radio call sign, KC+YV, and has temporary white upper surface camouflage applied.

Gruppe at Kirkenes. 2 August: 2.*Staffel* Ju 87 R–2 shot down by a fighter near Lake Nyornye, 1 KIA and 1 WIA. 13 August: 1.*Staffel* Ju 87 R–2 crashed into the Arctic off the coast, but the crew successfully baled out and was rescued by a German vessel. 19 August: 2.*Staffel* at Alakurtti. 27 September: 4.*Staffel* Ju 87 R–1 crashed at Bodo due to pilot error, 1 injured. 31 October: *Gruppenstab* with 1. – 3.*Staffeln* all at Kirkenes with 39 Ju 87 Rs and 4.*Staffel* detached at Bodo with 12 Ju 87 Rs. November: ordered to intensify attacks on the Murmansk railway line with most missions originating from Alakurtti under the overall command of *Nahkampfführer Alakurtti* (*Geschwaderstab*/J.G. 5), temporarily set up for this purpose. 13 November: Ju 87 R–4 shot up by a fighter while seeking targets along the Murmansk railway. 23 November: Ju 87 R–2 struck the ground during a low-level attack but returned to Alakurtti safely with moderate damage. 25 November: Ju 87 R–2 crashed at Olkajärvi due to technical problems, 1 KIA, but the pilot managed to bale out. 30 November: *Gruppenstab*, 2. and 3.*Staffeln* at Kirkenes, 1.*Staffel* at Alakurtti and 4.*Staffel* at Bodo. 1 December: *Gruppe* reported 33 Ju 87 R–2s, 9 Ju 87 R–1s and 9 Ju 87 R–4s on strength. 28 December: Ju 87 R shot down by AA fire over Kovda railway station, 1 KIA. January 1943: attacked Soviet artillery positions on the Rybachiy Peninsula and continued missions over the Murmansk rail line. 22 January: *Gruppenstab* and 1. – 3.*Staffeln* transferred to Gorodets/23 km south of Luga on the Leningrad front and reassigned to *Luftflotte* 1. At least part of the decision was based on the near-impossible winter flying conditions in the Finnish Arctic where air activity came almost to a standstill between November and March each year. But the primary reason appears to have been to support XXVI. *Armeekorps*/A.O.K. 18 which was attacked and driven back in the Schlüsselburg (Petrokrepost) area just east of Leningrad. Remained in the Leningrad area through June 1943 while 4.*Staffel* stayed back in North Norway and Finland.

Operations on the Leningrad Front and in Northern Norway and Finland (January 1943 – June 1943) 23 January: 4.*Staffel* temporarily moved from Bodo to Bardufoss/northern Norway; returned to Bodo a few weeks later. During this period the *Staffel* also at Alakurtti for a week or two to fly raids on the Murmansk railway line. 27 January: 2 Ju 87 R–2s shot down by AA and ground fire over the Leningrad front; a third shot up and damaged, *Staffelkapitän* of 2.*Staffel Major* Albert Busse WIA and 3 others KIA. 8 February: 2.*Staffel* Ju 87 R–2 shot up by AA fire north of Mga (45 km south-east of Leningrad). 9 February: 2.*Staffel* attacked targets south of Schlüsselburg/36 km east-south-east of Leningrad. 21 February: 3.*Staffel* Ju 87 R–4 shot up by AA fire over Matasovo, along the front 66 km south-south-east of Lake Ilmen. 27-28 February: meanwhile 4.*Staffel*, which had remained in North Finland, continued flying interdiction missions against the Murmansk railway line during February as the weather permitted, and on this date attacked the 29 ships of convoy JW 53, which had just arrived at Murmansk, damaging 3 of the freighters. To stage the attack, the *Staffel* undoubtedly moved forward from Bodo to Kirkenes. The *Staffel* reported no losses during February. 28 February: 3.*Staffel* Ju 87 R–4 shot down at Sekshino (Leningrad front area), 2 KIA. 10 March: 4.*Staffel* now at Alakurtti in north Finland, having transferred on or about this date from Bodo and/or Kirkenes. *Staffel* activity negligible during March due to poor flying conditions. 23 March: 1.*Staffel* Ju 87 D–3 shot down by a fighter south-west of Krasnibor (not located, but in Leningrad front area), 1 KIA and 1 WIA. April: 4.*Staffel* flew a total of 78 sorties in north Finland during April, losing only one plane. 24 April: 4.*Staffel* Ju 87 shot up and crashed near Konets along the Murmansk railway line, 1 WIA. 2 May: 4.*Staffel* Ju 87 R–4 crashed and burned near Chupa, which lies along the Murmansk railway line to the south-east of Alakurtti, 2 MIA. 16 May: 4.*Staffel* Ju 87 R–1 shot down by AA fire

Hans-Karl Stepp (RK-EL, DKG)

BORN 2 September 1914 in Giessen/Hesse, the son of a university professor, Stepp had four years of law school before his military service began and this, as much as his leadership abilities, accounts for his very rapid rise in rank. He joined the *Luftwaffe* on 6 April 1936 as a *Fahnenjunker* (candidate for a regular commission) and was assigned to II./St.G. 162 at Lübeck-Blankensee (later I./St.G. 76) in July 1936 for training. He later enrolled in cadet training at *Luftkriegsschule* Dresden. He was promoted to *Leutnant* on 1 January 1938.

When the war began in September 1939 Stepp was serving with I./St.G. 76 and was awarded the E.K. I on 15 June 1940. He transferred to *Stab*/St.G. 2 on May 1941 and was appointed *Geschwader-Adjutant*. He was awarded the *Ehrenpokal* on 9 September 1941 and the DKG on 15 October, both while serving as an *Oberleutnant* in 7./St.G. 2. He was appointed *Kapitän* of 7./St.G. 2 in January 1942 and provisional *Kommandeur* of I./St.G. 5 on 27 January 1942, and was awarded the *Ritterkreuz* on completion of 418 combat sorties on 4 February (recommended while serving as *Staka* of 7./St.G. 2). He became permanent *Kommandeur* of I./St.G. 5 on 23 June 1942. On 2 March 1943, *Hauptmann* Stepp was ordered to Rechlin on temporary duty and was appointed provisional *Kommandeur* of the *Versuchskommando für Panzer Bekampfung* (Experimental Detachment for Anti-Tank Warfare). On 18 May 1943 he was transferred to St.G. 1 and on 17 June took over command of II./St.G. 2, now with the rank of *Major*. On 1 October he was appointed *Kommodore* of St.G. 2, this unit being redesignated S.G. 2 on 18 October.

Stepp was awarded the *Eichenlaub zum Ritterkreuz* (Nr. 462) on 25 April 1944 on completion of 800 combat sorties. Promoted to *Oberstleutnant* (see photograph) on 1 May, he was transferred to various staff positions including the *Lw.Führungsstab* in Berlin in August 1944. Around December 1944 he was assigned to the staff of *Gen.d.Fl.* Ulrich Kessler, who had been appointed *Luftattaché Tokio*. Kessler had been assigned with a party to be aboard the submarine U-234, which was en route from Norway to Japan when the war ended. It was captured by the destroyer escort USS *Sutton* in the North Atlantic on 14 May 1945, but Stepp was not on board. He is believed to have had his assignment changed as Kessler's party awaited transportation to Japan and remained with the *LwFührungsstab* until the end of the war, but this has not been confirmed. Stepp was recommended for promotion to *Oberst* in April 1945. He was credited with some 900 combat missions. He worked as an attorney after the war and died on 12 December 2006 in Leipzig.

For operations in the snows of Norway and Finland, I./St.G. 5 had temporary white finish applied over their normally black green and dark green upper surfaces. This atmospheric photograph graphically illustrates the sub-zero temperatures under which the ground crews often had to toil.

During the winter of 1941/42 temperatures in Finland sank as low as -50°C which is well illustrated by this group of well wrapped-up pilots and radio operators from 1./St.G. 1 photographed at Rovaniemi. The unit had been formed from 10.(Stuka)/L.G. 1 on 27 January 1942, equipped with Ju 87 Rs.

Not long before it was renamed as the second I./St.G. 1, the first I./St.G. 5 began to receive the improved Ju 87 D model. This aircraft, L1+FU of the 1.Staffel was pictured on a Finnish airfield in an unserviceable condition.

near Mosha/90 km south-east of Alakurtti, 2 KIA. 18 May: 4.*Staffel* transferred half its aircraft from Alakurtti to Kirkenes around this date and from there flew a number of attacks on enemy artillery positions, observation posts and supply dumps on the Rybachiy Peninsula. 22 May: 2 Ju 87 D-3s from 2. and 3.*Staffeln* shot down by AA fire in the Volkhov-Dimenskaya area to the south-east of Leningrad, 2 MIA. 1 June: *Gruppe* reported 33 Ju 87 D-3s, 2 Ju 87 D-1s, 21 Ju 87 R-2s and 2 Ju 87 R-1s on strength. 1 June: 4.*Staffel* Ju 87 R-2 shot down by AA fire south-east of Lake Tishozero (not located), 2 MIA. 10 June: Ju 87 D-3 from the *Gruppenstab* shot down by AA fire over the Gulf of Finland, 2 KIA. 16 June: 4.*Staffel* Ju 87 shot down by a fighter north-west of Poyakonda/116 km south-east of Alakurtti, 2 KIA. 17 June: *Gruppenstab* and 1. - 3.*Staffeln* renamed I./St.G. 1 at Gorodets while 4.*Staffel* at Alakurtti was used as cadre for the formation of a new I./St.G. 5.

Codes: (L1+_E, U, V, W) until July 1942 then (L1+_B, H, K, L, M)

FpNs: *Gruppe*nstab and 1. - 3. (L 08798); 4. (L 41699)

Kommandeur:
Oblt. Hans-Karl Stepp (DKG, RK) (27 January 1942 - 18 May 1943)
Hptm. Horst Kaubisch (DKG, RK) (18 May 1943 - 17 June 1943)

I./St.G. 5 (Second Formation)

Formation (June 1943) Formed (new) 17 June 1943 at Bodo/northern Norway using trained crews from *Ergänzungsstaffel*/St.G. 5, fresh crews from Germany and later incorporating the former 4.*Staffel*/St.G. 5 at Alakurtti/Finland. New aircraft for the *Gruppe* were picked up at *Feldluftpark* 3/XI at Pori in northern Finland during July and August.

Operations in Northern Norway and Finland (June 1943 – October 1943) July: in formation at Bodo with 4.*Staffel* at Alakurtti in action along the Murmansk railway line with 11 Ju 87s. 1 July: aside from 4.*Staffel*, the *Gruppe* had not yet received any aircraft but did so during the month. 2 July: 4.*Staffel* Ju 87 shot down by AA fire south-west of Kovda/113 km south-east of Alakurtti along the Murmansk railway line, 1 KIA. 1 August: *Gruppe* reported 33 Ju 87 D-5s on strength. 18-20 August: formation now completed and fully equipped, I./St.G. 5 with *Gruppenstab* and 1. - 3.*Staffeln* transferred

from Pori to its assigned operational base at Nautsi, ca. 80 km south of Kirkenes. 28 August: the *Gruppe* flew its first mission, a raid by 26 *Stukas* on targets in a harbour on Muotka Fjord. 1 September: *Gruppe* at Nautsi with 36 Ju 87s. By this date 4.*Staffel* had been incorporated into the *Gruppe* and had lost its separate identity. During September, routine missions flown from Nautsi without loss, part of the ca. 1,800 sorties carried out by *Fliegerführer Nord (Ost)* over northern Finland. 1 October: Nautsi with 39 Ju 87s on strength. The Arctic weather began closing in during October and *Gruppe* combat activity was minimal. 13 October: Ju 87 D-5 crashed and burned at Nautsi, 2 KIA. 18 October: renamed I./S.G. 5.

Codes: (Q9+_B, H, K, L, M).

FpNs: I. *Stab* (L 54092); 1. (L 53109); 2. (L 55546); 3. (L 52823); 4. (L 41699)

Kommandeur:
Hptm. Martin Möbus (DKG, RK) (13 July 1943 - 18 October 1943)

Ergänzungsstaffel/St.G. 5

Formation (January 1942) Formed 27 January 1942 at Bardufoss in northern Norway by renaming *Ergänzungsstaffel* IV.(*Stuka*)/LG 1. The *Staffel* was equipped with Junkers Ju 87 dive-bombers and provided tactical training to replacement crews for St.G. 5.

North Norway and Finland (January 1942 – May 1943) 14 June: on the orders of *Luftflotte* 5, renamed 4.St./St.G. 5 and assigned to operations in northern Finland. A cadre of instructor personnel was held back and used to form a new Erg.St./St.G. 5 with fresh crews from Germany. Occasional training accidents and crashes were reported during 1942 and 1943. October: transferred from Bardufoss to Rovaniemi/north Finland during the second half of September or early October. 1 January: *Staffel* reported 7 Ju 87 R-2s, 4 Ju 87 B-2s and 1 Ju 87 B-1 on strength; these numbers remained relatively unchanged through May. 17 May: Rovaniemi - renamed 9.St./St.G. 151.

Codes: probably (L1+_F)

FpNs: (L 41699, 49011)

Staffelkapitän:
Lt./Oblt. Rudolf Neumann (1 May 1942 - 17 May 1943)

Sources for St.G. 5:

Unpublished and Archival:
BA-MA: *Flugzeug-Bereitstellungen* (Aircraft Availability
    Status Reports – FzB) in: M.Holm website.
BA-MA Freiburg: RL 2 III Gen.Qu.(6.Abt.) *Meldungen
    über Flugzeugunfälle und Verlust…* (LRs – Loss
    Reports).
PRO London: ADM 223 OIC/SI intelligence reports
    derived from ULTRA.
PRO London: AIR 40/1993.
K. Maesel - personal correspondence with H.L. deZeng;

Published:
[Anttonen – LiF] p. 17, 18;
[Anttonen – LiF2] p. 88, 89, 92, 94;
[Bergström – BC/RS-2] p. 142, 144, 172;
[Bergström – BC/RS-3] p. 92-94;

[Brütting – SA] p. 158, 235, 271;
[Carlsen – CM2] p. 338-344;
[Dierich – VdL] p. 204, 270;
[Hafsten – Hafsten] p. various;
[Kannapin – FPN] various;
[Mehner – FT] p. 54;
[Obermaier – RK2] p. 64, 65, 66, 87, 128,
    141, 150, 165, 171, 188, 247;
[Patzwall – LwR] p. various;
[Plocher – Rus42] p. 30;
[Rohwer – Chron] p. 140, 143, 148, 195;
[Scherzer – DKG] p. 614, 615;
[Smith – GA] p. 386;
[Tessin – Tes] p. 314, 369;
[Zweng – Zweng] p. various.

[Archiv #8 – A-8] p. 16.
[Holm – Website www.ww2.dk]

An external view showing the twin rearward firing MG 81 Z machine guns with the gunner seen peering through the purpose-made shaped internal armour protection. This armament was introduced in the Ju 87 D series together with the redesigned aerodynamic canopy.

A special version of the Junkers Stuka, the Ju 87 B-2/U4, was fitted with skis for landing on ice. Although this variant might have been very useful to St.G. 5 during its operations in northern Norway and Finland, it is thought that the variant was rarely, if ever, used operationally.

St.G. 51

Sturzkampfgeschwader 51

(Unit Code: 6G+)

Stab/St.G. 51

Formation (May 1939) Formed on 1 May 1939 at Schweinfurt under *Luftflotte* 3 by the redesignation of *Stab*/St.G. 165, but on or about 14 May 1939 it was redesignated as *Stab*/St.G. 77, with an effective date of 1 June 1939, by which time it was at Breslau-Schöngarten under *Luftflotte* 4.

FpN: *Stab* (L 04082)

Kommodore:
Obstlt. Günter Schwartzkopff (1 May 1939 - 14 May 1939)

I./St.G. 51

Formation (May 1939) Formed on 1 May 1939 at Kitzingen under *Luftflotte* 3 by the redesignation of I./St.G. 165, but on or about 14 May 1939 it was redesignated as I./St.G. 77, with an effective date of 1 June 1939, by which time it was at Brieg under *Luftflotte* 4. At the time it was equipped with Ju 87 A or Ju 87 B or a mixture of both.

FpN: I. (L 04206)

Kommandeur:
Hptm. Friedrich-Karl Dalwigk zu Lichtenfels (1 May 1939 - 14 May 1939)

II./St.G. 51

Formation (May 1939) Formed on 1 May 1939 at Schweinfurt under *Luftflotte* 3 by the redesignation of II./St.G. 165, but on or about 14 May 1939 it was redesignated as II./St.G. 77, with an effective date of 1 June 1939, by which time it was at Breslau-Schöngarten under *Luftflotte* 4. At the time it was equipped with Ju 87 A or Ju 87 B or a mixture of both.

FpN: II. (L 04499)

Kommandeur:
Hptm. Clemens Graf von Schönborn-Wiesentheid (1 May 1939 - 14 May 1939)

III./St.G. 51

Formation, Training (May 1939 – August 1939) Formed on 1 May 1939 at Wertheim under *Luftflotte* 3 with Ju 87 A and Ju 87 B by the redesignation of III./St.G. 165. It spent the summer of 1939 training at Wertheim. By 1 September, following mobilization orders during the last week of August, it transferred from Wertheim to Mannheim with 31 (29) Ju 87 B and 3 (3) Do 17 P and was placed under 6.*Fliegerdivision*.

Campaign in Poland and Standby in the West (September 1939 – May 1940) 8 September: transferred to Wiklow/Poland (not located) and commenced operations attached to St.G. 77, flying multiple daily missions against troop concentrations along the Vistula and against bridges and rail targets around Warsaw, Brest-Litovsk and Modlin, moving forward to Radom in the process. 8-13 September: relentlessly pounded a pocket containing 6 Polish divisions south of Radom (8-11 September) which led to the surrender of 60,000 men; attacked enemy positions west of Warsaw; took part in the reduction of the Ilza pocket and carried out operations against troop concentrations in the vicinity of Kutno. 20-30 September: on conclusion of the campaign during the last 10 days of September, the *Gruppe* returned to Wertheim to refit. The next 6 months were spent training and taking part in manoeuvres to prepare for forthcoming operations in the West.

9./St.G. 51 Emblem

A 550 lb SC 250 bomb being loaded beneath a Ju 87 B-2 of 9./St.G. 51 at the time of the invasion of France and the Low Countries in May 1940. The Gruppe carried the Geschwader code '6G' which was later transferred to II./St.G. 1. The individual letter 'J' and the ring around the spinner were painted yellow.

Members of 7./St.G. 51 are briefed on a forthcoming operation with one of the Staffel's Ju 87s, 6G+MR, in the background. The photograph may have been taken early in the campaign against France and the Low Countries.

Attack on France and the Low Countries (May 1940 – July 1940) 10 May: at Köln-Wahn with 39 Ju 87 Bs under I.*Fliegerkorps/Luftflotte* 3. Supported the advance of 6.*Armee* from the Aachen area via Maastricht - Liège - St-Trond - Namur - south of Brussels to the Lille area in north-eastern France. 14 May: in action vic Torgny, south of Virton. 17 May: 7 Ju 87 Bs shot down by Hurricanes over Valenciennes/south-east of Lille. 17 May: encountered enemy north-east of Landrecies. 18–30 May: flew daily missions in support of the advance with only an occasional loss. 31 May: attacked troop concentrations

south of Abbeville escorted by I.(J)/L.G. 2 and II./J.G. 3. 2 June: attacked ground targets on the Dunkirk beaches and evacuation shipping in the harbour. 7 June: in action vic Senarpont and Campneuseville. 11 June: a 9.*Staffel* Ju 87 B failed to return from operations around Poix (south-west of Amiens?). 12–30 June: the *Gruppe* reported no known combat losses, but there were a few accidents and crashes between Wertheim and France as replacement aircraft were brought forward and those needing repair work were flown back. The campaign ended on 22 June with the signing of an armistice between Germany and France. 1 July: now operating from Cherbourg – believed to have dive-bombed convoy *Jumbo* as it approached Plymouth, but no hits were scored. 4 July: dispatched some 33 *Stukas* for an undetected morning raid on Portland harbour, sinking the auxiliary anti-aircraft ship *Foyle Bank* (5,582 tons) and setting on fire an oil tanker in nearby Weymouth Bay. The *Gruppe* lost 1 Ju 87 B shot down by AA fire from the *Foyle Bank* plus another returned to Cherbourg shot up. 9 July: renamed II./St.G. 1.

Codes: III. (6G+_D, R, S, T); it is unknown if *Stab*, I. and II./St.G. 51 ever had the '6G' codes.

FpN: III. (L 04767, 31790)

Kommandeur:
Major Karl Christ (? – 1 July 1939)
Major Heinrich von Klitzing (1 July 1939 – 17 May 1940 KIA)
Hptm. Anton Keil (ca. June 1940 – 9 July 1940)

7./St.G. 51 Emblem

The distinctive yellow comet and black bull insignia which was carried by the Ju 87 Bs, 6G+AR, of 7./St.G. 51. Formed from 7./St.G. 165, the Staffel took part in the invasion of Poland and the attack on France and the Low Countries before it was redesignated 4./St.G. 1 on 9 July 1940.

Günter Schwartzkopff (RkHS, RK). General officer★

BORN 5 August 1898 in Forbach/Posen (now Poznan in western Poland). A veteran of the First World War, Schwartzkopff joined the *Fliegertruppe* in 1916 after being badly wounded at Verdun in 1915. He was later awarded the *Ritterkreuz des königlichen Hausordens von Höhenzollern mit Schwerter* together with a number of other First World War decorations. Between 1920 and 1933 he served in the *Reichswehr* with *Infanterie-Rgt.* 6. On 1 September 1933 he transferred to the *Luftwaffe* with the rank of *Hauptmann* and was appointed *Referent* in RLM (*Abt.Personal* – LP III) (specialist in the Aviation Ministry's personnel branch). A month later he became a *Lehrer* (instructor) with FFS Neuruppin; he was appointed *Lehrer* at FFS Celle on 1 December 1934 and *Kommandeur* on 1 April 1935. At the same time he also commanded *Fliegerhorst* Celle. He was promoted to *Major* on 1 July 1935 and became *Kdr.* of FFS C Celle-Wietzenbruch on 1 March 1936.

Schwartzkopff's first front line appointment came on 1 October 1936 when he became *Kommandeur* of I./St.G. 165 at Kitzingen, a duty which he shared with that of being airfield commander. On 1 September 1937 he was named *Kommandeur* of IV.(*Stuka*)/*Lehrgeschwader* (later *Lehrgeschwader* 1) at Barth, again sharing this duty with that of being airfield commander. He was promoted to *Oberstleutnant* (see photograph) on 1 October 1937. Some sources claim he served with the Legion Condor in Spain when his command, IV./LG. 1 at Barth sent three Ju 87 As with crews to Spain for trials but that claim is incorrect because Schwartzkopff remained at Barth. He was appointed *Kommodore* of St.G. 165 on 1 November 1938 and during the following year was involved in the setting up of *Stuka Fliegerschule* Kitzingen (later renamed *Stukaschule* 1). He became *Kommodore* of St.G. 51 on 1 May 1939 and *Kommodore* of St.G. 77 on 14 May 1940, having been promoted to *Oberst* on 1 April. He was killed in action on 14 May when his Ju 87 B-2 was shot down either by AA fire over Châtillon-sur-Bar or by RAF Hurricanes while dive-bombing targets at Le Chesne 24 km SW of Sedan. Schwartzkopff was promoted to *Generalmajor* on 28 June 1940 (RDA 1 May 1940) and was awarded the *Ritterkreuz* on 24 November 1940, both posthumously. He was considered the 'Father of the *Stuka*'.

★ Three different spellings of his name have appeared in official documents. 'Schwartzkopff' is as it appears on his tombstone, 'Schwarzkopff' appears in the records of the *Luftwaffenpersonalamt* and 'Schwartzkopf' has been found on several other official documents. An effort was made to find his birth certificate and his signature, but to no avail.

The 'Father of the Stuka', Oberst Günter Schwartzkopff, seen here in front of his Ju 87 B, became Kommodore of St.G. 51 on 1 May 1939. On the day of his appointment as Kommodore of St.G. 77 on 14 May 1940, he was killed when his Ju 87 B-2 was either shot down by anti-aircraft fire over Châtillon-sur-Bar or by RAF Hurricanes while dive-bombing targets at Le Chesne near Sedan.

Sources for St.G. 51:

Unpublished and Archival:
BA-MA Freiburg: RL 2 III Gen.Qu.(6.Abt.) *Meldungen über Flugzeugunfälle und Verlust* (LRs – Loss Reports).

Published:
[Aders – SG] p. 16, 28, 35, 36, 39, 41;
[Balke – KG2V1] p. 392, 404;
[Bateson – *Stuka*!] p. 11, 23, 27-29, 35;
[Bekker – LWD] p. 53;
[Brütting – SA] p. 153, 216, 265, 270;
[Dierich – VdL] p. 204, 205, 228;
[Griehl – KFZ] p. 121;
[Holm – Website www.ww2.dk];
[Kannapin – FPN] various;
[Mason – BovB] p. 310, 552;
[Mehner – FT] p. 54;
[Obermaier – RK2] p. 61, 87, 118, 125, 139, 180, 189;
[Patzwall – LwR] p. various;
[Prien – JG77] p. 270, 275, 308, 310;
[Ries – PhotoCol] p. 206, 216, 217;
[Shores – F] p. 17;
[Smith – SAW] p. 37, 40;
[Smith – StG77] p. 24, 38;
[Tessin – Form] p. 223;
[Tessin – Tes] p. various;
[Weal – *Stuka* 37-41] p. 18, 29, 66.

[Archiv #9 – A-9] p. 29.G. 76.

"You've forgotten your gun!" The pilot of this Ju 87 B of III./St.G. 51 hands his radio operator/gunner the rearward firing 7.9 mm MG 15 machine gun as they prepare for a mission. The unit code, 6G, was later carried by aircraft of II./St.G. 1.

A Ju 87 B of 9./St.G. 51, 6G+AT, photographed during the campaign against France with a Bf 109 in the background. After the Gruppe lost seven aircraft to Hurricanes over Valenciennes south-east of Lille on 17 May 1940, it was often escorted by Messerschmitts. For example, on 31 May it attacked troop concentrations south of Abbeville escorted by the Bf 109 Es of I.(J)/L.G. 2 and II./J.G. 3.

St.G. 76

Sturzkampfgeschwader 76
(Unit Code probably: S1+)

St.G. 76 consisted solely of I./St.G. 76. No evidence of other components has been found.

I./St.G. 76

Formation and Training (May 1939 – August 1939) Formed 1 May 1939 at Graz-Thalerhof/Austria by renaming I./St.G. 168. Equipped with Junkers Ju 87 B dive-bombers. On 15 August, while carrying out a dive-bombing and weapons demonstration at the Neuhammer training ground near Sagan in Silesia, 13 of the *Gruppe's Stukas*, including all of 2.*Staffel*, dove through heavy cloud cover and thick mist that had become trapped below the cloud layer, and crashed into the ground at high speed before a shocked array of high-ranking spectators. All 26 crew members were killed. The losses were immediately replaced and no responsibility was assigned to the *Gruppe* for this tragic mishap. The infamy of the incident put the *Gruppe* in the spotlight and it thereafter was nicknamed the *Grazer Gruppe* after its place of formation and home base.

Campaign in Poland and Standby in the West (September 1939 – May 1940) 1 September: at Nieder-Ellguth/25 km south-east of Oppeln in Silesia with 36 (28) Ju 87 Bs and 3 (3) Dornier Do 17 Ps. Assigned to *Fliegerführer z.b.V./Luftflotte* 4. Some sources give the *Gruppe's* location as Alt Siedel/20 km south-east of Oppeln, but Alt Siedel and Nieder-Ellguth may have been different names for the same airfield or they were adjacent strips separated by a mere 5 kilometres. 1-7 September: in company with St.G. 2, commenced operations with successful attacks on the Polish airfields at Krakow and Katowice, attacked enemy defences at Wielun, bombed the rail station at Piotrkow while troops were de-training and inflicted heavy losses (2 September), then struck rail targets around Radom. Moved forward to Oronsko/15 km south-west of Radom about 9-10 September. 8-13 September: relentlessly pounded a pocket containing 6 Polish divisions south of Radom (8-11 September) which led to the surrender of 60,000 men; attacked enemy positions west of Warsaw; and took part in the reduction of the Ilza pocket and carried out operations against troop concentrations in the

vicinity of Kutno. 14-20 September: moved forward to Kruszyna and then supported the ground advance towards Modlin/30 km north-west of Warsaw. 16 September: bombed bridges at Wisla south-east of Modlin. 21-26 September: struck targets in and around Warsaw, especially forts (Mokotow, Dobrowski, Czerniakow and Modlin) and related bunkers and defensive positions. By the end of the campaign on 27 September, the *Gruppe* had flown a total of 1,257 combat sorties over Poland. Returned to the Reich towards the end of September, probably to Graz-Thalerhof to refit and re-equip. October 1939 - April 1940: engaged in training and manoeuvres, probably after having moved to the Köln-Düsseldorf area where most *Stuka* units were assembled under VIII.*Fliegerkorps*.

Attack on France and the Low Countries (May 1940 – June 1940) 10-11 May: at Köln-Ostheim attached to *Geschwaderstab*/St.G. 2 with 39 (34) Ju 87 Bs. On the first two days of the attack, the *Gruppe* supported the initial breakthrough around Maastricht, hit enemy defences along the Albert Canal and assisted the subjugation of the Belgian fort at Eben-Emael by impeccably trained German glider troops on 10 May. Moved forward from Köln-Ostheim to Dockendorf to the north-west of Trier around 12 or 13 May. 12-14 May: supported the rapid advance by Reichenau's 6.*Armee* across eastern and central Belgium which was accompanied by heavy fighting around Liège and Namur, but managed to reach a north-south line along the River

A fully bombed-up Ju 87 B of I./St.G. 76 flies past the camera. This Gruppe was formed on 1 May 1939 at Graz-Thalerhof in Austria by renaming I./St.G. 168. Following operations against France and the Low Countries in May and June 1940, it was disbanded at Barly, with the main element going to form III./St.G. 77 and the lesser element establishing I./St.G. 3. Its Geschwader code, 'S1', was retained by the latter Gruppe.

Dyle between Antwerpen and Namur by 14 May. 12 May: attacked targets in the vicinity of Sedan in late morning. 12 May: Ju 87 shot down by a Hurricane over St-Trond/33 km north-west of Liège. 14 May: attacked French armour south of Sedan in late morning. 15-18 May: attacked enemy positions, troop concentrations and columns along the line of advance south of Brussels (taken 17 May by A.O.K. 6) towards the River Scheldt and Lille. Moved forward to Guise/25 km east-north-east of St-Quentin around 17 May. 19-24 May: shifted support to the 9 German *Panzer* divisions assembled in the St-Quentin - Péronne - Cambrai area which over the next several days advanced rapidly via Amiens for the Channel coast at Abbeville and then Boulogne. 25 May - 2 June: attacked British and French troops assembled in the Dunkirk bridgehead and evacuation shipping sent across the Channel to take them off the beaches and transport them to England (Operation *Dynamo*). 26 May: attacked shipping off Calais. 26-28 May: 2 Ju 87 shot down and another shot up, probably over the Dunkirk area. 28 May: in action against targets observed between Bailleul and Hazebrouck. 5 June: supported the main battle of France that began this date and drove south-west across the Rivers Somme, Aisne, Marne, Seine and on into the Loire Valley, clearing the way for A.O.K. 6 and *Panzergruppe Kleist*. 7-8 June: moved forward from Guise to Soissons/90 km north-east of Paris. 10 June: 2 Ju 87s lost in crashes at Zuss (not located, but may be Zussen near Maastricht/Belgium). 14 June: encountered enemy in the vicinity of La Chapelle, north of Romilly. 14 June: Ju 87 failed to return from operations – no details. 15-16 June: moved forward again, now from Soissons to Villenauxe/95 km east-south-east of Paris. 22 June: the campaign concluded with the signing of an armistice between Germany and France. 25-30 June: transferred to Barly/17 km west-south-west of Arras. 9 July: *Gruppe* disbanded at Barly, with the main element going to form III./St.G. 77 and the lesser element going to form I./St.G. 3.

Codes: I. (S1+_B, H, K, L)

FpNs: I. (L 07989, 33953)

I./St.G. 76 Emblem

Kommandeur:

Hptm. Walter Sigel (1 May 1939 - 9 July 1940)
Oblt. Dietrich Peltz (June 1940 - ?) – acting

Sources for St.G. 76:

Unpublished and Archival:

BA-MA Freiburg: RL 2 III Gen.Qu.(6.Abt.) *Meldungen über Flugzeugunfälle und Verlust…* (LRs – Loss Reports);
NARA WashDC: RG 242/T-971 roll 19.

Published Sources:

[Aders – SG] p. 16, 29, 36;
[Balke – KG 2V1] p. 395, 402;
[Bateson – *Stuka*!] p. 8-12, 22, 26, 29, 35;
[Bekker – LWD] p. 20, 37, 39, 41;
[Bracke – Bracke] p. 18;
[Brütting – BA] p. 68, 73;
[Brütting – SA] p. 143, 189, 192, 236;
[Dierich – VdL] p. 211, 212, 220;
[Griehl – KFZ] p. 121;
[Kannapin – FPN] various;
[Mehner – FT] p. 54;
[Nauroth – StG2] p. 52, 208;
[Obermaier – RK2] p. 42, 57, 64, 102, 164;
[Patzwall – LwR] p. various;
[Ries – Lw] p. 140;
[Ries – PhotoCol] p. 221;
[Rosch – Codes] p. 354-357;
[Scherzer – DKG] p. 318;
[Shores – F] p. 21;
[Smith – SAW] p. 17, 20;
[Smith – *Stuka*(1998)] p. 54, 55;
[Smith – StG 77] p. 31, 39, 65;
[Tessin – Form] p. 223;
[Tessin – Tes] p. 422;
[Weal – *Stuka* 37-41] p. 18, 29, 67.

[Archiv #9 – A-9] p. 30.

[Holm – Website www.ww2.dk]

At least two Ju 87s from I./St.G 76 were shot down between 26-28 May 1940 during Luftwaffe attempts to prevent British forces from evacuating Dunkirk. This aircraft carries the unit code 'S1' and the emblem of the Gruppe, a white beast with red tongue on a green shield edged in white. Shortly afterwards I./St.G. 76 was disbanded to form the basis of I./St.G. 3 and III./St.G. 77.

St.G. 77

Sturzkampfgeschwader 77
(Unit Code: S2+)

St.G. 77 Emblem

Stab/St.G. 77

Formation and Training (May 1939 – August 1939) Formed 1 (14?) May 1939 at Schweinfurt under *Luftflotte* 3 by renaming *Geschwaderstab*/St.G. 51 (previously St.G. 165. The *Kette* of 3 aircraft assigned to the *Stab* were later supplemented and upgraded to a *Stabsschwarm* and then to a *Stabsstaffel*. On 1 June 1939 the *Geschwaderstab* transferred to Breslau-Schöngarten, and then between 26 and 31 August moved forward to Neudorf/Silesia for the attack on Poland.

Polish Campaign, Training (September 1939 – April 1940) 1 September: Neudorf/Silesia under *Fliegerführer z.b.V./Luftflotte* 4 with 3 (3) Junkers Ju 87 B dive-bombers assigned to the *Stabskette*. The *Geschwaderstab* controlled assigned *Gruppen* in providing tactical ground support to German ground forces advancing across South Poland during the campaign. Besides one or more of its own *Gruppen*, III./St.G. 51 was attached on 8 September and IV.(St)/LG. 1 on 24 September. 29-30 September: returned to Breslau-Schöngarten on conclusion of the campaign. October 1939 - May 1940: the location of the *Geschwaderstab* is not known with certainty, but it is believed to have moved to Köln-Butzweilerhof in western Germany during October and remained there until May 1940. During winter 1939/40 and the following spring, the *Geschwader* trained and took part in manoeuvres.

Attack on France and the Low Countries (May 1940 – June 1940) 10 May: at Köln-Butzweilerhof under VIII.*Fliegerkorps/Luftflotte* 2 – the *Stabsstaffel* had 4 (3) Ju 87 Bs and 6 (5) Dornier Do 17 Ms on strength. The *Geschwader* attacked fortifications and positions in the Maastricht - Fort Eben-Emael area and along the Meuse south and south-east of Liège. 13 May: continued attacks on Allied positions and river crossings along the Meuse, particularly between Namur and Sedan. St.G.77 (the entire *Geschwader*) flew 200-plus sorties in just 5 hours on this date. 14 May: attacked armour south-west of Le Chesne in the late afternoon. 14 May: *Kommodore Oberst* Schwartzkopff KIA while dive-bombing targets at Le Chesne/24 km south-south-west of Sedan; his aircraft is believed to have been hit by French AA fire. 20 May:

Geschwaderstab moved forward and now at Rocroi to the north of Charleville Mézières, and still there on 27 May. 21 May: began to support encirclement operations along the Channel coast between Boulogne and Dunkirk, first hitting enemy concentrations around Arras and St-Pol. For the next 10 days, St.G. 77 bombed targets within the rapidly shrinking Dunkirk pocket as well as the shipping brought over from England to evacuate the troops trapped in the surrounded town and on the beaches. 29 May: attacked shipping in Dunkirk harbour as dusk approached. 5-18 June: together with the rest of VIII.*Fliegerkorps*, supported the drive across north-eastern France towards Paris and then south-east from Paris towards the Swiss border via Troyes and Dijon. From 19 to 22 June the *Geschwader* stood down pending further developments. 22 June: campaign in the West concluded with the signing of an armistice between France and Germany.

Air Offensive against England (Battle of Britain) (July 1940 – March 1941) July: *Geschwader* concentrated in the Caen-Cherbourg area of Normandy under VIII.*Fliegerkorps* towards the end of June and assigned to attack Channel shipping, ports and other targets along the south coast of England, with the first mission flown on 9 July when it went after a convoy (possibly a CE series convoy) off Portland. 22 July: *Stab* based at Caen. 13 August: at Caen under VIII.*Fliegerkorps/Luftflotte* 3 for the beginning of the main phase of the Battle of Britain this date – the *Stabsstaffel* had 4 (3) Ju 87 Bs and 4 (1) Do 17 Ms on strength. 18 August: in a disastrous full-*Geschwader* attack on two airfields (Thorney Island and Ford) and a radar station at Poling, St.G. 77 lost 17 *Stukas* plus 7 more damaged thus ending any meaningful further participation in the air offensive against England. Following this debacle, and the general inability of the Ju 87 to perform effectively in cross-Channel raids in the face of strong fighter opposition, the VIII.*Fliegerkorps'* *Stuka* force was effectively withdrawn from operations and held in standby for the planned invasion of England. The next 7 months were spent replacing losses and training. 7 December: alerted for Operation *Felix*, the planned attack on Gibraltar by elements of VIII.*Fliegerkorps* which was later cancelled. 13 March: Do 17 P damaged taxiing at Toussus-le-Noble airfield on the western outskirts of Paris. March 1941: ordered to

Romania towards the end of March for the attack on Yugoslavia and Greece.

Balkan Campaign (April 1941 – May 1941) 5 April: at Arad airfield in western Romania acting as *Fliegerführer Arad* under *Luftflotte* 4 for operations into Yugoslavia that began on 6 April with a devastating air attack on Belgrade – the *Stabsstaffel* had 3 (3) Ju 87 Bs and 5 (4) Bf 109 Es on strength. As *Fliegerführer Arad*, the *Stab* subordinated I./St.G. 77, III./St.G. 77, I./Z.G. 26, 4./J.G. 54, III./J.G. 54, II./J.G. 77 and III./J.G. 77 on the eve of the attack. 3 May: now at Megara/32 km west of Athens. 15 May: at Megara or Argos preparing for the airborne and air-landing assault on Crete that commenced on 20 May. 22 May: a Ju 87 belonging to the *Stabsstaffel* was lost during a mid-day attack on targets in the Suda Bay area, presumably shot down by AA fire. 2 June: Balkan campaign concluded, ordered to transfer to Sprottau/Silesia on or about this date to rest and refit before the attack on Russia.

Attack on the Soviet Union – Central Russia (June 1941 – July 1941) 19 June: transferred from Sprottau to Deblin in Central Poland and then the next day moved forward to Biala Podlaska/158 km east of Warsaw. 22 June: Biala Podlaska under II.*Fliegerkorps/Luftflotte* 2 for the invasion of the USSR beginning this date – the *Stabsstaffel* had 3 (1) Ju 87 Bs and 7 (6) Bf 110s on strength. 25 June: moved forward and now at Prusana/120 km west-north-west of Pinsk. 1 July: transferred from Prusana to northern Ukraine to support V.*Fliegerkorps/Luftflotte* 4.

Operations in South and Central Russia (July 1941 – December 1941) 11 July: 2 Ju 87 Bs from the

Stabsstaffel failed to return from operations – no details, *Hptm.* Gustav Pressler + 3 MIA, but all except for one of the men later returned to German control. 16 July: Bf 110 E-2 failed to return from operations – no details, *Oblt.* Willi Friedel + 2 KIA. 27 July: at Belaya Tserkov/75 km south-west of Kiev under V.*Fliegerkorps*. 5 August: still at Belaya Tserkov. 1 October: transferred to Konotop/210 km east-north-east of Kiev. The *Stab's* new assignment was to command ground support for 2.*Panzerarmee's* attack towards Moscow via Sevsk – Bryansk – Orel (3 October) – Mtsensk – Tula. 21 October: *Stab* at Orel. 23 October: *Geschwaderstab* and *Stabsstaffel* in transfer from Orel to Kherson-West/south Ukraine for reassignment to *Luftflotte* 4. 15 November: still at Kherson-West. ca. 30 November: from 22 June to approximately the end of November, the *Geschwader* was credited with the destruction of 234 Russian tanks, 92 batteries of artillery, 2,401 vehicles and 21 trains. December: *Stab* in the Taganrog-Stalino area supporting the advance on Rostov followed by a hasty withdrawal westward to winter positions. 11 December: *Stab* believed to be at Aleksandrovka/80 km east-south-east of Stalino.

Operations in Crimea, at Sevastopol, and in Caucasia (January 1942 – September 1942) 1 January: now at Sarabus in Crimea. With offensive activity at a relative standstill over the winter and the springtime's muddy period, there was little for the *Stab* to do until May. 17 February: transferred from Sarabus to Dnepropetrovsk-South. 1 March: *Stab* and *Stabsstaffel* reported 2 Ju 87 R-4s and 4 Bf 110s on strength. 15 April: *Geschwaderstab* and Ln.-Zug/St.G. 77 in transfer to Odessa. 22 April: Bf 110 reported missing in the Izyum area, 2 MIA. 11 May: *Geschwaderstab* arrived at Kharkov-Rogan this date from Sarabus. 17 May: St.G. 77 flew its

Three Ju 87 B-2s of St.G. 77 pictured in a cornfield at the time of the German invasion of the Soviet Union in June 1941. The Geschwader code, 'S2' is clearly visible on the rear fuselage of the aircraft nearest the camera.

20,000th combat sortie since the beginning of the war this date. 26 May: transferred from Kharkov-Rogan to Belgorod/70 km north-north-east of Kharkov. 1 June: *Stab* at Sarabus-North under VIII.*Fliegerkorps/Luftflotte* 4 and standing by to begin supporting the assault on fortress Sevastopol by 11.*Armee* and Romanian forces that began the next day. 29 June: Ju 87 D-3 shot down by AA fire near Inkerman on the eastern outskirts of Sevastopol, crew safe. 1 July: St.G. 77 reported flying 7,700 sorties against Sevastopol, which finally fell this date. 15 July: reaching another milestone, the *Geschwader* flew its 30,000th combat sortie. 20 July: transferred to Novo Lakedemonovka/30 km west of Taganrog. 22 July: Bf 110 failed to return on flight from Novocherkassk to Rostov, 1 WIA. 19 August: Bf 110 shot down by a fighter in the vicinity of Anapa/north Caucasia, 3 MIA. 27 August: *Hptm.* Werner Roell and his gunner *Ofw.* Karschewski from the *Geschwaderstab* claimed a SB-2 bomber in the Tuapse-Krasnodar area in north Caucasia. 28 August: Bf 110 E-3 bombed on the ground at Armavir/north Caucasia and damaged beyond repair. 29-31 August: ordered to Taganrog to rest and refit around this date. 29 September: Bf 110 crashed and destroyed on take-off from Belorechenskaya airstrip/77 km east-south-east of Krasnodar.

Operations in North Caucasia and West of Stalingrad (October 1942 – January 1943)

11 October: Ju 87 B-1 shot down by AA fire near Goech (not located), *Hptm.* Karl Fischer KIA + 1 WIA. 12 October: *Kommodore Major* Orthofer, apparently while sitting in the cockpit of his Ju 87 D and standing by to take off, KIA by shrapnel during a Soviet air attack on Belorechenskaya airfield. 23 October: 3 *Stabsstaffel* aircraft destroyed or damaged during a Russian air attack on Belorechenskaya: a Kl 35, a Bf 108 and a Ju 87 B-1. 11 November: still at Belorechenskaya. 19 November: the Soviets commenced a powerful counter-attack to the north and south of Stalingrad aimed at surrounding and destroying Axis forces between the River Don and the Donets Basin. Within a day or two, *Stab*/St.G. 77 was ordered from Caucasia north to Millerovo airfield/300 km west of Stalingrad. 25 November: *Lt.* Kintelmann and his gunner from the *Stabsstaffel* claimed an Il-2 *Shturmovik* ground-attack aircraft 25 km north-west of Bokovskaya/ 110 km east-north-east of Millerovo. 26 November: Bf 110 E failed to return from a sortie over the area west of Stalingrad, 3 MIA. 30 November: Bf 110 E returned to Millerovo after being shot up by AA fire. 1 December: *Stab* and *Stabsstaffel* reported 3 Ju 87 B/Rs and 7 Bf 110 D/Es on strength at Millerovo. 20-23 December: breakthroughs on the front by the Soviet 1st Guards Army threatened Millerovo and the *Stab* transferred to Kotelnikovo airfield/155 km south-west of Stalingrad. 25 December: 3 men from the *Stab* reported KIA during enemy air attack on Kotelnikovo airfield. January 1943: at Nikolayev/south Ukraine resting and refitting under IV.*Fliegerkorps*.

Operations in South and Central Russia (February 1943 – October 1943)

6 February: Bf 110 reported missing over the Bataisk area/10 km south of Rostov, 3 MIA. 19 February: *Kommodore Major* Enneccerus relieved of command for refusing to carry out orders that he deemed suicidal. 30 March: ordered to transfer to Kharkov-Voichenko. May: *Stab* now at Bobruisk/138 km

south-east of Minsk. 1 June: *Stabsstaffel* ordered to depart Russia and transfer immediately to Salonika-Sedes in north-east Greece with 12 crews for rapid training and incorporation into IV./LG. 1. A few days later the *Stabsstaffel's Feldpostnummer* was deleted from the postal directory confirming its disbanding. 1 July: at Kharkov – the *Stabskette* reported 1 Ju 87 D-1 and 2 Ju 87 D-3s on strength. During Operation *Zitadelle*, the German counter-offensive at Kursk, the *Geschwaderstab* commanded all three of its *Gruppen*. July - September: the day-to-day locations of the *Stab* following the German defeat at Kursk and the retreat westward have not been determined. 26 September: Ju 87 D-5 belonging to the *Stab* shot down by fighters over central Ukraine, 2 MIA. 18 October: renamed *Geschwaderstab*/S.G. 77 at Lvov (Lemberg) in south-east Poland.

FpNs: *Stab* (L 04082, 35172); *Stabsstaffel* (L 49031)

Kommodore:
Oberst Günter Schwartzkopff (16 May 1939 - 14 May 1940 KIA)
Obstlt. Clemens Graf von Schönborn-Wiesentheid (RK) (15 May 1940 - 20 July 1942)
Major Alfons Orthofer (RK) (25 July 1942 - 12 October 1942 KIA)
Major Walter Enneccerus (RK) (29 October 1942 - 19 February 1943) – relieved for disobeying orders.
Major Helmut Bruck (DKG, RK, EL) (20 February 1943 - 18 October 1943)

The original caption on this propaganda photograph records that this Ju 87 B-1 had its undercarriage shot away by an anti-aircraft shell. It adds that the aircraft flew 120 km in this state before making a successful belly-landing back at base. In fact is is probable that the photograph is a fake.

Walter Enneccerus (i.G.) (RK)

ENNECCERUS was born on 21 November 1911 in Trier. He joined the *Heer* (*Nachrichten*) Army (signals) on 1 April 1930, but transferred to the *Luftwaffe* on 1 January 1935, being sent to *Jagdfliegerschule* Schleissheim for training. Two months later he was made an instructor at JFS Schleissheim. On 1 April 1936, as an *Oberleutnant.*, he was assigned to I./St.G. 165 at Kitzingen following completion of training, being appointed *Staka* of 4./St.G. 165 in November. He was promoted to *Hauptmann.* on 1 January 1939 and awarded the E.K. II on 28 September 1939. Following the Polish campaign he took over command of II./St.G. 2 on 16 December 1939.

Enneccerus was awarded the E.K. I on 28 May 1940 and the *Ritterkreuz* on 21 July 1940 as a *Hauptmann*, and was promoted to *Major* (see photograph) on 25 July 1940. On 13 January 1942 he was made *Kommandeur.* of III./St.G. 3 until 1 March 1942. Twenty days later he became Ic (intelligence officer) in *Stab/Fliegerführer Afrika*. Transferred to Ob.d.L./RLM officer reserve and ordered to *Stab/Oberbefehlshaber Süd* for temporary duty on 1 May 1942. On 6 June 1942 he was appointed Ia op 1/*Luftgaukdo.* Rostow (operations officer – air in HQ Air District Rostov in south Russia). During the year he also acted as temporary *Kommodore* of St.G. 3. Appointed *Kommodore* of St.G. 77 on 29 October 1942 but relieved of duty on 19 February 1943 – reason unknown.

Enneccerus was transferred to *Frontflieger-Sammelgruppe* (operational aircrew collecting group) on 13 February 1943 and to the Qu.Abt. in *Stab/IX.Fliegerkorps* two weeks later. On 15 August 1943 he was appointed Ia of IX.*Fliegerkorps* and became an officer of the *Generalstab* d.Lw. on 1 September 1943 (although he did not attend the *Luftkriegsakademie*). Transferred to *Stab/Fliegerführer* West on 1 March 1944, and promoted to *Oberstleutnant* on 1 April 1944. Appointed Lw.-*Verbindungsoffizier* (*Luftwaffe* liaison officer) attached to commands in the *Luftflotte* 6 area on 29 July 1944. After the end of the war he served in the post-war *Bundeswehr*, retiring in 1967 as a *Brigadegeneral*. He died on 3 August 1971 in Troisdorf/20 km south-east of Köln.

I./St.G. 77

Stab/St.G. 77 Emblem

1./St.G. 77 Emblem

2./St.G. 77 Emblem

Formation (May 1939) Formed 14 May 1939 at Kitzingen by renaming I./St.G. 51. On 1 May 1939, I./St.G. 165 had been briefly renamed I./St.G. 51 on the date of the general renumbering of all (or nearly all) *Luftwaffe* air units because it was assigned to *Luftflotte* 3 at the time, and all *Luftflotte* 3 units had to carry numbers in the block 51-75. But just two weeks later *Luftflotte* 3 was ordered to hand I. and II./St.G. 51 over to *Luftflotte* 4, which used the number block 76-100. Accordingly, on 14 May I./St.G. 51 was renumbered I./St.G. 77. As a result of this reassignment, the *Gruppe* was transferred from Kitzingen (in *Luftflotte* 3's territory) to Brieg/Silesia (in *Luftflotte* 4's territory). Equipped with Junkers Ju 87 (*Stuka*) dive-bombers.

Polish Campaign and Standby in the West (September 1939 – April 1940) 26-31 August: moved forward from Brieg to Neudorf near Oppeln/Silesia for the attack on Poland. 1 September: Neudorf with 39 (34) Ju 87 Bs and 3 (3) Dornier Do 17 Ps under *Fliegerführer z.b.V./Luftflotte* 4. On the opening day of the campaign, bombed and annihilated a Polish cavalry brigade headquarters while supporting the initial assault of 10.*Armee* tank spearheads. Many of the crews flew four and five combat missions this date. 2-3 September: bombed troop concentrations around Radomsko, and possibly struck positions along the Pilica River. 6 September: dive-bombed targets in and around Warsaw. 8 September: flew continued support for armoured forces advancing towards the Vistula, moving forward from Neudorf to Czestochowa. 8-13 September: relentlessly pounded a pocket containing six Polish divisions south of Radom (8-11 September) that led to the surrender of 60,000 men; attacked enemy positions west of Warsaw; and took part in the reduction of the Ilza pocket and

carried out operations against troop concentrations in the vicinity of Kutno. 13 September: moved forward from Czestochowa and now based at Radom. 14-27 September: bombed targets in Warsaw and reduced the fortresses and bunker complexes around Warsaw, including the main fortress at Modlin, so they could be stormed by German infantry. 29-30 September: returned to Brieg on conclusion of the campaign. October: from October 1939 to April 1940 the *Gruppe* engaged in training and manoeuvres in preparation for forthcoming operations in the West. 5 December: now based at Celle near Hannover. 24 January 1940: 2.*Staffel* Ju 87 B crashed at Celle. 9 February: still at Celle, but transferred to Lippstadt by 19 February.

Attack on France and the Low Countries (May 1940 – June 1940) 10 May: at Köln-Butzweilerhof with 39 (31) Ju 87 Bs for the *Blitzkrieg* into Belgium and France under VIII.*Fliegerkorps*. On this date, flew multiple missions in the Maastricht area against Fort Eben-Emael in support of the initial advance, also attacks on Antwerpen. 11 May: moved forward from Köln-Butzweilerhof to Aachen – supported the crossing of the River Maas by 6.*Armee*. 12 May: operations in the Liège area followed by attacks on Belgian fortifications around Namur on 15 and 16 May. 14 May: attacked armour south-west of Le Chesne in the late afternoon. 14 May: 4 Ju 87 Bs lost south of Sedan, 3 of which were shot down by RAF Hurricanes. 16 May: moved forward to St-Trond/31 km north-west of Liège – began support for the drive to the Channel by armoured spearheads. One *Stuka* failed to return from operations in the Reims area this date. 19 May: advanced to Rocroi/ca. 20 km north of Charleville Mézières and remained there until at least 2 June. 22 May: bombed Merville airfield 20-25 km west of Lille and nearby British positions with one *Stuka* reported damaged. 23 May: attacked British troop

concentrations north of Arras and ships off Boulogne harbour, sinking the French destroyer *Orage* and damaging two other destroyers. 26 May 1940: 2 Ju 87 Bs failed to return from operations, but details are lacking. 27 May - 2 June: flew numerous missions against targets along the Dunkirk beaches and evacuation shipping assembled in the port and just off shore. 1 June: in action over Béthune. 2 June: began flying ground support missions to seek out and destroy French troop concentrations, positions and retreating columns south of the River Somme, and to support the crossing of the Rivers Marne, Seine and Loire by the advancing German Army, these missions continuing to the conclusion of hostilities on 22 June. 5 June: now operating from Guise-Crupilly/34 km east of St-Quentin. 9 June: transferred to Contescourt/6 km south-west of St-Quentin. 11 June: advanced to Maast/50 km west of Reims. 14 June: moved forward to Courgivaux/86 km east of Paris. 15 June: attacked French positions and strong points near Auxerre. 18 June: to Auxerre/156 km south-south-east of Paris. With combat virtually at an end, the *Gruppe* had about 8 to 10 days of respite at Auxerre and then transferred north around 25-28 June to La Ferté near Caen. There it busied itself with replenishment and training in preparation for the opening phase of the air offensive against the British Isles.

Air Offensive against England (Battle of Britain) (July 1940 – March 1941) 1 July: 3.*Staffel* removed from the *Gruppe* and redesignated 2./*Erprobungsgruppe* 210. A new 3.*Staffel* was immediately formed with fresh crews and assets. 2 July: all or elements of the *Gruppe* said to be at Flers/50 km south-west of Caen. 9 July: operating from Cherbourg-Théville, attacked a convoy off Portland damaging the 7,085-ton freighter *Empire Daffodil*, but *Kommandeur Hptm. Freiherr* von Dalwigk zu Lichtenfels was shot down by a Spitfire and killed. 21 July: from Théville, attacked a convoy off the Isle of Wight sinking two small ships. 25-30 July: bombed convoy *Bacon* in Weymouth Bay on 27 July losing a Ju 87 B shot down by fighters and then transferred to Maltot/8 km south-west of Caen towards the end of the month. August: engaged in intense training in northern France during the first half of August in preparation for the planned invasion of England (Operation *Seelöwe* or Sealion). 7 August: attacked convoy CW 9 near Dover, losing 3 a/c and 5 damaged. 13 August: at Maltot with 36 (33) Ju 87 Bs

under VIII.*Fliegerkorps* for the beginning of the main phase of the Battle of Britain. 18 August: 11 Ju 87 B-1s shot down by fighters and a further 4 damaged out of 28 dispatched during a disastrous raid on naval bases, airfields (Thorney Island and Ford) and a radar station in the Gosport-Littlehampton area. Among the dead and wounded was the *Gruppenkommandeur*, *Hptm.* Herbert Meisel. The debacle resulted in a withdrawal of the *Stuka* units from operations over southern England and their relegation to standby and training duties pending the planned invasion of England. Autumn 1940: continued training for the invasion, which was eventually postponed and later abandoned. 7 December: alerted for Operation *Felix*, the planned attack on Gibraltar by elements of VIII.*Fliegerkorps* that was later cancelled. 13 December: still based in the Caen area, probably at Maltot. January

Following a particularly disastrous raid by St.G. 77 on naval bases, airfields and a radar station on 18 August 1940, the Geschwader lost a total of 17 Ju 87s destroyed and seven damaged. This picture shows one of the Stukas that managed to limp back to the French Channel Coast where it made a belly-landing.

3./St.G. 77 Emblem

For operations in the Balkans, many Luftwaffe aircraft, such as this Ju 87 B, had their noses, rudders and patches beneath the wing tips, painted yellow. This aircraft, from the I.Gruppe Stab of St.G. 77 which was based at Arad at this time, took part in the early attacks on Yugoslav targets in the Belgrade area.

Camouflage could come in more than one form! Crews from 1./St.G. 77 smile for the camera around their Ju 87 B which carries the Staffel emblem, a pink flying pig on a yellow and white shield.

1941: temporarily based at Paris - Le Bourget, but then returned to its former base at Cherbourg-Théville. 31 March 1941: transferred from Cherbourg-Théville to Arad in north-west Romania for the attack on Yugoslavia and Greece (Operation *Marita*).

Balkan Campaign (April 1941 – May 1941) 6 April: Arad with 39 (33) Ju 87 Bs and 1 (1) Bf 110 C under *Fliegerführer Arad/Luftflotte* 4 – on the first day of the attack the *Gruppe* struck bridges and strong points in and around Belgrade, including the royal castle. 7 April: bombed troop columns around Belgrade. 14 April: hit enemy positions around Pancevo, then in the Bijeljina area of eastern Bosnia on 15 April. 19 April: transferred from Arad to Belgrade-Zemun, with elements detached at Bijeljina. A few days later, moved south to support the ground advance into central and southern Greece. 15 May: now at Argos/south Greece for the airborne and air-landing invasion of Crete on 20 May (Operation *Merkur* or Mercury). 23 May: 2.*Staffel* claimed a submarine and a minesweeper during raids on Suda Bay/Crete. Continued flying missions over and around Crete until 1 June. 2 June: Crete secured and campaign concluded, transferred from Argos to Sprottau in Silesia to rest and refit.

Attack on the Soviet Union – Central Russia. (June 1941 – July 1941) 19 June: transferred from Sprottau to Deblin in central Poland and then the next day moved forward to Biala Podlaska/158 km east of Warsaw. 21 June: at Biala Podlaska with 38 (31) Ju 87 Bs under II.*Fliegerkorps* for the opening of Operation *Barbarossa*, the massive invasion of Russia. 22-29 June: took part in the reduction of enemy fortifications along the River Bug and the stubbornly defended citadel at Brest-Litovsk using very large calibre bombs. 22 June: 1.*Staffel* Ju 87 B-1 shot down by AA fire near Brest-Litovsk, 2 KIA, and a 2.*Staffel* Ju 87 B-1 believed shot down by a fighter in the Kobryn area, *Oblt.* Karl Schmidt + 1 KIA. 28 June: non-aircrew casualties reported by the *Gruppe* at Slutsk airfield/100 km south of Minsk. 29 June: transferred to Tudora in north-east Romania to support the advance on Kiev, commencing these operations on 4 July.

Operations across Ukraine and the advance on Moscow. (July 1941 – October 1941) 6 July: moved forward to Iasi/north-east Romania. 7 July: 2 Ju 87 R-2s from 3.*Staffel* failed to return from operations – no details, *Oblt.* Franz Nehl + 1 MIA and 2 KIA. 10 July: 3.*Staffel* Ju 87 R-2 failed to return from operations – no details, 2 MIA. 17 July: advanced to Beltsy/Moldavia and from there supported the crossing of the Dniester River by A.O.K. 11 followed by pincer operations around Uman in western Ukraine. 11 August: now at Belaya Tserkov/75 km south-west of Kiev – supported the advance across the Dnieper River at Dnepropetrovsk and Kremenchug. 13 August: flew repeated attacks on bridges at Kanev to block the Soviet retreat across the Dnieper. 12-14 September: supported the closing of the German armoured pincers east of Kiev leading to the taking of some 600,000 prisoners over the following week. After the destruction of the Kiev pocket, the *Gruppe* was ordered north to the central sector of the front to support the drive on Moscow (Operation *Taifun* or Typhoon) that commenced on 2 October. 30 September: at Ponyatovka/111 km south of Smolensk. 1 October: transferred from Ponyatovka to Konotop/210 km east-north-east of Kiev. 9 October: 1.*Staffel* Ju 87 B-2 accidentally shot down by German AA fire at Minsk. 14 October: moved forward to Orel on or about this date, just a few days after the town was taken by the Germans. 21 October: from Orel flew support operations for ground forces advancing in the Bryansk area and around Vyazma. 23 October: no longer needed for the Moscow offensive, ordered to transfer from Orel to Kirovograd in Central Ukraine.

Operations in Crimea, East Ukraine, Refit in Germany and return to South Russia (November 1941 – July 1942) November - December: supported operations in Crimea, the advance on Rostov and along the Mius River. 13 November: operating from Taganrog airfield/60 km west of Rostov in close support of 1.*Panzerarmee's* advance east of the Mius, and then from 16 November south towards Rostov which was taken 20-21 November together with 10,000 prisoners. The Germans were driven from the city just 8 days later. 11 December: all of the *Gruppe's* ground personnel ordered to transfer from Mariupol/100 km west of Taganrog to Aleksandrovka/80 km east-south-east of Stalino this date. 18 December: ordered to transfer to Stalino for limited operations in the eastern Donets Basin as the winter weather allowed. 25-26 December: 2 Ju 87s from 2.*Staffel* shot down by AA fire in the Stalino area and 3 others damaged, but no casualties were reported. 13 January: transferred from Mariupol to Kharkov-Rogan. On arrival at Kharkov-Rogan the *Gruppe* began a 3-month period of rest, refit and re-equipping with new Ju 87s at Böblingen near Stuttgart while maintaining a rear echelon at Rogan. On 12 February, 3.*Staffel* rotated from Böblingen back to Kharkov and by 15 April the entire *Gruppe* was back, but now at Kharkov-Voichenko. 15 January: *Gruppenkommandeur Hptm.* Bruck claimed an I-15 biplane fighter 2 km south of Belgorod. 20 January: 2.*Staffel* Ju 87 shot down by AA fire near Kharkov, 2 MIA. 18 February: 2 ground servicing personnel from 2.*Staffel* WIA at Kharkov-Rogan. 1 March: *Gruppe* reported 13 Ju 87 B-1s, 9 Ju 87 B-2s, 1 Ju 87 R-1, 1 Ju 87 R-2 and 5 Ju 87 R-4 on strength. 7 March: Ju 87 B-2 shot up by AA fire near Kharkov. 18 April: transferred from Kharkov-Voichenko to Sarabus-South in Crimea. 7-12 May: took part in Operation *Trappenjagd*, the retaking of eastern Crimea by von Manstein's 11.*Armee*, blasting defensive positions, obstacles and anti-tank guns to open the way for the attacking infantry. 13-19 May: transferred to Kharkov-Rogan and began operations against a Soviet offensive that had broken through the lines between Kharkov and Izyum. All available air assets were rushed to this sector to support 6.*Armee* and *Armeegruppe Kleist* before the powerful Russian attack could encircle and retake Kharkov. *Stukas* and other ground-attack aircraft played a decisive role in turning back the Soviet advance and eventually plugging the breach in the lines. 20 May: the *Gruppe's* main mission this date was to destroy the bridges over the Donets River and thus cut off Russian forces west of the river. 31 May: returned to Sarabus-South. 2 June – 3 July: participated in the reduction and capture of Sevastopol with attacks on the fortress, harbour, adjacent artillery positions and Soviet relief ships off the Crimean coast. 9 July: transferred from Sarabus-South to a field airstrip 25 km south-east of Artemovsk in the Donets Basin and supported 1.*Panzerarmee* advances between Voroshilovgrad and Rovenki. 12 July: struck targets west of Rostov and rail station at Sutagan, and on 20 July hit positions ca. 12 km north-west of Rostov. 21 July: ordered to Lakedemonovka/89 km west of Rostov to support Pz.A.O.K. 1's drive on the city, which was taken on 24 July. The *Gruppe* was instrumental in enabling German troops to seize key bridges south of the city. 29 July: moved forward to Rostov and commenced tactical support for the opening phase of the drive into North Caucasia.

Operations in North Caucasia, Stalingrad Area and Donets Basin (August 1942 – February 1943)
5 August: transferred to Belaya Glina/north Caucasia and then to Kerch on the eastern tip of Crimea on 8 August. 20 August: ordered to transfer to Oblivskaya for the advance on Stalingrad, pounding defensive positions around the city. German infantry began fighting their way through the suburbs and into the city on 23 August with maximum support from *Luftflotte* 4 air units, including St.G. 77. 26 August: with the fighting still raging in and around Stalingrad, the *Gruppe* was relieved from operations – a *Staffel* at a time – and ordered to Breslau in Silesia for some 2 weeks of rest, refit and re-equipping. 29 August: 3.*Staffel* Ju 87 shot down by AA fire at Proletarskoye, 2 MIA. September: in addition to direct support missions for German troops fighting in and around Stalingrad, many missions were aimed at disrupting the constant flow of tiny to medium-size vessels crossing the Volga to feed replacements and supplies into the city. These boats, barges, ferries, etc. were bombed and strafed from first light to dusk nearly every day. 7 September: minor accidents at Oblivskaya, and the same for 16 and 19 September. 20 September: reported 35 (20) Ju 87s on strength. 26 September: 3.*Staffel* Ju 87 D shot down by AA fire near Kotluban/35 km north-west of Stalingrad, 2 MIA. 8 October: *Staffel* in Germany transferred from Breslau to Belorechenskaya/77 km east-south-east of Krasnodar in north Caucasia and

assigned to attack harbour installations and shipping at Tuapse and to provide tactical support for the ground fighting. 15 October: 3.*Staffel* operating from Karpovka/40 km west of Stalingrad. 6 November: Ju 87 D-1 shot down by a fighter at Fiagdon/104 km west-south-west of Grozny in North Caucasia, 1 MIA. 7 November: Ju 87 D-1 shot down by AA fire near Nogir/88 km west-south-west of Grozny, *Oblt.* Günter Hitz + 1 WIA. 19 November: a powerful Russian counter-attack to the north and south of Stalingrad rapidly tears open the front and encircles 6.*Armee* and many other German and Romanian forces deployed at and behind the front. 30 November: 1.*Staffel* Ju 87 D shot up and severely damaged by ground fire south-west of Stalingrad. December: covered the retreat westward from Stalingrad and also supported several weak counter-attacks that attempted to break through the encirclement. These missions continued during January. 1 December: *Gruppe* reported 25 Ju 87 D-1/D-3s on strength. 27 December: *Gruppe* reported a few ground personnel casualties near Kotelnikovo/155 km south-west of Stalingrad. 6 January 1943: transferred to Gigant/13 km west-north-west of Salsk in north Caucasia and attacked targets south of Stavropol. 13 January: Ju 87 D-3 shot down by fighters over Dubinski (not located), *Oblt.* Theodor Weber + 1 MIA. 14-19 January: attacked Russian forces advancing in the Manych River area near Salsk/162 km south-east of Rostov. 20 January: ordered to Rostov-North on or about this date – flew ceaseless attacks on Soviet tank spearheads advancing into the Donets Basin following the Russian counter-offensive at Stalingrad. 27 January: Ju 87 shot down by AA fire at Svoboda, 1 MIA. 1-8 February: operated from Rovenki and Stalino. 9-22 February: now at Kuteinikovo/125 km north-west of Rostov. 5 February: 2.*Staffel* Ju 87 D shot down by AA fire near Kazachiy (not located), *Oblt.* Kurt Rick + 1 KIA. 11 February: attacked tanks 50 km north-west of Stalino. 19 February: struck targets a few kilometres east of Taganrog where the front was stabilizing.

Retaking of Kharkov, Rest and Refit, and Attack on the Kursk Salient (February 1943 – July 1943)
22 February: transferred to Dnepropetrovsk-South and began attacks on Russian armoured spearheads around Pavlograd and then supported the advance on and retaking of Kharkov to 15 March. 9 March: 2.*Staffel* Ju 87 shot down by AA fire over Kharkov, 2 KIA. 16 March: moved from Dnepropetrovsk-South to Kharkov-Rogan to support the recapture of Belgorod, which lies to the north of Kharkov. On 18 March, 2.*Staffel* was at Poltava/130 km south-west of Kharkov. 30 March: ordered back to Nikolayev in south-central Ukraine to rest and refit during the April thaw. May: all or elements now at Bobruisk on the central sector of the front, but moved forward about 10 May. From 12 May, the *Gruppe* joined 1.*Fliegerdivision* attacks on railway and train station targets in the Kursk – Yelets – Voronezh triangle where a build-up of enemy forces had been noted. 14 May: 3.*Staffel* Ju 87 D-3 shot down by fighters at Shakhovka/55 km east of Roslavl, 2 MIA. 9 June: at Kharkov-North – 2.*Staffel* Ju 87 D-3 failed to return from operations in Kharkov area, 2 MIA. 1 July: *Gruppe* reported 35 Ju 87 D-3s and 5 Ju 87 D-1s on strength. 5-15 July: operating from Bogodukhov/55 km north-west of Kharkov, took part in the massive

German counter-offensive on the Kursk salient (Operation *Zitadelle*). 6 July: 2 Ju 87 D-3s shot down by fighters and AA fire over the Kursk salient and 2 others shot up and damaged, 2 KIA. 7 July: 2.*Staffel* claimed an Il-2 *Shturmovik* over the railway station at Churayevo/24 km south-east of Belgorod. 8 July: 3.*Staffel* Ju 87 D-3 shot down by fighters over the Kursk salient and another damaged, 1 KIA and 1 WIA. 9 July: 2.*Staffel* Ju 87 D-3 blew up in mid-air over the Kursk salient, 2 KIA.

Operation in the Donets Basin, around Kharkov and in Central Ukraine (July 1943 – October 1943)

17-20 July: *Gruppe* transferred south to Barvenkovo/130 km south-south-east of Kharkov to operate in the Donets Basin area and around Taganrog against Soviet forces pushing west across the Mius towards Stalino, and then moved back to the vicinity of Kharkov. These back and forth assignments continued to the end of August as the rejuvenated Red Army began pushing the Axis forces back along the entire front from Velikiye Luki to the Sea of Azov. During this period, many of the *Gruppe's* crews were flying 100 combat sorties a month. Tactical transfers were frequent: missions were flown from Barvenkovo (17 to ca. 25 July) and Tolokonoye/46 km north of Kharkov (end of July to ca. 5 August), Kharkov-Rogan (6-10 August), Poltava (12-29 August). 1-3 August: 2 Ju 87s were shot down by fighters and AA fire and 1.*Staffel* reported shooting down a LaGG-3 fighter near Tomarovka/26 km west-north-west of Belgorod on 3 August. Combat losses were also reported on 4 August near

Stalino and 19 August over the outskirts of Kharkov. 21 August: 3 Ju 87 D-3s from 3.*Staffel* shot down by fighters in the Romny-Sumy area to the north-west of Kharkov, 2 KIA and 1 WIA. 30 August: Ju 87 D-3 shot down by fighters in the Stalino area, 1 WIA. 30 August: transferred to a field strip (Krima) 94 km south-west of Kharkov and remained there to 11 September when it moved to Poltava, about 62 km further west. 16 September: transferred from Poltava to Vasilkov/35 km south of Kiev – from there flew daily attacks on Soviet spearheads east of the Dnieper. 24 September: *Hptm.* Heinz Schumann from 3.*Staffel* shot down a Yak-9 over the Dnieper north-east of Belaya Tserkov. 25 September: *Hptm.* Gehrmann from 3.*Staffel* claimed an Il-2 over the Dnieper north-east of Belaya Tserkov. 25 September: 1.*Staffel* Ju 87 D-3 shot down by AA fire over the Dnieper area south-east of Kiev, 2 KIA. 30 September: transferred from Vasilkov to Beresovka/100 km north-north-east of Nikolayev to attack Soviet attempts to cross the Dnieper. 3 October: Ju 87 D-5 shot down by AA fire at Pavlovka. 6 October: *Hptm.* Gehrmann from 3.*Staffel* reported downing 2 La-5 fighters over Gornostaypol/70 km north of Kiev. 12 October: returned to Vasilkov. 13 October: 1.*Staffel* Ju 87 D-5 shot down by AA fire over north-central Ukraine, 1 WIA. 14 October: 2 Ju 87 D-5s from 3.*Staffel* shot down by AA fire while attacking bridges along the Dnieper south-east of Kiev, *Hptm.* Wolfgang Kurth KIA and 2 MIA. 16 October: Ordered to Lvov this date, but the move was not carried out until a few days later. 18 October: renamed I./S.G. 77 at Vasilkov airfield near Kiev.

A Stuka pilot from the Stab of I./St.G. 77 is assisted into the cockpit of his Ju 87 B. The emblem of the unit, a black wolf's head with red tongue and white teeth, is plainly visible above the wing.

FpNs: *Gruppenstab* I. (L 04206, 35747); 1. (L 46264, 37997); 2. (L 47314, 38522); 3. (L 08758)

Kommandeur:

Hptm. Friedrich-Karl von Dalwigk zu Lichtenfels
   (1 May 1939 - 9 July 1940 KIA)

Hptm. Herbert Meisel (10 July 1940 - 18 August 1940 KIA)

Hptm. Helmut Bruck (DKG, RK) (28 August 1940 -
   19 February 1943)

Hptm. Werner Roell (DKG, RK) (20 February 1943 -
   18 October 1943) ★

★This is contradicted on p. 270 of *Das Waren die deutschen Stuka-Asse 1939-1945* by Brütting which states: *Major* Karl Henze (20 February 1943 - 18 October 1943)

II./St.G. 77

Formation (May 1939) Formed 1 May 1939 at Schweinfurt by renaming II./St.G. 51. On 1 May 1939, II./St.G. 165 had been briefly renamed II./St.G. 51 on the date of the general renumbering of all (or nearly all) *Luftwaffe* air units because it was assigned to *Luftflotte* 3 at the time, and all *Luftflotte* 3 units had to carry numbers in the block 51-75. But just two weeks later, *Luftflotte* 3 was ordered to hand I. and II./St.G. 51 over to *Luftflotte* 4, which used the number block 76-100. Accordingly, on 14 May II./St.G. 51 was renumbered II./St.G. 77. As a result of this reassignment, the *Gruppe* was transferred from Schweinfurt (in *Luftflotte* 3's territory) to Breslau-Schöngarten/Silesia (in *Luftflotte* 4's territory). Equipped with Junkers Ju 87 (*Stuka*) dive-bombers.

Polish Campaign and Standby in the West (September 1939 – April 1940) 26-31 August: moved forward from Breslau-Schöngarten to Neudorf near Oppeln/Silesia for the attack on Poland. 1 September: Neudorf with 39 (38) Ju 87 Bs and 3 (3) Dornier Do 17 Ps *Fliegerführer z.b.V./Luftflotte* 4. On the opening day of the campaign, and together with I./St.G. 77, bombed and annihilated a Polish cavalry brigade headquarters at Wielun while supporting the initial assault of 10.*Armee Panzer* spearheads. Many of the crews flew 4 and 5 combat missions this date. 8 September: flew continued support for armoured forces advancing towards the Vistula, moving forward from Neudorf to Kruszyna. 8-13 September: relentlessly pounded a pocket containing 6 Polish divisions south of Radom (8-11 September) which led to the surrender of 60,000 men; attacked enemy positions west of Warsaw; took part in the reduction of the Ilza pocket and carried out operations against troop concentrations in the vicinity of Kutno. 14-27 September: bombed targets in Warsaw and reduced the fortress at Modlin. 29-30 September: returned to Breslau-Schöngarten on conclusion of the campaign and then a week or two later reassigned to the *Luftflotte* 2 area in western Germany. October: from October 1939 to April 1940, the *Gruppe* engaged in training and manoeuvres in preparation for forthcoming operations in the West. April: based at Schweinfurt.

Stab II./St.G. 77 Emblem

St.G. 77 was perhaps the only Luftwaffe unit to adopt a standard basic emblem. This was a shield with a yellow base and a coloured, serrated, top. The top was white for the first Gruppe, red for the second, pale blue for the third and dark blue for the fourth. Each staff flight and Staffel incorporated a different symbol. This aircraft may have belonged to the II.Gruppe Stab which featured a black heraldic lion.

This close-up of the cockpit area of a Ju 87 B of Gruppe Stab of II./St.G. 77 shows the unit emblem painted in yellow with a red top and a black rampant lion. To the left of the emblem is the red oil filler point triangle with, to the right, the yellow 87 octane fuel filler point triangle.

4./St.G. 77 Emblem

5./St.G. 77 Emblem (early)

Attack on France and the Low Countries (May 1940 – June 1940) 10 May: at Köln-Butzweilerhof with 39 (30) Ju 87 Bs under VIII.*Fliegerkorps* for the *Blitzkrieg* into Belgium and France. On this date it flew multiple missions in the Maastricht area against Fort Eben-Emael in support of the glider-borne air-landing operations that were used to capture the fortress, which was key to opening the way for the initial advance into Belgium. 11 May: supported the crossing of the River Maas by 6.*Armee*. 13 May: struck French artillery and AA positions along the River Meuse allowing German forces to cross the river at Sedan; also reported the loss of 2 *Stukas* shot down by AA fire in the vicinity of Tirlemont/41 km east of Brussels. 21 May: attacked roads near Montreuil. 22 May: attacked roads east of St-Omer. 22 May: 4 Ju 87s lost in action, including at least one of which went down in the Rocroi area/ca. 20 km north of Charleville Mézières. 25 May: 1 Ju 87 failed to return from operations and another was reported damaged in action. 27 May - 2 June: flew numerous missions against targets along the Dunkirk beaches and evacuation shipping assembled in the port and just off shore. 29 May: attacked shipping in Dunkirk harbour during the late evening just before dusk. 1 June: attacked shipping off Dunkirk. 2 June: began flying ground support missions for the pursuit and destruction of French troop concentrations, positions and retreating columns south of the River Somme, and the crossing of the Rivers Marne, Seine and Loire by the advancing German Army to the conclusion of hostilities on 22 June. As the *Gruppe* advanced into north-central France, it made a number of base changes but these are not known. It is believed that they closely paralleled those of I./St.G. 77 and may in fact have been identical for the most part. 13 June: attacked Esternay railway station. 18 June: to the Auxerre area/156 km south-south-east of Paris. With combat virtually at an end, the *Gruppe* had about 8 to 10 days of respite and then transferred north around 25-28 June to the Caen area in Normandy. There it busied itself with replenishment and training in preparation for the opening phase of the air offensive against the British Isles.

Air Offensive against England (Battle of Britain) (July 1940 - March 1941) 3 July: Ju 87 damaged landing at Picauville field strip/33 km south-south-east of Cherbourg in the Cotentin Peninsula in Normandy. The *Gruppe's* activities are unclear for the next 5 weeks, but it probably refitted and participated in at least some of the July attacks on Channel convoys. 8 August: attacked Convoy CW 9 (*Peewit* convoy) off the Isle of Wight sharing in the sinking of 3 ships and the damaging of a number of others. The *Gruppe* lost 3 Ju 87 Bs shot down by fighters and 4 more damaged during the raid. Among the casualties, *Gruppenkommandeur Hptm*. Plewig was shot down by a Hurricane and taken prisoner. 13 August: at Caen with 37 (25) Ju 87 Bs under VIII.*Fliegerkorps*/*Luftflotte* 3 for the beginning of the main phase of the Battle of Britain. 18 August: during a disastrous raid on naval bases, airfields (Thorney Island and Ford) and a radar station in the Gosport–Littlehampton area by the entire *Geschwader*, the *Gruppe* lost 3 Ju 87 B-1s to RAF fighters out of the 28 it dispatched on the mission. The heavy losses for all three *Gruppen* of St.G. 77 resulted in a withdrawal of VIII.*Fliegerkorps'* *Stuka* units from operations over southern England and their relegation to standby and training duties pending the planned invasion of England. Autumn 1940: continued training for the invasion of England (Operation *Seelöwe* or Sealion), which was eventually postponed and later abandoned. 7 December: alerted for Operation *Felix*, the planned attack on Gibraltar by elements of VIII.*Fliegerkorps* that was later cancelled. 9 March: Ju 87 B-1 crashed on landing at Toussus-le-Noble airfield on the western outskirts of Paris, *Oblt*. Herbert Papst injured. 31 March: transferred from Caen to Graz-Thalerhof in Austria for the attack on Yugoslavia and Greece (Operation *Marita*).

Balkan Campaign (April 1941 – May 1941) 5 April: Graz-Thalerhof with 39 (34) Ju 87 Bs; assigned to *Geschwaderstab*/St.G. 3 (acting as *Fliegerführer Graz*)/*Luftflotte* 4 for the initial attack into Yugoslavia. 6 April: struck airfields in the Zagreb area, losing 4 *Stukas* during the first day of the invasion. The *Gruppe* was credited with destroying numerous Royal Yugoslav Air Force planes on the ground. 11 April: bombed Yugoslav airfields at Banja Luka, Bihac and Prijedor. 14 April: based at Zagreb. 15 May: now at Argos/south Greece preparing for the airborne and air-landing assault on Crete that commenced on 20 May. The specific activities of the *Gruppe* during the invasion are not known, but presumably it operated with the rest of St.G. 77 and attacked shipping in the waters around the island, struck ports and bombed selected ground targets in support of the German paratroops and air-landing infantry fighting to take Crete. 2 June 1941: Crete secured and campaign concluded, transferred from Argos to Sprottau in Silesia to rest and refit.

Attack on the Soviet Union – Central Russia (June 1941 – July 1941) 19 June: transferred from Sprottau to Deblin in Central Poland and then the next day moved forward to Woskrzenice Male/10 km east of Biala Podlaska in eastern Poland. 22 June: at Woskrzenice Male with 39 (27) Ju 87 Bs and 1 (1) Bf 110 under II.*Fliegerkorps*/*Luftflotte* 2 for the opening of Operation *Barbarossa*, the massive invasion of Russia. 22-29 June: took part in the reduction of enemy fortifications along the River Bug and the stubbornly defended citadel at Brest-Litovsk. 25 June 1941: operating from Prusana

Ground crews use a special truck to raise a bomb into position beneath a Ju 87 B of 5./St.G. 77. The yellow cowling would seem to indicate that the photograph was taken during operations in the Balkans during the spring of 1941. The badge of the Staffel, a black leopard on a yellow shield topped in red, was painted beneath the cockpit.

5./St.G. 77 Emblem

airfield/120 km west-north-west of Pinsk. 30 June – 12 July: provided tactical support to Guderian's *Panzergruppe* 2 and von Kluge's 4.*Armee* as they advanced rapidly past Minsk towards Borisov, Bobruisk, Mogilev and Smolensk. 6 July: attacked targets around Mogilev/205 km east of Minsk. 12-14 July: departed the central sector of the front and transferred to Iasi in Moldavia and Kishinev in Bessarabia to join the rest of the *Geschwader* in supporting the advance on Kiev, which had commenced on 4 July.

Operations across Ukraine, the Advance on Moscow, Refit in Poland (July 1941 – January 1942)
20 July: at Belaya Tserkov/75 km south-west of Kiev under V.*Fliegerkorps* in support of XIV.*Armeekorps* and 9.*Panzerdivision* advancing east and north-east of Belaya Tserkov. 22 July - 8 August: supported the surrounding of Russian forces in what became known as the Uman Pocket and resulted in the taking of some 103,000 prisoners and the capture of 317 tanks and 858 guns. August: supported the advance across the Dnieper at Dnepropetrovsk (taken 17 August) and Kremenchug. 23 August: transferred from Belaya Tserkov to Signayevka/84 km north-west of Kirovograd. 26 August: transferred to Schastivaya/30 km east of Vinnitsa. 18 September: Ju 87 B-1 shot up by AA fire near Poltava and rendered un-repairable 1 WIA. *Gruppe* was supporting the advance east of Kiev towards Kharkov. 21 September: attacked and sank the Soviet destroyer *Frunze*, the gunboat *Krasnaya Armeniya* and the tug *OP-8* off the Tendra Peninsula/63 km east of Odessa, these being elements of a much larger flotilla of vessels bringing reinforcements to Odessa. The next day, the *Gruppe* returned and severely damaged the destroyer *Besposhchadny* and damaged the destroyer *Bezuprechny*, the former having to be towed into Odessa harbour stern first by a tug. 28 September: now at Chernigov/130 km north-north-east of Kiev. 28-30 September: after

supporting the closing of the German armoured pincers east of Kiev on 12 September that led to the taking of some 600,000 prisoners, the *Gruppe* was ordered north to the central sector of the front to support the drive on Moscow (Operation *Taifun*) which commenced on 2 October. 3 October: 6.*Staffel* Ju 87 B shot up by a fighter and crashed on return to Seshchinskaya/40 km south-east of Roslavl, 2 KIA. 8 October: 4.*Staffel* Ju 87 B-1s operating from Vyazma airfield. 13 October: 5.*Staffel* Ju 87 B-1s operating from Orel. 17-19 October: 6 Ju 87 Bs returned to Orel shot up, 1 being written off and the other 5 damaged but repairable, no casualties. 21 October: operating from Orel in support of the drive on Moscow and the heavy fighting that developed as German ground forces drew closer to the city. The *Gruppe* announced that from 22 June to 21 October it had destroyed a total of 10 Russian warships, 27 other vessels, 140 tanks, 45 anti-aircraft batteries and 43 artillery positions. 25 October 1941: still at Orel, but ordered to Orsha a week or two later due to the need to refit and the worsening flying conditions along the front as winter closed in. 14-24 November: transferred from Orsha to Krakow in south Poland to rest and refit.

During the early part of the invasion of the Soviet Union II./St.G. 77 was heavily engaged, assisting German troops to surround Russian forces in what became known as the Uman Pocket. This resulted in the taking of some 103,000 prisoners and the capture of 317 tanks and 858 guns. This Ju 87 B of the 6.Staffel has its individual letter repeated on the outside of its wheel spats in yellow.

6./St.G. 77 Emblem

The second S2+AP crewed by the Staffelkapitän of 6./St.G 77, Hptm. Herbert Pabst and his radio operator, Fw. Woletz, was named 'Anton der Zweite' (Anton the Second) to reflect this fact. These photographs show the Ju 87 B-1 taxiing out for a sortie against Soviet targets probably in the late summer of 1941. The aircraft carries the leaping bull emblem of the Staffel.

A Ju 87 B-1 of 6./St.G. 77 taxies out for another mission against Soviet troops during the summer of 1941. This aircraft, S2+AP, was piloted by the Staffelkapitän, Hptm. Herbert Pabst, with Fw. Woletz in the radio operator's seat. Forward of the emblem of the 6.Staffel is the inscription 'Anton der Zweite' (Anton the second) in white. 'Anton' was 'A' in the German phonetic alphabet.

Operations in Crimea, Eastern Ukraine and Refit (January 1942 – September 1942) 6 January 1942: refit completed, ordered to move from Krakow to Kherson in south Ukraine. 13 January: allotted Stalino as its winter airfield and transferred there from Kherson between 2-11 February. Flew limited operations over the eastern Donets sector. 1 March: *Gruppe* reported 18 Ju 87 B-1s, 6 Ju 87 R-2s and 2 Ju 87 R-1s on strength. Same date, a Ju 87 was destroyed during a Russian air raid on Stalino. 2 March: 2 Ju 87 B-1s from 6.*Staffel* failed to return from operations in the Golubovka area, *Staffelkapitän Oblt.* Hermann Ruppert + 3 KIA. 25 March: temporarily at Kharkov due to a Russian attack on Stalino that developed into house-to-house fighting in the suburbs of the city. 5 April: now back at Stalino. 7-12 May: operating from Itschki-Grammatikovo (ca. 73 km north-east of Sarabus in Crimea), took part in Operation *Trappenjagd*, the retaking of eastern Crimea by von Manstein's 11.*Armee*, blasting defensive positions, obstacles and anti-tank guns to open the way for the attacking infantry. 8 May: 6.*Staffel* Ju 87 B-1 shot down by AA fire over the Isthmus of Parpach in eastern Crimea, 2 KIA; a second B-1 from 4.*Staffel* was shot up in the same location. 12-19 May: although it is not known with certainty, the *Gruppe* probably transferred to Kharkov-Rogan with I./St.G. 77 and began operations against a Soviet offensive that had broken through the lines between Kharkov and Izyum. 20 May: Ju 87 B-1 shot down by AA fire in the vicinity of Maksimovka/66 km west-north-west of Izyum, 2 KIA; 2 other Ju 87s were shot up and damaged in the same area. The *Gruppe's* main mission this date was to destroy the bridges over the Donets River and thus cut off Russian forces west of the river. 1 June: returned to

Crimea and now based at Sarabus from where the *Gruppe* participated in the reduction and capture of Sevastopol with attacks on the fortress, harbour, artillery positions and Soviet relief ships off the Crimean coast. The siege and capture of Sevastopol began on 2 June and ended around 3 July. 2 June: 5.*Staffel* Ju 87 B-1 shot down by AA fire over Sevastopol, *Oblt.* Wenzel Fink + 1 MIA. The *Stukas* flew maximum effort attacks on Sevastopol's heavily reinforced battery encasements and bunker complexes causing great wear and tear on both the aircraft and crews. July: on conclusion of the Sevastopol operation, ordered from Sarabus north (to Kharkov?) to support the advance to the River Don south of Voronezh in the A.O.K. 6 sector (Operation *Blau* – the German summer offensive towards Stalingrad and into north Caucasia). 16-19 July: 2 Ju 87 D-1s shot down in the vicinity of Voronezh, 2 KIA. 20 July: Ju 87 D-1 and D-3 both shot down by AA fire at Podgornoye near Rossosh along the Don, 4 MIA. 22 July: ordered to Lakedemonovka/89 km west of Rostov, but transferred to Bykovo/22 km north of Stary Oskol? These conflicting orders were evidently cancelled. August: with just 12 aircraft on strength, moved to Taganrog/60 km west of Rostov for a short rest and refit, but mainly to re-equip. According to the loss reports and monthly aircraft inventory reports for August and September, only a single Ju 87 was lost to enemy action and one to non-combat causes during this entire two month period, a *de facto* indication that the *Gruppe* had either been withdrawn from operations or was the beneficiary of some extremely good fortune. Thirty-two Ju 87 Ds were received over the course of September, probably while at Taganrog.

All hands to the pumps as the ground crew try to manoeuvre this Ju 87 B-2 out of an area of soft ground into which it had sunk. The machine carries the emblem of 5./St.G. 77, a black leopard on a yellow shield with a red top, painted forward of the cowling. Each component of St.G. 77 had a similar shield, with the coloured topping changing for each Gruppe: the first had a white top, the second, red, the third pale blue and the fourth, dark blue.

Operations in North Caucasia, Stalingrad Area and Donets Basin (October 1942 – February 1943)
3 October: again operational, several crashes and accidents occurred on arrival at Belorechenskaya/77 km east-south-east of Krasnodar in North Caucasia. Shortly after arriving, the *Gruppe* moved farther south to Soldatskaya airfield. North Caucasia had been taken by the Germans during August and September, and the front there had largely stabilized by early October. The *Gruppe* was assigned to support Pz. A.O.K. 1 and A.O.K. 17 as these two armies attempted to consolidate the German gains in North Caucasia against increasing Soviet opposition. 4 October: 5.*Staffel* Ju 87 D crashed at Soldatskaya and a second Ju 87 D shot down by AA fire near Tuapse on the Black Sea coast. Tuapse was a vital and heavily defended port. 20 October: at Soldatskaya – 4.*Staffel* Ju 87 D shot down by AA fire over Tuapse, *Hptm.* Walter Sanheck + 1 MIA. 10 November: now back at Belorechenskaya. 11 November: 6.*Staffel* Ju 87 D shot down by AA fire north-east of Tuapse, crew safe. 25 November: 4.*Staffel* Ju 87 D shot up and damaged by AA fire over Tuapse. 30 November: 5.*Staffel* Ju 87 D shot up by AA fire during a raid in the Tuapse area. 1 December: *Gruppe* reported 25 Ju 87 D-1/D-3s on strength. During December the *Gruppe* moved north to the Kotelnikovo-Salsk area to support the desperate defensive fighting south-west of Stalingrad following the powerful Russian counter-offensive to free the city that began on 19 November. 16-19 December: 1 Ju 87 D shot down and another damaged over the front south-west of Stalingrad. 28 December: ordered to transfer from Kotelnikovo/155 km south-west of Stalingrad to Konstantinovka in the Donets Basin as the Russians pushed rapidly west from Stalingrad. 29-30 December: 5 Ju 87 Ds blown up and burned by the *Gruppe* at Kotelnikovo to prevent them from falling into the hands of the enemy. 3 January 1943: 2 Ju 87 Ds from 4.*Staffel* failed to return from operations in the Salsk area to the south-east of Rostov, 4 MIA. 4 January: 5.*Staffel* Ju 87 D failed to return from operations in the Znamenka area, *Staffelkapitän Oblt.* Maus + 1 KIA. January 43: resting, refitting and re-equipping at Nikolayev/south Ukraine.

Operations Over Eastern Ukraine, the Taman Peninsula and Around Kharkov (February 1943 – July 1943) February - March: based mainly at Dnepropetrovsk-South – participated in the halting and destruction of a powerful Russian tank advance in the Pavlograd-Kramatorsk area before it could reach its objective at Zaporozhye (18-24 February); supported the recapture of Kharkov and Belgorod by Pz. A.O.K. 4 and the SS-Pz.Korps, destroying many retreating enemy troop and vehicle columns (early March). 27 March: 5.*Staffel* Ju 87 failed to return from operations at Bataisk just south of Rostov, 2 MIA. 30 March 1943: ordered to transfer from Dnepropetrovsk-South to Kharkov-Voichenko. April: at Kerch in eastern Crimea – the *Stuka* force at Kerch and surrounding airfields attacked Soviet positions in the Taman Peninsula in north Caucasia where the retreating German ground forces had set up defensive positions. 12-27 April: 4 Ju 87s shot up and damaged during operations over the Taman Peninsula. 30 April: 5.*Staffel* Ju 87 D-3 shot down by AA fire over Zaliman/east Ukraine, 2 KIA. 1-15 May: ordered to transfer from Kerch to Kharkov to operate against railway lines, train stations, supply columns, suspected fuel and

munitions dumps in the Kursk salient north and east of Belgorod where a huge build-up of Soviet forces had been observed. 19-21 May: 2 Ju 87 D-3s from 4.*Staffel* shot down by AA fire in the Chuguyev sector to the east of Kharkov, 2 MIA. 29 May: 4.*Staffel* Ju 87 D-3 shot down by a fighter in the Belgorod area north of Kharkov, crew safe. On the same date, and possibly the same mission, a crew from 5.*Staffel* reported shooting down a MiG-3 fighter to the north-north-west of Belgorod. 1 June: 5.*Staffel* Ju 87 D-3 shot down by AA fire to the south of Kharkov, 1 KIA and 1 WIA. 2 June: 2 Ju 87 D-3s from 6.*Staffel* shot down by fighters in the Belgorod area, 4 MIA; 2 other *Stukas* that had been shot up in the same melee were able to safely return to Kharkov-Voichenko. 8 June: 4.*Staffel* Ju 87 D-3 failed to return from operations over the Bulatelovka area (not located) and believed to have been shot down by AA fire, 2 MIA. 15 June: 6.*Staffel* Ju 87 D-3 shot down by AA fire in the vicinity of Belgorod, 2 KIA. 23 June: 5.*Staffel* Ju 87 D-3 shot down by fighters south-east of Kharkov, 1 WIA, and another from 6.*Staffel* crashed and burned south-east of Kursk, 2 KIA. 1 July: *Gruppe* reported 41 Ju 87 D-3s on strength.

Attack on the Kursk Salient and Operations in Eastern Ukraine (July 1943 – September 1943)
5 July: following 10 days of stand down to refit and be brought up to full strength, the *Gruppe* took part in the massive German counter-offensive on the Kursk salient to the north of Kharkov (Operation *Zitadelle*) that commenced this date. 6 July: 1 Ju 87 D-3 shot down by AA fire and fighters to the north-east of Kharkov and 2 others shot up and damaged, 2 KIA. 6-7 July: 5. and 6.*Staffel* claimed 2 Il-2 *Shturmoviks* and an La-5 around Churayevo in the Belgorod area. 8 July: 4 Ju 87 D-3s lost to fighters and mid-air collisions north-east of Kharkov, *Oblt.* Karl Fitzner + 5 KIA. 14 July: still engaged against targets to the north-east of Kharkov and north of Belgorod in support of XXXXVIII.*Panzerkorps*. Same date, 5.*Staffel* filed a claim for a LaGG-3 fighter ca. 30 km north of Belgorod. 17-19 July: ordered south to the Donets Basin area to attack the rapid build-up of Soviet forces along this sector of the front that were getting ready for an offensive to recapture the Donets and drive the Germans back across the Dnieper. 29-31 July: based at Makeyevka/12 km east of Stalino – 1 Ju 87 D shot down by AA fire in the area east of Stalino. 5 August: 1 Ju 87 D shot down, 3 shot up by fighters and 4 more damaged on the ground during a low-level Russian air attack on Tolokonnoye airstrip/46 km north of Kharkov where the entire *Gruppe* was based at the time. 6 August: 4.*Staffel* Ju 87 D-3 shot down by fighters to the north of Kharkov, 1 KIA and 1 WIA. 8 August: Fi 156 belonging to the *Gruppe* shot down by fighters in the Romny-Lubny area halfway between Kiev and Kharkov. 13 August: *Gruppe* was operating from Poltava and still there on 29 August. 30 August: 5.*Staffel* Ju 87 shot down by fighters in the Stalino area, crew safe. 4 September: 4.*Staffel* Ju 87 D-3 blew up in the air north-west of Kharkov, 2 MIA.

Operations in Central Ukraine and Redesignation (September 1943 – January 1944) 13-14 September: 2 Ju 87 D-3s accidentally struck the ground during a low-level attack on targets to the north-east of Kiev, 2 KIA. 14 September: 5.*Staffel* Ju 87 D-5 crash-landed at Nezhin airstrip/116 km north-east of Kiev due to blown tyres and then destroyed by the *Gruppe* to prevent it from

8./St.G. 77 Emblem

falling into the hands of the rapidly advancing enemy. 24 September: at Vasilkov airfield/35 km south of Kiev – daily attacks on Russian tanks and infantry advancing towards the Dnieper River to the east of Kiev. 1 October 1943: 4.*Staffel* claimed a LaGG-3 fighter over Mishurin Rog/46 km south-east of Kremenchug on the west bank of the Dnieper. 2 October: 4.*Staffel* Ju 87 D-3 shot up by fighters over Borodayevka/71 km north-west of Dnepropetrovsk. 18 October 1943: at Vasilkov – plans called for the *Gruppe* to be renamed III./S.G. 10 on this date, while 4.*Staffel* was renamed 4.(Pz)/S.G. 152 on 15 November 1944. However, the *Gruppe* (less 4.*Staffel*) continued to appear on the *Luftwaffe's* aircraft inventory books under its II./St.G. 77 designation to January 1944 (actually to 1 March 1944) due to its removal from the front to convert to the Fw 190 F. This confusion was caused by the fact that the *Gruppe* was intended to be redesignated II./S.G. 152 in January 1944 and based at Neudorf in Silesia, but the plan was belatedly changed and instead it became III./S.G. 10 during the second half of January at Neudorf.

FpNs: *Gruppenstab* II. (L 04499, 36638); 4. (L 45599, 16735); 5. (L 44663, 19395); 6. (L 43728, 26568)

Kommandeur:
Hptm. Clemens Graf von Schönborn-Wiesentheid (14 May 1939 - 15 May 1940)
Hptm. Waldemar Plewig (15 May 1940 - 8 August 1940 POW)
Hptm. Alfons Orthofer (RK) (15 August 1940 - 30 June 1942)
Major Kurt Huhn (RK, DKG) (1 July 1942 - 1 April 1943) – made permanent *Kdr.* 1 March 1943.★
Hptm. Georg Jakob (DKG, RK) (26 August 1942 - February 1943?) ★
Hptm. Helmut Leicht (DKG, RK) (1 April 1943 - September 1943) – acting
Hptm. Helmut Leicht (DKG, RK) (1 October 1943 - 18 October 1943)

★this conflict has proved impossible to resolve.

III./St.G. 77

Formation (July 1940) Formed 9 July 1940 at either Barly/17 km west-south-west of Arras in north-east France or at Caen in Normandy from elements of I./St.G. 76. Elements of II./K.G. 76, which had been ordered to commence conversion to the Ju 87 on 1 February 1940, are also believed to have been incorporated into the new *Gruppe*. On the other hand, some respected post-war authorities using archival evidence believe the majority of aircrew came from II.(St.)/K.G. 76, while only a few experienced crews and perhaps some ground personnel came from I./St.G. 76. Equipped with Junkers Ju 87 dive-bombers.

Air Offensive against England (Battle of Britain) (July 1940 – March 1941) July - August: following formation during July, engaged in intense training in northern France during most of July and the first half of August in preparation for the planned invasion of England (Operation *Seelöwe* or Sealion). 11 July: Ju 87 B destroyed in a landing accident at Flers airfield/50 km south-west of Caen. 13 August: at Caen with 38 (37) Ju 87 Bs under VIII.*Fliegerkorps/Luftflotte* 3. However,

there is a strong indication that the *Gruppe* was instead either based at Argentan/55 km south-south-east of Caen during August and September or using Argentan for operations or training. 18 August: 1 Ju 87 B-1 shot down by fighters, another shot up and crashed on return to France, and 2 more damaged out of 31 dispatched during a disastrous raid by St.G. 77 on naval bases, airfields (Thorney Island and Ford) and a radar station near Poling in the Gosport-Littlehampton area. The radar station was the specific target for III.*Gruppe*. The raid cost the *Geschwader* 17 *Stukas* destroyed and 7 damaged in all. The debacle resulted in a withdrawal of VIII.*Fliegerkorps Stuka* units from operations over southern England and their relegation to standby and training duties pending the planned invasion of England. Like the rest of St.G. 77, III.*Gruppe* apparently sat in France, relatively inactive, from September 1940 to the end of March 1941. 7 December: alerted for Operation *Felix*, the planned attack on Gibraltar by elements of VIII.*Fliegerkorps* that was later cancelled. 14 March: Ju 87 B-1 force-landed and moderately damaged at Étampes-Mondésir airfield/55 km south-south-west of Paris due to engine trouble.

III./St.G. 77 was formed from elements of I./St.G. 76 and II./K.G. 76 on 9 July 1940. Initially the unit retained the F1 *Geschwader* code allocated to II./K.G. 76. These close-up views show a Ju 87 B S1+MM of 7./St.G. 77 around the time of its formation. The individual (first) letter 'M' was painted white over a yellow rear fuselage band. The radio operator was provided with a single 7.9 mm MG 15 machine gun.

Following its formation in July 1940, III./St.G. 77, a Ju 87 from which is illustrated here, became engaged in intense training in northern France during preparations for Operation Sealion, the planned invasion of England. However, following the disastrous attack on a radar station near Poling in the Gosport-Littlehampton area on 18 August, the Gruppe, in common with other Luftwaffe dive-bomber units, was withdrawn from operations.

The radio operator waves as this Ju 87 B of 7./St.G. 77 leaves for a mission. The aircraft carries the Staffel emblem, a black eagle's head superimposed on a red and yellow shield. III./St.G. 77 had been formed on 9 July 1940 at either Barly (17 km west-south-west of Arras in north-east France) or at Caen in Normandy from elements of I./St.G. 76.

7./St.G. 77 Emblem

Balkan Campaign (April 1941 – May 1941) March 1941: transferred from France to Arad/Romania in late March. 6 April: Arad/north-west Romania with 40 (32) Ju 87 Bs under *Fliegerführer Arad* (*Stab*/St.G. 77)/ *Luftflotte* 4 for the attack on Yugoslavia and Greece – on the first day of the attack the *Gruppe*, operating together with I./St.G. 77, struck bridges and strong points in and around Belgrade, including the royal castle. 10 April: attacked targets in northern Greece, losing a Ju 87 near Lamia/150 km north-west of Athens. 15 April: now at Prilep-West/72 km south of Skoplje in Macedonia. 22 April: struck shipping and ground targets in the Athens area, losing a Ju 87 flown by *Oblt.* Wilde. 27 April: Ju 87 B shot down either by a Bristol Blenheim or by the destroyer *Hero* while dive-bombing a British evacuation convoy en route from Greece to Crete, *Oblt.* Harry Lachmann + 1 MIA. 15 May: now at Argos/south Greece for the airborne and air-landing invasion of Crete on 20 May. The specific activities of the *Gruppe* during the invasion are not known, but presumably it operated with the rest of St.G. 77 and attacked shipping in the waters around the island, struck ports and bombed selected ground targets in support of the German paratroops and air-landing infantry fighting to take Crete. 2 June: Crete secured and campaign concluded, transferred from Argos to Sprottau in Silesia to rest and refit. During the Balkan campaign, the *Gruppe* claimed 46,000 tons of shipping sunk and 86,000 tons damaged.

Attack on the Soviet Union – Central Russia (June 1941 – July 1941) 19 June: transferred from Sprottau to Deblin in Central Poland and then the next day moved forward to Woskrzenice Male field airstrip/10 km east of Biala Podlaska in eastern Poland. 22 June: at Woskrzenice Male with 35 (28) Ju 87 Bs under II.*Fliegerkorps*/*Luftflotte* 2 for the opening of Operation *Barbarossa*, the massive invasion of Russia. 22-29 June: took part in the reduction of enemy fortifications along the River Bug and the stubbornly defended citadel at Brest-Litovsk. 26 June: moved forward to Prusana airfield/120 km west-north-west of Pinsk in eastern Poland. During the first 5 days of operations, the *Gruppe* reported no combat losses and only 3 take-off and landing accidents. 27 June - 25 July: no mention of the *Gruppe* has been found in the surviving records. If it remained in operations, then it did so without loss.

Operations across Ukraine and the Advance on Moscow (July 1941 – October 1941) 27 July: at Belaya Tserkov-South/75 km south-west of Kiev operating under V.*Fliegerkorps*. 29 (or 30) July: attacked Soviet Marshal Timoshenko's quarters in Kiev. To 8 August, supported the surrounding of Russian forces in what became known as the Uman Pocket and resulted in the taking of some 103,000 prisoners and the capture of 317 tanks and 858 guns. 30 July: 2 Ju 87 Bs failed to return from operations – no details, *Hptm.* Wilhelm Rieger + 1 MIA. 9 August: transferred to Chmelevoye, a grass airstrip not far from Belaya Tserkov, and supported the advance across the Dnieper River at Dnepropetrovsk

(taken 17 August) and Kremenchug. 13 August: flew repeated attacks on bridges at Kanev to block the Soviet retreat across the Dnieper. 12-18 September: supported the closing of the German armoured pincers east of Kiev leading to the taking of some 600,000 prisoners over the following week. In particular, the *Gruppe* relentlessly bombed bunkers and artillery positions around the citadel in Kiev, allowing German infantry and engineers to finally take it on 19 September. 14 September: now at Schastivaya/30 km east of Vinnitsa. 18 September: Ju 87 R-4 shot up and destroyed by AA fire near Kiev, crew rescued. 20 September: at Belaya Tserkov. 21-24 September: softened up enemy defensive positions on the Perekop Isthmus for the advance into Crimea by A.O.K. 11. 2-7 October: operating from both Konotop and Kremenchug in support of the drive towards Kharkov and Kursk by 2.*Panzerarmee*. 8 October: at the end of the first week of October, well after the destruction of the Kiev pocket, the *Gruppe* in whole or part was ordered north to the Smolensk-Vyazma area on the central sector

Alfons Orthofer (RK)

'Ali' Orthofer was born on 7 December 1909 in Neustadt/Donau, 24 km east of Ingolstadt. He began his military service on 1 April 1930 with the *Heer* (*Infanterie-Rgt.* 20 in Regensburg) undertaking pre-military flight training with the D.V.S. Schleissheim until 31 March 1931. On 1 April 1935 he transferred to the *Luftwaffe* and was appointed *Kp.-Offz.* in *Fahr-Abt.* (Transport Detachment) Rendsburg. He was appointed *Adjutant* in *Flieger-Ers.Abt.* 15 in Neubiberg on 1 July 1935 and promoted to *Oberleutnant* on 1 October. He became an *Adjutant* in J.G. 134 at Dortmund on 12 March 1936 but was ordered on temporary duty to *Jagdgruppe* Lippstadt for fighter pilot training between 6 May and 30 July. He was awarded the *Luftwaffe* pilot licence on 1 August 1936 and assigned to I./St.G. 165 at Kitzingen a month later for further pilot training. On 1 March 1937 he transferred to II./St.G. 165 at Schweinfurt and a month later was ordered on temporary duty to *Fliegertechnische Schule* Jüterbog to attend the *Staffelkapitäne* training course. He was appointed *Staffelführer* in II./St.G. 165 at Schweinfurt on 1 July 1937 and awarded the *Luftwaffe* instrument flying certificate on 21 February 1938. Appointed *Staffelführer* and then *Staffelkapitän* in I./St.G. 162 at Jever on 1 January 1939, he was promoted to *Hauptmann* at the same time and ordered on temporary duty to attend the *Höh.Lw.-Schule* Berlin-Gatow (7. *Lehrgang*) between 5 January and 31 March. On 1 May 1939 he undertook *Generalstab* training at the *Luftkriegsakademie* Berlin-Gatow but did not complete the course.

Just before the Second World War, on 24 August 1939, Orthofer was temporarily assigned to *Stab/General* z.b.V. *Luftflotte* 4, and on 11 October to *Stab/Luftgaukdo.* XII. On 7 February 1940 he was appointed Ia (operations officer) in *Stab/Luftflotte* 2 and provisional or acting Ia in *Stab/Flieger-Div.* 7. He received the E.K. II on 25 May 1940 and was appointed *Kommandeur* of II./St.G. 77 on 15 August 1940. He was awarded the E.K. I on 19 July 1941 and the *Ritterkreuz* on either 21 October or 23 November 1941, was promoted to *Major* on 27 June 1942 and made *Kommandeur* of Stukaschule 1 and was appointed *Kommodore* of St.G. 77 on 25 July. On 12 October 1942 he was killed in action when his Ju 87 D was destroyed on the runway during a surprise Russian air attack on Belorechenskaya, a *Luftwaffe* field strip in North Caucasia. At the time of his death, Orthofer had completed 437 combat missions.

Two men from 7./St.G. 77 enjoy the Ukrainian sun during the summer of 1942, singing to an accordion accompaniment. The Ju 87 B-2 on which they are sitting carries the emblem of the Staffel, a black eagle's head with red beak and tongue on a yellow shield with a blue top.

from Soltsy to Vitebsk, although the actual transfer may not have been executed until 21 October. HQ 11.*Armee* (Manstein) and *Luftwaffe* assets had been ordered from the Leningrad front to Vitebsk to prepare for Operation *Taubenschlag* (or Dovecote), an offensive aimed at Toropets, but this was postponed and then cancelled. 21 October: 8.*Staffel* and 9.*Staffel* both reported Ju 87 B crashes and accidents at Vitebsk. 30 October: Fi 156 belonging to the *Gruppe* bombed on the ground at Vitebsk. November: not mentioned in the records, but believed to have departed Vitebsk and returned to *Luftwaffenkdo. Don* during the first half of the month.

Don Front, Refit in Germany and Training on Sardinia (December 1942 – May 1943)

1 December: *Gruppe* reported 12 Ju 87 B-1s, 11 Ju 87 B-2s, 6 Ju 87 R-2s and 1 Ju 87 R-1 on strength. 17-21 December: now operating again under *Luftwaffenkdo. Don*, 6 Ju 87 B-1s and R-2s shot down by fighters, AA fire and ground fire in the vicinity of Novaya Kalitva, Orreshevoye and Ivanovka, all of which are in the Don area between Rossosh and Stalingrad. The *Gruppe* was in support of the futile attempts being made by the Axis to slow down the second phase of the Russian Stalingrad counter-offensive (Operation *Malyy Saturn* or *Little Saturn*) that had commenced on 16 December, breaching the Italian 8th Army's positions along the Don. Over the next month, the Soviet 6th, 1st Guards, 3rd Guards and 5th Tank Armies pushed south and west forcing the Germans and their allies back towards Kharkov and Voroshilovgrad. 22 December: 8.*Staffel* Ju 87 hit by ground fire and exploded in the air north-east of Fisenkovo/37 km south-south-east of Rossosh (just west of the Don), *Staffelkapitän Oblt.* Theodor Langhardt + 1 KIA. January 1943: aircraft and crews withdrew to

Konotop during the first half of January. 11–31 January: 29 ground personnel belonging to the *Gruppe* reported as KIA or MIA along the line of retreat from Rossosh to Kharkov. February: decimated, transferred from Konotop and Bobruisk to Würzburg to rest, refit and re-equip. 15 April: transferred from Würzburg to Milis/95 km north-north-west of Cagliari on Sardinia with 37 Ju 87s and 245 officers and men to continue refitting and training. *Luftflotte* 2 and II.*Fliegerkorps* were both told that the *Gruppe* was to be left alone and used operationally only in the event of enemy landings on Sardinia. But Allied air attacks on Sardinian airfields proved so intense that it was ordered to depart on 27 April for reassignment to IV.*Fliegerkorps* in south Russia, arriving there by 8 May. 24 April: 2 Ju 87s destroyed in a mid-air collision over Orestano/Sardinia while training, *Oblt.* Georg Reichelt + 3 KIA.

Operations in the Donets Basin, Kursk Salient, Eastern and Central Ukraine (May 1943 – October 1943)

9 May: 8.*Staffel* Ju 87 D-3 crashed at Kuteynikovo airfield/125 km north-west of Rostov due to an engine fire, and same date a 9.*Staffel* Ju 87 D-3 failed to return from operations east of Kuteynikovo, 2 MIA. 12 May: 9.*Staffel* Ju 87 D-3 and another D-3 from 8.*Staffel* shot down by AA fire at Oboyan and Tamogovka in the Donets area, 2 KIA and 1 WIA. 24 May: 2 Ju 87 D-3s shot down by fighters and AA fire over Bataisk/10 km south of Rostov, 2 KIA and 2 MIA. On the same date and possibly the same mission, 7.*Staffel* claimed a LaGG-3 fighter near Azov/26 km south-west of Rostov. 28 May: 2 Ju 87 D-3s from 7. and 8.*Staffel* shot down by AA fire at Privolnoye, 2 KIA and 2 MIA. 7 June: 9.*Staffel* Ju 87 D-3 crashed ca. 30 km south-west of Kramatorskaya airfield in the Donets Basin due to engine trouble, 1 WIA. 18–22 June: transferred from Kramatorskaya to Pavlograd/62 km east of Dnepropetrovsk. 1 July: *Gruppe* reported 33 Ju 87 D-3s and 3 Ju 87 D-1s on strength. 1 July: 7.*Staffel* Ju 87 D-3 shot down by AA fire at Topalskiy, 2 KIA. 5–15 July: based in the Kharkov area (Kharkov-North? or Bogodukhov/55 km north-west of Kharkov?) for the German counter-offensive against the Kursk salient (Operation *Zitadelle*). 6 July: Ju 87 D-3 shot down by fighters and AA fire in the Belgorod area and 2 others shot up and damaged, 2 MIA. 11 July: five Ju 87 D-3s shot down by fighters and AA fire in the Prokhorovka area (Kursk salient) while supporting an advance by III.*Panzerkorps*, *Staffelkapitän Hptm.* Rudolf Blumenthal + 3 MIA and 1 KIA. 14 July: 8.*Staffel* Ju 87 D-3 shot down by fighters and AA fire north of Belgorod while supporting XXXXVIII.*Panzerkorps*, *Staffelkapitän Hptm.* Hans Werner + 1 KIA. 17–18 July: following the failure of the German's Kursk offensive and the shift to a defensive posture by German ground forces, the *Gruppe* was withdrawn from operations in this sector and ordered south to Kramatorskaya airfield in the Donets where the Russians were concentrating armour and infantry for a powerful offensive in this area. 20 July: 10 Ju 87 D-3s from 7.*Staffel* bombed on the ground at Kramatorskaya during a Russian air raid, this effectively putting the *Staffel* out of action for a week or two. 22 July: 9.*Staffel* Ju 87 D-3 shot up by AA fire and crashed on return to Kramatorskaya, 2 KIA. 27 July: attacked targets in area south of Stalino. 30 July: *Gruppe* claimed an La-5

Stab III./St.G. 77 Emblem

Major Franz Kieslich, the third Kommandeur of III./St.G. 77 sitting in the cockpit of his Ju 87 B. The emblem below the cockpit is the family coat of arms of Major Helmuth Bode, the first commander of the Gruppe.

Stab IV./St.G. 77 Emblem

!0./St.G. 77 Emblem

11./St.G. 77 Emblem

12./St.G. 77 Emblem

fighter around Chistyakovo (Torez)/60 km east of Stalino. 3 August: 8.*Staffel* Ju 87 D-3 bombed on ground at Kramatorskaya. 6-12 August: 4 Ju 87 D-3s shot down by AA fire in the Kharkov area as Soviet troops advanced on the city following the liberation of Belgorod on 5 August, and 3 others destroyed by the *Gruppe* to prevent them from falling into enemy hands; another could not be demolished in time and was seized undamaged by the Russians. 17 August: *Gruppe* now at Poltava. 18 August: 4 Ju 87 D-3s from 7.*Staffel* shot down by fighters and AA fire in the Sumy area to the north-west of Kharkov, 4 KIA and 2 WIA. 25 August: 8.*Staffel* Ju 87 D-5 shot down by AA fire on the south-west outskirts of Kharkov, 1 WIA. 30 August: all or elements now operating from Stalino in the Donets. 2-3 September: three Ju 87 D-3s shot down by AA fire in the Kharkov area, *Oblt.* Alfons Auer + 1 MIA and 2 KIA. 5 September: 2 Ju 87 D-3s from 7. and 9.*Staffel* shot down by AA fire just south of Kharkov, 2 MIA and 2 WIA. The *Gruppe* departed Poltava about 19 September and continued to support ground forces retreating from the Kharkov area towards the Dnieper River at Kiev. 4 October: 8.*Staffel* Ju 87 D-3 shot up by AA fire in the Mirgorod-Lubny area between Kharkov and Kiev. 10 October: reassigned to *Luftflotte* 6 on or about this date and ordered to the central sector of the Eastern Front to reinforce air assets concentrating to hinder the Soviet advance west and north-west from Smolensk.

Operations in Central Russia (October 1943)
15 October: 8.*Staffel* Ju 87 D-3 shot up and belly-landed at Ulla airstrip/59 km west of Vitebsk. 17 October: 9.*Staffel* Ju 87 D-3 shot down by AA fire west of Polotsk, 2 MIA. 18 October: renamed III./S.G. 77 (at Vitebsk?).

Codes: up to July 1942 (F1+_C, M, N, P), then (S2+_D, R, S, T)

FpNs: *Gruppenstab* III. (L 31683, 37393); 7. (L 42879, 30344); 8. (L 41933, 31192); 9. (L 40148, 31796)

Kommandeur:
Oblt. Dietrich Peltz (June 1940?) – acting
Hptm./Major Helmuth Bode (RK) (9 July 1940 – 25 August 1942)★
Hptm./Major Georg Jakob (DKG, RK) (26 August 1942 – February 1943?) ★★
Major Franz Kieslich (DKG, RK) (1 January 1943? – 18 October 1943) – acting?

★ Bode's first name is consistently misspelled as 'Helmut' in the secondary literature. 'Helmuth' is correct.
★★ *Major* Georg Jakob, according to official orders issued by the *Luftwaffen-Personalamt*, was changed from acting to full *Kommandeur* of III.*Gruppe* effective 1 March 1943, and subsequent orders show him to still be the *Kommandeur* of III./St.G. 77 in August 1943. As this conflicts with published references the reader is cautioned.

IV.(Erg.)/St.G. 77

Formation and Organization (February 1941) Formed February 1941 at Schweinfurt from elements of *Stuka-Ergänzungsstaffel*/VIII.*Fliegerkorps* as *Ergänzungsstaffel*/St.G. 77 and responsible for providing 6 to 8 weeks of operational formation and dive-bombing training to green crews fresh out of the schools that had been assigned to *Sturzkampfgeschwader* 77. Expanded from one to two *Staffeln* during autumn 1942 and redesignated IV.(Erg.)/St.G. 77 on or about 17 November 1942.

Training in Germany and South Russia (March 1941 – May 1943) March - June 1941: routine Ju 87 B-1 training crashes and accidents at Schweinfurt, Wertheim and the surrounding area. July 1941 - January 1942: not mentioned in the Loss Reports. 17 February: Ju 87 B-1 damaged landing at Schweinfurt. March – September 1942: not mentioned in the Loss Reports. 24 June: transferred from Schweinfurt to Sarabus/Crimea. 5 October: 2 Ju 87 Ds destroyed in a mid-air collision over Biyuk-Onlar to the south of Stalingrad, 1 KIA. December: following the Soviet Stalingrad counter-offensive on 19 November, the *Gruppe* was ordered to form an operational unit for use over the Taman Peninsula. Known as *Einsatzstaffel* 'Sattler', it was assigned to *LuftwaffenGruppe Kaukasus* for employment. *Oblt.* Sattler was killed a month or so after the *Staffel* began operations (see below). 1 January 1943: *Gruppe* reported 16 Ju 87 B-1/B-2s, 7 Ju 87 R-1/R-4s, 2 Ju 87 D-1s, 6 Fw 56s and 1 Fw 58 on strength. 13 January: Ju 87 B-1 crashed north-east of Krymskaya in the Taman Peninsula due to engine fire, *Oblt.* Hans-Karl Sattler + 1 KIA. January: transferred from Sarabus to Nikolayev-East. 25 March: Ju 87 B-1 destroyed in a mid-air collision over Nikolayev-East, 2 KIA. 1 April: *Gruppe* reported 18 Ju 87 B-1/B-2s, 4 Ju 87 R-1/R-4s, 2 Ju 87 D-1s and 3 Ju 87 D-3s on strength. April: transferred from Nikolayev-East to Wertheim/30 km west of Würzburg in south Germany. 17 May: renamed IV./St.G. 151.

FpNs: (L 43675, 37723)

Staffelkapitän/Gruppenkommandeur:
Oblt. Helmut Leicht (? - 27 February 1941 - ?)
Hptm. Herbert Pabst (1 September 1941 - 31 July 1942)
Oblt. Hans-Karl Sattler (RK) (1942 - 13 January 1943) KIA
Hptm. Alexander Gläser (DKG, RK) (April 1943 - 16 May 1943)

LS-Ausb.Abt./St.G. 77

Formation and History (March 1943 – May 1943) Formed 9 March 1943 at Wertheim near Würzburg with Junkers Ju 87s and DFS 230 gliders. Before this little training detachment could really get up and running, it was joined with LS-Ausb.Kdo./St.G. 1 and together renamed LS-*Ausbildungsstaffel für Sturzkampfverbände* (FpN L 52415) on or about 17 May 1943. The *Abteilung* reported no losses during its brief existence.

FpN: none assigned

Kommandeur:
Hptm. Gerhard Stüdemann (DKG) (9 March 1943 –
    June 1943)

Sources for St.G. 77:

Unpublished and Archival:
AFHRA Maxwell AFB: Karlsruhe Collection.
BA-MA Freiburg: RL 2 III Gen.Qu.(6.Abt.) *Meldungen
    über Flugzeugunfälle und Verlust…* (LRs – Loss
    Reports);
BA-MA - *Flugzeug-Bereitstellungen* (Aircraft Availability
    Status Reports – FzB) in: Holm-op website;
BA-MA Freiburg: *Signatur* RL 20/274-77, RL 20/281-
    84;
NARA WashDC: RG 242/T-313 roll 89 frame 245;
    T-971 roll 19;
PRO London: AIR 40/files 1965, 1966, 1967, 1968,
    1971, 1975, 1977, 1978, 1979, 1980, 1982, 1986,
    1995.
PRO London: DEFE 3 ULTRA signals VM9299,
    VM9391, ML475, ML1756, ML3174.

Published:
[Aders – SG] p. 29, 36, 41, 59, 89, 110, 115;
[Balke – KG 2V1] p. 395, 402, 411, 414, 417;
[Bateson – *Stuka!*] p. 8-12, 21-27, 29-31, 35, 38, 42, 47,
    50, 52, 54, 59;
[Bekker – LWD] p. 4, 20, 41, 53, 157, 167, 211, 230,
    316;
[Bergström – BC/RS-1] p. 102, 104-106, 153, 212, 227;
[Bergström – BC/RS-2] p. 128, 129, 132, 135, 167, 202;
[Bergström – BC/RS-3] p. 19, 46, 127, 155;
[Brütting – SA] p. 152-154, 160-164, 169, 178, 182,
    184-186, 191, 195, 210, 220, 233, 234, 236, 242, 245-
    247, 253, 255, 257, 260, 269, 270;
[Carlsen – CM2] p. 281-284, 340;
[Dierich – KG51] p. 50, 51;
[Dierich – VdL] p. 227-230, 270;
[Foreman – Forg] p. 188;
[Gundelach – Med] p. 55;
[Griehl – KFZ] p. 121;
[Hayward – Stopped] p. 181;
[Holm – Website www.ww2.dk];
[Kannapin – FPN] various;
[Mason – BovB] p. 552;
[Mehner – FT] p. 54;
[Nauroth – StG2] p. 217, 244;
[Obermaier – RK2] p. 60, 61, 66, 68, 69, 71, 76, 77, 81,
    84, 90, 91, 96, 112, 119, 125, 131, 153, 165, 169, 176,
    178, 181, 183, 184, 187-189, 192, 198, 199, 204, 206,
    215;
[Patzwall – LwR] p. various;
[Plocher – Rus41] p. 66, 69, 130, 227;
[Plocher – Rus42] p. 160, 162, 189, 190, 193;
[Plocher – Rus43] p. 37, 76, 122;
[Ramsey – B-1] p. 184;
[Ries – Lw] p. 140;
[Ries – PhotoRec] p. 65, 67, 103, 120, 142, 156;
[Rosch – Codes] p. 354-357;
[Scheibert – EP] p. various;
[Scherzer – DKG] p. various;
[Shores – F] p. 21;
[Shores – Yugo] p. 180, 195, 221, 239, 278, 301, 337, 359;
[Smith – GA] p. 383-385, 388-390;
[Smith – SAW] p. 19, 20, 31, 37, 40, 41, 43, 44, 72;

[Smith – StG 77] p. 24-27, 30-32, 35, 36, 38, 39, 44, 46-
    48, 50, 51, 53, 56, 57, 62, 65, 66, 68, 72, 74, 76-82,
    84, 85, 87, 89, 90, 93-95, 97-100, 102, 104-109, 113-
    115, 118-120, 125-127, 129, 131-139, 142-145, 148-
    152, 154-159, 161, 162, 164, 165, 186, 187;
[Tessin – Form] p. 223;
[Tessin – Tes] p. 425, 426;
[Tuider – LwOst] p. 118;
[Vasco – Bomb] p. 10;
[Weal – 37-41] p. 18, 26, 29, 31, 32, 46, 48, 50, 55,
67, 80-83.

[Archiv #8 – A-8] p. 13, 16;
[Archiv #9 – A-9] p. 30.

M.Holm – website www.ww2.dk

St.G. 151

Sturzkampfgeschwader 151
(Unit Code: 6Q+)

Stab/St.G. 151

Formation (May 1943) Ordered formed 17 May 1943, but the actual formation of the *Geschwaderstab* at Zagreb/Croatia was somewhat delayed and may not have occurred until June, July or early August. The *Geschwader* was a consolidation of all of the *Ergänzungsgruppen* and *Ergänzungsstaffeln* of the *Stuka* arm under one roof, so to speak, although few of these widely scattered units actually changed location.

Yugoslavia (June 1943 – October 1943) 12 October 1943: Bf 108 D-1 belonging to the *Geschwaderstab* crash-landed at Udine/north-east Italy due to engine failure. 18 October: renamed *Stab/Schlachtgeschwader* 151.

FpN: *Geschwaderstab* (L 52210)

Kommodore:
Oberst Karl Christ (DKG) (5 June 1943 - 18 October 1943)

I./St.G. 151

Formation (May 1943) Ordered formed 17 May 1943 at Belgrade-Pancevo in Serbia by renaming IV.(Erg.)/St.G. 1. Organized with a *Gruppenstab* and 1. - 2.*Staffel*. Equipped with Junkers Ju 87 dive-bombers.

Yugoslavia and Germany (May 1943 – October 1943) 1 June: *Gruppe* reported 12 Ju 87 D-3s, 32 Ju 87 B-1/B-2s and 7 Ju 87 R-1/R-2s on strength – a total of 51 *Stukas*. 4 June: Ju 87 D-1 crashed at Belgrade-Pancevo, 2 KIA. July: many training crashes and accidents at Belgrade-Pancevo. 4 August: elements of the *Gruppe* transferred to Memmingen in south Germany. 1 September: *Gruppe* reported 16 Ju 87 D-3s, 6 Ju 87 B-1/B-2s, 5 Ju 87 R-2s and 11 Ju 87 D-1s on strength. 15 September: Ju 87 D-3 crashed at Belgrade-Pancevo, 2 KIA. 16 September: Ju 87 D-3 Trop crashed and burned at Zagreb-Lucko, 1 KIA. 27 September: Ju 87 D-3 crashed at Memmingen and moderately damaged due to engine fire. 18 October 1943: renamed I./S.G. 151.

FpN: I. *Stab* and 1., 2. (L 37989)

Kommandeur:
Hptm. Karl Schrepfer (DKG, RK) (17 May 1943 - 18 October 1943)

II./St.G. 151

Formation (May 1943) Ordered formed 17 May 1943 at Zagreb/Croatia by renaming IV.(Erg.)/St.G. 2. Organized with a *Gruppenstab* and 4. - 5.*Staffel*. Equipped with Junkers Ju 87 dive-bombers.

Yugoslavia (May 1943 – October 1943) 1 June: *Gruppe* reported 14 Ju 87 B-1/B-2s, 1 Ju 87 R-2, 2 Ju 87 D-1s and 7 Ju 87 D-3s on strength. 9 July: a DFS 230 glider belonging to the *Gruppe* crashed at Ostrice/ 51 km north-east of Zagreb near Varazdin, *Gruppenkommandeur Hptm.* Thiede, *Hptm.* Karl Hohmann, *Oblt.* Hellmuth Winter + 3 others all killed. 4 August: Ju 87 D-3 crashed west of Zagreb, 2 killed. 1 September: *Gruppe* reported 6 Ju 87 B-1/B-2s, 5 Ju 87 D-1s and 25 Ju 87 D-3s on strength. 9 September: assigned to *Fliegerführer Kroatien* and ordered to operate from Zadar, Mostar and Sarajevo-Butmir against Italian forces along the Dalmatian coast following the capitulation of Italy on 8 September (Operation *Achse*). 11 September: flew 35 sorties against shipping along the Dalmatian coast claiming one 1,200-ton ship in Dubrovnik harbour and near-misses on 2 others. These missions continued over the next week to 10 days until Allied fighters from Italy forced the *Gruppe* to return to Zagreb-Lucko. 14 September: Ju 87 D-1 crashed at Belgrade-Pancevo due to pilot error, 1 killed. 24 September: Ju 87 D-1 failed to return from a mission in the vicinity of Berac Island off the Dalmatian coast, 2 MIA. 17 October: Ju 87 D-3 crash-landed at Zagreb-Lucko due to engine failure, pilot injured. 18 October 1943: renamed II./S.G. 151 at Zagreb-Lucko.

FpN: II. *Stab*, 4., 5. (L 19339)

Kommandeur:
Hptm. Armin Thiede (DKG, RK) (17 May 1943 - 2 July 1943) – KIA 9 July 1943
Hptm. Gerhard Küffner (2 July 1943 - 18 October 1943)

Photographs of St.G. 151 are relatively rare. These two views show Ju 87 Ds of the II.Gruppe preparing for take-off during the early summer of 1943. The Gruppe had been formed on 17 May 1943 at Zagreb in Croatia by renaming IV.(Erg.)/St.G. 2. St.G. 151 was basically an operational training unit but flew combat sorties against Italian forces along the Dalmatian coast following the capitulation of Italy on 8 September. It was redesignated II./S.G. 151 on 18 October 1943 Zagreb-Lucko.

III./St.G. 151

Formation (May 1943) Ordered formed 17 May 1943 at Athens-Kalamaki and/or Athens-Tatoi in Greece by renaming IV.(Erg.)/St.G. 3. Organized with a *Gruppenstab* and 7. - 8.*Staffel*. Equipped with Junkers Ju 87 dive-bombers.

Greece and Yugoslavia (May 1943 – October 1943) May: *Gruppe* was using both Kalamaki and Tatoi, one of which was its official airfield. 1 June: *Gruppe* reported 8 Ju 87 R-2s, 1 Ju 87 R-4, 10 Ju 87 D-1s, 5 Ju 87 D-3s, 3 Bf 109 E-7s and 1 Bf 109 E-4 on strength. 16 August: Ju 87 D-3 crashed east of Skoplje/Macedonia – no details. This crash is believed to have occurred while the *Gruppe* was in-transfer from Athens to Zirkle (Cirklje) airfield/35 km north-west of Zagreb where it was still located in October. 1 September: *Gruppe* reported 6 Ju 87 R-2/R-4s, 2 Ju 87 D-1s, 28 Ju 87 D-3s and 1 Bf 109 E-7 on strength. 1 September: 2 Ju 87 D-3s collided in mid-air over the village of Rann near Zirkle, 1 KIA. 24 September: Ju 87 D-3 shot down by AA fire (Italian, Partisan or German AA fire?) over Trilj/25 km north-east of Split in Dalmatia, 1 KIA. 18 October: renamed III./S.G. 151.

FpN: III. *Stab*, 7., 8. (L 31153)

Kommandeur:
Oblt. Siegfried Göbel (DKG, RK) (17 May 1943 – 17 September 1943)
Hptm. Heinrich Heins (DKG) (20 September 1943 – 18 October 1943)

St.G. 162

Sturzkampfgeschwader 162
(Unit Code: 23+)

The first Luftwaffe dive-bomb unit to be formed was Fliegergruppe Schwerin. On 3 April 1935 this Gruppe was awarded the honorary title of Geschwader Immelmann, named after the famous fighter ace of the First World War, Max Immelmann. The designation Fliegergruppe Schwerin was retained until 1 October 1935 when it became I./St.G. 162 Immelmann. Aircrew assigned to the unit were allowed to carry the name of their unit on the right sleeve cuff of their uniforms.

Stab/St.G. 162

Formation (October 1935) I./St.G. 162 was formed on 1 October 1935 under *Luftkreis* II by the redesignation of the former *Fliegergruppe* Schwerin at Schwerin, and was equipped with 24 He 50 dive-bombers.

Training, Re-Equipping and Redesignation (October 1935 – April 1937) Early 1936: received some He 51s to supplement the He 50 As which had poor aerodynamics. February 1936: contributed to the creation of I./St.G. 165 at Kitzingen. 7 March: due to the Rhineland crisis the *Gruppe* moved temporarily to Düsseldorf, then later returned to Schwerin. Late March 1936: contributed to the formation of II./St.G. 162 at Lübeck-Blankensee. ca. 1 October 1936: loaned to the *Lehrgeschwader* Greifswald for peacetime development work but in the event of mobilization it would resume its identity as I./St.G. 162 at Schwerin. 15 March 1937: still at Schwerin, contributed to the formation of 7./St.G. 162 at Kolberg. 16 March: exchanged its He 51s for Ju 87s. 1 April 1937: the temporary association with the *Lehrgeschwader* became permanent when the *Gruppe* was redesignated IV.(St)/*Lehrgeschwader* with mainly Ju 87 As. ca. 15 July 1937: moved from Schwerin to Barth.

Kommandeur:
Major Wolfgang von Chamier-Glisczinski (1 April 1935 – July 1935).
Major Werner Junck (1 August 1935 - 11 March 1936).
Hptm. Hans-Hugo Witt (12 March 1936 - 31 December 1936). – acting
Major Hans-Hugo Witt (1 January 1937 - 28 February 1937).

I./St.G. 162 (Second Formation)

Background (June 1938 – October 1938) With the Sudeten crisis looming, on about 10 June 1938 a number of tactical support *Gruppen* were ordered to be formed *ad hoc*, making use of whatever aircraft and personnel that could hurriedly be assembled. One of these was *Fliegergruppe* 30, formed 1 August 1938 at Fassberg and equipped initially with obsolescent a/c such as He 46s and/or He 51s, and subordinated to *Stab/FliegerGeschwader* 100. On 1 September, the *Gruppe* was thought to be still at Fassberg but by 20 September it was believed to be at Straubing equipped with Hs 123. The *Gruppe* took part in the occupation of the Sudetenland and by 13 October it was probably at Marienbad. With the end of the Sudeten crisis, these temporary *Gruppen* faced dissolution but *Fliegergruppe* 30 was instead incorporated into a new *Gruppe*.

Formation (November 1938) The second I./St.G. 162 was formed on 1 November 1938 at Barth by the redesignation and reorganization of *Fliegergruppe* 30 and the incorporation of new personnel. Most likely it was equipped with Hs 123s.

Training and Redesignation (November 1938 – April 1939) The prime activity of this *Gruppe* was to incorporate and train new personnel and convert to Ju 87 Bs at Barth and later at Jever. In April of 1939 it moved from Jever to Stolp-Reitz and on 1 May 1939 it was redesignated II./St.G. 2.

Kommandeur:
Hptm. Siegfried von Eschwege (1 August 1938 - December 1938).

Kommandeur:
Obstlt. Alexander Holle (1 July 1935 - 30 September
1937)
Major Wilhelm Dannenberg (August 1938 - 1939?) – ?
Major Oskar Dinort (February 1939 - 30 April 1939)

II./St.G. 163

Background (June 1938 – October 1938) Due to
mounting tension over the Sudeten crisis, on or
around 10 June 1938 the formation of five *ad hoc* ground-
attack (ie: *Schlacht*) *Gruppen* was ordered. One of these
units was *Fliegergruppe* 50, officially created on 1 August
1938 at Lechfeld with Hs 123 As and placed under *Stab/
FliegerGeschwader* 100. Most personnel came from FEA 23
(Air Force Replacement Detachment 23) at Kaufbeuren.
Training and organization was hasty and the unit suffered
from inexperience. On around 20 September, the *Gruppe*
moved from Lechfeld to Grottkau/Silesia where it was
still equipped with Hs 123s and subordinated to
Fliegerdivision z.b.V. In October it relocated to Paulsgrund
near Ratibor to support the troops advancing into the
Sudetenland. With the end of the crisis these temporary
Fliegergruppen were dissolved and *Fliegergruppe* 50 was
incorporated into a new *Stukagruppe*.

**Formation, Training, Re-Equipping and
Redesignation (November 1938 – April 1939)**
Formed on 1 November 1938 at Langensalza with
Hs 123s by the incorporation and reorganization of the
former *Fliegergruppe* 50 and the addition of new aircraft
and personnel. While subordinated to *Lw.
Gruppenkommando* 1, the *Gruppe* continued with training
at Breslau-Schöngarten over the winter and into the
spring while at the same time converting to Ju 87 B-1s.
II./St.G. 163 was redesignated III./St.G. 2 at Langensalza
on 1 May 1939.

Codes: for Fl.Gr. 50 (▲50+nn), where nn represents
the individual aircraft numerical identifier. For II./
St.G. 163 the code was (35+_20, 24, 25, 26)

Kommandeur:
Hptm. Hans-Gunter von Kornatzki (1 November 1938 - ?)
Hptm. Ernst Ott (January 1939 - 30 April 1939)

Sources for St.G. 163:
[Balke – KG2V1] p. 21;
[Brütting – SA] p. 215, 267, 268, 278;
[Deichmann – Support] p. 33;
[Dierich –VdL] p. 211;
[Dressel – FP87A] p. 19;
[Obermaier – RK2] p. 48, 60, 93, 95, 134, 138, 176;
[Nauroth – StG2] p. 21, 23, 24, 31-33, 37, 38, 41-46, 48,
50, 363, 365, 366;
[Ries – Lw] p. 139, 140, 145, 200;
[Smith – GA] p. 318;
[Smith – StG77] p. 24;
[Tessin – Form] p. 85, 87, 223;
[Völker – dDL] p. 284.

During the winter of 1937-38, I./St.G. 163 was re-equipped with the Ju 87 A at Breslau-Strachwitz in Silesia. At this time the unit adopted as its badge the well-known German 'Vater und Sohn' newspaper cartoon character drawn by Erich Ohser. After moving to Cottbus in April 1939 and converting to the Ju 87 B-1 the unit was finally redesignated I./St.G. 2.

I./St.G. 163 was one of the first units to re-equip with the Ju 87 B-1. This aircraft has just been delivered and is still in its pre-war camouflage and before the unit identification has been applied. The dive brakes beneath the wings are shown fully extended.

I./St.G. 165 Badge.

St.G. 165

Sturzkampfgeschwader 165
(Unit Code: 52+)

Stab/St.G. 165

Formation and Redesignation (April 1937 – April 1939) The *Geschwaderstab* was formed on 1 April 1937 at Kitzingen from a cadre provided by *Gruppenstab* I./St.G. 165 and new personnel, and was equipped with Hs 123s. Little is known about the *Geschwaderstab*, but it eventually moved to Schweinfurt. On 1 May 1939, it was redesignated as *Stab*/St.G. 51 at Schweinfurt and was equipped with Ju 87 Bs.

Kommodore:
Major Eberhard Baier (1 April 1937 - October 1938?)
Major Günter Schwartzkopff (1 November 1938 – 30 April 1939)

I./St.G. 165

Background (Autumn 1935 – April 1936) The origins of this *Gruppe* date back approximately to the autumn of 1935 when personnel and aircraft were being gathered at Kitzingen. It was informally called *Fliegergruppe* Kitzingen but its official name is unknown. The process of building up the unit was inhibited by a lack of equipment, which consisted of a few He 51s and Ar 65s. With the approach of the Rhineland remilitarization crisis, there was a hurried attempt to put the unit into some sort of operational status. It had received a cadre from I./St.G. 162 and now consisted of three *Staffeln*, each with 3 He 50s and the remainder filled with He 51s and Ar 65s. On or about 7 March 1936, it sent two *Staffeln* to Frankfurt/Main and one to Mannheim. In the event of a French military occupation of the Rheinland the *Fliegergruppe* was to put up what resistance it could. Before the end of the month the *Gruppe* returned to Kitzingen.

A Kette of three Hs 123 A-1s from 3./St.G. 165 coming in to land at Kitzingen airfield sometime in 1937. By August of the following year the Gruppe had completely re-equipped with the Ju 87. Visible in the photograph are 52+X13 and 52+N13 with their individual letters painted white.

In impeccable formation these three Hs 123 As of 3./St.G. 165 perform for the camera. This Staffel was equipped with the Henschel dive-bomber between April 1937 and August 1938, during which time it was detached from Kitzingen to Schweinfurt to form the basis of the new II./St.G. 165.

Formation (April 1936) The *Gruppe* was officially formed on 1 April 1936 at Kitzingen under *Luftkreis* IV by the redesignation of *Fliegergruppe Kitzingen*.

Training, Re-Equipping and Redesignation (April 1936 – April 1939) April 1936 - March 1937: based at Kitzingen, conducted essential training and incorporated new personnel. Autumn 1936: began to receive Hs 123s to replace the original He 50s, He 51s and Ar 65s. ca. 15 March 1937: 3.*Staffel* was removed from the *Gruppe* to create a cadre for the new II./St.G. 165 at Schweinfurt. 1 April: at Kitzingen with Hs 123s. April 1937 - August 1938: training and building up the *Gruppe* continued at Kitzingen. By August 1938: converted to Ju 87 As. September: during the Sudeten crisis the *Gruppe* was at Jena-Rödingen with Ju 87 As, but had returned to Kitzingen by 20 September. November 1938 - April 1939: training at Kitzingen under *Lw.-Gruppenkommando* 3. 1 May 1939: redesignated I./St.G. 51 at Kitzingen, probably with Ju 87 As.

Clemens Graf von Schönborn-Wiesentheid (RK)

BORN on 3 April 1905 in München, Schönborn-Wiesentheid was with the *Deutsche Verkehrs-Fliegerschule* (German Civil Aviation Flight School) at Schleissheim between 1928 and 1934. He began military training in April 1934 with 10.(Sax)/*Infanterie-Rgt.* but transferred to the *Luftwaffe,* becoming *Stabskp.-Chef* in II./J.G. 132 between 1935 and 1936. In March 1936 he was appointed *Staka* of 4/J.G. 132 and in September 1937 he became *Kommandeur* of II./St.G. 165. As a *Hauptmann* he remained commander of this unit when it became II./St.G 51 on 1 May 1939 and II./St.G. 77 on 14 May 1939.

On 16 April 1940 Schönborn-Wiesentheid, now a *Major*, took over command of III./St.G. 2 but, following the death of Günter Schwartzkopff on 14 May 1940, he was appointed *Kommodore* of St.G 77 on 15 May, a post which he held until 20 July 1942. He was awarded the *Ritterkreuz* on 21 July 1940 and subsequently took up two additional posts: *Fliegerführer* Arad between ca. 30 March 1941 and ca. 15 April 1941, and *Nahkampfflieger Süd* in August 1941, both as an *Oberstleutnant* (as in photograph). On 25 July 1942 he was appointed *Kommandeur* of *Stukaschule* 1 and on 8 December he became *Kommodore* of St.G. 101. Promoted to *Oberst* on 1 June 1943, he became (acting?) *Kommodore* of St.G. 1 (probably to 11 June 1943). In October 1943 he took over as *Kommodore* of S.G. 103 and was appointed *Luftattaché Sofia* (probably in July 1944). Schönborn-Wiesentheid died on 30 August 1944 when his Fi 156 *Storch* crashed in or near Sofia/Bulgaria.

Kommandeur:

Major Werner Junck (12 March 1936 – 30 September 1936)

Major Günter Schwartzkopff (1 October 1936 – 30 August 1937)

Major Oskar Dinort (1 September 1937 – February 1939?)

Hptm. Friedrich-Karl von Dalwigk zu Lichtenfels (? – 30 April 1939)

II./St.G. 165

Formation, Training, Re-Equipping and Redesignation (April 1937 – April 1939) The *Gruppe* was formed officially on 1 April 1937 at Schweinfurt using the former 3./St.G. 165 as a cadre of experience personnel plus an allotment of new replacements fresh from the schools. It was planned that it was to be equipped with He 70s but apparently they received only Hs 123s. From about August 1938, the

This Hs 123 A of 2./St.G. 165, 52+A12, W.Nr. 831, crash-landed during the autumn manoeuvres of 1937. The aircraft's individual letter 'A' was painted white and repeated above the centre of the top wing in the same colour.

Four Ju 87 A-1s of II./St.G. 165 photographed at Schweinfurt airfield shortly after the unit was re-equipped with the type in August 1938. They carry the brown, green and grey upper surface splinter camouflage scheme adopted by most pre-war Luftwaffe military aircraft. The Ju 87 to the right of the photograph was coded 52+A2. This indicates individual aircraft 'A' of II.Gruppe Stab, theoretically at least, that of the Kommandeur, Hptm. Clemens Graf von Schönborn-Wiesentheid.

Gruppe started to convert to Ju 87 As from the Hs 123s. Training was the primary activity of the Gruppe until at least the advent of the Sudeten crisis. It is unknown if it had anything to do with the occupation of the Sudetenland, but on 1 November 1938 it was still at Schweinfurt under Lw.-Gruppenkommando 3. On 1 May 1939, it was redesignated II./St.G. 51 at Schweinfurt under Luftflotte 3.

Ground crews manoeuvre this Ju 87 A-2 into its take-off position. The aircraft carries the code 52+D24 of 4./St.G. 165, this Staffel, based at Schweinfurt, being temporarily redesignated 4./St.G. 51 on 1 May 1939 before becoming 4./St.G. 77 two weeks later. This change was due to an order for the unit to be transferred from Luftflotte 3 (which used the number block 51-75) to Luftflotte 4 (which used the number block 76-100).

This trio of Ju 87 A-1 dive-bombers from 4./St.G. 165 make an ideal picture for the propaganda photographer and show the very jagged camouflage splinter pattern of RLM colours 61, 62 and 63 to advantage. The aircraft nearest the camera carries the 52+C24. The numbers in this code, when read backwards, indicate that the aircraft belonged to the 4th Staffel of the 2nd Gruppe of the 2nd Geschwader to be formed with Luftkreiskommando 5.

This photograph of an Hs 123 A-1, W.Nr. 968 of St.G. 165, graphically illustrates the jagged three colour 'splinter' pattern adopted by most Luftwaffe aircraft during the late 1930s. The national insignia, at this time, featured narrow white outlines with the black Hakenkreuz or swastika painted over a white circle on a red band.

Kommandeur:

Hptm. Clemens Graf von Schönborn-Wiesentheid
(September 1937 - 30 April 1939)

III./St.G. 165

Formation, Training, Re-Equipping and Redesignation (April 1937 – April 1939) Formed on 1 April 1937 at Fürstenfeldbruck using a cadre from II./St.G. 162 and new personnel. Initially equipped with Hs 123s, it was supposed to have started conversion to Ju 87 As by mid-1937. With the completion of the base at Wertheim, the *Gruppe* moved there from Fürstenfeldbruck on 1 October 1937, while still equipped with Hs 123s. As of 1 April 1938, it had 34 Hs 123s at Wertheim and was still based there on 1 November under *Lw.-Gruppenkommando* 3. On 1 May 1939, it was redesignated III./St.G. 51 at Wertheim and had finally been equipped with Ju 87 As and Ju 87 Bs.

Kommandeur:

Hptm. Anton Keil (October 1937 - 30 April 1939)
Hptm. Heinrich von Klitzing (? - 30 April 1939)

Sources for St.G. 165:

NARA WashDC: RG 242/T-971, roll 107, frames 1103-09

[Bateson – *Stuka!*] p. 6;
[Brütting – SA] p. 136, 142, 153, 162, 189, 191, 233, 265, 270;
[Dierich – VdL] p. 204, 227;
[Dressel – FP87A] p. 19;
[Green – WotTR] p. 381, 432;
[Obermaier – RK2] p. 53, 56, 61, 68, 71, 78, 86, 125, 129, 130, 131, 141, 168, 177, 180, 189, 192, 199;
[Ries – Lw] p. 70, 139, 140, 141, 185, 189, 195, 200, 203, 206, 209, 229;
[Ries – PhotoRec] p. 35, 37;
[Schliephake – BotL] p. 41, various;
[Smith – GA] p. 318;
[Smith – LCV4] p. 142;
[Smith – StG77] p. 11, 13, 14, 15, 17, 18, 22-25, 28;
[Tessin – Form] p. 81, 83, 84, 222, 223;
[Völker – dDL] p. 100, 148, 275.

AIR International V15-2 p. 75;
AIR Enthusiast No. 36 p. 16.

St.G. 167

Sturzkampfgeschwader 167
(Unit Code: 73+)

Stab/St.G. 167

There is no evidence that a *Geschwaderstab* ever existed.

I./St.G. 167

Formation (April 1937) The *Gruppe* was formed on 1 April 1937 at Lübeck-Blankensee under *Luftkreis* VII by the redesignation of II./St.G. 162. Initial equipment consisted of Hs 123s.

Training, Re-Equipping, Redesignation (April 1937 – April 1938) It primarily carried out training activities over the year of its existence, during which it is believed to have converted to Ju 87s. On 1 April 1938, the *Gruppe* was redesignated I./St.G. 168 and at about the same time it relocated from Lübeck-Blankensee to Graz/Austria.

Kommandeur:
Unknown.

Although the unit to which these Hs 123s belonged had yet to be established, they would have been typical of the aircraft flown by I./St.G. 167. It was common practice for the aircraft's individual identification letter to be painted above the centre of the upper wing in white.

St.G. 168

Sturzkampfgeschwader 168
(Unit Code: 81+)

Stab/St.G. 168

There is no evidence of a *Geschwaderstab* having existed.

I./St.G. 168

Formation (April 1938) The *Gruppe* was formed on 1 April 1938 at Graz/Austria by the redesignation of I./St.G. 167. It may have been equipped with Ju 87 As.

Training, Re-Equipping, Redesignation (April 1938 – April 1939) Conducted general training activities during its year of existence and it is likely that it re-equipped with Ju 87 Bs during the winter of 1938-1939. On 1 May 1939, it was renamed I./St.G. 76 at Graz and had Ju 87 Bs by that time.

Kommandeur:
Hptm. Walter Sigel ?? (? – 1 May 1939?) – a speculation.

Sources for St.G. 168:

[Brütting – SA] p. 268;
[Dierich – VdL] p. 220;
[Dressel – FP87A] p. 19;
[Obermaier – RK2] p. 42, 57, 64, 69, 91, 96, 145, 212;
[Ries – Lw] p. 139, 140, 203;
[Ries – PhotoRec] p. 35;
[Schliephake – BotL] p. various;
[Smith – StG77] p. 28, 31;
[Tessin – Form] p. 223.

Although I./St.G. 168 only existed between 1 April 1938 and 1 May 1939, it is thought that it was originally equipped with the Ju 87 A-1. Powered by a 600 hp Jumo 210 Ca 12 cylinder liquid-cooled in-line engine, the variant had an armament of two 7.9 mm machine guns and could carry a 250 kg bomb beneath the fuselage.

St.G. 262

Sturzkampfgeschwader 262
(Unit Code: none)

Planned formation (April 1937). This Gruppe never actually existed. It had been planned for formation at Kolberg from elements of St.G. 162 with Ju 87 As, but expediency resulted in the formation of III./St.G. 162 from the same cadre elements at Anklam instead.

Sources for St.G. 262:
[Green – WotTR] p. 430;
[Smith – GA] p. 318;
[Ries – Moles] p. 139?;
[Völker – Form] p. 83, 222.

A rear-view photograph taken around the end of 1937 of Ju 87 A-1, D-IEAU showing the early pre-war camouflage splinter pattern and tail markings. Had the planned formation of St.G. 262 gone ahead in 1937 the unit would have been equipped with this variant or the A-2.

Schlachtfliegerverbände (Ground-Attack Formations)

General Background

Although Germany had direct ground support air units during World War I and experimented with specialized ground-attack doctrine and tactics during the Spanish Civil War, mainly with the Heinkel He 51 biplane fighter and to a far lesser extent with the Henschel Hs 123, the *Luftwaffe* entered World War II with only one formation of this type: II.(*Schlacht*)/*Lehrgeschwader* 2, equipped with Hs 123 biplanes and consisting of a *Gruppenstab* and 3 *SchlachtStaffeln*. That is all that the *Luftwaffe* mobilization plan of 1 July 1939 called for to be operational by 1 September 1939. In fact, the ground-attack arm remained woefully underdeveloped and neglected until the beginning of 1942. On 2 September 1939, for example, there were just 40 ground-attack aircraft assigned to operational units; by 11 May 1940 the number had increased to just 50 and by 21 June 1941 to 60. In all three cases, this was less than 1% - 1½% of the *Luftwaffe's* active aircraft strength on these dates. The arm was finally expanded at the beginning of 1942, due to the course of events on the Eastern Front and a shift in policy by the *Luftwaffe* general staff, with the formation of *Schlachtgeschwader* 1 followed 10 months later by *Schlachtgeschwader* 2. The aircraft employed were Bf 109 single-engine fighters, Hs 123 biplanes (these being phased out over the next year) and Hs 129 twin-engine ground-attack aircraft, with Fw 190 single-engine fighters gradually replacing most of the Bf 109s from 1943 on.

On 18 October 1943 all *Nahkampfflieger* (close support) categories, e.g., *Stuka-, Schlacht-, Panzerjäger-* and *Schnellkampf-*, were consolidated and redesignated as a second generation of *Schlachtgeschwader* numbered 1, 2, 3, 4, 5, 9, 10 and 77. In addition to their primary ground-attack mission, those *Schlachtgruppen* and *SchlachtStaffeln* equipped with Fw 190s increasingly found themselves embroiled in dogfights over the front area and some of the pilots ran up quite respectable scores in air-to-air combat during the last two years of the war. For those interested in pursuing the developmental and technical history of the ground-attack arm further, an excellent account can be found in Martin Pegg's *Hs 129 Panzerjäger!* cited in the bibliography.

Tables of Organization

Not all of the *Kriegsstärkenachweisungen* (KStNs – tables of organization and equipment) survived the mass destruction of *Luftwaffe* records during the last year of the war, but what is known of the numerical designation for the main ones for the ground-attack arm is listed below:

1196 (L)	*Nachrichtenzug (mot) einer Schlachtgruppe* (Signals Platoon of a Ground-Attack *Gruppe*).
1255 (L)	*Stab eines Schlachtgeschwaders* (Staff of a Ground-Attack *Geschwader*).
1255 t (L)	*Stab eines Schlachtgeschwaders/Trop* (Staff of a Ground-Attack *Geschwader* (Tropical)).
1256 (L)	*Stab einer Schlachtgruppe* (Staff of a Ground-Attack *Gruppe*).
1256 t (L)	*Stab einer Schlachtgruppe/Trop* (Staff of a Ground-Attack *Gruppe* (Tropical)).
1257 (L)	*SchlachtStaffel* (Ground-Attack *Staffel*).
1257 t (L)	*SchlachtStaffel/Trop* (Ground-Attack *Staffel* (Tropical)).
1258 (L)	*Stabskompanie einer Schlachtgruppe* (Staff Company of a Ground-Attack *Gruppe*).
1258 t (L)	*Stabskompanie einer Schlachtgruppe/Trop* (Staff Company of a Ground-Attack *Gruppe* (Tropical)).
1454 (L)	*Ergänzungs-SchlachtStaffel (v)* (Reserve Training Ground-Attack *Staffel*) (transferable).
1455 (L)	*Stab einer Ergänzungs-Schlachtgruppe* (Staff of a Reserve Training Ground-Attack *Gruppe*).
1456 (L)	*Stabskompanie einer Ergänzungs-Schlachtgruppe* (Staff Company of a Reserve Training Ground-Attack *Gruppe*).
1475 a, b, c (L)	(Separate KStNs for *Schlachtgeschwader* 151)
1827 b (L)	*Stab einer Gruppe eines Schlachtgeschwaders* (Staff of a *Gruppe* of a *Schlachtgeschwader*).
3364 a (L)	*Stabsnachrichtenzug (mot) eines Schlachtgeschwaders (Ju 87)* (Headquarters Signals Platoon (motorized) of a *Schlachtgeschwader* (Ju 87)).
3364 b (L)	*Gruppennachrichtenzug (mot) eines Schlachtgeschwaders (Ju 87)* (Group Signals Platoon (motorized) of a *Schlachtgeschwader* (Ju 87)).
3365 a (L)	(Identical to 3364 a, but for a *Schlachtgeschwader* equipped with Fw 190s).
3365 b (L)	(Identical to 3364 b, but for a *Schlachtgeschwader* equipped with Fw 190s).

For non-tactical, general administrative matters concerning doctrine, tactics, staffing, promotion and awards recommendations, inspections, etc., the ground-attack arm was managed by a branch of the *Luftwaffe* general staff in Berlin that was reorganized, redesignated and/or changed several times during the war:

Inspekteur der Jagd-, Zerstörer- und Schlachtflieger (February 1939 - 15 September 1941)
General der Jagdflieger (15 September 1941 - ca. July 1942)
Inspekteur der Schlacht- und Zerstörerflieger (ca. July 1942 - 7 September 1943)
General der Nahkampfflieger (7 September 1943 - 7 October 1943)
General der Schlachtflieger (7 October 1943 - 8 May 1945)

Sources for the Introduction:
AFHRA Maxwell AFB, Montgomery, Alabama: decimal 512, A.I.12 (Post Hostilities section) study Y/29 'G.A.F. Establishment Schedule Numbers';
NARA WashDC: RG 242/T-321 roll 104 frames 530-38.

Balke, Ulf- *Der Luftkrieg in Europa: Die Operativen Einsätze des KampfGeschwader 2 im Zweiten Weltkrieg*, 2 Bde (Koblenz: Bernhard & Graefe Verlag, 1989-90), Teil 1, p. 419;
Boog, Horst-*Die deutsche Luftwaffenführung 1935-1945: Führungsprobleme-Spitzengliederung-Generalstabsausbildung* (Stuttgart: Deutsche Verlags-Anstalt, 1982), index;
Dierich, Wolfgang-*Die Verbände der Luftwaffe 1935-1945* (Stuttgart: Motorbuch Verlag, 1976), p. 193-200, 233-35;
Murray, Williamson-*Strategy for Defeat: The Luftwaffe 1933-1945* (Secaucus (NJ): Chartwell Books, 1986), p. 35;
Pegg, Martin-*Hs 129 Panzerjäger!* (Burgess Hill/West Sussex: Classic Publications, 1997), p. 16-24;
Ries, Karl-*Luftwaffen Story 1935-1939* (Mainz: Verlag Dieter Hoffmann, 1974), p. 140 and 145;
Ries, Karl and Hans Ring-*The Legion Condor: A History of the Luftwaffe in the Spanish Civil War 1936-1939* (Atglen/PA: Schiffer Publishing Ltd., 1992), various;
Weal, John-*Luftwaffe Schlachtgruppen*. Osprey Aviation Elite Units (Botley, Oxford: Osprey Publishing, 2003), p. 6-16.

Schlachtfliegergeschwader and *Gruppen*

Stab/Fliegergeschwader 100

Due to mounting tension over the Sudeten crisis, on about 10 June 1938 the formation of five *ad hoc* ground-attack (i.e: *Schlacht*) *Gruppen* was ordered. These were officially created on 1 August 1938 and placed under *Stab/FliegerGeschwader* 100. They were hastily thrown together from whatever assets could be quickly found. Personnel were primarily directly from the training schools with small cadres of more experienced personnel taken from various units. Aircraft initially were in small quantities of inappropriate types, such as Fw 44s, He 45s, He 46s and He 51s, in order to have something to practise with. As soon as possible these were replaced with Hs 123s. The five *Gruppen* were highly deficient in effectiveness, but in the event they saw no action during *Fall Grün* (Case Green), the planned operation to seize the Sudeten territories by force. Some patrols and shows of strength were flown before they returned to Germany in early October. With the end of the crisis, these temporary *Fliegergruppen* were dissolved and the remains incorporated into new units.

**Kommodore*:
Unknown.

Fliegergruppe 10

(June 1938 – October 1938) *Fliegergruppe* 10 was officially created on 1 August 1938 at Tutow with Hs 123 As and placed under *Stab/FliegerGeschwader* 100. The personnel and aircraft were obtained from multiple sources, and the training and organization were hasty due to the crisis atmosphere regarding the Sudetenland territories. As of 1 September it was still at Tutow but by 20 September it had moved to Brieg, still equipped with Hs 123s. The *Gruppe's* actual activities in support of the troops advancing into the Sudetenland are unknown. With the end of the crisis, the assets of *Fliegergruppe* 10 were incorporated into other units, most of it going into the creation of I./St.G. 160 with Hs 123s at Insterburg on 1 November 1938, and subordinated to *Lw.-Gruppenkommando Ostpreussen*.

Codes: (▲10+nn). The code is prefixed by a triangle. The nn represents the number of the individual aircraft.

**Kommandeur*:
Hptm. Dietrich Graf von Pfeil und Ellguth (31 July 1938 - October 1938?) – acting

Sources:
[Balke – KG2V1] p. 21;
[Brütting – SA] p. 278;
[Dierich –VdL] p. 235;
[Fast – JG 52V4] p. 289;
[Obermaier –RK2] p. 60, 103, 186;
[Ries – Lw] p. 140, 145, 200;
[Schliephake – BotL] p. App H;
[Smith – GA] p. 316;
[Tessin – Form] p. 233;
[Völker – dDL] p. 284;
[AIR V15 – 2] p. 76.

Fliegergruppe 20

(July 1938 – October 1938) Stemming from an order issued ca. 10 June 1938, *Fliegergruppe* 20 was formed *ad hoc* at Tutow by 1 August 1938 and placed under *Stab/FliegerGeschwader* 100. During the course of the Sudeten crisis, the unit was stationed at Breslau where it tried determinedly to raise its operational capabilities with a mixture of He 45, He 51, Ar 68 aircraft. By 1 September 1938, the *Gruppe* was back at Tutow anticipating re-equipping on the Hs 123. With the end of the Sudeten crisis at the beginning of October, it was intended to be dissolved like the other four *Gruppen* in this series and its assets returned from whence they had come, but instead *Fliegergruppe* 20 was redesignated II.(Sch.)/LG. 2 at Tutow on 1 November 1938, with a *Staffel* forming the basis of I./St.G. 160. Its conversion to the Hs 123 had only just been started by the date of redesignation.

Codes: (▲20+nn). The code is prefixed by a triangle. The nn represents the number of the individual aircraft.

Kommandeur:
Hptm. Werner Rentsch (1 July 1938 - 31 October 1938)

Sources:
[Balke – KG2V1] p. 21;
[Brütting – SA] p. 155,278;
[Deichmann – Support] p. 33;
[Dierich –Vdl] p. 221;
[Obermaier – RK2] p. 40, 59, 157, 172, 248;
[Ries – Lw] p. 140, 145, 172, 200;
[Schliephake – BotL] p. App H;
[Tessin – Form] p. 85;
[Völker – dDL] p. 284.

Fliegergruppe 30

(June 1938 – October 1938) *Fliegergruppe* 30 was formed on 1 August 1938 at Fassberg and equipped initially with obsolescent a/c such as the He 46 and/or He 51, and subordinated to *Stab/FliegerGeschwader* 100. As of 1 September, the *Gruppe* was thought to still be at Fassberg but by 20 September it was believed to be at Straubing equipped with the Hs 123. The *Gruppe* took part in the occupation of the Sudetenland and by 13 October it was at Marienbad before it was ordered back to Fassberg on 22 October. On 1 November 1938, *Fliegergruppe* 30 became the second I./St.G. 162 at Barth with Hs 123.

Codes: (▲30+nn). The code is prefixed by a triangle. The nn represents the number of the individual aircraft.

Kommandeur:
Hptm. Siegfried von Eschwege (1 August 1938 - 31 October 1938?)

Sources:
[Balke – KG2V1] p. 21;
[Brütting – SA] p. 278;
[Deichmann – Support] p. 33;
[Fast – JG 52V4] p. 290;
[Obermaier – RK2] p. 201;
[Ries – Lw] p. 139,140, 145,204, 206;
[Schliephake – BotL] p. App H;
[Tessin – Form] p. 85;
[Völker – dDL] p. 284.

Fliegergruppe 40

(July 1938 – October 1938) Stemming from an order issued approximately 10 June 1938, *Fliegergruppe* 40 was formed as a provisional or temporary unit for the Sudeten crisis on 1 July 1938 at Fassberg under *Stab/ FliegerGeschwader* 100. While it was intended to have 3 *Staffeln*, by 1 August the unit possessed only one He 45 and 39 (30) crews, although by the end of August 1938 it had 39 He 45s and 39 (39) crews. On 1 September 1938, the *Gruppe* was still at Fassberg but by late September the 3.*Staffel* was at the Messerschmitt factory airfield at Regensburg with the rest of the *Gruppe* at Obertraubling. The *Gruppe* reportedly flew demonstration flights over Czechoslovakia during the crisis and dropped leaflets. After the end of the Sudeten crisis, *Fliegergruppe* 40 was split up, with *Gruppenstab* and 1. and 2.*Staffeln* staying at

Obertraubling to later become the basis of II.(Sch.)/LG. 2 on 1 November 1938, while 3.*Staffel* and the greater part of the ground personnel, technicians and observers left for Cottbus on 18 October to become part of I./K.G. 252 on 1 November 1938.

Codes: (▲40+nn). The code is prefixed by a triangle. The nn represents the number of the individual aircraft.

Kommandeur:
Major Werner Spielvogel (1 July 1938 - 31 October 1938)

Sources:
[Balke-KG2V1] p. 21,22, 23, 33;
[Balke-KG2V2] p. 407, 408;
[Brütting -SA] p. 278;
[Deichmann-Support] p. 33;
[Obermaier-RK2] p. 54, 71;
[Ries-Lw] p. 124, 140, 145, 194, 204;
[Schliephake- BotL] p. App H;
[Tessin -Form] p. 85;
[Völker -dDL] p. 284.

Fliegergruppe 50

(June 1938 – October 1938) *Fliegergruppe* 50 was officially created on 1 August 1938 at Lechfeld with Hs 123 As and placed under *Stab/FliegerGeschwader* 100. Most of the personnel were received from the F.E.A. 23 (Air Force Replacement Battalion 23) at Kaufbeuren. Training and organization was hasty and the unit suffered from inexperience. In the autumn, the *Gruppe* moved from Lechfeld to Grottkau/Silesia and was located there on 20 September under *Fliegerdivision z.b.V.* and still equipped with the Hs 123. In October, it relocated to Paulsgrund near Ratibor to support the troops advancing into the Sudetenland. With the end of the crisis, *Fliegergruppe* 50 received new personnel and equipment (Hs 123s), then reorganized and was redesignated II./St.G. 163 on 1 November 1938 at Langensalza under *Lw.-Gruppenkommando* 1.

Codes: (50+nn). The code is prefixed by a triangle. The nn represents the number of the individual aircraft.

Kommandeur:
Hptm. Hans-Günther von Kornatzki (1 August 1938 - 31 October 1938?) – acting?
Hptm. Ernst Ott (ca. October 1938 - 31 October 1938?)

Sources:
[Balke – KG2V1] p. 21;
[Brütting – SA] p. 215, 278;
[Deichmann – Support] p. 33;
[Obermaier – RK2] p. 93, 138;
[Nauroth – IMM] p. 23, 24, 31,32, 33, 37, 363, 365, 366;
[Ries – Lw] p. 139, 140, 145, 200;
[Schliephake – BotL] p. App H;
[Smith – GA] p. 318;
[Tessin – Form] p. 85;
[Völker – dDL] p. 284;
[AIR V15-2] p.76.

II.(*Schlacht*)/L.G. 2

II.(Schlacht)/Lehrgeschwader 2
(Unit Code: L2+)

[**Note:** II.(*Schlacht*)/L.G. 2 can also be found in *Bomber Units of the Luftwaffe 1933-1945: A Reference Source*, Volume 2, pages 377-79, by the same authors and publisher. An expanded and more detailed history is given below because while the *Gruppe* belonged organizationally to *Lehrgeschwader* 2, it also belongs functionally with the *Schlachtflieger* units.]

Formation and Early History (November 1938 – August 1939) Formed 1 November 1938 at Tutow/near Demmin in north Germany by renaming *Gruppenstab*, 1. and 2.*Staffeln* of *Fliegergruppe* 40 and one *Staffel* from *Fliegergruppe* 20. There is wide disagreement in the published literature over the lineage of II.(Schl.)/L.G. 2, but the two most authoritative sources (Karl-Heinz Völker and Karl Ries) have been used here. Equipped with Heinkel He 45 biplanes, which were replaced with Henschel Hs 123 biplanes in early 1939. Plans called for an eventual conversion to Ju 87s, but this was never carried out. Based at Tutow, the *Gruppe* conducted training exercises until the general mobilization order was received on 26 August 1939. At the beginning of hostilities, the *Staffelkapitäne* were *Hptm.* Otto Weiss (4.*Staffel*), *Oblt.* Adolf Galland (5.*Staffel*) and an unidentified officer (6.*Staffel*). A number of the pilots were experienced veterans of the *Legion Condor* in Spain.

Polish Campaign (September 1939) 1 September: transferred from Tutow to Altsiedel (also known as Alt-Siedel)/20 km south-east of Oppeln in Silesia by 1 September for assignment to *Fliegerführer z.b.V./Luftflotte* 4 with 40 (37) Hs 123s. After moving forward to Alt-Rosenberg, just 15 km from the German-Polish border, flew the Second World War's first ground-attack mission at the break of dawn on the first day of hostilities, striking enemy positions ahead of 1. and 4.*Panzer* Divisions as they opened a breach through the lines, and then attacked Polish Army positions at Przystajn/31 km west-north-west of Czestochowa and near Panki (5 km from Przystajn) as well as other targets. Most of the Henschels carried four 50 kg (110 lb) bombs as well as a pair of 7.9 mm fuselage-mounted MG 17 machine guns. Moved forward with XVI.*Armeekorps*/10.*Armee*, and for next 6 days continued to support the spearheads of 1. Pz.Div. and 4. Pz.Div. as they drove rapidly north-east

towards Lodz and Warsaw. From a forward airstrip at Wolborz/39 km south-south-east of Lodz, participated in the battles of encirclement at Radom, where from 8-12 September the *Gruppe* took part in the destruction of a Polish army in a forest area around Ilza to the south of Radom, and along the Bzura River to the west of Warsaw where the Polish Army Poznan launched a strong counter-attack during the evening of 9 September just south of Kutno. On 13 September, *Gruppenkommandeur Major* Spielvogel failed to return from an early morning Fi 156 reconnaissance sortie and was reported missing (later amended to KIA). His little single-engine *Storch* had been shot down by AA fire over the southern outskirts of Warsaw. 13-18 September: flew continuous missions against the now defeated Army Poznan as it tried to make its way into a thickly wooded area north-west of Warsaw, but it was reduced to remnants during heavy ground and air attacks and 120,000 prisoners were rounded up a few days later. 22 September: with the campaign in Poland all but over, ordered to transfer west to Braunschweig in north-western Germany for reassignment to *Luftflotte* 2 and to train and stand by for forthcoming operations. Known airfields used by the *Gruppe* during the campaign in Poland: Altsiedel, Witkowice, Wolborz, Mazowszany-Kacin, Grojec and Zalesie.

Standby in the West and Attack on France and the Low Countries (October 1939 – June 1940) 1 February 1940: after four quiet months at Braunschweig, most of the *Gruppe* was ordered to München-Gladbach (Mönchengladbach)/25 km west of Düsseldorf and a short distance from the Dutch border. From 11 February to late April, II.(Schl.)/L.G. 2 exercised at Dedelsdorf with *Sturmabteilung Koch*, the *Luftwaffe* airborne/glider-borne paratroops assigned to take the powerful Belgian fortresses and three key bridges along the Albert Canal. 4 May: *Gruppe* lost 1 killed and 9 wounded when a bomb accidently detonated during final preparations for offensive action. 10 May: at Lauffenberg/near Neuss under VIII.*Fliegerkorps/Luftflotte* 2 with 49 (38) Hs 123 As. (**Note:** the airfield 'Lauffenberg' or 'Laufenberg' is ill-defined and may actually be Neuss-Kaarst). Supported the seizure of key bridges to open the way for the advance of the 6.*Armee's Panzer* divisions into Belgium, taking part in the decisive

A formation of Henschel Hs 123s of 4.(Schlacht)/L.G. 2 operating during the German invasion of Poland in September 1939. The aircraft nearest the camera, L2+PM, still has the early type national insignia on the fuselage sides with narrow white edging.

Otto Weiss (RK-EL)

WEISS was born on 25 September 1907 in Breslau and joined the *Polizei* (police) on 15 April 1926. After a distinguished career with that force he enrolled in pilot training with D.V.S. Braunschweig on 1 March 1933 until 16 June. On 4 June 1934 he continued pilot training at the *Aufklärungsfliegerschule* Braunschweig and on 1 October 1934 transferred from the *Landespolizei* to the *Luftwaffe*, being assigned to *Fliegergruppe* Cottbus as a pilot. He was transferred to Aufkl.Gr. 212 at Cottbus on 12 March 1936 and promoted to *Hptm.* on 1 April 1936. Appointed *Chef* (company commander) of *Stabs*-Kp. I./J.G. 134 Horst Wessel at Dortmund on 1 December 1936, Weiss was ordered to *Luftkreisschule* II Berlin-Gatow for training with the 4. *Lehrgang* to 14 February 1937. He transferred to Fassberg for a *Schlachtflieger* course on 1 July 1938 and a month later was appointed *Staka* of 1./*Fliegergruppe* 40, with the rank of *Hptm.* On 1 November 1938 he took over 4.(Schl.)/LG. 2 and was *Kommandeur* of II.(Schl.)/LG. 2 thirteen months later.

Awarded the E.K. II on 13 September 1939, the E.K. I on 30 September and the *Ritterkreuz* on 18 May 1940, Weiss was promoted to *Major* on 1 July 1940 and enrolled in *Generalstab* training at the *Luftkriegsakademie* Berlin-Gatow (3.*Kurz-Lehrgang*) on 15 October that year. He was awarded the *Ehrenpokal* on 9 November 1940, appointed Ia of *Jagdfliegerführer* 2 on 16 February 1941, was reappointed *Kommandeur* of II.(Schl.)/LG. 2 on 26 May 1941, and awarded the *Eichenlaub zum Ritterkreuz* (No. 52) on 31 December 1941. He may have become *Kommandeur* of I./St.G. 2 on 4 January 1942 but was appointed *Kommodore* of Schl.G. 1 nine days later and *Kommodore* of St.G. 1 on 24 April.

Weiss transferred to the *Führer-Reserve* (officer reserve) Ob.d.L./RLM on 18 June 1942 and was made *Inspekteur der Schlacht-u.Zerstörerflieger* (L.In.2/3)/RLM on 8 July 1942. He was promoted to *Oberstleutnant* (see photograph) on 1 September 1942, apparently simultaneously commanding *Versuchskommando für Panzerbekämpfung* (Experimental Detachment for Anti-Tank Warfare) in December 1942. In February 1943 he was appointed *Führer der Panzerjägerstaffeln* (again possibly concurrently). On 1 August 1943 he was removed from the list of Lw. *Generalstab* candidates as it was felt he had more value as a unit commander. He was promoted to *Oberst* on 1 November 1943 and during 1944 was with the *Stab/Luftflotte* 6. Around January 1945 he was appointed *Jagdfliegerführer Westpreussen* but approximately a month later he returned to *Stab/Luftflotte* 6. Credited with over 500 combat missions, he died on 19 August 1955 in Kiel.

On 22 May 1940 II.(Schlacht)/L.G. 2 distinguished itself by helping to block a breakthrough by British tanks about 35 kilometres north of Arras in France. Both Hs 123s shown here belonged to the 6.Staffel. The aircraft (ABOVE) carries the unit code L2+GP, the individual identification letter 'G' in yellow edged in black. The forward fuselage of the aircraft (BELOW) carries the badge of the squadron – a black cat carrying a sword and lantern, superimposed on a silver circle. Following the completion of the campaign in June 1940 the Gruppe began to exchange its Hs 123s for Bf 109 Es.

battles around Maastricht and Eben Emael. At Eben Emael on 10 May, the *Gruppe* and elements of St.G. 2 mauled an infantry division that attempted to relieve the fort's garrison and prevented it from getting through. Ordered south to Guise/25 km east-north-east of St-Quentin to support the drive by XIX.*Panzerkorps* across the Meuse and the fighting around Sedan, Liège and Namur. On 14 May, an Hs 123 was shot up by AA fire near Tirlemont and reduced to salvage. 16 May: ordered from Duras/54 km east of Brussels south to the Sedan-Neufchâteau area to support 12.*Armee's* advance to the Channel coast. 19-20 May: flew repeated missions against troop concentrations in the vicinity of Douai and Le Cateau. Transferred to Cambrai on 21 May and shortly after arrival credited with the destruction of nearly 40 French tanks and numerous supporting infantry that were massing north of Cambrai. On 22 May the *Gruppe* distinguished itself by helping to block a breakthrough by British tanks about 35 kilometres north of Arras. Remained active in north-eastern France over the next 10 days, mainly in support of *Panzergruppe Kleist*, flying from St-Pol as well as other forward airfields. 5 June: following operations around Dunkirk, moved to Puisieux/19 km south of Arras to support the crossing of the Somme and the advance south-west towards Paris, and then into Normandy and Brittany in the final battles for France as a component of VIII.*Fliegerkorps* in support of *Panzergruppe* Kleist, A.O.K. 6 and A.O.K. 9. One combat loss to French fighters was reported on 5 June, although two other Hs 123s are said to have been so badly shot up they barely made it back to base. Another Henschel was lost to a French fighter on 15 June, and by 17 June the *Gruppe* was operating in the Dijon area. On conclusion of the campaign on 22 June, ordered to Braunschweig-Waggum for conversion to the Bf 109 E, then to Böblingen to begin fighter-bomber training.

Air Offensive against England (Battle of Britain) (July 1940 – March 1941) 13 August: at Böblingen for training at the Rohrau weapons range with 39 (31) Bf 109 E-7s, which concluded with a transfer to Calais-Marck on 4 September (other sources place it at St-Omer - Arques or both). However, a week earlier elements of the *Gruppe* moved to the Pas de Calais ahead of the main body and raided RAF Station Biggin Hill on 31 August. 2 September: hit Hornchurch and Detling airfields, and the next day struck RAF Station Manston, Maidstone airfield and Ramsgate harbour. Suffered its first losses in the air offensive against England on 6 September, with two Bf 109 E-7s shot down by fighters at Canterbury and off Herne Bay (other sources claim these were shot down by naval AA fire over Chatham during a raid on shipping in the Thames Estuary), followed by another over Ashford in Kent on 14 September during a raid on London. A turning point was reached in the Battle of Britain on 15 September when the *Luftwaffe* suffered extraordinary losses, forcing it to shift the main effort to night bombing. Daylight operations after this date relied increasingly on nuisance raids along England's south coast by the fighter-bombers of II.(Schl.)/L.G. 2. 18 September: took part in an attack on the docks at Tilbury. 20 September: hit London again. Second half of September: 5.*Staffel* tested the Hs 129 A-0 and Fw 189 V6 for suitability for ground assault. London was the *Gruppe's* target again on 21, 28 and 29 September and on 13 days during October. On 7 October two 4.*Staffel* Bf 109 E-4s were shot down by fighters over southern England during fighter-bomber sorties to London followed by two more on 29 October, these falling to Hurricanes during an attack on North Weald air base. One of the pilots lost on 29 October was *Oblt.* Hans-Benno von Schenck, *Staffelkapitän* of 5.*Staffel*. 5 December: 4.*Staffel* lost its *Staka*, *Oblt.* Heinz Vogeler, when he failed to return from an attack on Channel

Infantry assault badge

During the winter of 1940/1941 a second Hs 123-equipped Staffel was added to the Lehrgeschwader under the designation 10.(Schlacht)/L.G. 2. Formed at Braunschweig-Waggum the squadron moved to Bulgaria to support Luftwaffe operations in the invasion of Greece which began on 6 April 1941. This aircraft carried the black triangle marking which was later adopted by Schl.G. 1 and 2 and the red letter 'T' outlined in white. Its engine cowling, rudder and undersides of the top wing tips were painted yellow.

Following the conclusion of the campaign against France on 22 June 1940, II.(Schlacht)/ L.G. 2 was ordered to Braunschweig-Waggum for conversion to the Bf 109 E. However, the unit retained a number of the biplane dive-bombers up until its dissolution in January 1942. Here, two aircraft from the unit stand idle on a German airfield with a number of Bf 109 Es in the background. The Hs 123 nearest the camera appears to be unmarked while the second machine carries the unit code L2+A?

shipping, and *Oblt.* Viktor Kraft from the *Gruppenstab* was lost to a Spitfire on 11 December during a fighter-bomber sweep over Kent. 5 February 1941: a Bf 109 E-4 crashed at Cognac airfield in south-west France, killing the *Kapitän* of 6.*Staffel*, *Oblt.* Paul Widmann. 8 February: 5.*Staffel* lost a Bf 109 E-7 to AA fire over RAF Station Hawkinge during a low-level, high-speed attack on the airfield by just two aircraft. 9 March: Bf 109 E-7 bombed on ground and destroyed during an RAF raid on Calais-Marck. 15 March: Bf 109 E-7 shot down by 3 Hurricanes flying convoy escort off Dungeness/Kent.

Balkan Campaign (April 1941 – May 1941)

29 March: transferred from Calais-Marck to Bulgaria for the Balkan campaign via Köln-Butzweilerhof, stationed at Sofia-Bozhurishte under VIII.*Fliegerkorps*, two *Staffeln* with 29 (23) Bf 109 E-7/Bs and one *Staffel* with Hs 123 As. Other sources place the *Gruppe* at Sofia-Vrazdebna with a second Henschel *Staffel* (10.*Staffel*) based at Krainici to the south of Sofia. The second Hs 123 *Staffel* had been formed at Braunschweig-Waggum some time between autumn 1940 and March 1941. The two Hs 123 *Staffeln* together had a total of 32 (20) machines on hand. The attack began on 6 April and the *Gruppe* was assigned to bomb and strafe several airfields, including Skopje in Macedonia. 7 April: said to have attacked airfields at Kumanovo and Skopje and troop concentrations in the vicinity of Stip, Veles and Gradsko. Supported the advance through Serbia, Macedonia and into Greece, and on 26 April strafed ground targets and flew cover for the airborne and glider assault on the Corinth Canal by the *Luftwaffe's* 2nd Parachute Regiment (*Fallschirmjäger*-Rgt. 2). By early May the *Gruppe* was at Molaoi/150 km south-west of Athens. It did not participate in the airborne and air-landing assault on Crete that began on 20 May due to the distance from Molaoi to Maleme/Crete exceeding the *Gruppe's* operational range with a bomb load. June: ordered from

Molaoi to Praschnitz (Przasnysz)/85 km north of Warsaw in north-east Poland in early June for the forthcoming invasion of Russia with subordination to VIII.*Fliegerkorps/Luftflotte* 2.

Attack on the Soviet Union – Central and North Russia (June 1941 – January 1942)

22 June: Praschnitz with 38 (37) Bf 109 Es in the *Gruppenstab* and 4. - 6.*Staffel*, and 10.*Staffel* with 22 (17) Hs 123s; attached to St.G. 2 and under VIII.*Fliegerkorps/Luftflotte* 2. Operated from Suwalki and Berzniki in support of A.O.K. 9 and *Panzergruppe* 3 as the lead armour and infantry smashed through the border defences and annihilated the Grodno-Bialystok pocket during the initial advance into the Soviet Union. 24 June: a 10.*Staffel* Hs 123 B-1 failed to return from operations in the Grodno area. 3-4 July: several 10.*Staffel* Hs 123 B-1 accidents at Repicki (not located), a forward field strip along the line of advance. 5 July: moved forward to Sloboda for operations in the Minsk area and the destruction of Soviet forces encircled there. It then supported the advance of *Panzergruppe* 2 to and across the Dnieper River and the thrust forward to take Smolensk. 6 July: 10.*Staffel* Hs 123 B-1 shot down by AA fire at Bosheikovo (not located). 6 July: ordered to Lepel to fly Bf 109 escort for I./St.G. 2 *Stukas*. 8-11 July: lost two Bf 109 E-7s in the Lepel-Vitebsk area supporting the drive towards Smolensk, moving to Vitebsk by 24 July. 26 July: two Bf 109 Es shot down by fighters while attacking a strong Russian counter-attack against *Panzergruppe* 2 to the east and south of Smolensk. 26 July: there is no further mention of 10.*Staffel* in the surviving documents for the next two months following this date, which suggests that it must have had a run of extraordinarily good fortune to avoid any losses, crashes or accidents for that long a period, or that it had been withdrawn to refit, perhaps in the Warsaw area. 3 August: transferred to the northern sector of the front with VIII.*Fliegerkorps* and attached to *Stab*/J.G. 27 for

On 29 March 1941, II.(Schlacht)/L.G. 2 was transferred from Calais-Marck to Sofia-Bozhurishte in Bulgaria for the Balkan campaign. At this time the two Hs 123 Staffeln had a total of 32 machines on hand. Here, ground crews look on as an Hs 123, W.Nr. 7132, is prepared for a sortie against Macedonia airfields. It carries the triangle marking together with a bright yellow engine cowling and rudder used by most Luftwaffe in this theatre at this time.

employment, with action in the Dno – Staraya Russa area south-west of Lake Ilmen by 8 August. For the remainder of the month, the *Gruppe* supported 16.*Armee* south of Lake Ilmen and then the advance of armoured forces from Novgorod towards Chudovo and Lyuban. 25 August: based at Spaskaya/north-north-east of Novgorod, where two Bf 109 E-7s were destroyed on the ground in a Russian air attack. Moved to Lyuban/southeast of Leningrad by 29 August. September: supported attack by *Panzergruppe* 4 towards Leningrad and

Schlüsselburg at the south end of Lake Ladoga. 15 September: 10.*Staffel* Hs 123 crashed near Warsaw due to engine failure. 25 September: 10.*Staffel* now back at the front, several landing and taxiing accidents were reported at Lyuban airstrip/south-east of Leningrad. At the end of September, transferred from Lyuban back to the central sector with VIII.*Fliegerkorps* for the attack on Moscow, flying direct support for the battles around Bryansk on 2 October. October – November: moved to field strips at Belyy and Moshna a few days later to support 9.*Armee*,

Two Hs 123 A-1s of 5.(Schlacht)/L.G. 2 photographed at Thalerdorf in Austria later in 1941. The aircraft in the foreground, L2+MN, W.Nr. 2292, carries the Staffel badge. This comprised a bear standing on his hind legs chopping up the British Prime Minister, Neville Chamberlain's, famous umbrella with an axe. It was painted on the forward fuselage just behind the cowling.

This Hs 123 in standard splinter camouflage belonging to II.(Schlacht)/L.G. 2 stands under camouflage netting with its engine running is about to set off on a mission. Note the 'Berlin Bear' emblem on the nose.

Mickey Mouse Emblem introduced by II.(Schlacht)/L.G. 2

Panzergruppe 3 and 6.*Panzer-Division* in action around Vyazma and the offensive towards Kalinin. On 14 October, 3 Bf 109 E-7s were lost in heavy fighting in the Kalinin area, and three more damaged there on 18 October. At Kalinin-South on 21-22 October where the *Gruppe* flew near round the clock attacks on Russian forces that had cut off and isolated 1.*Panzer-Div.* The little Hs 123 biplanes particularly distinguished themselves in the desperate fighting around Kalinin. While there, the Bf 109 pilots also received orders to engage and shoot

After arrival in Russia II.(Schlacht)/L.G. 2 painted this on the wall of its quarters. It includes the Gruppe's Mickey Mouse badge together with a listing of some of the successive bases which it used.

down every enemy plane encountered over the Kalinin sector. Back at Belyy on 24 October, but then returned to Kalinin-Luchinovka by the end of the month. November: supported the continuing drive towards Moscow, although many missions were scrubbed due to bad flying weather. 27 November: 10.*Staffel* was operating from Staraya Russa at the south end of Lake Ilmen where heavy fighting was underway. December: by December the *Gruppe* was in support of the intense defensive fighting along the entire front from Moscow north-west to Lake Ilmen that began with the Soviet counter-offensive on 5 December. Base changes were rapid and frequent as the *Gruppe* attempted to support the German retreat towards the west. On 13 December, 4.*Staffel* (at least) is known to have been operating from Staraya Russa at the south end of Lake Ilmen. 6 January: now based at Dugino/65 km south of Rzhev, where it was renamed I./*Schlachtgeschwader* 1 on 13 January 1942. 10.*Staffel* was probably renamed 8. (Pz)/*Schlachtgeschwader* 1 on the same date, although the lineage is not absolutely clear.

FpNs: II. *Stab* (L 36352, 34346); 4. (L 36533, 35341); 5. (L 37154, 35777); 6. (L 32907, 36673); 10. (no FpN found)

Kommandeur:
Major Werner Spielvogel (1 November 1938 – 9 September 1939 KIA)
Major Wolfgang Neudörffer (ca. 14 September 1939 – 1 December 1939)
Major Otto Weiss (RK) (1 December 1939 – 15 October 1940)

Following the completion of the campaign against France and the Low Countries, II.(Schlacht)/L.G. 2 began to re-equip with the Bf 109 E-7, but by the time of Operation Barbarossa in June 1941 the Gruppe was still flying a mixture of this type and the Hs 123. Here, a Bf 109 E of the Gruppe is pictured behind the remains of a Soviet aircraft, many of which were destroyed in ground-attack sorties carried out by the unit.

Hptm. Egon Thiem (RK) (15 October 1940 – 26 May 1941)
Major Otto Weiss (RK, EL) (26 May 1941 – 13 January 1942)

Sources for II.(Schl.)/L.G. 2:

Unpublished and Archival:

BA-MA Freiburg: RL 2 III *Meldungen über Flugzeugunfälle*.....(Loss Reports – LRs);
PRO London: AIR 40 intelligence documents derived from ULTRA and 'Y' Service intercepts;
PRO London: AIR 40/folders 1966, 1968, 1975, 1976.

Correspondence:
Heinz Guelzow - private correspondence with H.L. deZeng dated 18 May 1999.

Published Sources:
[Balke – KG2V1] p. 395,402,411,415,418;
[Bergström – BC/RS-1] p. 62, 117, 234;
[Brütting – SA] p. 138-40;
[Carlsen – CM1] p. 89;
[Dierich –VdL]
[Foreman – Forg] p. 168;
[Goss – LFBoB] p. 36, 40, 44, 47, 49, 51, 52, 54, 57, 58;
[Green – WotTR] p. 380-381;
[Hooten – Phoenix] p. 181-82,185,209,243,251,258;
[Kannapin – FPN]
[Ramsey – B-2] see index;
[Ries – Lw] p. 145;
[Shores –Yugo] see index;
[Tessin – Tes]
[Toliver – FG] p. 59-61, 122;
[Völker – dDL] p. 104-105;

[Weal – LS] p. 6-37;
[Zaloga – Poland] p. 36-89.

A 550 lb SC 250 bomb fitted on a Bf 109 E/B fighter-bomber in Russia.

Schl.G. 1

Schlachtgeschwader 1
(Unit Code: none)

Stab/Schl.G. 1

Formation & Work-up (January 1942 – April 1942) The *Stab* of the *Geschwader* was formed on 13 January 1942 at Werl, near Dortmund, using personnel from the *Gruppenstab* of II.(*Schlacht*)/LG 2. On 1 March, the *Geschwaderstab* reported a total of 3 Bf 109 E-7s on strength. Training was completed by the end of April and the *Geschwader* was ordered to Crimea for duty with IV.*Fliegerkorps* of *Luftflotte* 4. The *Stab* departed for Itshki-Grammatikovo on 2 May.

Crimea and South Russia (May 1942 – November 1942) After arrival, operations started almost immediately with ground-attack missions in the Eastern Crimea from 8 to 15 May, and then switching to the Izyum Salient south-east of Kharkov to the end of the month. Altogether, Schl.G. 1 flew 1,467 sorties during the month with 1,028 Bf 109, 259 Hs 123 and 180 Hs 129 missions. The *Stab* transferred to Kharkov towards the end of May and then moved to Tatsinskaya in July and Tusov in August to support the advance on Stalingrad under command of IV.*Fliegerkorps* and VIII.*Fliegerkorps*. About late September or early October it relocated to Oblivskaya.

Stalingrad Encirclement, Retreats, Re-equipment (November 1942 – June 1943) On 22 November, the *Stab* was forced to blow up two of its unserviceable Bf 109 E-7s, just three days after the opening of the Soviet counter-offensive at Stalingrad which eventually encircled the German 6th Army. The *Stab* was forced to abandon its base at Oblivskaya on 26 November and withdraw west, probably to Morosovskaya and then to Millerovo or Voroshilovgrad. Meanwhile, the *Stabsschwarm's* aircraft had been quickly replaced and on 1 December it reported 4 Bf 109 E-7s on hand. During early 1943 the *Stab* remained in the Donets Basin area and was stationed at Barvenkovo-South in May. The *Geschwader's* two *Gruppen* continued operations during the spring and summer while converting one at a time to the Fw 190. In April, the *Stabsschwarm* also received its first Fw 190s, with 4 Fw 190 A-5 or F-3 models generally being on strength through the summer and autumn.

Kursk Offensive, Retreats, Dissolution (July 1943 – October 1943) Headquarters locations for the *Stab* are not known with certainty after May 1943, but it was probably at either Barvenkovo or Varvarovka in July at the time of the Kursk offensive (Operation *Zitadelle*), followed by a few weeks at Orel and then gradually withdrew to Kiev where it was stationed in October 1943. On 18 October the *Stab* was ordered disbanded at Kiev and the personnel used to form the *Stäbe* of IV./S.G. 9, NSGr. 3 and NSGr. 7.

FpN: *Stab* (L 15361)

***Kommodore*:**
Major Otto Weiss (RK, EL) (23 April 1942 – 18 June 1942)
Hptm./Major Hubertus Hitschhold (RK, EL) (18 June 1942 – 25 June 1943)

I./Schl.G. 1

Formation, Central Russia (January 1942 – April 1942) The I.*Gruppe* was formed on 13 January 1942 at Werl by renaming II.(*Schlacht*)/L.G. 2, which was still in central Russia at Dugino, north of Vyazma. It continued to operate with Bf 109 Es from Dugino until mid-March, mainly due to the critical situation along the front west of Moscow, before transferring to Werl to rest, refit and reorganize. On 1 March, while still at Dugino, the *Gruppe* reported 18 Bf 109 E-7s and 18 Henschel Hs 123s on strength. Its organization was perhaps unique for the usually methodical Germans in that I.*Gruppe* controlled four *Staffeln*, 1., 2., 3. (all from II.(*Schlacht*)/L.G. 2), and 8./Schl.G. 1. The latter was redesignated from the independent 10.(*Schlacht*)/L.G. 2. It retained its original Hs 123 A biplanes until it arrived at Werl where they were transferred to the newly formed 7.*Staffel*. Normally, the subordinate *Staffeln* of a *Gruppe* were numbered in sequence, but not *Schlachtgeschwader* 1, as all the Henschel-equipped *Staffeln* were put under II.*Gruppe*.

Hubertus Hitschhold (RK-EL). General officer

BORN 7 July 1912 in Kurwien/East Prussia, Hitschhold began his military service on 1 April 1930 serving with the *Reichswehr* (*Kavallerie*). On 30 September 1931 he commenced pre-military flight training with D.V.S. Schleissheim and then in Russia, receiving the interim *Luftwaffe* pilot licence B on 27 October 1932. On 1 October 1934 (or 1 January 1935?) he was officially transferred from the *Heer* (Army) to the *Luftwaffe* with the rank of *Lt.* and assigned to *Jagdfliegerschule* Schleissheim for fighter pilot training. Promoted to *Oblt.* on 1 September 1935 and transferred as a pilot to *Fliegergruppe* I./St.G. 162 at Schwerin on 1 April 1936, he moved to the II.*Gruppe* at Lübeck on 1 September 1936 and received the permanent *Luftwaffe* pilot licence ten days later. Further transfers included a move to III./St.G. 2 at Anklam on 1 March 1937 and to I./St.G. 163 at Breslau-Strachwitz on 1 October 1937.

Hitschhold was promoted to *Hptm.* on 1 January 1939 and made *Staka* in I./St.G. 2 at Breslau on 1 May 1939. He was awarded the E.K. II on 6 October for operations in Poland, and appointed *Kdr.* of I./St.G. 2 ten days later. He received the E.K. I on 15 May 1940 and was promoted to *Major* on 1 July 1940. For conspicuous action during the invasion of France and the Low Countries, he was awarded the *Ritterkreuz* on 21 July. On 23 June 1941 he was shot down while flying a low-level attack on Russian troop columns along the Vilnius-Kaunas road in Lithuania, but another *Stuka* quickly landed along the road in the middle of the enemy, picked up Hitschhold and his radio operator, and flew them to safety.

Hitschhold was appointed *Kommandeur* of *Stukaschule* 1 at Wertheim on 16 October 1941 and awarded the *Eichenlaub zum Ritterkreuz* (No. 57) on 31 December. He took over Schl.G. 1 as *Kommodore* on 18 June 1942 and was promoted to *Obstlt.* on 1 February 1943. Ordered to *Luftflotte* 2 in the Mediterranean on 10 June 1943, he was appointed *Fliegerführer* Sardinien nine days later. This appointment only lasted until 26 June 1943 when he became *Fliegerführer* 2 (*Luftflotte* 2). He was promoted to *Oberst* on 1 July 1943 and appointed *Kommodore* of St.G. 101.★ On 12 November 1943 he became the *General der Schlachtflieger* (L.In.2/3)/RLM and was promoted to *Gen.Maj.* on 1 January 1945. He was taken Allied prisoner of war on 8 May 1945 but was released from custody in June 1947. He died on 10 March 1966 in Starnberger See (Söcking?) of a sudden illness.

★ (**Note**: his assignments for summer 1943 originate from reliable sources but there is disagreement; the 26 June 1943 appointment as *Fliegerführer* 2 can be found in LPA *Personalveränderungen in der Dienstaltersliste* A (*Truppenoffiziere*) Nr. 662/A *geheim* dated 26 June 1943, page 3, but his appointment as *Kommodore* of St.G. 101 is from a slightly less reliable published source, questionable and needs confirmation before it can be accepted).

During operations in the Soviet winter many Luftwaffe aircraft had their dark green upper surface camouflage over-painted in temporary white finish. The black triangle marking of this Bf 109 E-7 of 1./Schl.G. 1 has been completely obscured, the individual letter 'R' (in white edged in black) remaining as the only visible unit marking.

On 1 March 1942, I./Schl.G. 1 reported 18 Bf 109 E-7s and 18 Hs 123s on strength at Dugino north of Vyazma in central Russia. These four Henschels from the 3.Staffel, are coded 'yellow L, H, M and B' respectively and all carry the unit's familiar black equilateral triangle and infantry assault badge. Three of the aircraft have their wheel spats removed to ease maintenance, a practice often adopted by many Ju 87s.

A 550 lb SC 250 bomb being loaded aboard a Bf 109 E/B fighter-bomber based on the Russian Front. When formed from II.(Schlacht)/L.G. 2 at Dugino, I./Schl.G. 1 was equipped with a mixture of the Bf 109s and Hs 123s. The bomb on this aircraft bears an inscription which can be roughly translated as 'Greetings to Ivan'.

Operations in Crimea (May 1942) Equipped with Bf 109 E-7s, I./Schl.G. 1 was ordered to Crimea during the first week of May. After arriving at Itshki-Grammatikovo, the *Gruppe* was assigned to VIII.*Fliegerkorps* for support of 11.*Armee's* re-conquest of the Kerch Peninsula (Operation *Trappenjagd*). Attacks were carried out against Soviet positions along the front and on troop and supply columns immediately behind the front with such a concentrated effect that the German infantry assault units were able to break through the forward defences on 8 May, the first day of the attack. A few days later, on 12 May, *Oblt.* Werner Dörnbrack scored the *Gruppe's* first victory claiming an I-16 Rata fighter near Martovka. The German spearheads moved rapidly across the peninsula and took the town of Kerch on 15 May. Losses to the *Gruppe* were limited to two Bf 109 E-7s on 11 May over the eastern tip of the peninsula, both probably shot down by AA fire around Kerch. One further victory, a MiG-3, was claimed on 18 May before the *Gruppe* departed Crimea.

Izyum Salient, Kharkov and the Advance to Stalingrad (May 1942 – September 1942) With the entire Crimea now firmly in German hands, excluding the fortress of Sevastopol, I./Schl.G. 1 transferred north to Konstantinovka, Kharkov and Barvenkovo/130 km south-south-east of Kharkov to stem a Soviet offensive launched from the Izyum Salient and directed at Kharkov. The *Gruppe* was heavily engaged in ground attacks against Soviet armour, troop concentrations and supply columns until the salient was eliminated on 28 May. The *Gruppe* then moved to Kharkov-Rogan on 30 May for its next assignment, which was to attack enemy tank

concentrations east of Kharkov and to support the 6th Army during the drive to the Don, and later Stalingrad, which began on 25 June. For the beginning of the attack, the *Gruppe* moved temporarily to Shatalovka on the central sector of the Eastern Front on 24 June and remained there until 5 July. Few losses were recorded during intense action against retreating Soviet troops, but the *Gruppe* did lose two Bf 109 E-7s, one shot down over Voronezh and the other along the Don south of the city, both on 4 July. The rapid advance of the German forces resulted in the *Gruppe* being transferred via several intermediate field strips to Tatsinskaya on 18 July and then to Frolov-West, a small airstrip a few kilometres from Oblivskaya, on 31 July. In the two months to the end of July, the *Gruppe* claimed 5 more victories, including an R-5 reconnaissance biplane over Voronezh on 5 July and two Il-2s along the Don south-east of Voronezh in the Kalach area on 24 and 28 July. A major ground-attack victory was scored on 27 July when the *Gruppe* struck the Russian airfield at Illarionovskoye (Illarionovskiy/58 km west of Stalingrad) and destroyed 15 aircraft on the ground, mostly Yak fighters, and damaged 13 more. During the rapid advance towards Stalingrad the pilots were frequently called upon to fly up to 8 missions a day against artillery positions, troop concentrations, retreating columns, bridges and other targets. On or shortly before 11 August, a further move was made to Tusov (Tuzov)/99 km west of Stalingrad and for the next several days supported the elimination of a pocket of Russian troops around Kalach. Tusov remained the home base for the *Gruppe* until late November. On 1 September, the *Gruppe* reported 37 Bf 109 E-7s on strength. Shortly after the *Gruppe* settled in at Tusov, 1.*Staffel* claimed a LaGG-3

This Bf 109 E-7 was probably piloted by the Major Alfred Druschel who commanded I./Sch.G. 1 from the time of its formation on 13 January 1942 to 1 March 1943. The aircraft carries the familiar black equilateral triangle marking adopted by the first Schlachtgruppen together with a double chevron forward of the fuselage Balkenkreuz. The latter symbol, originally adopted by the fighter units, indicated the aircraft of a Gruppe Kommandeur. The engine cowling and rear fuselage band were painted yellow.

Georg Dörffel (RK-EL, DKG)

'Orge' Dörffel was born 27 July 1914 at Rengersdorf/Kreis Görlitz in Silesia. He joined the *Heer* (Army) in 1935, serving with *Infanterie-Rgt.* 22. Two years later he transferred to the *Luftwaffe* with the rank of *Oberfähnrich* (senior officer candidate) and was initially trained and assigned as a *Beobachter* (observer/navigator) in a *Kampfgruppe* before volunteering for the *Schlachtflieger* branch. On 1 July 1939, now promoted to *Leutnant*, he transferred from II.(Schl.)/L.G. 2 to III.(Aufkl.)/L.G. 2 for a short period. When Germany invaded France and the Low Countries on 10 May 1940, he was serving with 5.(Schl.)/L.G. 2. On 21 May he received the E.K. I and the E.K. II at the same time in recognition of his outstanding performance in demolishing a French tank and infantry attack north of Cambrai a few days earlier.

On 30 October 1940 Dörffel was appointed *Staffelkapitän* of 5./LG. 2 as an *Oberleutnant*, (see photograph) and was awarded the *Ritterkreuz* on 21 August and the *Ehrenpokal* on 17 November 1941. On 13 January 1942 he became *Staka* of 5./Schl.G. 1 and received the DKG eleven days later. He was appointed acting *Kommandeur* of I./Schl.G. 1 (to September 1943) and awarded the *Eichenlaub zum Ritterkreuz* (No. 231) on 14 April 1943 as *Hauptmann* and *Kommandeur* of I./Schl.G. 1 for completing over 600 combat missions. He was made permanent *Kommandeur* of I./Sch.G. 1 on 11 June 1943 and took over leadership of the *Erg.Schlachtgruppe* on 24 September until 15 November. On 7 October 1943 he flew his 1,001st combat mission but was banned from further operational flying, although he chose not to obey this order immediately. He claimed his 30th aerial victory (a Russian fighter in the vicinity of Vitebsk) on 12 October 1943 – an extraordinarily large number for a *Schlachtflieger*. He became *Kommandeur* of I./S.G. 152 on 15 November 1943 and was promoted to *Major* and appointed *Kommodore* of S.G. 4 in May 1944, but was killed on the 26th when his Fw 190 F-8 was shot down north of Rome while engaging a formation of P-47s escorting 4-engine bombers from the US 15th Air Force. Another, more recent and better researched, account states that he engaged P-47 fighter bombers in the vicinity of Lake Bracciano on 26 May 1944 and baled out 15 km NW of Rome, and that no 4-engine bombers operated that day. Dörffel was posthumously promoted to *Obstlt.* and credited with 1,004 combat missions and at least 30 air victories.

Hptm. Georg Dörffel, acting Kommandeur of I./Schl.G. 1, is congratulated by his fellow pilots possibly after completing his 600th combat mission in April 1943. One of the unit's Bf 109 E-7s can be seen in the background.

over Abganerovo/73 km south of Stalingrad on 20 August and an Il-2 in the same area on 30 August, but no more enemy planes were reported shot down for the next three months. The main act of the Stalingrad epic opened on 13 September as the ill-fated 6.*Armee* launched its assault into the heart of the city preceded by swarms of bombers, dive-bombers and ground-attack aircraft, including Schl.G. 1, that were to destroy defensive positions and open a path for the troops. The street fighting raged in the destroyed city for months, and it was not until 18 November before the Germans had taken most of it.

Stalingrad and the Aftermath (October 1942 – March 1943) Air operations for the *Gruppe* in the Stalingrad area were continuous but at a somewhat reduced level throughout the autumn, and a number of aircraft were damaged by Soviet infantry and AA fire but only a few outright losses were recorded. One exception was the *Staffelkapitän* of 3.*Staffel*, *Oblt.* Heinz Frank, who was severely injured in a crash-landing at Tusov on 15 October. The Soviet counter-offensive at Stalingrad erupted on 19 November causing total surprise and mayhem. Now operating from Oblivskaya, four Bf 109 E-7s were lost between 30 November and 19 December, at least two of these to Soviet fighters, as the *Gruppe* was forced back to Millerovo. On 31 December, 3.*Staffel* lost its new *Staffelkapitän*, *Oblt.* Josef Graf von und zu Honsbrock, who was killed by ground fire. In isolated engagements over the front from 30 November to 26 December while flying in terrible

weather conditions, I./Schl.G. 1 claimed 6 Russian fighters and ground-attack aircraft including a pair of Il-2s on 17 December. In February, support missions were flown from Gorlovka/96 km south-west of Voroshilovgrad in an attempt to blunt the onward advance of the Red Army through the Donets Basin, with two Bf 109 E-7s from 2.*Staffel* lost to enemy fire at Kramatorskaya on 10 February. A few days later, on 16 February, the Soviets recaptured Kharkov and the Germans began a counter-attack to retake the city two weeks later. The *Gruppe* supported this effort, and as soon as the city was back under German control it moved to Kharkov-North on 14 March. During the first ten days of February, 2.*Staffel* claimed five aircraft and these were the only ones reported until the end of May.

Conversion to the Fw 190, Eastern Ukraine and Kursk (April 1943 – July 1943) With a temporary lull in the fighting, the *Gruppe* began conversion to the Fw 190, which was completed by the end of April, though a few Bf 109s remained on strength. By mid-May another move had been made to Barvenkovo and Varvarovka, just behind the front lines south-west of Izyum. In heavy fighting over the next six weeks, two Fw 190 A-5s, an Fw 190 F-3 and a Bf 109 were lost to Russian fighters and AA fire around Izyum. On the plus side, 3 Il-2s and 3 LaGG-5s were claimed between 28 May and 24 June by 1. and 3.*Staffel*, these going down in the Varvarovka-Barvenkovo area along the Don on the northern end of the Donets Basin. On 1 July 1943, the *Gruppe* reported 52 Fw 190 A-5s on strength. Another

By the end of April 1943 I./Schl.G. 1 had converted to the Fw 190 A-5 and F 3. This aircraft retained the equilateral triangle marking of the early ground-attack units together with the individual letter 'F'. By mid-May the Gruppe had moved to Barvenkovo and Varvarovka, just behind the front lines south-west of Izyum.

four Fw 190 A-5s and F-3s were lost between 4 and 7 July in the same area as the long-delayed German offensive at Kursk (Operation *Zitadelle*) got underway. Russian strength in the area was substantially greater than German estimates and the attack on the Kursk salient ground to a halt by the end of the first week. I./Schl.G. 1 was ordered north to Orel to help break up the Soviet counter-offensive in that area. In bitter, non-stop operations between 8 July and 2 August, the *Gruppe* lost at least eight Fw 190s to AA fire, including an Fw 190 F-3 piloted by *Obstlt*. Horst-Wilhelm Hossfeld, a general staff officer doing a career-required combat stint as an acting *Staffelkapitän*, on 17 July. However, the three *Staffeln* scored heavily during the intense air action of the first 5 days of the offensive (5-9 July) claiming 12 Il-2s, 2 LaGG-3s and 1 LaGG-5, the majority of these in the vicinity of Belgorod.

Kursk Aftermath, Central Ukraine, Redesignation (August 1943 – October 1943) As the Soviets continued to advance, Orel fell on 4 August and I.*Gruppe* was forced back, first to Karachev and then to Bryansk. In heavy action during the latter part of July and most of August, the *Gruppe* claimed a LaGG-3 over Orel on 20 July, an Il-2 30 km north-north-east of Orel on 25 July, an Il-2 just north of Karachev airfield on 4 August, a LaGG-5 100 km north of Bryansk on 15 August and a Pe-2 in the Sevsk area/123 km north-west of Kursk on 26 August. At the beginning of September, the *Gruppe* was shifted south to Konotop and then to Nezhin in the northern part of Ukraine to fly missions against the Soviet spearheads aimed at Kiev. *Hptm*. Johannes Meinecke, *Staffelkapitän* of 1.*Staffel*, was killed when his Fw 190 A-6 was shot down by AA fire near Mutino on 4 September. Nezhin fell on 15 September and the exhausted pilots and ground personnel moved to Kiev-South to continue operations as best they could. Three Fw 190 F-3s were lost on 27 September and another F-3 and an Fw 190 A-6 were shot down by AA fire on 6 October while attacking Soviet spearheads driving south-west from around Nezhin. The latter was flown by the recently appointed *Staffelkapitän* of 1.*Staffel*, *Hptm*. Josef Menapace, who was killed. On the same date, 6 October, 1. and 2.*Staffeln* filed claims for a LaGG-3, 2 LaGG-5s and an Il-2 in the general area 25 km south-south-east of Chernobyl which lies to the north of Kiev. A week later, on 13 October, two more Fw 190 F-3s were shot down by Soviet fighters north-west of Starnevka with the loss of both pilots. On or about 18 October 1943, the *Gruppe* was renamed II./S.G. 77, except for 1.*Staffel*, which was disbanded and its assets incorporated into the other *Staffeln*.

FpNs: I. *Stab* (L 34346, 16447); 1. (L 35341, 16447); 2. (L 35777, 16849, 52379); 3. (L 36673, 17667, 54639)

Kommandeur:
Major Alfred Druschel (RK) (13 January 1942 - ?)
  – acting
Major Alfred Druschel (RK, EL, SW) (3 September 1942 - 1 March 1943)
Hptm. Georg Dörffel (DKG, RK) (2 March 1943 - September 1943) – acting
Hptm. Siegfried Steinhoff (DKG) (September 1943 - 18 October 1943)

4.(Pz)/Schl.G. 1

Formation and Conversion (January 1942 – April 1942) The *Staffel* was formed on 13 January 1942 at Dugino on the central sector of the Eastern Front as an independent component of II./Schl.G. 1 with Bf 109 Es provided by the disbanded II.(*Schlacht*)/L.G. 2. It was based at Dugino and Rzhev under VIII.*Fliegerkorps* until early April. Sources indicate that it received 16 Hs 129 B-1s by 28 March, presumably at Lippstadt, and then left for Crimea, arriving on 6 May.

Crimea, Izyum and Advance to Stalingrad (May 1942 – April 1943) Commenced operations on 7 May from Grammatikovo/Crimea with some 15 Hs 129s as part of of II.*Gruppe*, although the rest of II.*Gruppe* was still en route. Over the next several days, 4.*Staffel* attacked various ground targets, shot down an I-16 fighter and destroyed an estimated 40 other aircraft during a low-level strafing attack on an enemy airfield in Eastern Crimea. It moved north to Konstantinovka in mid-May with the rest of II.*Gruppe* and took part in the heavy fighting against Soviet incursions in the Barvenkovo-Izyum-Chuguyev-Kupyansk sector to the south and south-east of Kharkov. Ordered to Kharkov-Rogan in early June for outfitting with the new underbelly 30 mm MK 101 cannon installation, and took these armour-piercing weapons into action against Soviet tanks retreating from east of Kharkov towards Voronezh on the Don River, apparently operating without loss until July 1942 when an Hs 129 belonging to 4.*Staffel* was reported lost in the Kobyla-Sterya area on 6 July and another Hs 129 was shot down by Russian fighters at Voronezh two days later. On 1 August operational at Tatsinskaya under VIII.*Fliegerkorps*/*Luftflotte* 4, reporting no aircraft on

The aircraft of 4.(Pz)/Schl.G. 1 carried this 'Panzerbär' (panzer bear) emblem. The bear was chosen as a badge as it was the symbol of Berlin where the Henschel company had its main factory.

4.(Pz)/Schl.G. 1 was formed on 13 January 1942, initially equipped with Bf 109 Es. In March it began to re-equip with the new Hs 129 B-1 at Lippstadt, receiving 16 aircraft by the end of the month. This aircraft, 'blue K', W.Nr. 0166, also carries the black triangle marking of the Schlachtflieger. After re-equipment, the Staffel left for the Crimea, arriving on 6 May.

1 October, but 12 Hs 129 B-1s on 1 November and 18 (17) on 20 November. Following the Soviet counter-offensive at Stalingrad that began on 19 November, the *Staffel* was deployed along the Chir front to the west of the beleaguered city. On 22 December, while the rest of II.*Gruppe* pulled back to Voroshilovgrad, 4.(Pz) remained forward at Tatsinskaya until Russian tanks approached the airfield two weeks later and then it withdrew to Stalino. Two Hs 129s were reportedly lost in action on 27 and 28 December. On 5 January 1943 another Hs 129 B-1 crashed, killing the *Staffelkapitän*, *Oblt.* Eduard Kent. After withdrawing to Stalino, it was subsequently re-equipped with the new Hs 129 B-2, which was just then coming off the production line, and ordered to transfer to Poltava on 14 March and then to Stalino-North during the first half of April.

North Caucasia, Kursk and Central Ukraine (May 1943 – October 1943) By the beginning of May, the *Staffel* was flying in support of hard-pressed German ground forces on the Taman Peninsula in North Caucasia to the south-west of Rostov, losing two Hs 129 B-2s near Krymskaya on 8 and 13 May. It was ordered back to the Reich (Deblin-Irena in Poland?) in June, possibly to have all or a number of its B-2s fitted with the new 30 mm MK 103 armour-piercing cannon, and then returned to Russia with station at Varvarovka for the upcoming German attack on the Kursk salient (Operation *Zitadelle*) that commenced on 5 July. On 1 July the *Staffel* reported 17 Hs 129 B-2s on strength. Losses were heavy during the month with seven Hs 129 B-2s falling to Soviet AA fire and at least three more heavily damaged between 12 and 30 July. Three pilots were killed and two missing in these engagements. Although active from the beginning of *Zitadelle*, its big day was the massive tank battle around Prokhorovka/49 km north of Belgorod on 12 July during

which 4.(Pz)/Schl.G. 1, I./Schl.G. 1, Pz.Jäg.St./J.G. 51 and *Stukas* from St.G. 2 and St.G. 77, destroyed and disabled huge numbers of Soviet tanks (300 to all causes). Meanwhile, the *Staffel* had been ordered from Varvarovka to Orel-West on 14 July to bolster the defence against the Soviet counter-attack towards Orel that began on 13 July. The Henschels flew from dawn to dusk against advancing tanks and losses among the anti-tank *Staffeln* reached 30% between 14 and 25 July. As Soviet forces drove the Germans westward, 4.(Pz) pulled back to Konotop during the first half of August and then moved to Poltava at the end of August. An Hs 129 B-2 was destroyed on the ground at Zaporozhye-East during a Soviet low-level air attack on 5 September and another five were lost over the course of the month as the *Staffel* retreated from eastern Ukraine into central Ukraine. It was at Kiev-Post Volinski on 21 September, at Askania Nova (123 km west-south-west of Melitopol) on 30 September, and on 6 October it was ordered to transfer to Orsha on the central sector of the Eastern Front, but there is no evidence that this was carried out. On 18 October it was renamed 10.(Pz)/S.G. 9.

FpNs: (L 18335, 53215)

Staffelkapitän:
Oblt. Bruno Meyer (RK) (February 1942 - July 1942?)
Hptm. Bruno Meyer (RK) (30 September 1942 - March 1943 MIA)
Hptm. Dietrich Gerhardt (January 1943 - 20 January 1943) – acting
Oblt. Georg Dornemann (January 1943 - 18 October 1943)
Major Matuschek (April 1943? - 19 July 1943 KIA) – acting?

II./Schl.G. 1

Formation and Work-up (January 1942 – April 1942) The *Gruppe* was raised at Lippstadt on 13 January 1942 with 5. and 6.*Staffeln* equipped with Henschel Hs 129 B-1s and 7.*Staffel* with Hs 123 As, the latter unit taking over the aircraft of 8.*Staffel* in April. On 1 March, II.*Gruppe* reported 16 Hs 129s and 3 Hs 123s on strength. After formation and work-up was completed by the end of April, it was ordered to southern Russia for assignment with *Luftflotte* 4.

Crimea, Izyum, Advance to Stalingrad and 5.*Staffel* to Tunisia (May 1942 – November 1942) The first combat loss occurred on 9 May when a Hs 129 B-1 was shot down by Soviet AA fire, possibly over eastern Crimea. The pilot, *Hptm.* Max Eck, was listed as missing. In mid-May, while based at Konstantinovka, operations centred on the Izyum Salient and around Stalino. It was there that three Hs 129 B-1s were shot down by Russian AA fire on 23 May, a severe blow at this relatively early stage of the war for this newly formed unit. The main effort shifted to the Kursk area and east towards Voronezh at the end of June and into the first half of July. The *Gruppe* was temporarily split up during this period with the *Staffeln* operating independently from Volchansk, Kharkov, Shatalovka, Orel, and Kursk on the central sector of the front. While flying from these airfields, 6.*Staffel* lost two Hs 129 B-1s to AA fire on 28 June and three Hs 123 As from 7.*Staffel* failed to return from the Shchigry area north-east of Kursk on 29 June. From mid-July, the *Gruppe* concentrated on supporting the drive to Stalingrad, moving to Tatsinskaya, Frolov, and Tusov by mid-August. On 1 August,

II./Schl.G. 1 reported 25 Hs 129s and 20 Hs 123s on strength. Towards the end of the month, 5.*Staffel* was sent back to Orel and temporarily attached to J.G. 51. A strength return for the *Gruppe* dated 20 September reported a total of 46 Hs 129s and Hs 123s on hand with 28 serviceable. Losses that autumn in the Stalingrad area were very light. *Lt.* Josef Menapace, *Staffelkapitän* of 7.*Staffel*, was wounded on 13 September when his Hs 123 was shot up by a Soviet fighter over Stalingrad, and 6.*Staffel* reported Hs 129 losses on both 2 and 11 November. 7.*Staffel* received some Bf 109 Es during the summer to supplement its stock of Hs 123 As. Meanwhile, 5.*Staffel* was transferred to Jesau in East Prussia in October to rest, refit and re-equip with Hs 129 B-2s. It departed for North Africa on 5 November and arrived at Tunis-El Aounina on 29 November after being delayed en route by bad weather. It flew its first combat mission the next day against British tanks and vehicle columns near Tebourba, followed by numerous successful missions to the end of the month. It was renamed 8.(Pz)/Schl.G. 2 in January 1943. A new 5.*Staffel* for Schl.G. 1 was formed a few weeks later in Germany with Fw 190s.

Retreat from Stalingrad (November 1942 – January 1943) The Soviet counter-offensive at Stalingrad on 19 November brought a rapid turn of events. After moving from Millerovo to Frolov and Oblivskaya by 26 November, the *Gruppe* began a maximum effort around Stalingrad at the cost of at least eight Hs 129 Bs, Hs 123 As and Bf 109 Es lost in ground-attack missions or blown up to prevent capture by the on-coming Russians. On 1 December the *Gruppe* reported 5 Hs 129s, 10 Bf 109 E-7s and 11 Hs 123s on strength.

An Hs 123 A-1 of 7./Schl.G. 1 in flight over Russia, photographed from a second aircraft. The first Schlachtgeschwader (Schl.G. 1 and 2) could be identified by a black triangle marking edged in white and the infantry assault badge painted behind the cowling in white. The aircraft's individual letter 'B' was painted black, edged in white over the yellow rear fuselage band.

This Hs 129 B-1 of 5./Schl.G. 1, W.Nr. 0191, was shot down by anti-aircraft fire on 23 May 1942. It was subsequently repaired but was finally destroyed on 21 February 1944 during a bombing attack on Diepholz airfield. The bear and axe badge originally carried by 5.(Schlacht)/L.G. 2 was retained by this Staffel.

On 1 August 1942 II./Schl.G. 1 reported that it had a total of 25 Hs 129s and 20 Hs 123s. Although probably pictured a little later in the year, this Hs 123 of the 7.Staffel 'yellow E' was typical of the Gruppe's aircraft at this time.

A Bf 109 E-7 of I./Schl.G. 1 taxies towards take-off carrying a full load of four 50 kg bombs. Note the 'Schlacht' black triangle outlined in white, which continued in use until the end of April 1943; on the orders of the RLM all such markings and badges were to be deleted.

Due to the poor forward visibility afforded by single-engined fighters, it was sometimes necessary for a ground crewman to guide the pilot through the rough ground to the take-off point. Here, the pilot of a Bf 109 E-7, loaded with four 50 kg bombs, is being shown directions by a mechanic sitting on the wing giving hand signals.

From around 6 December, the *Gruppenstab* and 6.*Staffel* were operating from Rossosh, just west of the Don River and to the north-east of Kharkov, shooting up Russian tanks that were driving deep into the Romanian Third and Italian Eighth Armies, while 7.*Staffel* appears to have remained in the Stalingrad area with its Hs 123s, flying from Morosovskaya. By 22 December, what was left of II./Schl.G. 1 had pulled back to Voroshilovgrad. In a summary of the year's operations, II.*Gruppe* reported flying a total of 3,128 Hs 129 sorties, 1,532 Hs 123 sorties, and 1,938 Bf 109 sorties since formation, claimed 107 aircraft shot down or destroyed, 91 enemy tanks and

The Staffelkapitän of 5./Schl.G. 1, Oblt. Georg Dörffel, relaxes on the wing of his Bf 109 E in southern Russia during the summer of 1942. Variations of the Mickey Mouse emblem were adopted by German airmen as early as 1937. This version was originally carried by 4.(Schlacht)/L.G. 2 before being taken over by the whole of Schl.G. 1 following its formation. Dörffel was killed on 26 May 1944 near Rome while commanding S.G. 4, his Fw 190 F-8 probably shot down by P-47s.

Photographed as it sweeps past the camera in southern Russia, this Hs 129 B-1 of II./Schl.G. 1 carries the Staffel emblem of the Berlin Bear behind the cockpit with a white chevron and letter 'O' forward of the fuselage Balkenkreuz and a white edged black triangle aft.

Berlin Bear Emblem

1,354 vehicles blown up on the ground, while losing 20 Hs 129s, 16 Bf 109s, and 5 Hs 123s due to enemy action. While operating from Voroshilovgrad II at the beginning of 1943, the *Gruppe* claimed 13 tanks destroyed from 1 to 16 January.

Conversion and Operations over North Caucasia (January 1943 – June 1943) In mid-January 1943, the surviving personnel left for Deblin-Irena in Poland to rest and convert to the Fw 190, except for 7.*Staffel* which continued to fly the Hs 123. A few Hs 129s and crews from the other *Staffeln* were also left behind in South Russia. The *Gruppenkommandeur*, *Hptm*. Frank Neubert, was shot down and wounded by Soviet AA fire on 30 January near Skurbiy. Based at Nikolayev-East from 6 February, the conversion to Fw 190 A-5s was completed by the first week in March. The *Gruppe* was then transferred to Pavlograd in the east-central part of the Ukraine for a month of training and work-ups before moving back to the front in mid-April. Its new home was Anapa in North Caucasia where it remained until the beginning of July. The ground-attack missions from Anapa in support of 17.*Armee*, which had been cut off in the constantly shrinking Kuban bridgehead on the Taman Peninsula, were intense and costly. The Soviet Air Force had concentrated vastly superior forces in this sector and outnumbered the *Luftwaffe* four to one and, in addition, had heavily reinforced the numbers of AA guns in the area. Anapa was bombed on 19 April for the loss of two of 7.*Staffel's* Hs 123s. Between 10 and 17 May at least seven Fw 190 A-5s were shot down while attacking targets around Abinskaya and Krymskaya, most falling to AA fire. On 26 May, 6.*Staffel* claimed an Il-2 to the north-east of Krymskaya, this being the first enemy plane shot down by the *Gruppe* since returning to the front in mid-April. The Russians bombed Anapa again on 12 June, destroying an Fw 190 A-6. The month of June also saw the arrival of some of the new Fw 190 F-3s which were better designed for the ground-attack role and featured better armour protection. One Fw 190 F-3 was shot down on the 17th and two more destroyed in a runway collision at Novorossisk on 1 July when a bomb on one of them accidentally detonated. The *Gruppe's* strength return for 1 July reported 15 Fw 190 A-5s, 18 Fw 190 F-3s and 16 Hs 123 B-1s on hand.

Kursk Offensive, Kharkov and Redesignation (July 1943 – October 1943) The Kursk Offensive (Operation *Zitadelle*) took priority over support of the Kuban bridgehead and the *Gruppe* was ordered north to Varvarovka on 2-3 July to operate against Soviet forces along the Donets River south-east of Kharkov. Operation *Zitadelle* commenced on 5 July, but II./Schl.G. 1 did not get mixed in with the heavy fighting until Russian spearheads began to close around the defending Germans in early August, or so it appears. Another explanation might be that it participated in full but experienced very few losses. Nevertheless, the *Gruppe* did file claims for four victories during the second half of July: a LaGG-3 50 km north of Belgorod on 13 July and an Il-2 10 km north of Izyum on 18 July. On 29 July, the *Gruppe* moved south to Kuteinikovo/125 km north-west of Rostov to attack a Soviet breakthrough along the Mius by tanks and cavalry. While there, claims were made for 2 LaGG-5s to the north of Shakhty in the south-eastern part of the Donets on 31 July before returning to Varvarovka on 1 August and then transferring to Kharkov-Rogan on 5 August. In five days, between 3 and 7 August, one Fw 190 F-3 and an Hs 123 A were shot down by Russian fighters, six more Fw 190s were damaged in action south of Kharkov, and a further four Fw 190s were destroyed or damaged in a Soviet raid on Varvarovka. A claim for an Il-2 shot down north-west of Belgorod was also made on 3 August. The *Gruppe* was forced back to Rudka/18 km north-north-west of Poltava on 11 August and from there flew continuously in the defence of Kharkov, losing at least four Fw 190s, with two more damaged, while claiming another Il-2 on 17 August. The Red Army finally took the city on 22 August. On 28 August, II.*Gruppe* moved to Stalino-North to support defensive measures around that city before it fell to the advancing Russians a week or so later. From 4 to 8 September II./Schl.G. 1 withdrew west, this time to Kiev-South, where it rested for 14 days while the aircraft were overhauled. It also flew a few missions against Soviet armoured columns driving rapidly on the Ukrainian capital. Accordingly, losses during September and October were extremely light, averaging only about one aircraft a week. On 18 October 1943, II./Schl.G. 1 was renamed II./S.G. 2 at Kiev-South, with 5.*Staffel* becoming 8.*Staffel* while the others retained their previous numbers.

FpNs: II. *Stab* (L 18016); 5. (L 18682, 52553); 6. (L 19138, 54989); 7. (L 19369, 55201)

Kommandeur:
Hptm. Paul-Friedrich Darjes (RK) (28 February 1942 – September 1942?)
Hptm. Frank Neubert (DKG, RK) (October 1942 – September 1943)
Major Heinz Frank (DKG, RK, EL) (September 1943 – 18 October 1943)

Infantry assault badge

LEFT AND ABOVE: Time for a chat as Luftwaffe ground staff from 7./Schl.G. 1 bask in the heat of the Russian summer while preparing for another mission. The Hs 123s have the German infantry assault badge painted on the sides of their fuselages behind the engine cowlings. This proved a popular emblem for II.(Schlacht)/L.G. 2, and both Schl.G. 1 and 2. Note the two 110 lb SC 50 blast bombs mounted beneath the wing of one of the aircraft.

This Hs 123 B-1 of II./Schl.G. 1 may have been flown by the Gruppe Kommandeur, Hptm. Paul-Friedrich Darjes. It carries a black single chevron forward of the fuselage cross and a white II.Gruppe horizontal bar aft. Note the Stabo extensions fitted to the two underwing bombs. In mid-January 1943, II./Schl.G. 1 converted to the Fw 190 with the exception of the 7.Staffel which retained the type until its dissolution in October 1943.

Lt. Josef Menapace, Staffelkapitän of 7./Schl.G. 1 stands in front of his Hs 123 A-1 just after being awarded the Ritterkreuz on 20 August 1942. The aircraft carries the infantry assault and Schl.G. 1 badges in addition to the name 'Rudolf von Zahradniczek'. This was in memory of Menapace's friend who had been shot down by Soviet flak on 4 February 1942. Menapace himself was killed on 6 October 1943 while leading 1./Schl.G. 1 when his Fw 190 A-6, W.Nr. 550432, 'white N', was shot down by Russian anti-aircraft fire near Strascholessje.

8.(Pz)/Schl.G. 1 was formed from 10.(Schlacht)/L.G. 2 on 13 January 1942 at Dugino airfield in central Russia. This Hs 123 A-1 from the Staffel, photographed during the spring of 1942, carries the blue individual letter 'X' outlined in white and has the familiar black equilateral forward of the fuselage Balkenkreuz. The Staffel only flew the Hs 123 until April 1942 when it returned to Germany and was re-equipped with the Bf 109 E-7.

As the winter snows begin to recede the ground crews of 8.(Pz)/Schl.G. 1 have removed the cowling of this Hs 123, W.Nr. 2325, so that a service can be carried out on its BMW 132 radial engine. The aircraft was coded 'blue X', the letter positioned over the yellow rear fuselage band.

8.(Pz)/Schl.G. 1

Formation, Re-equipment (January 1942 – April 1942) 8./Schl.G. 1 was formed from 10.(*Schlacht*)/L.G. 2 on 13 January 1942 at Dugino airfield in central Russia, where it continued to operate under VIII.*Fliegerkorps* until the beginning of April. It then returned to Germany (Lippstadt?), disbanded, and was then immediately re-established with Bf 109 E-7s. The *Staffel's* Hs 123 biplanes were turned over to 7.*Staffel*. Although 8.(Pz) was organizationally a component of I.*Gruppe* from 13 January 1942 until the *Geschwader's* reorganization in January-February 1943, it is carried separately here because of its conversion to the Hs 129 in December 1942 and redesignation as a *Panzerjägerstaffel* shortly thereafter.

South Russia, Conversion to Anti-tank role (May 1942 – February 1943) It was transferred to the south-eastern part of the Ukraine via Lvov, Poland, on 5 May and flew support missions in the fighting around the Izyum salient in May, moved forward to Kharkov in early June, but did not report any losses until 26 July, when a Bf 109 E-7 returned to Morosovskaya-West badly damaged after being shot up by a Russian fighter. It remained active in the Stalingrad area with bases at Tusov in September and Morosovskaya until some time in November. However, by late November it was withdrawn for rest and conversion to the Hs 129, probably at Deblin-Irena in Poland or possibly in Germany. On 1 December the *Staffel* reported 12 Hs 129 B-1s/B-2s on strength. It was then redesignated 8.(Pz)/Schl.G. 1 and became semi-independent.

South Russia, North Caucasia and Central Russia, Redesignation (February 1943 – October 1943) The *Staffel* returned to south Russia by the end of February and reported some training crashes at Zaporozhye-East on 22 February and at Kharkov on 21 March. At the beginning of April, it was sent to North Caucasia to support operations in the Kuban bridgehead on the Taman Peninsula, with bases at Kerch and Anapa. Very heavy losses were suffered in the bitter fighting over the beleaguered Kuban. An Hs 129 B-2 went down to AA fire on 5 April; two more were lost in the Krymskaya-Bakanskaya area on 16 April, another on 3 May; two fell to AA fire on 5 May, two more on 27 May; the last was lost to Russian AA fire and fighters on 29 May. The survivors were withdrawn to Zaporozhye in south-eastern Ukraine in early June to rest, refit, and re-equip. On 1 July the *Staffel* reported 16 Hs 129 B-2s on strength, and the next day, on 2 July, 8.(Pz) was transferred to Mikoyanovka, 8 kilometres south-west of Belgorod, for Operation *Zitadelle*, the German offensive against the Kursk salient. Losses were again heavy as the *Staffel* pounded Soviet armour east of Kursk. As the Germans were forced over to the defensive at the height of the battle, the *Staffel* was ordered to Orel-West in the central sector of the Eastern Front on 14 July to help blunt the powerful Soviet counter-attack towards Orel that had begun two days before. The Henschels flew from dawn to dusk against advancing tanks and losses among the anti-tank *Staffeln* reached 30% between 14 and 25 July. By the end of July it was based at Karachev, about 75 kilometres west-north-west of Orel, probably at Konotop during August and then moved to Poltava around the beginning of September. From there the

Hptm. Rudolf-Heinz Ruffer photographed sitting in the heavily armoured cockpit of his Hs 129. Ruffer led 8.(Pz)/Schl.G. 1 until October 1943 and then 10.(Pz)/S.G. 9 until he was killed on 16 July 1944 when his Hs 129 B-2 was shot down by AA fire north of Volkasusanska.

Staffel was committed in the fierce rear guard fighting between Kharkov and Kiev before transferring on 21 September to Zaporozhye. After losing five Hs 129 B-2s over the course of the month, the next move was to Kiev on or about 30 September as the Soviet spearheads approached Zaporozhye. While based at Kiev 8.(Pz) was renamed 11.(Pz)/S.G. 9 on 18 October 1943.

FpNs: (L 19491, 52899)

Staffelkapitän:
Lt./Oblt. Hans Stollnberger (DKG) (? - 14 October 1942 - June 1943?)
Oblt.? Rudolf-Heinz Ruffer (8 April 1943 - ca. 18 October 1943).

Erg. Staffel/Schl.G. 1

Formation and History (January 1942 – December 1942) Formed on 13 January 1942 at Lippstadt by renaming Erg.*Staffel* (*Schlacht*)/L.G. 2. Its subsequent base locations are not known although one source places it at Novocherkassk, 36 km north-east of Rostov, in the late summer and early autumn of 1942. It was disbanded in December 1942 following the Soviet counter-offensive at Stalingrad and the withdrawal of Schl.G. 1 from the front for conversion to the Fw 190.

Note: Carlsen/Meyer p. 344 claims that the Erg.*Staffel* was renamed 5./*Erg.JagdGruppe Ost* in March 1942, but this is probably incorrect. *Erg. JagdGruppe Ost* only had 4 *Staffeln* - (1. - 4.) - as far as is known. Further, Erg.St./Schl.G. 1's FpN (L 37446) remained assigned to it under that designation until approximately December 1942 before it was stricken from the *Feldpostübersicht* (Field Postal Directory) and fell into disuse. In any event, the assertion in Carlsen/Meyer needs to be corroborated with solid evidence before it can be accepted.

FpN: (L 37446)

Staffelkapitän:
Oblt. Heinrich Estl (13 January 1942 - February 1943?)

Sources for Schl.G. 1:

Unpublished and Archival:
BA-MA Freiburg: *Flugzeug-Bereitstellungen* (Aircraft Availability Status Reports – FzB) in: M.Holm website;
BA-MA Freiburg: RL 2 III *Meldungen über Flugzeugunfälle*…..(Loss Reports – LRs);
BA-MA Freiburg: *Luftwaffen-Personalamt* L.P.(A)5 (V) (OKL *Chef für Ausz. und Disziplin*). 18 rolls of microfilm consisting of partial daily log sheets and summaries of *Luftwaffe* enemy aircraft victory to the end of 1944. The material has been keyed to a data base and can be found at website tonywood.cjb.net under the short title 'O.K.L. Fighter Claims'.
NARA WashDC: RG 242/T-312 (A.O.K. 11 various daily reports and attachments);
PRO London: AIR 40 intelligence documents derived from ULTRA and 'Y' Service intercepts;
PRO London: AIR 40/folders 1977, 1978, 1979, 1980 and 1988;

Published Sources:
[Bateson – *Stuka!*] p. 59;
[Bekker – LWD] p. 436;
[Bergström – BC/RS-3] p. 59-60, 63-64, 151;
[Bergström – Kursk] p. 76-81, 102-103;
[Brütting – SA] p. 140, 142, 143, 149, 150, 155, 156, 173, 198, 228, 231, 253, 270, 272, 273, 276;
[Carlsen – CM2] p. 344;
[Dierich –VdL] p. 217, 235, 237, 238;
[Green – WotTR] p. 381, 382, 386;
[Held – Mölders] p. 61;
[Holm – Website www.ww2.dk];
[Kannapin – FpN] p. various;
[Mehner – FT] p. 55;
[Obermaier – RK2] p. 40, 54, 55, 59, 63, 71, 86, 88, 97, 110, 121, 156, 157, 163, 164, 189, 197, 200, 204, 211, 249, 258;
[Patzwall – LwR] p. various;
[Pegg – PzJgr] p. (throughout);
[Ries – PhotoRec] p. 148;
[Scheibert – EP] p. various;
[Scherzer – DKG] p. 61, 73, 81, 233, 279, 328;
[Smith – GA] p. 195, 320, 321, 333, 334, 336;
[Smith – LCV3] p. 53, 71, 72;
[Tessin – Tes] p. 329;
[Zweng – Zweng] p. various.

[Archiv #8 – A-8] p. 15;
AIR Vol. 19-6 p. 282, 283.

Schl.G. 2

Schlachtgeschwader 2
(Unit Code: none)

Stab/Schl.G. 2

Formation **(December 1942)** *Geschwaderstab* formed 17 December 1942 at Gleiwitz (Gliwice) in Upper Silesia (now south-west Poland). Other sources give Deblin-Irena/97 km south-south-east of Warsaw as the place of formation. A *Stabsschwarm* of 4 aircraft was attached to the *Geschwaderstab* on initial formation.

Reich, Tunisia, Sicily, Sardinia, Italy (December 1942 – October 1943) 1 April: *Stabsschwarm* reported 4 Fw 190 A-5 on strength. 12 April: *Geschwaderstab* in transfer to Tunisia. 18 April: arrived at Bizerte - Sidi Ahmed this date. 7 May: following a very brief stay at Bizerte, *Stab* departed Tunisia as the Axis position there

collapsed and now at Gerbini-North in Sicily and still there 8 June. 12 June: *Stab* now at Trapani/west Sicily. 15 June: *Geschwaderstab* ordered to transfer from Trapani to Milis in west-central Sardinia, but this order appears to have been rescinded. 5 July: back at Gerbini-North. 17 July: withdrew from Sicily following the Allied invasion on 10 July and now at Aquino/110 km south-east of Rome under II.*Fliegerkorps/Luftflotte* 2. 25 July: *Stab* ordered to depart Aquino and move to Ottana in central Sardinia. 1 September: no aircraft assigned to the *Geschwaderstab* according to status report this date. 9 September: *Stab* departed Ottana this date for the Italian mainland, eventually relocating to Piacenza in north Italy. 18 October: redesignated *Geschwaderstab/ S.G.* 4.

Wolfgang Schenck was the first Kommodore of Schl.G. 2, leading the unit from 17 December 1942 until 18 October 1943 when he took over the newly-formed S.G. 4. He is shown here sitting in the cockpit of his Fw 190 giving instructions to two of his pilots. The signature on the photograph is his.

FpN: *Geschwaderstab* (L 52152)

Kommodore:

Hptm. Wolfgang Schenck (RK, EL) (17 December 1942 - 16 May 1943) – acting

Major Wolfgang Schenck (RK, EL) (17 May 1943 - 18 October 1943)

I./Schl.G. 2

Formation (September 1942) Ordered formed 28 September 1942 at Comiso/Sicily by renaming *Jabo-Gruppe Afrika* (*Jagdbomber-Gruppe Afrika*, also known as *JagdGruppe Oberbefehlshaber Süd*), which consisted of the Bf 109-equipped 10.(Jabo)/J.G. 27 and 10.(Jabo)/J.G. 53, these forming 1. and 2.*Staffeln*, and by also incorporating elements of the Bf 109-equipped III./ZG 1 as 3.*Staffel*. The various components of the *Gruppe* were engaged in North Africa at the time orders were issued for formation and were not assembled at Comiso until two weeks later.

Sicily, Egypt and Libya (September 1942 – January 1943) 29 September: Bf 109 F-4 landing and take-off accidents at Bir el Abd on the El Alamein front. 1 October: *Gruppe* reported 32 Bf 109 E-7 on strength. 2 October: Bf 109 F-4 landing and take-off accidents at Bir el Abd. 10 October: Bf 109 F-4 Trop shot down by AA fire at El Ruweisat along the front south of El Alamein, pilot safe. 11-12 October: 1 Bf 109 F-4 Trop accident at Bir el Abd and 2 more at Bari in south Italy, 1 pilot killed. 15 October: from Comiso, began flying Bf 109 fighter-bomber (Jabo) missions against targets on Malta as part of the final mass attacks against the island bastion by II.*Fliegerkorps*, which continued to at least 2 November, although the *Gruppe* was ordered back to western Egypt after only a week of operations. The raids on Malta cost 3.*Staffel* 3 Bf 109s lost in combat. 15-22 October: 4 Bf 109 F-4 Trop crashes at Comiso. 22 October: 2 Bf 109 F-4 Trop shot down south of El Alamein, probably by AA fire, both pilots MIA. During the evening of the following day, the British 8th Army (Montgomery) launched its well-prepared offensive along the El Alamein front that over the next 3 months drove the Axis forces out of Egypt and Libya. 26 October: Bf 109 shot down over the front area, pilot KIA. 28 October: ordered to pull back from Bir el Abd on the El Alamein front to Qasaba (Quasaba)/30 km south-east of Mersa Matruh. 31 October: Bf 109 E failed to return from operations, pilot KIA. 4 November: Bf 109 F shot down while attacking British tanks, pilot KIA when his parachute failed to open. 5-17 November: *Gruppe* reported the total loss of 21 Bf 109 Es and Fs at airfields Bir el Abd, Qasaba (Quasaba), Gambut and Martuba as it retreated west from the El Alamein front; 16 of these aircraft were intentionally destroyed by *Gruppe* personnel to keep them from falling into enemy hands. 24 November: at Arco (Arco Philanorum)/195 km south-south-west of Benghazi – Bf 109 F-4 Trop collided with an Italian aircraft while either landing or taking off, pilot KIA. 29 November: Bf 109 F crashed at Arco, *Staffelkapitän* of 1.*Staffel Oblt.* Wolf Zipper KIA. 2 December: Bf 109 F lost in action east of El Agheila/225 km south-south-west of Benghazi. 4 December: another Bf 109 F lost in action east of El Agheila. 12 December: transferred from Merduma (Bir el Merduma)/250 km south west of Benghazi to Tamet/48 km west-north-west of Sirte. 30 December: 1 to 3 Bf 109 Fs shot down by P-40 Kittyhawks while strafing enemy troops in the Bir el Zidan area. 6-7 January 1943: elements at Bir Dufan/165 km south-east of Tripoli flying Jabo attacks on enemy-occupied airfields in the Sirte-Hamraiet area, losing 1 Bf 109 F-4 shot down on 6 January and several more damaged in landing and take-off accidents at Bir Dufan. 13 January: main body transferred from Zarzur to Bir Dufan to continue operations under *Fliegerführer Afrika* in *Gruppe* strength. 17 January: transferred to Tripoli - El Asabaa.

Tunisia (January 1943 – April 1943) 23 January: now at Oudref landing ground near Tripoli. February: flew fighter-bomber missions against British 8th Army forces along the front in southern Tunisia. 10 February: at Medenine/68 km south-east of Gabes (Qäbis)/south-east Tunisia under *Fliegerkorps Tunis*. 15 February: Medenine airfield evacuated and destroyed by the Germans this date and the *Gruppe* transferred up the coast to Gabes-West. 20 February: Bf 109 F-4 shot down by AA fire over Oran/Tunisia, pilot WIA, and a second F-4 shot down by a fighter in the Gabes-Gafsa area in central Tunisia, pilot WIA. 24 February: *Gruppe* now at La Fauconnerie-South/60 km north-west of Sfax (Safäqis) with 1.*Staffel* detached at Gabes-West. 27 February: 2.*Staffel* Bf 109 F-4 shot down south of Medenine, probably by a fighter, pilot MIA. March: operated mainly along the Mareth defensive line located just south of Gabes until this was breached and outflanked at the end of March and beginning of April. 1 March: *Gruppe* reported 21 Bf 109 F-4 Trops on strength. 12 March: 2 Bf 109 F-4s shot down by AA fire in the Dernaia - Bir el Hofra area near Kasserine in west-central Tunisia where U.S. forces were beginning an advance towards Gafsa (liberated 18 March), both pilots MIA. 21-23 March: 5 Bf 109 F-4s lost in operations around Gafsa, Djel-Guelia and Wadi Keddab, *Staffelführer* of 1.*Staffel Lt.* Wilhelm Vetter MIA. 24-28 March: 5 Bf 109 F-4s damaged in force-landings and crash-landings in the Gabes-Sfax area due to being shot up in combat. 7 April: transferred from La Fauconnerie-South to Bourdjine (not located). 10 April: now at Ste-Marie du Zit/44 km south-south-east of Tunis in northern Tunisia. 15 April: handed over all remaining aircraft to III./S.K.G. 10 in mid-April and then departed Tunisia for Italy to re-equip with Fw 190s.

Sicily, Sardinia and Italy (May 1943 – October 1943) 7 May: all or elements at Gerbini/east Sicily. 24 May: now at Brindisi/south-east Italy re-equipping. 7 June: ordered to transfer as soon as possible from Brindisi to Milis in west-central Sardinia. This order was subsequently rescinded or delayed. 20 June: in transfer from Brindisi to Milis. 2 July: at Milis with 37 (22) Fw 190 A-5s (25 of these) and F-3s (12 of these). 3 July: 3 Fw 190 A-5s bombed on the ground and reduced to scrap during Allied air attack on Milis. 12 July: transferred from Milis to Gerbini and ordered to begin continuous attacks on Allied invasion forces that began landing on Sicily on 10 July. To what extent I./Schl.G. 2 flew fighter-bomber missions in Sicily is unclear as it reported no losses that can be connected to Sicily between 12 and 17 July. 17 July: withdrew from Sicily to Aquino/110 km south-east of Rome. 25 July: now back on Sardinia and most likely based at Ottana in central Sardinia. 1 September 1943: *Gruppe* reported no aircraft on strength. October: now at Piacenza/north Italy – ordered to Graz/Austria to rest and refit. 18 October: redesignated I./S.G. 10.

FpNs: I. *Stab* (L 49307), 1. (L 50257), 2. (L 51064), 3. (L 49746)

Kommandeur:

Hptm. Johann Drescher (DKG) (28 September 1942 - 18 November 1942 WIA POW but escaped)

Hptm. Wolf-Dietrich Peitsmeyer (10 December 1942 - 10 December 1942 KIA) ★

Oblt. Hermann Langemann (ca. 19 November 1942 - May 1943?)

Hptm. Hanns Fischer (January 1943?) acting? – a speculation

★ **Note**: Peitsmeyer was appointed but MIA aboard a BV 222 shot down into the sea while flying from Taranto/Italy to Africa.

4.(Pz)/Schl.G. 2

Formation (September 1942) Formed on or about 30 September 1942 at Deblin-Irena (97 km south-south-east of Warsaw) by renaming 3./Ergänzungs-Zerstörer*Gruppe*, equipped with 12 Hs 129 Bs for anti-tank operations.

North Africa and Italy (November 1942 – March 1943) 2 November: departed Deblin-Irena for assignment in North Africa, flying via Krakow, Belgrade and Athens. 7 November: arrived at El Adem/26 km south-south-west of Tobruk in North Africa after 5 days en route with Hs 129 Bs equipped with the 30 mm MK 101 anti-tank gun, and first went into action at Bir el Abd on 17 November under the direct tactical control of *Fliegerführer Afrika* during the German retreat along the Libyan coast from El Alamein. After some initial success against British armoured cars and Crusader tanks, the *Staffel* withdrew via Sollum, Benghazi (20 November)

and Misurata (22 November). Some of the aircraft were unable to complete more than just two or three missions, and all of the Henschels had to be withdrawn from operations and flown to Tripoli for overhaul due to engine problems caused by ineffective sand filters. 1 December: *Staffel* reported 6 Hs 129 B-1s on strength. 31 December: arrived at Castel Benito/26 km south-south-west of Tripoli with 7 remaining Hs 129s. 13 January 1943: at Castel Benito – lost 3 Henschels on the ground there during an Allied raid on the airfield with fragmentation bombs. 17 January: ordered to depart Africa, with personnel to go to Bari/south-east Italy to be re-equipped with new Hs 129 B-2s without the MK 101 cannon and all remaining aircraft and spare parts at Castel Benito to be handed over to 8.(Pz)/Schl.G. 2. 1 March: at Bari with 4 Hs 129s on strength. 11 March: ordered to transfer immediately from Bari to Berlin-Staaken, pick up factory-new Hs 129 Bs, then proceed to Zaporozhye/south-east Ukraine for assignment to *Luftflotte* 4.

This Hs 129 B-2 of 4.(Pz)/Schl.G. 2, W.Nr. 0296, 'blue A', was the first aircraft of its type to be examined by the RAF. It made a bad landing at El Adem airfield which resulted in the collapse of the port undercarriage leg. The Germans then attempted to destroy the aircraft, but the remains were found by advancing British forces and provided valuable intelligence. The aircraft was armed with a 30 mm MK 101 cannon beneath the fuselage.

Pilots from 4.(Pz)/Schl.G. 2 gather round for a briefing prior to a sortie from Castel Benito. Both Hs 129 Bs had sand yellow (RLM colour 79) upper surfaces over-sprayed with dark green (80) mottling and white rear fuselage bands. The two aircraft were coded 'blue C', W.Nr. 0297 and 'blue O', W.Nr. 0310.

Another photograph of 'blue O', W.Nr. 0310 of 4.(Pz)/Schl.G. 2 . The white chevron and metal triangular pennant on the radio mast may indicate that this Hs 129 B-2 was flown at one time by the Staffelkapitän, Hptm. Bruno Meyer. This aircraft was later captured by British troops at Castel Benito airfield.

Crimea, Kursk and Ukraine (April 1943 – October 1943) 14 April: in reserve at Zaporozhye under *Führer der Panzerjägerstaffeln*. May: *Staffel* now at Kerch on the eastern tip of Crimea and in action over the Taman Peninsula. 1 June: Hs 129 B-2 shot down and 2 more shot up around Krymskaya on the Taman Peninsula, 1 pilot MIA. June: returned to Zaporozhye in early June to rest and refit. 1 July: *Staffel* reported 17 Hs 129 B-2 on strength. 2 July: transferred from Zaporozhye to Varvarovka/north-west of Kharkov and Mikoyanovka/8 km south-west of Belgorod on or about this date to take part in the German offensive against the Kursk salient (Operation *Zitadelle*) which commenced on 5 July. 5-15 July: flew anti-tank missions over the salient, but no record of its performance has so far been found. 14 July: transferred to Orel-West to help blunt the powerful Soviet counter-attack aimed at Orel that began on 13 July. The Henschels flew from dawn to dusk against advancing tanks and losses among the anti-tank *Staffeln* reached 30% between 14 and 25 July. 17-20 July: Orel-West – 3 Hs 129 Bs shot down plus 3 more shot up, *Staffelkapitän Major* Matuschek KIA when he flew his plane directly into a Russian T-34 tank on 19 July after using up all of his ammunition. August: pulled back to Konotop/210 km east-north-east of Kiev at the beginning of August and then ordered to Poltava a week or so later. 4 August: 2 unserviceable Hs 129s

destroyed by *Staffel* personnel at Varvarovka on evacuation of the airfield. 7 August: operating from Poltava, Hs 129 B-2 shot down by AA fire near Bogodukhov/north-west of Kharkov. During August and September, 4.(Pz)/Schl.G. 2 was kept busy trying to blunt the armoured forces of Voronezh front and Steppe front that were charging west and south-west from the Kharkov area. 9 August: Hs 129 shot up by AA fire in the Bogodukhov area. 15 August: Hs 129 shot down north-north-east of Poltava, pilot KIA. 17 August: Hs 129 damaged taxiing at Bol. Rudka airstrip/18 km north-north-west of Poltava. 21 August: Hs 129 shot down by AA fire north-east of Krimchka (not located), pilot KIA. 2 September: Hs 129 B-2 crashed in Ukraine due to technical problems. 26 September: Hs 129 B-2 crashed to the north of Kiev due to technical problems, pilot injured. 30 September: now at Krivoy Rog/140 km south-west of Dnepropetrovsk. 12 October: Hs 129 B-2 shot down by ground fire in the Kiev area, pilot KIA. 18 October: renamed 12.(Pz)/S.G. 9.

FpN: (L 49336)

Staffelkapitän:
Hptm. Bruno Meyer (RK) (30 September 1942 – March 1943)

II./Schl.G. 2

Formation (December 1942) Formed on 17 December 1942 at Gleiwitz (Gliwice)/Upper Silesia with Fw 190 A-3/A-5 fighter-bombers. The new *Gruppe* consisted of a *Gruppenstab* with 5. – 7. *Staffeln* and most of the personnel came from replacement training units (*Ergänzungsverbände*).

Tunisia (December 1942 – May 1943) December 1942 - mid March 1943: training and work-up. 1 March: reported 26 Fw 190 A-5s on strength. March: transferred from Gleiwitz to Brindisi/Italy where it completed its training. 16 March: Fw 190 A crashed at Vicenza/north Italy probably while transferring. 18 March: Fw 190 A-5 force-landed near Höhenbrunn (93 km north-north-west of Linz) in north Austria probably in transfer from Gleiwitz. 21 March: crash noted at Bari/south-east Italy. 12 April: in transfer to Tunisia with orders to relieve I./Schl.G. 2. 18 April: arrived at Bizerta - Sidi Ahmed and assigned to operate against enemy tank spearheads in support of German ground forces. 19 April: flew first mission in Tunisia, an attack on targets in the Medjez-el-Bab area south-west of Tunis. 20 April: ordered to depart for San Pietro/Sicily due to intense Allied air attacks on Tunisian airfields, but this order was not carried out in the full sense in that only the bulk of the personnel were evacuated while the Fw 190s and key mechanics remained. 25 April: flew 43 sorties against British armour advancing east of Goubellat/ca. 55 km south-west of Tunis and claimed numerous tanks, trucks and other vehicles and weapons destroyed or damaged. 27 April:

struck Allied armour in the Medjez el Bab area in 27 sorties flown for the day. 28 April: at Protville-West (23 km north-north-west of Tunis) with 20 Fw 190 A-5s under *Fliegerkorps Tunis* and put up 63 sorties between early morning and dusk. 29 April: claimed 21 vehicles, a tank and a munitions dump during missions in the Tebourba and Béja areas. 3 May: moved to a dispersal strip 6 km east-south-east of Protville and continued to mount 20+ sorties a day in the face of overwhelming Allied fighter superiority. 9-10 May: operating from the tip of the Cap Bon peninsula since 7 May, the remnants of the *Gruppe* evacuated to San Pietro/Sicily by air and then moved to Gerbini-North.

Sicily, Sardinia, Italy (June 1943 – October 1943) June: operating from Gerbini, San Pietro and Castelvetrano in south Sicily, flew a large number of fighter-bomber attacks on Allied surface vessels and landing craft in the Straits of Sicily and off the Tunisian coast. 8 June: still at Gerbini-North. 11-12 June: from Castelvetrano, attacked British 1st Division landings on the island of Pantelleria, and on 11 June 2 Fw 190 A-5s were shot down by fighters over Pantelleria, both pilots MIA. A third Fw 190 from 7. *Staffel* is also believed to have been shot down over the island on this mission. 13 June: 21 Fw 190 As took off from Castelvetrano to attack shipping at Pantelleria with 250 kg bombs. On the return leg one of the Fw 190 A-4s was intercepted by a Spitfire and shot down into the sea and the pilot reported MIA. A second Fw 190 was shot up and crashed on return to Castelvetrano. 15 June: an Fw 190 A, a Junkers W 34 and a Fi 156 belonging to the *Gruppe* were severely

This Fw 190 A-5/U3 Trop of 5./Schl.G. 2 was fitted with an ER 4 supplementary bomb carrier beneath its fuselage-mounted ETC 501 rack which could mount four SC 50 bombs. Standing next to the aircraft is Reinhold Omert, brother of Lt. Emil Omert who was awarded the Ritterkreuz on 19 March 1942 while serving with 8./J.G. 77.

The forerunner of the F-series, the Fw 190 A-5/U3 was fitted with racks for two 50 kg bombs under each wing. This aircraft, 'black F' of 6./Schl.G. 2, crashed at Protville in Tunisia in May 1943.

damaged during an Allied air attack on Castelvetrano. 15 June: ordered to transfer from Castelvetrano to Alghero/north-west Sardinia, the move being carried out on 19 June with 31 Fw 190s. This was in response to German fear of an impending invasion of Sardinia, since they were aware of the massive build-up of Allied troops and landing craft in Algerian and Tunisian ports. 28 June: 3 Fw 190s severely damaged during Allied raid on Alghero. 2 July: transferred from Alghero to Ottana/central Sardinia. 12 July: transferred from Ottana to an emergency field at Enna/central Sicily to begin attacks on Allied forces invading Sicily. 17 July: withdrew from Sicily and now at Aquino (110 km south-east of Rome) under II.*Fliegerkorps*/*Luftflotte* 2. 23 July: Aquino airfield hit by North-west African Strategic Air Force (NASAF), B-26 Marauders destroying many of the *Gruppe*'s planes on the ground. The pilots were then sent to Bari by Ju 52 to pick up new Fw 190s. 25 July: ordered from Aquino back to Sardinia, with station initially at Alghero and then a few days later at Ottana in the central part of the island.

8 August: at Ottana with 37 (24) Fw 190s. 14 August: 6.*Staffel* Fw 190 A-5 force-landed east of Ottana and caught fire, *Staffelkapitän Oblt.* Ernst Hermann MIA. 3 September: 7.*Staffel* Fw 190 F-3 shot down by a fighter south of Ottana, pilot MIA. 9 September: relocated from Ottana to the Italian mainland, probably going to Piacenza a short time later. The absence of direct combat losses and other evidence suggests the *Gruppe* experienced very little operational activity during September and the first half of October. 24 September: two Fw 190 A-5s destroyed by German personnel at Chisionaccia (not located) apparently to prevent capture. 4 October: Fw 190 A bombed on the ground during Allied raid on Grosseto airfield on the Italian west coast opposite Corsica. 18 October: redesignated as I./S.G. 4 at Guidonia (22 km north-east of Rome) with *Gruppenstab* becoming *Gruppenstab* of I./S.G. 4, 6.*Staffel* became 3./S.G. 4, 5.*Staffel* split up and divided among the *Staffeln* of I./S.G. 2 in Russia, and 7.*Staffel* became 3./S.G. 2 in Russia.

FpNs: II. *Stab* (L 55808), 5. (L 54245), 6. (L 53104), 7. (L 53251)

Kommandeur:

Hptm. Werner Dörnbrack (RK) (17 December 1942 – 18 October 1943)

BELOW AND OPPOSITE: Found abandoned by British troops on a Tunisian airfield in 1943, this Fw 190 A-5/U3 of II./Schl.G. 2 carried single coloured identification letter as distinct from the aircraft of the Jagdgeschwader and Schnellkampfgeschwader which utilised colour numbers. The colour of these letters/numbers were, however, similar: green for the Stab, white for the first Staffel, red for the second, yellow for the third and blue for the fourth. 'White D' of 5./Sch.G. 2 (the first Staffel in the second Gruppe) carried the Mickey Mouse riding a bomb emblem which was later used by I./S.G. 4.

8.(Pz)/Schl.G. 2

Mickey Mouse Emblem of II./Schl.G. 2

Formation (December 1942) Ordered formed on or about 17 December 1942 at Tunis - El Aouina/Tunisia by renaming 5./Schl.G. 1 reinforced with additional personnel from elements of J.G. 27 and J.G. 53 that were based in Tunisia. Equipped with Henschel Hs 129 Bs for anti-tank operations.

Tunisia and Sardinia (December 1942 – July 1943) 22 December: Hs 129 B-2 shot down by P-38 Lightnings north-west of Kairouan/Tunisia, pilot KIA. 28 December: Hs 129 B-2 shot down by P-38s and Spitfires near Pont-du-Fahs/north Tunisia, pilot KIA. 18 January: 1 Hs 129 B-2 shot down by AA fire and a second severely shot up while the pair attacked a British armoured column in the Bou Arada area, *Oblt.* Fritz Krause KIA and *Staffelkapitän Oblt.* Franz Oswald WIA. 20 January: as of this date, the *Staffel* under this new designation had not yet flown any anti-tank operations. 1 February: ordered to transfer to Gabes/south-east Tunisia for operations against the British 8th Army but this order was soon cancelled. 10 February: based at Tunis - El Aouina under *Fliegerkorps Tunis* with 10 (5) Hs 129s. 23 February: still at El Aouina under *Fliegerkorps Tunis*. 22 March: 2 Hs 129s failed to return from operations, one of which fell at Messouna, both pilots safe. 25 March: now at La Fauconnerie-South (60 km north-west of Sfax (Safāqis)) with elements at Tunis. 27 March: 3 Hs 129s

ABOVE AND BELOW: 8.(Pz)/Sch.G. 2 was formed during the middle of December 1942 at Tunis - El Aouina by renaming 5./Schl.G. 1. It was also reinforced with additional personnel from elements of J.G. 27 and J.G. 53 that were based in Tunisia. These Hs 129 B-2s from the unit photographed at El Aouina airfield have pale grey 'wave mirror' camouflage over their dark green upper surfaces. The aircraft in the colour picture carries the letter 'C' in red.

An American GI sits in the cockpit of a wrecked Hs 129 B-2, W.Nr. 0278, of 8.(Pz)/Schl.G. 1 at El Aouina airfield. The machine retained its radio call sign DQ+ZN (painted in black beneath the wings), but had the letter 'X' painted forward of the fuselage Balkenkreuz. According to the Allied crash report the colour of this letter was 'purple' but this odd colour may have been the result of the desert sun altering the shade which theoretically should have been blue.

operating from La Fauconnerie, escorted by a handful of Bf 109 Gs from II./J.G. 77, ordered to attack British tanks in the El Hamma area to the south-west of Gabes, but the formation was jumped by Spitfires in the target area. Two Spitfires claimed by II./J.G. 77 for the loss of 1 Messerschmitt while 2 Hs 129s went down either to ground fire or as victims of the fighters. Of the two Hs 129 pilots, 1 KIA and the other WIA. 5 April: lost 2 Hs 129s during Allied raid on Tunis - El Aouina. 10 April: reported 16 (2) Hs 129s on strength at Tunis - El Aouina. 19 April: half of Staffel with at least 8 aircraft ordered to transfer from Tunis to Decimomannu (18 km north-west of Cagliari/south Sardinia). 20-25 April: after a stopover at Trapani/Sicily, the half Staffel arrived at Decimomannu. 23 April: meanwhile the other half attacked Allied armour at Pont du Fahs/north Tunisia. 28 April: elements still at Tunis with 8 Hs 129s under *Fliegerkorps Tunis*. 5 May: Hs 129 shot down by AA fire at Mateur (Mätir) (50 km north-west of Tunis), pilot KIA. 6 May: departed Tunisia for Decimomannu and reassigned to *Fliegerführer Sardinien*. 1 July: reported 10 Hs 129 B-1/B-2s. Second half of July: left Decimomannu to refit and re-equip at Deblin-Irena in central Poland. 24 July: Hs 129 crashed and burned at Monte Moneta (77 km north-west of Naples), probably during the transfer to Poland.

Eastern and Central Ukraine (August 1943 – October 1943) Beginning of August: refitted and re-equipped, transferred from Deblin-Irena to South Russia to support the westward retreat by German forces following the Soviet counter-offensive along the entire southern sector of the front that began in the Kursk salient in mid-July. 7-8 August: based at Poltava - 4 Hs 129 B-2s shot down by AA fire near Bogodukhov (north-west of Kharkov), 1 pilot KIA and 2 MIA. 10 September: Hs 129 shot down by AA fire in the Poltava area, pilot KIA. 21 September: transferred to Zaporozhye. 30 September: evacuated Zaporozhye on or about this date and withdrew to Kirovograd. A week or so later the Staffel moved to Krivoy Rog to cover the fighting retreat of A.O.K. 6 in the Dnepropetrovsk area. Also operated from Apostolovo (42 km south-east of Krivoy Rog) during this period. 18 October: redesignated 13.(Pz)/S.G. 9.

Oblt. Franz Oswald, pictured during the summer of 1942 while serving as technical officer of 5./Schl.G. 1. He is standing in front of the communications truck which also carries the Staffel emblem. On 17 December 1942, the unit was redesignated 8.(Pz)/Schl.G. 2 with Oswald being made Kapitän. Shortly afterwards, on 18 January his Hs 129 was severely damaged while attacking a British armoured column in the Bou Arada area. Oswald was wounded.

THIS PAGE AND OPPOSITE: This Hs 129 B-2 from 8.(Pz)/Schl.G. 2, W.Nr. 0364, had the letter 'J' and II.Gruppe bar painted in red outlined in white. The infantry assault badge was painted on both sides of the fuselage, in white, above the gun bulge and a total of 23 tank 'kill' markings appeared on the port side of the rudder. This aircraft was shot down by AA fire on 27 May 1943 in the Kuban Peninsula in Russia. This sequence of photographs show the aircraft being refuelled and made ready for a mission.

The 'Infantry Assault' badge
as applied to red 'J'

FpN: (L 18682)

Staffelkapitän:
Oblt. Franz Oswald (DKG) (ca. 1 January 1943 -
    18 October 1943)
Lt. Hans-Werner Jurck (19 January 1943 - ?) – acting
    St.Fü. ★
★**Note**: from *Fighters Over Tunisia*, p. 159

Sources for Schl.G. 2:

Unpublished and Archival:
AFHRA Maxwell: decimal 512 (British Air Ministry)
    P/W interrogation report CSDIC AFHQ A.42.
AFHRA Maxwell/PRO London: CSDIC AFHQ A.55,
    A.252.
BA-MA Freiburg: RL 2 III Gen.Qu.(6.Abt.) *Meldungen
    über Flugzeugunfälle und Verlust…* (LRs – Loss
    Reports);
BA-MA - *Flugzeug-Bereitstellungen* (Aircraft Availability
    Status Reports – FzB) in: Holm-op cit.
PRO London: AIR 40/file. 1988, 1995, 1996.
PRO London: DEFE 3 ULTRA signals ML539,
ML1350, ML1494, ML2662, ML2700, ML3693,
ML3742, ML4109, ML4153, ML4271, ML4337,
ML4402, ML4469, ML4681, ML4757, ML5292,
ML7104, ML7314, ML7369, ML9018, VM1711,
VM3049, VM4851, VM5637, VM6346, VM7525,
VM8328, VM8827, VM9050, VM9180, VM9267,
VM9744, VM9860, VM9926.
M. Pegg: personal letter to H.L. deZeng dated 17 April
    1994.

Published:
[Aders – SG] p. 60, 83, 91, 118, 139;

[Arthy – 190] p. 140-150;
[Bergström – Kursk] p. 102-103;
[Brütting – SA] p. 149, 170, 189, 272, 273, 275, 276;
[Dierich – VdL] p. 238-240;
[Green – WotTR] p. 382, 393-396;
[Gundelach – Med] p. 487, 488, 534, 611;
[Hammel – AWE] p. 157;
[Kannapin – FPN] various;
[Mehner – FT] p. 55;
[Obermaier – RK2] p. 58, 71, 157, 158, 169, 172, 188,
    249;
[Patzwall – LwR] p. various;
[Pegg – Hs129] p. 102-108, 116, 122, 123, 130, 144, 145,
    150, 154, 155;
[Prien – JG53] p. 717;
[Prien – JG77] p. 1494;
[Scheibert – EP] p. 219, 299;
[Scherzer – DKG] p. 62, 242;
[Shores – FotD] p. 195, 204, 210, 213, 216;
[Shores – FOT] p. 82, 111, 116, 122, 135, 136, 159, 197,
    203, 212, 226, 228, 241, 242, 259, 271, 278, 297, 303,
    307, 339, 366, 372, 377, 379;
[Shores – MAW3] p. 104, 107;
[Shores – Malta-S] p. 565, 608, 618, 634, 637, 643, 671;
[Smith – GA] p. 180, 182, 195, 321, 333, 334, 336,
[Smith – Hs129Prof] p. 255;
[Tessin – Tes] p. 321;
[Vasco – Bomb] p. 60;
[Zweng – Zweng] p. various.

[Archiv #13 – A-13] p. 31
AIR Vol. 19-6 p. 279, 282, 283.

[Holm – Website www.ww2.dk]

The pilot of this Hs 129 B-2 of 8.(Pz)/S.G. 2 stands in the heavily armoured cockpit of his aircraft with three other Hs 129s and a Ju 52/3m transport in the background. The infantry assault badge was carried by both the Hs 123 and Hs 129 of the first Schlachtgeschwader.